Ethical Economy

Studies in Economic Ethics and Philosophy

Volume 62

Series Editors
Alexander Brink, Wirtschafts- und Unternehmensethik, University of Bayreuth, Bayreuth, Germany
Jacob Dahl Rendtorff, Department of Social Sciences and Business, Roskilde University, Roskilde, Denmark

Editorial Board Members
John Boatright, Loyola University, CHICAGO, IL, USA
George Brenkert, Business Ethics Inst, Maguire Hall 209B, Georgetown Univ, Georgetown, WASHINGTON, DC, USA
Allan K. K. Chan, Lee Shau Kee School of Business & Admi, The Open University of Hong Kong, Homantin, Hong Kong
Christopher Cowton, University of Huddersfield, Huddersfield, UK
Richard T. de George, University of Kansas, Lawrence, KS, USA
Jon Elster, Columbia University, New York, USA
Amitai Etzioni, George Washington University, WASHINGTON, DC, USA
Ingo Pies, Lehrstuhl für Wirtschaftsethik, Martin-Luther-Univ Halle-Wittenberg, Halle (Saale), Sachsen-Anhalt, Germany
Michaela Haase, Marketing, Freie Universität Berlin, Berlin, Germany
Carlos Hoevel, Facultad de Ciencias Economicas, Universidad Catolica Argentina, Buenos Aires, Argentina
Yuichi Shionoya, Hitotsubashi University, Kunitachi, Tokyo, Japan
Philippe Van Parijs, Chaire Hoover d'Ethique Economique, Universite Catholique de Louvain, Louvain-la-Neuve, Belgium
Gedeon J. Rossouw, Hadefields Office Park, Ethics Institute of Africa, Hatfield, Pretoria, South Africa
Josef Wieland, LEIZ, Zeppelin Universität, Friedrichshafen, Baden-Württemberg, Germany

Ethical Economy describes the theory of the ethical preconditions of the economy and of business as well as the theory of the ethical foundations of economic systems. It analyzes the impact of rules, virtues, and goods or values on economic action and management. *Ethical Economy* understands ethics as a means to increase trust and to reduce transaction costs. It forms a foundational theory for business ethics and business culture. The Series *Ethical Economy. Studies in Economic Ethics and Philosophy* is devoted to the investigation of interdisciplinary issues concerning economics, management, ethics, and philosophy. These issues fall in the categories of economic ethics, business ethics, management theory, economic culture, and economic philosophy, the latter including the epistemology and ontology of economics. Economic culture comprises cultural and hermeneutic studies of the economy. One goal of the series is to extend the discussion of the philosophical, ethical, and cultural foundations of economics and economic systems. The series is intended to serve as an international forum for scholarly publications, such as monographs, conference proceedings, and collections of essays. Primary emphasis is placed on originality, clarity, and interdisciplinary synthesis of elements from economics, management theory, ethics, and philosophy.

The book series has been accepted into SCOPUS (March 2019) and will be visible on the Scopus website within a few months.

Niels Kærgård
Editor

Market, Ethics and Religion

The Market and its Limitations

Springer

Editor
Niels Kærgård
Department of Food and Resource Economics
University of Copenhagen
Frederiksberg C, Denmark

ISSN 2211-2707   ISSN 2211-2723 (electronic)
Ethical Economy
ISBN 978-3-031-08461-4   ISBN 978-3-031-08462-1 (eBook)
https://doi.org/10.1007/978-3-031-08462-1

© The Editor(s) (if applicable) and The Author(s), under exclusive license to Springer Nature Switzerland AG 2023

This work is subject to copyright. All rights are solely and exclusively licensed by the Publisher, whether the whole or part of the material is concerned, specifically the rights of translation, reprinting, reuse of illustrations, recitation, broadcasting, reproduction on microfilms or in any other physical way, and transmission or information storage and retrieval, electronic adaptation, computer software, or by similar or dissimilar methodology now known or hereafter developed.

The use of general descriptive names, registered names, trademarks, service marks, etc. in this publication does not imply, even in the absence of a specific statement, that such names are exempt from the relevant protective laws and regulations and therefore free for general use.

The publisher, the authors, and the editors are safe to assume that the advice and information in this book are believed to be true and accurate at the date of publication. Neither the publisher nor the authors or the editors give a warranty, expressed or implied, with respect to the material contained herein or for any errors or omissions that may have been made. The publisher remains neutral with regard to jurisdictional claims in published maps and institutional affiliations.

This Springer imprint is published by the registered company Springer Nature Switzerland AG
The registered company address is: Gewerbestrasse 11, 6330 Cham, Switzerland

Preface

For more than a 100 years, many scientific disciplines, including economics, have strived to achieve the ideal of being a real science, that is, objectivity, formalization, and statistical testing. The change of name from "political economy" to the "science of economics" is an indication of the movement. Economics, like almost all other disciplines, has been more focused on the specific core of the discipline, that is, in the case of economics, on the market mechanism. Many other topics have been handed over to sociology, anthropology, and political science.

This specialization in the scientific disciplines and the ideal of objectivity, more exact models, and statistical tests have many advantages but does, however, also have drawbacks. Interdisciplinary research became more difficult among modern specialists than among old-time generalists, and a stronger separation between a political discussion of how the world ought to be and a scientific discussion of how the world really is hindered fruitful parts of the public debate.

These problems have, over the last decade, led to a number of contributions on the topics of economics, ethics, and religion, all of which have tried to fill the gap. Some theologians entered the debate about economic problems, for example, Philip Goodchild with the book *Theology of Money* from 2009, and economists became more interested in ethical questions, for example, Tomas Sedlacek with the book *Economics of Good and Evil* from 2011. A further notable example is political scientist Michael J. Sandel's book *What money can't buy: The Moral Limits of Markets*. Recognition of the broader debate within the disciplines was also signalled by the award of a Nobel Prize in 2017 to the behavioural economist Richard Thaler with the parole "Economists work more with Homo Sapiens and less with Homo Economicus than a decade ago". Another indication is that corporate economics has changed from being completely concentrated on profit maximizing for shareholders to taking social responsibility seriously and having a broader group of stakeholders at its core.

As a result of these debates, an interdisciplinary workshop on market, ethics, and religion was arranged by Niels Kærgård in 2014 at The Royal Danish Academy of Science and Letters, sponsored by the Carlsberg Foundation. Here, economists, theologians, and representatives of other disciplines discussed the forces and the limitations of the market and different ethical and religious attitudes to the market economy. The aim was not to promote alternatives to the market economy but to provide a framework for a constructive discussion of the attitudes of mainstream economics and other disciplines to the advantages and disadvantages of the market mechanism. It was decided at the time to publish the collected papers in book form.

Danish research in market orientation and theology, however, changed direction just after the workshop. In the autumn 2014, a major project was started, entitled "What money can't buy", led by the theologian Hans Raun Iversen. It was started and financed by a large grant from The Danish Council for Independent Research: Culture and Communication. The research related to analysing marketization, and the cooperation between economists and theologians was collected in this project, and the results published in the book *Individualisation, Marketisation and Social Capital in a Cultural Institution* edited by Hans Raun Iversen, Lisbet Christoffersen, Niels Kærgård, and Margit Warburg in 2019.

Subsequently, there has now once again been time to resume work on publishing a book about the topics from the workshop in 2014, and the present book is the result. Not all the topics from the workshop are included, and new ones have been added. Twelve of the book's 20 chapters do, however, still have their origins in papers from the workshop.

Heartfelt thanks to the many persons involved are extremely justified. To the original authors for their patience in accepting the delay in the project; to the newcomers who have joined the project, some of whom with rather short deadlines; to the Carlsberg Foundation and the Danish Council for Independent Research: Culture and Communication for economic support to different stages of the research process; and to Springer Press for following the process ever since 2014. They have all made contributions which made the book possible. A necessary condition for these many different disciplines to form a coherent mosaic has been that a number of the authors have shown an admirable flexibility and willingness to discuss issues in the periphery of their discipline's core. And it must be remembered that participation in a debate about the appropriate design of a society can be felt irrelevant both for economists seeking the objective truth about the economic laws and for theologians analysing individuals' conscience and belief.

Frederiksberg C, Denmark   Niels Kærgård

Contents

1 **Introduction: Market, Ethics and Religion** 1
Niels Kærgård

Part I Economics of the Market

2 **The Market in Economics: Behavioural Assumptions
and Value Judgments** 19
Agnar Sandmo

3 **Market Failures and What to Do About It?** 41
Peder Andersen

4 **Unproductive Market Ideology** 55
Hans Aage

5 **Happiness in the Hands of Empirical Economists** 71
Peder J. Pedersen

6 **Economics, Religion, and Ethics: Economics of Good and Evil** 85
Tomas Sedlacek

Part II Religion and the Market

7 **Lutheran Social Ethics** 103
Svend Andersen

8 **Theology of Money: Rationalisation and Spiritual Goods** 115
Philip Goodchild

9 **Two Bishops on the Ethics of the Market Economy** 131
Niels Kærgård

10 **K.E. Løgstrup's Ethics: Is There a Christian Alternative
to Economics?** 145
Niels Kærgård

11	Reading Genesis 1.28 with a Plea for Planetary Responsibility Ole Jensen	159
12	Religion, Politics, and Moral in Recent Denmark Peter Lüchau	171
13	Economic Life and the Social Doctrine of the Catholic Church Else-Britt Nilsen	181
14	On Muslim Attitudes to Modern Capitalism and to What It Brought Along Jakob Skovgaard-Petersen	197

Part III   The Limitation of the Market: Some Cases

15	Markets for Human Body Parts: The Case of Commercial Surrogacy Kirsten Halsnæs and Thomas Ploug	211
16	Gender, Sex and Market – "Can Sex Be a Service Like Any Other?" Hanne Petersen	221
17	The Problem of Interest for Luther and the Danish Reformers Martin Schwarz Lausten	237
18	Poverty, Income Distribution, Lutheran Christianity and the Danish Welfare State Jørn Henrik Petersen	251
19	The Company as a Good Citizen: Institutional Responsibility and Cosmopolitanism Jacob Dahl Rendtorff	267
20	Climate Problems: Market and Ethics Kirsten Halsnæs and Niels Kærgård	285

Index... 297

Chapter 1
Introduction: Market, Ethics and Religion

Niels Kærgård

Abstract The conflict between unlimited needs and scarce resources means that some restrictions on human behaviour become necessary, and regulation has always been an important part of every society. Many different institutions, e.g., ethics, religion, and markets, can directly or indirectly regulate the interrelation between people, and between people and society. The interplay between these institutions is, however, very complicated and an important part of the public debate. To get a solid foundation for analysing these fundamental topics, scientific insight from different disciplines is a necessity; social science, humanities and theology all play an important role.

Keywords Regulation · Scarce resources · Market · Ethics · Religion

1.1 Introduction

The interplay between market, ethics and religion is very complicated and very important as a part of the public debate dealing with the key questions: What is a "valuable behaviour", and how can a society provide the right framework for such a behaviour. The public debate deals with many topics, but a key topic in all public debates has always been how people interact, often in relation to which goods and services should be produced and how the products should be allocated between members of the society. To get a solid foundation for analysing these fundamental topics, scientific insight from different disciplines is a necessity; social science, humanities and theology all play an important role.

Over the centuries, many of the scientific disciplines have gradually developed instruments to cope with the challenge posed by "valuable behaviour". Central to these is the science of economics dealing with the society's use of scarce resources

---

N. Kærgård (✉)
Department of Food and Resource Economics, University of Copenhagen, Frederiksberg C, Denmark
e-mail: nik@ifro.ku.dk

and distribution of these resources among people. The key topic of economics is the market and the markets' role in society.

The main starting point of economics is that human needs are unlimited, whilst the number of commodities and resources are scarce. The main problem facing society in this context was ably presented by The Rolling Stones in their hit "You can't always get what you want", and in formal economic terms in the Nobel prize winning economist Paul Samuelsson's definition of economics: "Economics is the study of how societies use scarce resources" (Samuelson 1948). The conflict between unlimited needs and scarce resources means that some restrictions on human behaviour become necessary.

The interaction between people and between people and the institutions of society needs consequently to be regulated, which can be done in many different ways. Part of this is to regulate behaviour to obtain various political priorities. This is not only the point of departure for economics; for ethics and theology it is also a main topic to discuss how a fair position for the weak shall be constructed.

1.2 Regulations Necessary

Regulation has always been an important part of every society. A society without regulations has never been seen as an attractive possibility, but rather as an ominous scenario to be avoided. The best-known description of such a society without regulations is presumably Thomas Hobbes well-known formulation dating back to 1651:

> *In such conditions, there is no place for industry, because the fruit thereof is uncertain, and consequently no culture of the earth, no navigation, nor use of the commodities that may be imported by sea, no commodious building, no instruments of moving and removing such things as require much force, no knowledge of the face of the earth, no account of time, no arts, no letters, no society, and which is worst of all, continual fear, and danger of violent death, and the life of man, solitary, poor, nasty, brutish and short. (*Hobbes 1651, XIII, 9*).*

But whereas everyone agrees that regulation and restriction on behaviour is necessary, there has hardly ever been any consensus about what the optimal form of regulation is. Many different institutions, e.g., law, ethics, religion, and markets, can directly or indirectly regulate the interrelation between people, and between people and society. These institutions all restrict people from doing things that can be harmful to other members of society or to society itself. The most direct regulation is by law, the observance of which is enforced by the police and the military; Thomas Hobbes argued e.g., for an absolute monarchy giving all power to the strongest. But there are many other forms of possible regulation. Ethics, moral or religious rules are often considered as "soft laws". Such "soft laws" can have many forms and their origin can be mixed and debatable.

It is a very old observation that the different forms of regulation are interchangeable. If people are honest and moral, there is less need for law and police. This is formulated already in the preamble of the first national law in Denmark, "Jyske Lov":

> *With law shall land be built, but if all men would be content with what is theirs, and let others enjoy the same rights, there would be no need of law. But no law shall be perceived and*

followed as the truth, however where there is doubt about what is truth, the law shall show what is the truth. If the land had no law, then he would have the most who could grab the most. Law shall hence be made in the interest of all for the just and peaceable and blameless to enjoy their peace, and such as the unjust and evil may be daunted by the letters of the law and hence will not dare to carry out their evil intent. It shall further be the truth that where men are not swayed to do the good out of fear of God and love of the right, then the fear of authorities and the penal code of the land shall prevent them from doing evil and punish them if they do (Fenger and Jansen 1991, *Translation from Danish*).

An attractive society without a need for many police officers can be created by religion or ethics, but only if all members - as formulated in the quotation – *"do the good out of fear of God or love of the right"*.

If law or ethics ensure that private ownership is to be respected, the market mechanism is – at least by economists – seen as an effective regulation mechanism. Each of the three, – religion, ethics, and the market – are all part of the institutions that make a modern society function in an appropriate manner. They do supplement each other.

But the regulation can take different forms and stress different type of motivations. Theologians and ethicists stress our responsibility in relation to other members of the society as, for instance, formulated by the Danish theologian and philosopher K.E. Løgstrup:

The demands made by ethics derive from the basic parameters according to which we must live, and which we cannot change, i.e., that the life of any individual is entwined with that of other individuals, in that it requires that we take care of the other's life, to the extent to which that life is delivered into our hands. (Translated from Løgstrup 1971, p. 211)

Or in the Bible

Suppose there are brothers or sisters who need clothes and don't have enough to eat. What good is there in your saying to them, "God bless you! Keep warm and eat well!" – if you don't give them the necessities of life? (James 2:15–16)

Economists normally stress completely different motivations.

1.3 The Economists and the Market

Most economists' hold almost the opposite view. They accepted selfishness and are sceptical to benevolence; the following quotation of the "Father of economics", Adam Smith, is well known:

He (the businessman) intends only his own gain, and he is in this, as in many other cases, led by an invisible hand to promote an end which was no part of his intention. Nor is it always the worse for society that it was not part of it. By pursuing his own interest, he frequently promotes that of the society more effectively than when he really intends to promote it. I have never known much good to be done by those who affected to trade for the public good. It is an affectation, indeed, not very common among merchants, and very few words need be employed in dissuading them from it. (Smith 1776 Book IV chapter 2).

It is not people trying to help the society that is the solution to scarcity problems, but, rather, it is the market mechanism. Scarcity means high prices; high prices mean high profit, and the high profits attract new producers, and the needed higher production is created as if steered by an invisible hand. Examples of praise for the market mechanism can be found amongst economists since 1776, e.g., Friedrich Hayek (Nobel Prize winner 1974):

> *I am convinced that if (the price mechanism) were the result of deliberate human design, and if people guided by the price changes understood that their decisions have significance far beyond their immediate aim, this mechanism would have been acclaimed as one of the greatest triumphs of the human mind. Its misfortune is the double one, that it is not the product of human design and, that the people guided by it usually do not know why they are made to do what they do.* (Hayek 1948)

See also Kenneth J. Arrow (Nobel prize winner 1972) and Frank H. Hahn supporting this point of view:

> *The immediate "common sense" answer to the question "What will an economy motivated by individual greed and controlled by a very large number of different agents look like?" is probably: There will be chaos --- Our answer is somewhat different. There is by now a long and fairly imposing line of economists from Adam Smith to the present who have sought to show that a decentralised economy motivated by self-interest and guided by price signals would be compatible with a coherent disposition of economic resources that could be regarded, in a well-defined sense, as superior to a large class of possible alternative dispositions* (Arrow and Hahn 1971).

Many, perhaps most, economists' views can perhaps be summarized in a quotation of the prominent researcher in the history of economic thoughts, Laurence S. Moss:

> *The economics that I know and love had its origins in the work of that accused seventeenth century atheist Thomas Hobbes, who asked how a community of selfish and cheating individuals could ever get organized. Bernard de Mandeville, the Dutch cynic of the early Eighteenth Century, suggested it is the private vices of the masses that supply the social glue. Adam Smith argued that in a well-governed society, self-interest could promote the public interest, and in the Twentieth Century economists such as Ludwig von Mises defined a "well governed" society as one in which property rights were clearly defined and private contracts about the exchange of those rights enforced. The great insight of our discipline – most recently sensationalized in the Coase theorem – is that competition can serve to secure efficiency and meaningful organization.* (Moss 1996, p. 493).

For more than a century, the trend has gone in the direction of letting bigger and bigger parts of society be regulated by the market. A very early example is the Danish agricultural reforms in the 1780s, where a traditional agriculture regulated by common decisions in the villages and without individual ownership of the farms was transformed into a system with individual privately owned, profit maximizing farms producing for the market. In 1857, free competition was generally introduced in Danish industry replacing the guild systems and their rules of behaviour. This trend has accelerated both in Denmark and most other western countries over the last couple of decades, where a considerable part of public infrastructure, hospitals, education etc. has been transformed from being a part of the public sector to become managed by market-oriented profit maximizing firms e.g., telephone, energy, and train companies.

1.4 Limitations of the Market

But the optimality of the market does build on several assumptions which, in a number of cases, are not fulfilled in the real world. A main assumption is that the commodities are "normal" goods, which means that they are "rivalrous" and "excludable". "Rivalrous" means that if one consumer uses the good other consumer cannot. If I drink a beer, another person cannot drink the same beer. "Excludable" means that it is possible to exclude others from using the commodity. These two characteristics are obvious for most normal traded goods: food, shoes, houses, beer, clothes etc. There are, however, a considerable number of *public goods* in which these properties are not found, as first discussed by Paul Samuelson (1954). The textbook case is fireworks. If the utility of fireworks is to provide a visual display (rather than just to be an object for ignition), a rocket in a residential neighbourhood can be seen by all its inhabitants, i.e., it is not rivalrous. Everybody can stand in his or her own garden and see the fireworks; it is not excludable. In such a situation there is a free-rider problem. If someone pays for the fireworks everyone can share the utility of it. This means that the individual maximizing consumer will hope that somebody else will pay and that he can get the pleasure without paying. If the market distributes public goods among selfish agents, the consequences are that very few will be paying, and that consumption will be sub-optimally small. In the real world there are many public goods: Broadcasting, national defence, police, street lighting and parts of the health care system are traditional examples of public goods. Environmental commodities such as fresh air, attractive landscapes, biodiversity, and beautiful sunsets are all examples of public goods.

Even "normal" goods can be problematic if some products are market regulated and other not. The unregulated products caused *market external effects* or *externalities*. A factory produces goods for the market but the production results in smoke and noise, and in an unregulated market economy the cost for society of smoke and noise is not paid for by the factory. The cost attributed to the factory is too low because not all that cost is paid by the factory. This means that the price of the factory's market-oriented production is too low and, consequently, the sold amount of goods and the production are too high. The externalities can also be positive. The beekeeper sells honey, but his bees do an important and unpaid job by pollinating cultivated and wild plants. So, honey will be too expensive because not all parts of the production is paid for, and the production in an unregulated market is too small. There needs some sort of intervention. For a more profound discussion of public goods and externalities see Chap. 3 below.

Game theory deals with decision-making in a situation with a number of decision makers with conflicting interests. von Neumann and Morgenstern (1944) is considered as the foundation for the discipline, which has subsequently flourished and produced about a dozen Nobel Prize winners in economics. There are two possible concepts of equilibrium. A Nash equilibrium is a situation where all the decision makers are satisfied with their own decisions when they learn what the other decision makers have decided[1]. Because everyone is satisfied, there are no incentives to change, and the equilibrium is stable. Such an equilibrium need not, however, be the best possible for the decision makers. If they cooperate, it will in many cases be possible to reach a better situation for all. But such a cooperative equilibrium will normally be unstable, as individual decision makers might seek advantage by breaking the cooperative agreement. This dilemma can be illustrated by the case of a community of fishermen around a lake. All of them will get the biggest catch of fish if they do not fish too intensively. This is the cooperative equilibrium. But if a single fisherman fishes more intensively than others he will net a bigger catch. Everyone has an individual incentive to fish more intensively than in the cooperative equilibrium. The problem has been discussed intensively in the literature known as "The tragedy of the common", of which Garrett Hardin's article is the classic example (Hardin 1968). The central point is that there needs to be some sort of formal or informal restriction on individual actions on the market if an optimal situation is to be achieved. The market cannot provide rational management on its own.

A normal individual decision-maker has a time preference. He will weight his cost and benefit according to the point in time at which they incur. A benefit incurred today is seen as more valuable than a benefit of the same size incurred in the distant future. We discount the cost and benefit with a discount rate e.g., an interest rate. In Denmark, The Ministry of Economic Affairs normally uses a discount rate of 6 per cent per year. This means that a benefit next year is worth 6 per cent less than the same benefit today. A benefit of 100,000 will if it is realized 25 years from now be worth only 21,300, and if it takes place 50 years from now it will be worth only 4500, measured in present day money. We all tend to discount the value of future events, although we do so at different individually perceived discount rates. This means, however, that the distant future will be neglected or at least play a minor role in such a decision process. This is of particular significance in relation to major long-term problems such as climate change, the growing world population, and a potential scarcity of non-renewable natural resources. Even if it can be rational for me to neglect my own distant future by following an unhealthy lifestyle and by not saving money for my pension, it seems unethical to neglect the interests of my children and grandchildren. This has resulted in a definition of *sustainability*. We must not consume more than will allow future generations to have at least the same living conditions as our own generation. The basic idea was forcefully introduced into the public debate by the Brundtland Report to the United Nations (United Nations: 1987) and has since been formalized and discussed, for example by Arrow et al. (2004). The central point in relation to our topic is the fact that some restrictions on human activity are necessary to secure a long-run acceptable equilibrium. A rational market equilibrium is not able, even under ideal conditions, to secure satisfactory living conditions for future generations. For a more profound discussion of sustainability see Chap. 20 below.

---

[1] The Nash equilibrium is named after the American mathematician John F. Nash (born 1928) who was awarded the Nobel Prize in economics in 1994. His genius and schizophrenia is described in the book and film "A beautiful Mind" from 2001.

A central part of a fair society and of the political debate is just and fair income distribution. *Fair income distribution* is not, however, a characteristic of a market equilibrium – on the contrary. Income and wages are determined by scarcity. If there are three skilled and industrious bakers and one lazy butcher in a village, no doubt the butcher will get the highest income. One of the Danish professors introducing this point of view in Denmark in the early twentieth century, L. V. Birch, had a student in economics to an examination at the university and asked, "Why do I get so high a wage" No answer, so the professor continued: "Is it because I am clever or because I am beautiful?" Suddenly the student remembered his curriculum and answered: "No, you are neither clever nor beautiful, you are rare". And this is the basic assumption behind a market economy. But this need not to be fair. The function of incomes and wages in a market economy is not to be ethically fair, but to stimulate movement of resources from occupations where there is enough to occupations where there is too little. If there are many unskilled workers, they can be exploited by those in a stronger position. This is not fair, but the incentives are optimal.

This discussion of Christianity and the responsibility for the poor has, in the last half century, been followed by a debate about Christianity and the welfare state. The grand old man in this debate is Jørn Henrik Petersen. His most recent books related to this topic are Petersen (2016, 2017, 2018), see also Kærgård (2013 and 2017). There are arguments in Luther's work against market and capitalism which can be seen as early indication of an aim of constructing a "welfare state" instead of an unregulated market economy. But the first trace of the modern welfare state are the poor laws and the debate in 1870s, see Chap. 9 in this book. And there are 300 years with Lutheran rulers between Luther and the first modern arguments for a welfare state. So, it seems reasonable to be rather cautious about the causal chain from Luther to the Scandinavian welfare state. A recent book by theologians is, however, more assertive in claiming a chain from Luther to the welfare state, see Koefoed & Holm (2021).

1.5 Moral Restrictions as Alternatives to Economic Incentives

The conclusion of the previous sections is that it is impossible to achieve an ideal situation with a sufficient supply of public goods, a cooperative equilibrium in the games, a sustainable long-run development, and a fair income distribution without restrictions on the market and regulations of individual private interests. Such restriction is not intrinsic to an unregulated market economy and can take many forms e.g., laws or guidelines in the form of advice, recommendations, and morals. In many cases formal laws are difficult to formulate and control, so ethical guidelines seem in many situations more attractive, if they are respected without formal control and punishment.

Nobel Prize winner Elinor Ostrom argued that a structure of local organizations in a polycentric governance system, even if looking "terribly messy and hard to understand", can be a more sustainable system for the solution of "tragedy of the common" problems. Social norms in smaller communities can do a better job than seemingly rational general regulations (Ostrom 1999). "A frequent finding is that when the users of a common-pool resource organize themselves and enforce some of their own basic rules, they tend to manage local resources more sustainably than when rules are externally imposed on them" (Ostrom 2000, p. 148), and "individuals achieve results that are "better than rational" by building conditions where reciprocity, reputation, and trust can help to overcome the strong temptations of short-term self-interest" (Ostrom 1998, p. 1).

It is furthermore important to stress that the use of "rational" economic incentives can have a crowding-out effect in relation to social norms; if people are paid, the social norms for doing such work are weakened, see Frey et al. (1996), Frey and Oberholzer-Gee (1997) and Frey and Jegen (2001). The conclusion can very well be "pay enough or don't pay at all", see Gneezy and Rustichini (2000). An example where systems using economic incentives have been in direct confrontation with systems using morality and a belief of altruism is the case of blood donors. Richard Titmuss book "The Gift Relationship: From Human blood to Social Policy" from 1971 argued that the US system using economic incentives is much less effective than the British system, which builds on volunteers (Titmuss 1971). This has subsequently caused an intensive debate, but Titmuss arguments have been so convincing that WHO for the last 40 years has recommended not using economic incentives. But this point of view has been contradicted by e.g., Lacetera et al. (Lacetera et al. 2012). For a recent overview see e.g., Slonim et al. (2014) arguing for material but non-monetary incentives. See Chap. 15 below.

In most of the discussed cases in the section above the long-term optimal situation is in conflict with the individuals' short-term self-interest. This means that guidelines and moral restrictions, to be effective, will need to be perceived as very binding. Moral rules may be strengthened if they can achieve the status of religious rules or taboos, and no doubt some of the religious rules are important rational maxims crystallised into religious dogmas.

A number of cases provide evidence of an appropriate effect of taboos. Colding (1998) indicates that food taboos are effective means of achieving sustainable hunting patterns in part of Brazil. Afe (2013) argues that taboos can be a necessary and complementary tool in achieving a sustainable social order and moral rectitude in Ondo Province in Nigeria. "Taboo was one of the mechanisms used by the traditional institution to maintain peace, law and order" (Afe 2013, p. 107). "Many resource and habitat taboos have functions similar to those of formal institutions for nature conservation in contemporary society but have not been sufficiently recognized in this capacity" (Colding and Folke 2001 p. 584). All this means that also more theoretical economists are beginning to analyse morals and taboos, see e.g., Benabou and Tirole (2011).

Sacred texts such as the Christian Bible obviously do not use terms such as "public goods" or "cooperative equilibrium". But the main idea in relation to both public goods and cooperative equilibrium is that some problems can only be handled in common, and this is a main tenet of Christianity and of many other religions. This is the opposite of the Margaret Thatcher quotation: "There is no such thing as society". The demand for charity and solidarity are common to many religions - "Love your neighbour as yourself" (e.g., Matthew 22: 37) is an indication of interpersonal interdependency. The analogy of a body with individuals as its limbs is a more specific description of this attitude.[2] The quotation "Do nothing out of selfish ambition or vain conceit, but in humility consider others better than you. Each of you should look not only to your own interests, but also to the interests of others" (Paul's letter to Philippians 2: 3–4), could perhaps be translated as "Do not search for a Nash equilibrium, try to find a cooperative one".

Sustainability and ecological stewardship can also find support in the Bible, e.g., the instruction to Noah to take care of biodiversity: "Take with you seven of every kind of clean animal, a male and its mate; and two of every kind of unclean animals, a male and its mate; and also, seven of every kind of bird, male and female, to keep their various kinds alive throughout the earth" (Genesis 7: 2–3). It is so precise that the main article in modern economic theory about biodiversity is called "The Noah's Ark problem" (Weitzman 1998). Here the problem is which species you should take care of if there is not enough room in the ark and the landscape for all of them. For a more profound interpretation of Genesis in relation to stewardship of nature see Chap. 11 below.

Income distribution is also intensively dealt with in the Bible, and many of the authors are rather explicit in the call to care for the poor. For instance, in Acta 20:35: "In everything I did, I have showed you that by this kind of hard work we must help the weak, remembering the words of the Lord Jesus himself said, 'It is more blessed to give than to receive'" and in Luke 6:20: "Blessed are you who are poor, for yours is the Kingdom of God". A third case is Deuteronomy 24: 19–22: "When you are harvesting in your field and you overlook a sheaf, do not go back to get it. Leave it for the alien, the fatherless and the widow, so that the Lord your God may bless you in all the work of your hands. When you beat the olives from your trees, do not go over the branches a second time. Leave what remains for the alien, the fatherless and the widow. When you harvest the grapes in your vineyard, do not go over the wines again. Leave what remains for the alien, the fatherless and the widow. Remember that you were slaves in Egypt."

An example which shows a call for solidarity with both the poor and with nature is found in Exodus 23: 10–11: "For six years you are to sow your fields and harvest

---

[2] E.g., Paul's first letter to Corinthians 12: 25–27: "So that there may be no division in the body, but that its parts should have equal concern for each another. If one part suffers, every part suffers with it; if one part is honoured, every part rejoices with it". Or Paul's letter to the Romans 12:4–8: "Just as each of us has one body with many members, and these members do not all have the same function, so in Christ we who are many form one body, and each member belongs to all the others. We have different gifts, according to the grace given to us. If a man's gift is prophesying, let him use it in proportion to his faith. If it is serving, let him serve; if it is teaching, let him teach; if it is encouraging, let him encourage; if it is contributing to the needs of others, let him give generously; if it is leadership, let him govern diligently; if it is showing mercy, let him do it cheerfully."

the crops, but during the seventh year let the land lie unploughed and unused. Then the poor among your people may get food from it, and the wild animals may eat what is left over. Do the same with your vineyard and your olive grove". This quotation can be seen as both a rational restriction on the crop rotation in form of religious barriers against the temptation to deplete the soil, and as a call to take care of the weak and of nature.

Religion and taboos can of course be barriers to a harmonious and happy development. Both religion and taboos are, however, many different things, and a number of chapters in this book argue that religion and taboos can also be instrumental in securing rational interest of the common and the long term. Such interests may well be neglected in a traditional market economy. Institutions based on traditions, moral and religion may well, by taking care of a broader palette of interests, be more optimal than seemingly more rational institutions based on individual utility maximizing, unregulated markets, and new public management.

1.6 The Role of Market, Ethics, and Religion in Regulating Society

Religion, ethics, and the markets seem to supplement each other when a society's resources should be distributed and exchanged between the members of the society. All three can be mechanisms by which the society's resources can be distributed and exchanged in a regulated manner without too many conflicts and without too much violence. But the mechanisms do not only supplement each other. There can also be situations as mentioned where one mechanism crowds another one out. People can feel a call to do something specific for their society, but, if such tasks are commercialized by economic incentives on a market, the call can be weakened or disappear. There are a considerable number of cases where soft ethical regulations are crowded out by incentives that are more schematic and commercial. The donor blood examples has been mentioned. Time tracking and accord payment can kill volunteering and the "Lutheran work ethic". Economic incentives can have the opposite effect of the expected. If a fine is introduced – for instance for lateness - it can have the effect that people no longer feel a bad conscience about being late. They feel that when they pay for it themselves there is no reason for bad conscience, and in many cases bad conscience has a stronger effect than economic incentives. Such arguments are recently becoming more common among mainstream economists in what is called "behavioural economics" which clearly indicates that ethics and the market cannot be seen in isolation from each other.

But in many relationships, there seems to be a clear division of labour between the three. Religion and ethics deal with what are fair and just, the market with what is efficient. High wages and incomes in a market economy are not intended to reflect some sort of justice but to give the right incentive to allocate the labour force and the resources in an optimal way. To move resources from areas where they are plentiful

1 Introduction: Market, Ethics and Religion

to an area where they are scarce is the aim of the market. This is done by the price mechanism. If a commodity is scarce, it will be expensive. To make a society successful their needs, however, to be a reasonable amount of both fairness and efficiency. If the market creates a very unequal income distribution, the society will not be successful. But neither will it succeed without incentives.

Different scientific disciplines handle different problems and start from different points of view. This is also the case in relation to regulation, markets, and distribution of commodities. Each of the disciplines focuses on specific issues. And to get a balanced picture of the society and a rational solution of the problems it is consequently often necessary to combine the different points of view. The whole truth can neither be found by the economists' deep analysis of a rational market, nor by the lawyer's construction of precise laws, by the philosopher's profound thoughts about ethics, or by the theologian's deliberations about right and wrong. There needs to be a debate between them and a combination of the different viewpoints – and this is the aim of this book. The book includes 20 chapters, which is divided in three main parts, one about economics, one about religion and one with specific cases.

1.7 First Part: Economics

The first part includes five chapters dealing with arguments for and against the market economy and the theory about it. All written by economists. It covers arguments for the rationality and irrationality of the market seen from an economic point of view and discusses what might be seen as problems and limitations for the market when addressed from such an economic point of view. The section discusses basic assumptions in mainstream economics, external effects and pollution, unjust distribution of income, and happiness. In other words, rationality and irrationalities, optimality and exception from optimality discussed by economists. The function of this section is to give a basic understanding of how economist thinks about the topics discussed in this book.

This starts with a general introduction to behavioural assumptions and value judgment in the economic theory of the market. In this chapter, *Agnar Sandmo* discusses the normal implicit assumption behind the economic market models. In the following chapter, *Peder Andersen* analyses how market failure is handled in mainstream economic theory. Problems like external effects and public goods are explained and what to do about them are discussed. These two chapters describe the assumptions and results in standard mainstream economics.

The following three chapters discuss more specific problems related to economics and the good society. Can and shall economics take part in the debate about how a society shall be organized? After all, the father of economics, Adam Smith, was a professor of moral philosophy, but for many modern economists is the ideal to be a real science with objective and formalized models. The answer is far from obvious. In the third chapter, *Hans Aage* discusses exactly the limitation of economics. Economics has a consistent and well-developed theory of the market economy but, unfortunately, economists often used the theory on problems where it isn't adequate. According to Hans Aage, the discipline has to accept its limitations when discussing environment, health care, culture and income distribution. This is followed by a chapter of *Peder J. Pedersen* about happiness; can happiness be a legitimate part of an economic analysis and contribute to it? It is obvious that a happy life is based on many other things than economy, but what is the relationship between economic wealth and happiness? It is empirical investigated how important economic variables like income are in creating personal happiness. In the last chapter in the part, the economist *Tomáš Sedláček* analysis the relation between religion and economics. Both the influence that economics had on religion and vice versa. The chapter compares the fruit of economic ethics compared with Christian ethics in order to encourage a new debate over the spirit of capitalism.

It is not the intention of this section to let the economists take part in the ethical and philosophical debate on a common basic with ethicists, theologians, and philosophers. Today's scientific disciplines have so different methods and concepts that this is almost impossible. Nevertheless, an interdisciplinary dialogue is necessary, and this section attempts to describe how economists think about questions of common interests, in economic terminology, but hopefully understandable for other disciplines.

1.8 Second Part: Religion and Society

This part includes eight chapters and deals with religious attitude to the market society, social problems, and capitalism. What positions do the different religions hold on questions of market, social problems and politics? There is, however, even among theologians, no agreement about the basic starting point: The question of whether a religious view of life needs to have implications for social and political attitudes has result in harsh debates. Many theologians are of the opinion that it does; people from very different religions have often condemned usury, exploitation of the weak, profit maximizing or capitalism. Even if there are many different religions, and even if there are strong conflicts within the specific religions, there have been numerous debates about such questions in almost all major religions.

This section does not discuss all religions worldwide but is concentrated on those common in Western Europe: Lutheran Christianity, the Catholic Church and Islam. The section starts with two protestant theologians' analyses of these questions. *Svend Andersen* discusses Lutheran social ethics. The chapter takes its point of departure in a classical text but finishes by discussing the possibility of formulating a Lutheran social ethics for our time. *Philip Goodchild* stresses that modern rationalization proceed life to quantification, generating evidence and models, and the more we subject life to codification, generating systems, regulations, and procedures, then the less we understand of who we are and what we do.

In the following two chapters *Niels Kærgård* describes two earlier debates with participation of leading Danish theologians about Christianity and the market economy. First, the very profound debate in the 1870s between two of the most famous theologians in Denmark about the Christian church's attitude to social ethics and the market. The one theologian was very critical to the market distribution of wealth between rich and poor, whilst the other had no intention of participating in economic and political affairs but made a clear separation between Christianity and economic arguments. Secondly, in the following chapter, *Niels Kærgård* considers the Danish philosopher and theologian K. E. Løgstrup's ethics and discusses whether they can be seen as an alternative to the economists' theory about a selfish and egocentric homo economicus.

In the next chapter, *Ole Jensen* discusses mankind's relation to nature, biodiversity, and climate; an interpretation of the myth of Creation given in Genesis 1:28 has resulted in an anthropocentric perspective on life, according to which mankind has a right to exploit nature and other species to its own advantage. This interpretation is rejected, and an alternative is set out.

After these theological discussions, the following chapter by *Peter Lüchau* deals with a sociological description of the actual attitudes in the Danish population; the interrelation between religious, political, and moral attitudes and their impact on the Danish society is investigated. The influence of religion on political and moral values in Denmark at the present time seems to be rather limited.

The last two chapters in this part deal with non-Lutheran attitudes to the social questions. *Else-Britt Nilsen* describes the Catholic Church's social ethics and *Jakob Skovgaard-Petersen* summarizes the Islamic attitude to the market and the social question as presented in the course of this religion's history.

1.9 Third Part: Different Cases

This last part deals with the limitations of the market mechanism. Economists do often appreciate the market but some of the uses are highly questionable. Trade with human organs and sexual services is often - perhaps normally - seen as unethical. Usury and exploitation of weak members of society must, according to ethics and religion, often be condemned, sometimes directly forbidden. Profit maximization is by many seen as greed and unethical. Income equality is an important aim not taken care of by the market economy. This is such border line cases which are discussed in this third part.

In many of the cases, where market regulation is inappropriate or unethical, morality and religion are used and relevant in the regulation of the behaviour. Religion and taboos can be instrumental in the creation of a successful society securing sufficient safety for weak individuals, a sustainable use of limited resources and a fair income distribution. Such important aims can easily be neglected in a traditional commercial market. The permanent debates about "stakeholders" versus "shareholders" and about "gemeinschaft" versus "gesellschaft" are indications of how important such debates on the limitations of market regulation have become.

The part starts with a chapter by *Kirsten Halsnæs & Thomas Ploug* about ethical considerations in relation to trade with human body parts, with commercial surrogacy as example. Whether commercial trade with such "goods" are ethical defendable is highly debated. Consequently, different countries have different rules. The same is the case for sexual "services", addressed in the following chapter by *Hanne Petersen,* who writes about the – often hidden – market for sexual services; is it at all ethical to have markets for such services? Even among the Western European countries, some have forbidden it and punish both sellers and buyers whilst, in others, there are open and official markets.

In the third chapter in this part of special markets and cases, ecclesiastical historian *Martin Schwarz Lausten* describes the credit market and the debate in the sixteenth century on the prohibition of interest. Is the money market a fair and normal market or is money like surrogacy and sexual services too specialised to be considered as normal tradable goods? At the time of Denmark's transition to the Lutheran faith, there was an interesting debate and conflicts between Lutheran theologians and economic pragmatists.

The focus changes in the following chapters to more societal institutions. The grand old man in the discussion of the Danish welfare state and the relation between Christianity and the welfare state, *Jørn Henrik Petersen,* discusses the Danish (and Scandinavian) welfare state. Is such a type of society at all possible without a strong religious or ethically founded solidarity binding its inhabitants together?

Chapter 19 deals with corporate ethical responsibility. *Jacob Dahl Rendtorff* analyses corporate social responsibility and its foundation in general ethical considerations. The company is not only a profit maximizing unity but need to be a good citizen showing institutional responsibility and cosmopolitanism. The firms are clearly not only responsible in relation to the shareholder but to many other stakeholders.

The last chapter deals with the climate crisis. The division between market and ethics is also here central, but the problem is different. The problem here is the very long run and the transgressive character of the problem. This places the relation between generations and consequently sustainability in a central position and put the question whether the market mechanism can handle such problem in a situation where countries have incentives to free ride. *Kirsten Halsnæs & Niels Kærgård*'s analyses these problems in this chapter.

References

Afe, A.E. 2013. Taboos and the maintenance of social order in the Old Ondo Province, Southwestern Nigeria. *African Research Review* 7 (1): 95–109.
Arrow, K.J., and F.H. Hahn. 1971. *General competitive analyses.* San Francisco: Holden Day.
Arrow, K., P. Dasgupta, L. Goulder, G. Daily, P. Ehrlich, G. Heal, S. Levin, K.-G. Mäler, S. Schneider, D. Starret, and B. Walker. 2004. Are we consuming too much? *Journal of Economic Perspective* 18 (3): 147–172.

Benabou, R., and J. Tirole. 2011. Identity morals, and taboos: Beliefs as assets. *Quarterly Journal of Economics* 126 (2): 805–855.

Colding, J. 1998. Analysis of hunting options by the use of general food taboos. *Ecological Modelling* 110 (1): 5–17.

Colding, J., and C. Folke. 2001. Social taboos: "invisible" Systems of Local Resource Management and Biological Conservation. *Ecological Applications* 11 (2): 584–600.

Fenger, O., and C.R. Jansen, eds. 1991. *Jyske lov i 750 år*. Viborg: Udgiverselskabet ved Landsarkivet for Nørrejylland.

Frey, B.S., and R. Jegen. 2001. Motivation crowding theory. *Journal of Economic Surveys* 15 (5): 591–611.

Frey, B.S., and F. Oberholzer-Gee. 1997. The cost of Price incentives: An empirical analysis of motivation crowding-out. *American Economic Review* 87 (4): 746–755.

Frey, B.S., F. Oberholzer-Gee, and R. Eichenberger. 1996. The old lady visits your backyard: A tale of morals and markets. *Journal of Political Economy* 104 (6): 1297–1313.

Gneezy, U., and A. Rustichini. 2000. Pay enough or don't pay at all. *Quarterly Journal of Economics* 115 (3): 791–810.

Hardin, G. 1968. The tragedy of the commons. *Science* 162 (2859): 1243–1248.

Hayek, F.A. 1948. *Individualism and economic order*. Chicago: Chicago University Press.

Hobbes, T. 1651. *Leviathan or the matter, Forme and power of a commonwealth ecclesiastical and civil*, several editions among others Jan Shapire (ed.) New Haven: Yale University Press, 2010.

Kærgård, Niels. 2013. Religion und Wohlfahrtstaatlichkeit in Dänemark. Der Wohlfahrtstaat als Produkt gottesfürchtiger Christen oder mächtiger Politiker? In *Religion und Wohlfahtsstaatlichkeit in Europa*, ed. K. Gabriel, H.-R. Reuther, A. Kurschat, and S. Leibold. Tübingen: Mohr Siebeck.

———. 2017. *Hvorfor er vi så rige og lykkelige?* Eksistensen, Copenhagen: Reformationen og økonomien.

Koefoed, N. J., and B. K. Holm. 2021. *Pligt og omsorg – velfærdsstatens lutherske rødder*, Copenhagen: Gads Forlag.

Lacetera, N., M. Macis, and R. Slonim. 2012. Will there be blood? Incentives and substitution effects in pro-social behavior. *American Economic Journal: Economic Policy* 4 (19): 186–123.

Løgstrup, K. E. 1971. Etiske begreber og problemer. In G. Wingreen (Ed.), *Etik og Kristen tro* (pp. 205–286), Gyldendal, Copenhagen.

Moss, L.S. 1996. Review of H.G. Brennan & A.M.C. Waterman (ed.) Economics and religion: Are they distinct? *European Journal of History of Economic Thought* 3: 490–494.

Ostrom, E. 1998. A behavioral approach to the rational choice theory of collective action - presidential address, American Political Science Association 1997. *American Political Science Review* 92 (1): 1–22.

———. 1999. Coping with tragedies of the commons. *Annual Review of Political Science* 1999 (2): 493–535.

———. 2000. Collective action and the evolution of social norms. *Journal of Economic Perspectives* 14 (3): 137–158.

Petersen, Jørn Henrik. 2016. *Fra Luther til Konkurrencestaten*. Odense: Syddansk Universitetsforlag.

———. 2017. *Luthers socialetik og det moderne samfund*. Odense: Syddansk Universitetsforlag.

———. 2018. *Den glemte Luther*. Odense: Syddansk Universitetsforlag.

Samuelson, P.A. 1948. *Economics: An introductory analysis*. Nev York: McGraw-Hill.

———. 1954. The pure theory of public expenditure. *Review of Economics and Statistics* 36 (4): 387–389.

Slonim, R., C. Wang, and E. Garbarino. 2014. The market for blood. *Journal of Economic Perspectives* 28: 177–196.

Smith, A. 1776. *An inquiry into the nature and causes of the wealth of nations*. London: Methuen & Co. (a huge number of later reprints).
Titmuss, R. 1971. *The gift relationship: From human blood to social policy*. New York: Random house.
United Nations. 1987. *Our common future, World Commission on Environment and Development*. Oxford: Oxford University Press.
von Neumann, John, and Oskar Morgenstern. 1944. *Theory of game and economic behavior*. Princeton University Press.
Weitzman, M.L. 1998. The Noah's ark problem. *Econometrica* 66 (6): 1279–1298.

Niels Kærgård born 1942, since 1993 professor of agricultural economics and policy at University of Copenhagen. First chairman of the Danish Board of Economic Advisors 1995–2001. In the board of University of Copenhagen 2008–2013, vice-president of The Danish Academy of Science and Letters 2008–2013.

Part I
Economics of the Market

Chapter 2
The Market in Economics: Behavioural Assumptions and Value Judgments

Agnar Sandmo

Abstract The market in terms of the interplay between utility-maximizing consumers and profit-maximizing producers plays a central role in modern economics. Since the time of Adam Smith economists have been concerned with the development of the internal logic of their models of markets, sometimes with the consequence that too little attention has been paid to the broader, sometimes implicit, social context in which market transactions take place. For an enlightened understanding of economic theory, it is, however, essential to keep in mind that economists do not always find it necessary to present a full account of human motivation in the analysis of each and every piece of analysis. The article will discuss the often implicit behavioural assumptions and the value judgments more explicitly.

Keywords Market economy · Behavioural assumptions · Value judgments · Normative and positive economics

2.1 Introduction

The study of markets plays a central role in economics; naturally enough in view of the fact that the market mechanism is of crucial importance for modern economies and has been so throughout history. There are to be sure examples of economic systems – most notably the communist economies of the Soviet Union and its sphere of influence – where governments have tried to suppress the operation of the market mechanism and replace it with central planning. However, it is a remarkable feature of these attempts that they have not proved to be viable; detailed central planning has turned out to encounter so many difficulties that the market system has

---

A. Sandmo (deceased)
Norwegian School of Economics, Bergen, Norway
e-mail: nik@ifro.ku.dk

© The Author(s), under exclusive license to Springer Nature Switzerland AG 2023
N. Kærgård (ed.), *Market, Ethics and Religion*, Ethical Economy 62,
https://doi.org/10.1007/978-3-031-08462-1_2

reestablished itself in the reformed economies of Russia and Eastern Europe. Another notable aspect of central planning is that the theory of the market economy has been an important point of reference for the proper understanding of how a system of economic planning works. This reference has sometimes taken the form of setting the efficient market up as a contrast to an inefficient system of central planning, but it has also played a more subtle role in the debate about alternative economic systems. Thus, in the interwar period, the Polish economist Oskar Lange coined the phrase "market socialism" to describe his interesting blueprint for an efficiently functioning socialist economy. In Lange's system, the central planning committee of the socialist state would design its system so that it would work like a smoothly functioning market economy but without the market failures that are important features of real market economies and which also lie in the central field of interest of the theoretical economist (see Lange and Taylor 1938).

There are obviously a large number of markets in the modern economy, and many of these have special features that distinguish them from the markets for other goods. Markets for services have characteristics that make them different from the markets for physical commodities, and within the service sector there are a number of differences between e.g. the market for financial services and that for health care. In the markets for ordinary consumer goods, agricultural markets in many countries operate in an institutional framework that is different from the markets for industrial products, and in order to fully understand the markets for durable goods like housing and paintings one has to acquire specialized knowledge that goes beyond a general insight in economic theory.

In spite of these complexities, economists have since the beginning of their science assumed that there are some general features of all markets that can form a useful framework for the study both of individual markets and of their interaction with other markets, and it is this general framework that I will focus on in the following discussion. This must not be taken to mean that there is a fixed body of theory that all academic economists adhere to in every respect. In an evolving science there must necessarily be a number of researchers that are dissatisfied with the present state of the subject and are engaged in its further improvement. In addition, there is naturally less than complete agreement about the new directions that economics in general and the economic theory of markets in particular should take. If this were not the case, economics would be a stationary subject with little appeal to the intellectually curious. But within the confines of a single chapter I cannot possibly cover all new developments in the study of the market economy and have to limit my focus to what the majority of the profession would probably agree on as being the central features of the study of markets.

What we usually refer to as the market economy cannot be understood by focusing on the markets alone. In any market economy there is a substantial public sector that allocates resources by the use of planning and bureaucracy without the use of markets, and some parts of resource allocation take place within firms, families and voluntary organizations. Throughout the history of economics there has been a lively debate on the appropriate roles of the private and public sectors in the economy, especially on the role of markets versus planning. This requires a normative analysis of what markets can and cannot do and to what extent the achievements of markets are in accordance with some notion of social welfare or the common good. Thus, the theory of markets has both positive (descriptive) and normative aspects, and both aspects will be discussed in the following. I begin with positive economics.

2.2 Supply and Demand

In the centre of the theory of markets is the concept of a commodity (which could be a physical good, a service or even a financial asset or liability). Grouped around the commodity are the market agents, i.e. the consumers and producers or buyers and sellers. Consumers are buyers in the markets for consumer goods and sellers in the markets for factors of production, in particular in the labour market. For producers it is the other way round; they are sellers in the markets for consumer goods and buyers in the markets for factors of production.[1] Whatever the market, we can identify a set of buyers and sellers. For the buyers, it is natural to assume that they will wish to buy more of the commodity in question the lower is the price, assuming that all other prices remain the same. For producers, an equally natural assumption is that they will wish to produce and sell more, the higher is the price. The price that is such that the quantity demanded equals the quantity supplied is the *equilibrium price*. If the actual price is higher than this, there is excess supply, and the price will tend to fall. If the price is lower than the equilibrium price, there is a situation of excess demand, and the price will rise. The equilibrium price is in other words that towards which the actual market price will tend to converge, although at a particular moment of time it might deviate from it.

This account depicts the theory of supply, demand and price determination with reference to a single market and is therefore often referred to as partial equilibrium theory. But markets are interrelated: The demand for cars depends not only on the price of cars but also on the prices of petrol and railway tickets, just like the demand for petrol depends on the prices of cars and railway tickets. In fact, since on the demand side all consumer goods compete for the consumers' money, the demand for every consumer good depends in principle on the prices of all consumer goods. Likewise, on the supply side an increase in the price of a particular good tends to lead producers to produce more of it, while an increase in the price of a factor of production creates incentives for producers to use less of it and instead use more of other factors of production that have become relatively cheaper. Production decisions with regard to inputs and outputs therefore depend on the prices of all inputs and outputs in the economy. If we try to construct a model of the whole economy, or at least of the whole market system in the economy, we have to introduce the notion of the equilibrium set of prices instead of just the equilibrium price, and this

---

[1] In addition, there are the markets for intermediate goods where firms produce factors of production, like machinery and raw materials, for use in production by other firms.

set of prices is such that it leads to equality of supply and demand in all markets. This is the definition of *general equilibrium*.

The general equilibrium theory of the market economy, as it was first formulated by Léon Walras (1874–77), is a very ambitious theory. In principle, it claims to determine the quantities produced and consumed of all goods and factors of production in the economy as well as the distribution of income as the result of the interplay of the forces of supply and demand. The general model has a number of special versions that can be adapted to the study of particular aspects of economic life. The use of these models is typically to study the effects on prices, industrial structure and income distribution of changes in such exogenous data as world market prices, various types of technical progress and the discovery of new supplies of natural resources. They offer an understanding of why some industries decline and others expand, why the wages of some professions fall and others rise, and why the holdings of some forms of capital become more profitable while others become less attractive to investors.

Two remarks are in order at this point. First of all, as regards the issue of what the model determines, I must emphasize strongly the qualification implicit in the term "in principle". Naturally, the economist cannot possibly claim that he is able to explain or predict all prices and quantities in the market economy; such a claim would border on the ridiculous. What the analysis provides is a general framework for analysis, a certain way of thinking, that can be applied to more concrete cases both by theoretical adaptation of the general model and numerical calculation. One set of cases relate to the problems that arise in an open economy, where models address issues like the effects of trade liberalization or increases in migration on the domestic economy. Another class of models are especially adapted to study the interaction between the private and public sectors and are concerned e.g. with the effect of alternative tax systems on the allocation of labour and capital between industries.

A second point worth emphasizing is that the theory of general equilibrium in the market economy outlined above is strictly speaking only valid for a special case of a market economy, viz. that of perfect competition. Perfect competition is the case where no agent has sufficient power to have appreciable influence on the market prices; instead he takes the prices of goods and factors of production as determined by impersonal market forces. The real market economy is not quite like that. In some branches there are just a few producers, sometimes no more than one, and these often do have the power to influence market prices and sometimes even the power to influence the choice of economic policies adopted by the government.

Whatever the market form, it remains a general conclusion of the analysis that prices are determined by the interplay of supply and demand forces. To better understand what these forces are, we need to go behind the notions of supply and demand and look at what the theory says about the goals and incentives of consumers and producers.

2.3 Utility Maximization and Consumer Behavior

In the early days of economic theory the demand side of the economy was not given very much attention, and theorists of the market economy were not much concerned with explaining the decisions made by consumers.[2] Thus, Adam Smith in his great work *The Wealth of Nations* (Smith 1776) refers rather loosely to the individual as pursuing his own interest, but he does not go deeper into the question of what the individual's interest is or exactly how he goes about pursuing it. The establishment of such a deeper theory was a task left for economists of the nineteenth and twentieth centuries and is based on the notion of utility maximization.

Utility is not an easy concept, and its conceptual content has changed greatly over time. To begin with it was seen as a property that goods possessed, and this was why goods were desired. This perception of the concept gradually changed to become a measure of the consumer's preferences; that one good had more utility than another was simply an expression of the fact that the first good was more preferred that the second. Naturally, the new view led to the realization that since utility must be seen as a subjective and not an objective property of goods, it could not be directly compared between persons. But it could still function as a basis for the theory of consumer demand. The most interesting property of utility then became that of *marginal utility* as first suggested by Gossen (1854). Marginal utility is the increase in utility that you get by consuming an extra unit of the commodity. It is reasonable to assume that marginal utility is decreasing; the more you consume, the less valuable is the extra unit. Would you be willing to buy the extra unit? This requires a comparison between marginal utility and price. As long as marginal utility is higher than the price, you would like to buy more of the good. If marginal utility is lower than the price, you would wish to reduce your consumption. Your optimal level of consumption is where price and marginal utility coincide. This is very abstract. But note that the theory has one empirical implication that is empirically testable: If, at your chosen optimum, the price of a particular commodity goes up the quantity demanded will fall; similarly, if the price goes down demand will increase. The assumption of utility maximization, together with that of decreasing marginal utility, implies the hypothesis that the demand curve – the curve showing the relationship between the quantity demanded and the price – is downward sloping.

The theory as sketched here, which roughly corresponds to its state at the end of the nineteenth century, is in many respects unsatisfactory. During the next century it was refined in a number of ways. First of all, it was realized that one had to take account of the consumer's budget constraint, requiring that the sum of expenditure

---

[2] For simplicity I refer to individual agents as consumers, although, as indicated above, the explanation of individual behaviour covers both the demand for consumer goods and the supply of factors of production like labour.

on all goods cannot exceed his income.[3] This implies that one cannot simply analyze the demand for one commodity at a time; one has to study the joint determination of the demand for all commodities. The second refinement relates to the concept of utility. Many economists felt uneasy about this both because it seemed to associate economics too closely with utilitarian philosophy and because it seemed to build on some very simplistic psychological assumptions. Beginning with Vilfredo Pareto (1909), economics gradually came to discard the traditional concept of utility and substitute the notion of a preference ordering. The only assumption that was required for a theory of rational consumer choice was that the individual was able to rank all available alternatives in terms of preferences. The principle of choice then became to choose that among all available alternatives which is ranked highest in the consumer's preference ordering. Remarkably, even this extremely general approach turned out to have implications for demand behavior that were empirically meaningful. But although this meant that economic theory could do without the concept of utility, utility maximization survived as a convenient representation of the more general but cumbersome principle of choosing among available alternatives according to one's preference ordering.

Whether one considers the theory of utility maximization in its nineteenth century version or in its most recent and more general formulation, the picture that it presents of the individual consumer in the market economy is basically the same. The individual attempts to achieve the best possible result for himself, given the constraints imposed by his resources. This perspective is applied not only to the allocation of his household budget between consumer goods, but also to saving and portfolio decisions and to the explanation of labour supply and occupational choice. In recent decades there has also been a strong tendency to apply the economic theory of utility maximization and rational choice to areas that were previously considered to lie outside the scope of economic analysis. This tendency, which has been characterized as "economic imperialism" (Lazear 2000) is particularly associated with Gary Becker, who has applied the theory to such areas as crime and punishment (Becker 1968) and family decisions, including marriage, child-bearing and divorce (Becker 1981).

2.4 Profit Maximization and Producer Decisions

The theory of utility maximization attempts to describe demand behavior in the market. On the supply side, the corresponding assumption is that of profit maximization. The firm is assumed to maximize the difference between sales revenue and costs. A central concept in this theory is the production function, which relates

---

[3] In an extension of the theory, one can analyze the consumer's expenditure over time. Then, although equality between expenditure and income must hold over the consumer's lifetime, in any one period such as a week or a year, expenditure could be either greater than or less than income, depending on the adjustment of cash balances and borrowing and lending transactions.

output to the input of factors of production like various types of labour and capital. The effect on output of a unit's increase in the input of a particular factor of production is called the factor's *marginal productivity*. The standard assumption is that marginal productivity is positive and decreasing; with successive increases of a particular factor of production, the marginal effect on output goes down. In considering whether or not to add an additional unit of input, the firm will compare the value of the additional output that this generates with the cost of the additional unit, which is simply its price. If the value of marginal productivity exceeds the price of the factor, the additional unit should be bought. If the reverse inequality holds, input should be reduced. The firm's optimum is achieved where the value of the marginal productivity is equal to the factor price. An obvious implication of this is that an increase in the price of the factor will lead to a reduction in demand. In other words, the demand curve for a factor of production is downward sloping. By using a similar reasoning, one can show that the supply curve, showing the relationship between the price of the output and the amount produced, is upward sloping.

The theory can be reformulated in a number of ways relative to the simple textbook version that has been sketched here. The time dimension can be taken into account by assuming that the firm maximizes the present value of future revenues and costs, and there is a large body of literature which is based on the view that the firm maximizes its stock market value. A common feature of all these formulations is that they see the firm's objective as being the maximization of the income from the firm that accrues to the owners, while the owners are assumed to have no other interest in the firm than as a source of private income.

Compared to the hypothesis of utility maximization, profit maximization is a much more specific assumption. One could imagine a much richer formulation of the firm's objectives to include a number of additional elements. Some of these could be of a social nature, such as the provision of meaningful jobs, environmental responsibility and product quality, while others could relate to the private concerns of the management, including on the one hand their personal morality, the size and prestige of the firm and managers' salaries. So why focus on the narrower hypothesis? One line of defense is that of explanatory power: If the simple assumption can explain commodity supply and factor demand in a way that is consistent with empirical observation, there is no need for a more complex hypothesis about objectives. Another line of defense is based on the basic logic of the market economy. If the present owners and managers of the firm fail to exploit its earnings potential, there will be investors in the market who realize that they can make a profit through a take-over bid: By offering the present owners to buy the firm at its present market valuation and install a new management they can make a financial gain by running the firm according to the principles of profit maximization. According to this logic, if owners and managers want the firm to survive in their own hands, they have in fact no choice about which objective to adopt: The only alternative is profit maximization.

These are fairly convincing arguments in favour of the realism of this hypothesis. However, it would perhaps be hasty to conclude that there is no need to think further along these lines. On the one hand, there may be sectors of the economy where the competitive pressure is not so high as to exclude the possibility of pursuing alternative or additional objectives. Second, from the point of view of social organization, some people would take the position that government should encourage a modification of the competitive system to allow more scope for firms to take account of wider objectives. In order to understand where such a policy might lead, it is clearly necessary to explore what implications it would have for firm behavior.

2.5 The Market Mechanism and the Public Interest

The foregoing has been a sketch of the economist's positive theory of the market economy: How do markets work? What are the assumptions underlying the economic theory of market behavior? But ever since its beginnings, economics has also approached the study of markets from another angle which raises normative and critical questions about its social function.

The question of whether the market mechanism functions in the public interest – whether it can be considered to promote social welfare – is a question that has concerned economists at least since the time of Adam Smith. The question is a natural one because, in a free market where there are no forced transactions, all parties to a particular trade must be assumed to gain from it; otherwise, they would be better off abstaining from the transaction. If individuals are free to enter into any type of transaction with each other, all possibilities for mutually advantageous transactions will be exploited, and the result will be the best possible use of society's resources. This set of ideas must have been at the back of the minds of many economists when they considered the meaning of the famous pronouncement of Adam Smith:

> *Every individual necessarily labours to render the annual revenue of society as great as he can. He generally, indeed, neither intends to promote the publick interest, nor knows how much he is promoting it. ... He intends only his own gain, and he is in this, as in so many other cases, led by an invisible hand to promote an end which was no part of his intention* (Smith 1776, 1976, p. 456)

The invisible hand became Smith's most famous single formulation and has become a popular point of reference for both market enthusiasts and critics ever since.

The context in which the quotation appears has given rise to some controversy about "what Smith really meant": It is to be found in a chapter on home versus foreign investment and not as part of a general analysis of the social benefits of markets. But the conventional interpretation of the invisible hand metaphor gains support from the presence of a number of similar statements elsewhere in the *Wealth of Nations*.[4] The reasonable interpretation is that Smith meant it as a general characterization of the workings of a market economy with free competition or, as he

---

[4] For a more detailed discussion of the interpretation of the quotation and references to later discussions of it see Sandmo (2011).

expressed it, "a system of perfect liberty." The challenge for later economists has been partly to consider in more depth how one could arrive at a more precisely definition of the public interest, and partly to explore the issue of what kind of market competition that is required for Smith's statement to be true.

Smith does not himself propose any definition of the public interest, although the term "annual revenue of society" suggests that what he had in mind was something like the modern concept of national income or product. Obviously, the maximization of national income implies that the total amount of resources available for the population is as large as possible. Nevertheless, this measure of the public interest also raises some difficult issues. Many of Smith's policy recommendations involved the dismantling of private and public regulation of competition in favour of free markets. It is easy to imagine that a reform in this direction, although leading to an increase in national income, would at the same time boost the real income for some citizens and lower it for others. Is it reasonable to conclude that the reform is unequivocally in the public interest if the gains to the winners exceed the losses to the losers? In particular, is this true even if the winners are rich and the losers poor? Some economists found an escape from this dilemma in the principles of utilitarian philosophy. Suppose that we identify the total welfare of society with the sum of utility enjoyed by its members rather than the sum of their income. Further, let us assume that the marginal utility of income is greater for the poor than for the rich. A market oriented reform then leads to a gain for society only if total utility increases, but the losses to the poor are now given more weight than the gains to the rich. Thus, even if national income were to increase it might be that social welfare could go down, since the utilitarian measure takes account both of the size of the national income and its distribution between individuals.[5]

The utilitarian approach to social welfare is in many ways an attractive one, but many economists have been skeptical about the underlying assumption that utility is objectively measurable and comparable between persons. If utility is simply a measure of preferences, it is hard to see that it makes sense to speak of sums of utility. Pareto took a strong point of view regarding this issue:

> *The utility for one individual and the utility for another individual are heterogeneous quantities. We can neither add them together nor compare them. A sum of utility enjoyed by different individuals does not exist; it is an expression which has no meaning.* (Pareto 1909, 1971, p. 192)

If we accept this view, is there then no way on the basis of which we can conclude that a social reform will lead to a gain for society? According to Pareto, the only case in which such a conclusion is possible is where everyone gains from the reform, or at least that some gain and nobody loses. From this idea follows the criterion for social efficiency that is known as *Pareto optimality*: A Pareto optimum or an efficient use of resources is such that it is not possible to reallocate resources so as to

---

[5] There are a number of passages in *The Wealth of Nations* where Smith expresses his sympathy for the poor in society, so one may guess that he would have been sympathetic to the utilitarian approach.

increase the utility of some without decreasing the utility of others. Note that this criterion does not require the possibility of interpersonal comparisons of utility. Whether utility for an individual goes up or down is simply an expression of his or her preferences.

Using only the criterion of Pareto optimality there are unlikely to be many reforms or other developments in the economy that could be clearly identified as representing progress regarding the public interest - or social welfare, to use a more modern terminology. But many economists would be prepared to go further and identify social progress with reforms or events that improve life for the great majority of citizens, or that clearly lead to a more egalitarian distribution of resources, even if some individuals lose in the process. This may mean overstepping the line between neutral economic judgment and moral philosophy,[6] but many economists have taken this step over the years – with greater or less awareness of what they are doing.

Turning now to the nature of competition, Adam Smith's notion of free competition was somewhat loose. The crucial element of his definition was freedom of entry. A single firm that for some reason enjoyed protection from competition was a monopoly and as such had the ability to charge higher prices than would be possible under free competition; in fact, he states that the price that the monopolist will charge is "the highest that can be squeezed out of the buyers" (Smith 1776, 1976, p. 79). But if an attempt to charge monopoly prices could be challenged by new entrants, the monopoly position would become worthless. So the absence of limits to entry in this sense leads to a market equilibrium that is similar to that of perfect competition even with only one or a few producers.[7] Later developments in economic theory presented a more diversified picture of competition where firms had the possibility to exert market power although they did not have a monopoly. In the limit, the absence of market power was identified with the case of perfect competition where all consumers and producers make their buying and selling decisions on the assumption that market prices are beyond their control. When market prices are such that demand is equal to supply in all markets, we have a situation of *competitive equilibrium*.

One of the main insights of economic theory is now that a competitive equilibrium is a Pareto optimum. This means that in such a state of the economy it is not possible to reallocate resources between individuals so as to make some of them better off while making no one worse off. In other words, the competitive equilibrium is socially efficient; there is no waste of resources.

Note that this result says nothing about the justice or fairness of the distribution of resources or income between individuals. The competitive market economy makes it possible for all individuals to do as well for themselves as their resources and the market prices allow. But the distribution of income and wealth may be

---

[6] It is possible to argue, however, that the criterion of Pareto optimality is not ethically neutral either, since the view that individuals are the best judges of their own interests is itself based on a certain conception of social welfare.

[7] For further discussion of Smith's thoughts on the nature of competition see Sandmo (2016).

equally or unequally distributed. The equivalence between Pareto optimality and competitive equilibrium has nothing to say about justice in the distribution of resources between individuals.

A further point worth emphasizing is the following: Since the market equilibrium is socially efficient, it might be tempting to conclude that the market agents themselves must have adequate incentives to sustain competition. But it is easy to see that this is not the case. The producers in a particular line of industry might find in their interest to combine to form a monopoly so as to reap the extra profits that such a position allows. This possibility was clearly realized by Adam Smith, who wrote:

> *People of the same trade seldom meet together, even for merriment and diversion, but the conversation ends in a conspiracy against the public, or in some contrivance to raise prices. It is impossible indeed to prevent such meetings, by any law which either could be executed, or would be consistent with liberty and justice. But though the law cannot hinder people of the same trade from sometimes assembling together, it ought to do nothing to facilitate such assemblies; much less to render them necessary.* (Smith 1776, 1976, p. 145).

So even if competition is beneficial to society (abstracting from the complications of distributive justice) the market agents do not themselves have the proper incentives to uphold the system. Even though Smith apparently took a pessimistic view of the state's ability to take on this task, it is hard to escape the conclusion that there is no other agent that can do so. An efficiently functioning market economy must be based on a symbiosis between the market and the state.

2.6 What Markets Cannot Do

As we have seen, a central conclusion of economic theory is that markets have the ability to allocate goods efficiently both with regard to production and consumption. But this conclusion has its limitations which have to do with the nature of the goods that we consider. The most obvious case where markets fail is that of public goods. A public good is such that once it has been provided everyone is able to benefit from it. A classic example is national defense. Your defense is my defense. If I were able to buy more defense for myself, you would benefit from it as much as I do. Consequently, if in such a situation I am mainly guided by my own interests, I have very weak private incentives to provide national defense, since the cost of my effort would fall entirely on me while the benefits would accrue to the whole population. But since all agents face the same incentives, a system of public goods provision that were based on voluntary contributions would be likely to result in underprovision. For national defense as well as for other cases of national infrastructure related to e.g. political institutions, police, courts of law and basic research, and for the wide class of cases that concerns the protection of the natural environment, one needs an agent that can overcome these adverse incentives. This agent is the state, which can take a broader view of benefits and costs than any individual consumer or firm. The market as a system is inadequate when it comes to the allocation of resources to public goods.

Another class of market failure emerges with so-called externalities that may arise both with regard to consumption and production decision. In the present context, the most relevant case of externalities is where private decisions have as a side effect a negative or positive effect on the quantity or quality of the availability of a public good. The most obvious examples relate to the natural environment. To take just one: Hunting for endangered species presumably provides private benefits for the hunter and for the people who buy his trophies. But hunting also imposes costs (or negative benefits) on the wider group of individuals who appreciate the public good of biological diversity. For that reason, hunting must be regulated in some way in order to improve the alignment of social benefits and costs, and the agents themselves cannot in general be relied upon to do it. There are basically two reasons for this. One is that individual incentives are not right: The individual huntsman may see little point in restraining his hunting since he compares the possibly substantial cost to himself with the infinitesimal increase in benefits that he derives from his own contribution to the public good (assuming that he too cares about biological diversity). The other reason lies in the cost of organization: If huntsmen realize that a solution to the problem lies in forcing themselves to act together, they face the cost of organizing collective action. If there are many huntsmen – more generally many agents who are involved in the process that contribute to the deterioration of the public good – this cost may be so large that individually organized common action may be difficult to achieve.[8] Once again, we need the power of the state as a supplement to the market mechanism.

This conclusion may need some modification. If the number of individuals involved in the process is not too large, and if the sets of agents who bear the costs and reap the benefits of collective action coincide, there are reasons to expect that both the incentives and organization problems may be overcome. Cases where this actually happens have been documented and analyzed in the research of Elinor Ostrom; see e.g. the survey presented in her Nobel lecture (Ostrom 2009).

2.7 Equality Versus Efficiency

The strong point of the market economy from the broader social perspective is that markets – with some qualifications – generate an efficient allocation of resources. But in addition the allocation of resources has implications for the distribution of income and standards of living between individuals in society. The shape of this distribution is not mainly the result of moral deliberations about fairness and rights (although ideas about fair wages and reasonable differentials undoubtedly play

---

[8]This class of cases is sometimes referred to as the tragedy of the commons, a term introduced in a famous article by Garret Hardin (Hardin 1968).

some role in wage formation) but of market forces that reward productivity and ownership. These factors are only partly under the control of the individual, especially since the crucial point about them is not physical productivity and ownership, but the *value* of productivity and ownership as determined by market prices. The rewards to work and investment, as seen from the point of view of the individual, is therefore determined partly by skill and effort, partly by historical accident and sheer luck. On this background, it is not surprising that governments in modern societies have seen it as one of their tasks to modify the distribution of income and wealth to which the market economy gives rise. They do this through such policies as income support, social security arrangements and progressive income taxation. The objective of all these measures is to shift the market distribution of income in the direction of more equality and modify the impact of market movements on individual standards of living.

Implicit in this line of argument is the belief that the market mechanism generates inequality. But this is a view that should be considered with a great deal of care. It is certainly true that a system that systematically rewards productivity necessarily leads to some inequalities of income. However, if the presumption is that the market economy leads to more inequality than would otherwise have been the case, it is important that one asks what "otherwise" means. What is the alternative system against which the inequality of the market economy is to be judged? This has to be one that systematically rewards work and investment on some other basis. Of the systems that have actually been tried out in practice, we know that the ideology of communist societies was to break the link with productivity by rewarding each according to his needs, but by doing this one also severed the link between income and effort, thereby causing adverse effects on productivity. In practice, moreover, the system of rewards tended to a considerable extent to reflect political privilege. It is far from clear that this was a more attractive system from the point of view of egalitarianism.

Ideally, one could imagine a society where there is a perfect distribution of tasks between the market and the state. While competitive markets ensure the efficient use of resources with regard to private goods, the government imposes taxes that are designed both to finance public expenditure and to redistribute incomes so as to achieve a high degree of equality. The challenge that this ideal solution faces is that almost all taxes tend to reduce the efficiency of the market mechanism. A good example is the progressive income tax which involves taxing the rich at higher rates than the poor. This modifies the distribution of income in the direction of more equality but at the same time it tends to discourage labour effort and saving by reducing the private returns to these activities. An increase in the degree of progression in order to achieve more equality tends to reduce the efficiency of the economy: Aggregate income falls and the total amount available for redistribution shrinks. This is what Arthur Okun referred to as "the big tradeoff": More equality has a cost in the form of less efficiency (Okun 1975). In other words, the more equally one wishes to divide the pie, the more it shrinks. How large the cost of redistribution actually is, is of course an empirical question, depending on such issues as the effectiveness of the progressive tax in redistributing income and the sensitivity of labour supply to high tax rates.

The equality-efficiency tradeoff facing public policy in a market economy is a fundamental insight. However, there may be cases where progressive taxation and other redistributive policies are efficiency-enhancing rather than the opposite. One such case is where inequalities of income are not mainly explained by productivity differences, but rather by protected monopoly positions and other privileges; in this case progressive taxation may actually serve to bring after-tax wages more in line with productivity. Another case whose importance has been argued by a number of researchers is where the experience of living in a society with small income differentials increases productivity because it fosters a spirit of solidarity and cooperation between social classes and diminishes the amount of social conflict. Several economists have seen this as the main explanation of why the Scandinavian welfare states with their compressed wage structure and large tax distortions have nevertheless been able to do so well in terms of productivity and economic growth.

2.8 The Nature of Preferences

The economic analysis of markets has always come in for a good deal of criticism. Some of the criticism has clearly been misguided in that the critics have mistaken analysis for apology: The economic explanation of how markets work has been misinterpreted as a justification for all that the critics see as the negative aspects of the market economy. But much of the critical literature – which has originated both inside and outside of the economics profession - has also been well taken and should be seriously considered.

Part of the criticism has been aimed at the assumptions that economists use to explain the driving forces of market behavior: These are said to reflect a simple view of man as greedy and self-seeking. Some of the responsibility for this kind of interpretation should clearly be placed in the economics community itself; there are examples of textbooks that use a very similar terminology to describe the theory of market behavior. At the same time, leading economists have always been sensitive to this kind of criticism. In his debates with the critics of economics in the early nineteenth century, John Stuart Mill strongly emphasized the point that the effort to understand and predict actual social and economic developments did not involve any moral acceptance of them. Half a century later, in his influential treatise on economic theory Alfred Marshall took a broad view of human motivation when he wrote that

> [e]veryone who is worth anything carries his higher nature with him into business; and, there as elsewhere, he is influenced by his personal affections, by his conceptions of duty and his reverence for high ideals. (Marshall 1890, 1920, p. 14).

It is fair to say, however, that this broad view of man's nature plays a fairly minor role in Marshall's more analytical contributions to economic analysis, as it does in the economic theory that is presented in much of the modern literature. In the textbook accounts of the utility-maximizing consumer whose preferences only concern the amount of different goods that he himself consumes, and the firm whose only concern is with the maximization of income for the owners, the critical reader may well ask what has become of the "higher nature" of economic agents that Marshall refers to.

However, a point that should be born in mind when interpreting modern economic theory is that economists are keen adherents of the principle of Occam's razor: Never use complicated theories to explain your observations when simpler theories will do. When applied to the economics of consumer behavior, the principle implies that it is unnecessary to take account of people's preferences over public goods like defense, law enforcement and biological diversity if the object of the analysis is simply to study how the demand for consumer goods depends on prices and incomes. Nevertheless, when one moves from the study of consumption demand to the field of public finance and the analysis of public goods, this more general assumption about the nature of preferences becomes of essential importance. Several economists have also taken an interest in the analysis of charitable giving, and in order to provide a theoretical basis for empirical studies in this area it is natural to postulate that the individual consumer has preferences that take account not only of his own consumption but also on that of others. All of this shows that the theory of the utility-maximizing consumer is not in the nature of a specific hypothesis of what the individual cares about; it is an analytical approach that can be applied to a wide variety of issues. It does not by necessity incorporate a general view of man as egoistic and self-seeking. In any particular theoretical application, the specific assumptions made about the nature of preferences reflect the context in which the theory is to be used. In some arenas of economic activity a narrow view of preferences is sufficient to explain behavior, while in others a broader set of assumptions will be necessary. But economists have not been very good at explaining the connection between the broader view of economic behavior and the more narrow assumptions that are adopted for the explanation of specific problems. This failure no doubt lies at the root of at least some of the criticism that has been directed against the economist's allegedly simplistic view of human nature.

These remarks should not be taken to imply that there is nothing in the standard theory of market behaviour that is in need of revision and extension. Thus, a view that is mostly implicit in the literature is that the individual's preferences are autonomous. They appear to have their origin in his or her personality and can be analyzed in isolation from the social context. Social influences, norms, ethical concerns and religious convictions are usually absent from the analysis. A few examples are sufficient to illustrate this point.

Some people would never consider having pork meat on their plate or drink wine with their meal. In a few cases this might be because they simply do not like pork or wine but a more likely explanation is that they are obeying the demands of their religion. They might actually know from previous experience that they like pork and wine; nevertheless, the preferences revealed in their market behaviour suggest that they do not. What are their "true" preferences? The majority of economists would probably argue that whatever the true preferences are, the ones that are relevant for the study of market behavior are the revealed preferences, and for this purpose it is irrelevant whether these preferences have their origin in the individual's physiological and psychological makeup or in his religious views. But this argument may be too superficial. On the one hand, taking account of religious views could play a role in positive economics since predictions of the rise or decline of religious convictions might be helpful for long run forecasts of consumer demand. From a normative perspective, moreover, peoples' judgments concerning social welfare might be heavily influenced by religious views that do not respect the principle of consumer sovereignty, i.e. the principle that it is the individual's own preferences that should count in an evaluation of what is good for society.

A second example concerns the analysis of labour supply. Understanding individual decisions about how much and what kind of work to supply is central for the understanding of how modern economies work. It is crucial for the analysis of welfare state policies and for long run economic development. The economic theory of labour supply is based on a model of utility maximization where the individual makes his choice of hours worked on the basis of an evaluation of the utility of consumption on the one hand and leisure on the other. The more leisure he gives up to work, the higher becomes his earnings and the more he is able to consume. His optimum choice is where his subjective valuation of leisure in terms of consumption is equal to the hourly wage rate. The model leads to the prediction that a higher wage rate leads to increased labour supply while a lower wage rate leads to a contraction of labour supply.[9] Note that the relevant wage rate is the after-tax wage. Thus, a positive incentive to supply more labour could come about both as a result of an increase in the market wage or as a reduction of the marginal tax rate on earnings.

Where do these labour-leisure preferences come from? Most expositions of the theory are silent on this point but leave one with the impression that the preferences originate in some way with the individuals themselves and that it is unnecessary to consider the social environment in which they live. However, there have been alternative and influential views on this issue. The sociologist Max Weber (Weber 1904) claimed that the protestant ethic led to attitudes to work, saving and economic activity that in turn generated economic prosperity for society, and similar views were advanced by the economic historian Richard Tawney (Tawney 1926). They did not present these views in the formalized manner of modern economic theory, but the basic idea clearly implies that the labour-leisure preferences of modern textbooks must be seen as being formed by the social environment, in this case by the work ethic inspired by peoples' religious views. One could imagine this set of ethical beliefs leading to e.g. a higher rate of labour market participation, later retirement,

---

[9] A qualification is in order: The increase in the wage rate means that the worker has higher earnings at his initial level of labour supply. He might react to this by wanting to buy more leisure, i.e. to reduce his labour supply. This income effect pulls in the opposite direction from the incentive or substitution effect.

and less utilization of social security benefits than would otherwise have been the case.

The general point that the two examples illustrate is that the individual preferences that are expressed in people's market behavior cannot be seen in isolation from ethical and religious beliefs; more generally, they are conditioned by the social environment in which people live.

2.9 Economics as an Influence on Society

Positive economics is concerned with the study of how the actual economy works. Normative economics, on the other hand, tries to derive criteria for economic welfare and to design reforms that can make the economic system perform better. One should not be surprised that the conclusions of normative economic studies often turn out to be more controversial that the findings of positive economics. This is especially true in recent times when many observers have argued that economists tend to recommend the introduction of the mindset of the market in areas of life where this way of thinking is misplaced. Before turning to the recent debate, however, I will consider a historical case that may throw some light on modern concerns.

Edwin Chadwick (1800–1890) was an English civil servant who was much influenced by the utilitarian philosopher Jeremy Bentham as well as by the economist and philosopher John Stuart Mill, and in his work in various areas of social reform he was keen to utilize the ideas that he found in the literature on economics. During his long and very active career as a public administrator he made a number of important contributions to the design of policy and pioneered both in the creative design of incentive-based mechanisms and in the use of empirical data. An interesting example of Chadwick's inventiveness in the exploitation of incentives for administrative improvement is his initiative regarding the transportation of British criminals to Australia. According to the account of Ekelund and Hébert (1997), the captains of the vessels in charge of the transports were originally paid a flat fee per prisoner taken on board in the port of departure. When at Sidgwick's suggestion the scheme was changed so that the captains were paid per prisoner who disembarked alive in Australia, the survival rate among the convicts increased from 40% to 98.5%! Most economists would not hesitate in characterizing this as a triumph of economic analysis in designing a reform based on market incentives that conveys obvious benefits on all parties concerned as well as on society as a whole.[10]

On second thoughts, however, perhaps there is an aspect of the story that may be a cause for concern. When we look at the initial system of incentives, the captains would seem to have had virtually no economic motivation to keep the prisoners

---

[10] In his popular book on the history of everyday life, Bill Bryson writes that Chadwick was an "intense and cheerless figure" and that almost nobody liked him (Bryson 2010, 510). But as this story shows, some had good reason to like him very much, at least if they judged him by the results of his efforts.

alive during the sea voyage; still, 40% of the convicts were in fact alive on arrival in Australia. Since the 40% was an average for all transports, the survival rate for some voyages must have been considerably higher, indicating that some captains must after all have taken reasonably good care of their charges without the type of incentives embodied in Sidgwick's scheme. For these captains, the new financial incentives took the place of the moral incentives that had previously guided their behavior. To use the concepts of Bénabou and Tirole (2003), the extrinsic incentives of the new payments system "crowded out" the intrinsic incentives that apparently guided the behavior of at least some of the captains. Or as it has been put by Bruno Frey in a different context "a constitution for knaves crowds out public virtues" (Frey 1997).

In the context of this particular historical example, the concern for the weakening of moral motivation may seem absurd. The documented effects of the new set of incentives were so overwhelmingly positive that any such objection to it must be regarded as being of minor importance if not cynical. However, the example is not without relevance for the understanding of some of the criticism of more recent proposals to introduce economic incentives and markets in fields that have traditionally been governed by different principles. In the words of the philosopher Michael Sandel, "market values and market reasoning increasingly reach into spheres of life previously governed by nonmarket norms." He goes on to argue that "this tendency is troubling; putting a price on every human activity erodes certain moral and civic goods worth caring about" (Sandel 2012, 2013, p. 121). He lists a number of areas where market thinking has been introduced and where in his opinion it has adversely affected attitudes and values. These areas include pregnancy for pay, trade in human organs, the sale of lobbying services, selling the right to kill endangered species and many others. A basic objection to these practices, in Sandel's view, is that subjecting the activity or good in question to market thinking degrades it from a social and moral point of view; reorganizing society to extend the domain of the market should not be regarded as a value neutral reform.[11]

This line of argument is of course not new; thus, slavery and corruption have been denounced by leading economists since the early days of the subject. In these areas it has long been recognized that individuals do not enter into transactions on a voluntary basis or that they are reasonably well informed about the consequences of their actions; the market mechanism is therefore likely to lead to socially undesirable results. The difficult issue is obviously where to draw the line between desirable and undesirable extensions of the market paradigm. A general answer is difficult to provide, but a couple of examples may illustrate the issues involved.

The problem of global warming is undoubtedly the most massive case of market failure that the world has ever seen. Economists have proposed a number of market-based incentive mechanisms to try to come to grips with the problem, including "green taxes" on environmentally harmful goods and activities as well as tradable emission quotas. These policy instruments have great potential for achieving

---

[11] For critical discussions of Sandel's views see Besley (2013) and Bruni and Sugden (2013). A more descriptive analysis of the social legitimacy of different systems for the allocation of resources that respond to both efficiency and equity concerns can be found in Elster (1993).

substantial results, and to argue that they are socially inferior to appeals to individual morality represents a severe underestimation of the incentive problems that arise with regard to individual provision of a global public good. In this case, the argument that extrinsic incentives crowd out intrinsic motivation seems to me to carry little weight relative to the enormity of the social problems that are at stake and that need to be solved within a fairly short time horizon.

Creating stronger incentives in the workplace has been a central topic for discussion in proposals to make public institutions in areas like health and education perform more efficiently. Good performance should according to these proposals be rewarded, as when academics are paid a bonus for publication in a high-quality journal. Among the objections that have been raised against this practice is the argument that it instils an attitude that you are not expected to perform well if you are not paid for it. Since academics are employed in institutions where they are expected to perform multiple tasks (such as administration, teaching and popular writing), monetary reward for one type of activity may lead them to downgrade the importance of the other activities. A possible response to this objection is obviously to introduce rewards for good performance in the other activities also, but this easily leads into a system that is too complicated to operate efficiently.

There is obviously much more to be said about the introduction of market incentives and mechanisms in areas where they have not previously been tried. But the two examples may at least indicate that there is no easy conclusion to be drawn regarding its desirability. The environmental case is one where the conscious use of the market incentives has the promise to do a lot of good for society, and where the concern for the effects on intrinsic incentives must be considered to be of the second order of importance. The discussion of incentives in the workplace makes us aware that extrinsic incentives may sometimes have undesirable side effects and that in ensuring a high quality of work performance one cannot do without a strong work ethic and intrinsic incentives. The validity of this conclusion must certainly hold beyond the case of formalized employment relationship and be at least as relevant for the voluntary sector that plays such a large role in our societies.

2.10 Concluding Remarks

The analysis of the market economy in terms of the interplay between utility-maximizing consumers and profit-maximizing producers plays a central role in modern economics. Since the time of Adam Smith economists have been concerned with the development of the internal logic of their models of markets, sometimes with the consequence that too little attention has been paid to the broader social context in which market transactions take place. However, some of this social context is in fact implicit in the standard models, and the present chapter has attempted to bring some of these hidden assumptions out in the open. A common criticism of economists is that they base their analyses and policy recommendations on a narrow view of man as egoistic and self-seeking. No doubt there are some economists who in fact hold this view, but it is not a necessary implication of economic theory. For an enlightened understanding of economic theory it is essential to keep in mind that economists do not find it necessary to present a full account of human motivation in the analysis of each and every piece of analysis. We may subscribe to Alfred Marshall's view of man's "higher nature" and at the same time acknowledge that he was right in leaving it out from his analysis of the demand for fish.

The normative study of the properties of the market mechanism has over time led to a deeper understanding of what markets can do and what they cannot do. In recent years there has developed an increased interest in extending the market paradigm to areas that have traditionally been governed by other systems of resource allocation. The wisdom of some of these extensions has been questioned by critics both from the inside and outside of the economics profession, and the debate has raised important issues that will no doubt be discussed further in the years ahead.

References

Becker, G.S. 1968. Crime and Punishment: An Economic Approach. *Journal of Political Economy* 76: 169–217.

———. 1981. *A Treatise on the Family*. Cambridge: Harvard University Press.

Bénabou, R., and J. Tirole. 2003. Intrinsic and Extrinsic Motivation. *Review of Economic Studies* 70: 489–520.

Besley, T. 2013. What's the Good of the Market? An Essay on Michael Sandel's What Money Can't Buy. *Journal of Economic Literature* 51: 478–495.

Bruni, L., and R. Sugden. 2013. Reclaiming Virtue Ethics for Economics. *Journal of Economic Perspectives* 27 (4): 141–164.

Bryson, B. 2010. *At Home. A Short History of Private Life*, 2011. London. Black Swan Paperback Edition: Doubleday.

Ekelund, R.B., and R.F. Hébert. 1997. *A History of Economic Theory and Method*. 4th ed. New York: McGraw-Hill.

Elster, J. 1993. *Local Justice. How Institutions Allocate Scarce Goods and Necessary Burdens*. New York: Russell Sage Foundation.

Frey, Bruno. 1997. A Constitution for Knaves Crowds Out Public Virtues. *Economic Journal* 107: 1043–1053.

Gossen, H.H. 1854. *Entwickelung der Gesetze des menschlichen Verkehrs und der daraus fliessenden Regeln für menschliches Handeln*. Cambridge: MIT Press, 1983.

Hardin, G. 1968. The Tragedy of the Commons. *Science* 162: 1243–1248.

Lange, O., and F.M. Taylor. 1938. *On the Economic Theory of Socialism*, 1964. New York: McGraw-Hill Paperbacks.

Lazear, E.P. 2000. Economic Imperialism. *Quarterly Journal of Economics* 115: 99–146.

Marshall, A. 1890. *Principles of Economics*. 8th ed, 1920. London: Macmillan.

Okun, A.M. 1975. *Equality and Efficiency*. Washington, D.C.: Brookings Institution.

Ostrom, E. 2009. Beyond Markets and States: Polycentric Governance of Complex Economic Systems. *American Economic Review* 100: 641–672.

Pareto, V. 1909. *Manuel d'économie politique*. London: Macmillan, 1971.

Sandel, Michael J. 2012. *What Money Can't Buy. The Moral Limits of Markets*. Vol. 2013. London: Penguin Paperback Edition.

Sandel, M. 2013. Market Reasoning as Moral Reasoning: Why Economists Should Re-engage with Political Philosophy. *Journal of Economic Perspectives* 27 (4): 121–140.

Sandmo, A. 2011. *Economics Evolving. A History of Economic Thought*. Princeton: Princeton University Press.

———. 2016. Adam Smith and Modern Economics. In *Adam Smith: His Life, Thought and Legacy*, ed. H. Ryan, 231–246. Princeton: Princeton University Press.

Smith, A. 1776. *An Inquiry into the Nature and Causes of the Wealth of Nations*. Bicentenary ed., ed. R.H. Campbell, & A.S. Skinner. Oxford: Oxford University Press, 1976.

Tawney, R. 1926. *Religion and the Rise of Capitalism*. London: Murray.

Walras, L (1874–77), *Éléments d'économie politique pure*. Homewood: Irwin, 1954.

Weber M. 1904. *Die Protestantische Ethik und der Geist des Kapitalismus*. New York: Scribner, 1930.

Agnar Sandmo 1938–2019, professor of economics at the Norwegian Business School, Bergen, 1971–2007; from 2007 professor emeritus until he passed away 2019. President of European Economic Association 1990 and a lot of other merits. The grand old man of Scandinavian economics, Agnar Sandmo, was a leading Scandinavian economist and we were very happy when he accepted to participate in our workshop and the book, and he was one of the first to deliver a manuscript. But he passed away in 2019 before the book was finished. The text in the chapter is unchanged in relation to Agnar Sandmo's manuscript but an abstract and a few changes in layout have been made after Agnar Sandmo passed away.

Chapter 3
Market Failures and What to Do About It?

Peder Andersen

Abstract It is common knowledge in economic science that a free, non-regulated market economy does, generally speaking, fail to allocate good and services efficiently and does not result in a fair distribution between individuals due to market failures. Some of the most important market failures are related to the existence of public goods and externalities. To secure a society's overall welfare, there is a need for regulation and interventions to correct for market failures.

Keywords Market failures · Public goods · externalities

3.1 Introduction

The markets and market mechanism can deliver results measured in efficient terms that no planning agency can do better if the right conditions are in place. The markets can allocate goods and services efficiently both with regard to production and consumption. However, the outcome of the market processes might not be a fair distribution of resources or welfare between individuals, see Chap. 2.

It is common knowledge in economic science that a free, non-regulated market economy does, generally speaking, fails to allocate good and services efficiently and do not results in a fair distribution between individuals due to market failures. To secure a society's overall welfare, there is a need for regulation and interventions to correct for market failures and by doing so to secure a society's overall welfare.

In the following, the conditions for an efficient market economy will be presented, various types of market failures are explained and examples of how to correct for markets failures will be given. We present the concepts "public goods" and "externalities", explain why markets do not work efficiently when we have public

P. Andersen (✉)
Department of Food and Resource Economics, University of Copenhagen, Frederiksberg C, Denmark
e-mail: pean@ifro.ku.dk

goods and externalities and what we can do about it. We applied an anthropocentric approach, meaning that only benefit and cost for human beings count. Although a non-anthropocentric approach might appeal to some for moral or ethical reasons, it is important to acknowledge that an anthropocentric approach includes moral and ethics values being of importance for human beings.

3.2 Conditions for Efficiency in Market Solutions

All standard textbooks in economics present the conditions that are necessary for obtaining market competition and no market failures and needed if the market has to deliver production and consumption efficiency, see e.g. Varian (2014). The most important conditions are

1. Large number of agents (producers and buyers)
2. Homogeneous product
3. Free entry and exit
4. No government regulation or restrictions
5. Perfect mobility of factors of production and no transaction costs
6. Perfect knowledge
7. No externalities and public goods

The first six are the standard conditions for having perfect completion. To have a perfect competitive market we need many agents, producers and buyers so a single agent cannot influence the price of identical or almost identical products. If e.g. there is only one or few producers, the price of the product will be too high and the producer will gain pure profit. This means that a monopoly will prevent perfect competition. To get competition we also need easily entry and exit to the market. This will e.g. allow high productive producers to get access to the market. If a government introduces taxes or restrictions this will violate the market forces to use production factors in the most efficient way. This is also the case if barriers prevent mobility and restrict the use of goods and factors of production in the most efficient way. Finally, regarding perfect competition it is important that agents are well informed about current and future products and prices to make decisions that support market forces to work.

It is obvious that the conditions for obtaining perfect competition rarely are met. Economic science uses the perfect competition model as a basis for analyzing the consequences of lack of competition. Furthermore, the model is applicable to find ways to correct for lack of perfect competition to improve the outcome, given the society's objectives, see the introduction of positive and normative economics in Chap. 2.

The implication of incomplete competition (e.g. few agents), externalities (e.g. pollution) and public goods (e.g. defense) is that the market fails to deliver results, measured in goods and services that, generally speaking, are acceptable for society. The key question is how to correct for market failures or at least for some of the failures by imposing regulations to the market forces by using incentives and restrictions. In this chapter, we will concentrate on these questions by looking at a number of examples of market failures due to the existence of public goods and externalities.[1]

3.3 Public Goods

A pure public good has two important characteristics or properties. The first is that a pure public good or service is non-rival and the second that a pure public good is non-excludable. Non-rival means that it has no positive or negative impact on existing agents' (consumers, firms or organizations) welfare or profit if the number of agents expands. Non-excludable means that it is impossible to exclude an agent from enjoying the good and service. In standard economic terms this means that the marginal cost of proving the good or service to one more agent is zero (non-rival) and it is technically impossible to exclude the agent from enjoying a pure public good (Samuelson 1954). Of course, these two properties are very rare in the real world but we have many goods that are close to public goods. Classical examples are a country's defense, human rights, freedom of religion, pure basic research, and local public goods like police services, traffic lights and lighthouses. If the two characteristics are partly fulfilled, we get club goods that are non-rival and non-excludable for club members to a great degree but within rules formulated by the club.

The key differences between a pure public good and a private good like food and gasoline are obvious. If you eat your burger, I cannot enjoy the same burger but will have to buy my own burger. When a company uses gasoline in the production, another company cannot use the very same gasoline but will need to purchase gasoline.

It is also of interest to be aware of the cases where only one of the properties are in place. If it is easy to exclude an agent for enjoying a wilderness area and the area is so large that one more visitor has no impact on other visitors´ benefit of the wilderness, it will be a loss of welfare to allow for excludability. If there is open-access to exploit a natural resource like a fish stock, non-excludability will result in too many fishers and the stock will be economically overfished. The use of a fish stock is rival, as the stock decreases when fishing increases. The potential outcome is the tragedy of the commons, see Hardin (1968). The existence of public goods also means that the market does not reveal nor deliver the optimal level of production of the public good. Agents will benefit of being free riders and not reveal the true willingness to pay for the public good. The true demand is the sum of willingness to pay by all agents. This has to be compared with the cost of production of the public good

---

[1] Monopoly and imperfect competition are other important market failures and in almost all countries regulated by law and by public competition authorities.

at different level to find the optimal level. This is a very difficult exercise as no methods to reveal true willingness to pay are perfect, and the cost of production of the public good has to be financed. As a pure public good is non-excludable, the most common way to finance public goods is by income or consumption taxation. To make things even more complicated it is a fact that an income or a consumption tax is a distorting tax, meaning that such a tax results in loss of efficiency as e.g. labor supply will decrease as taxes go up.

To find balanced solutions to the trade-offs between the production of public goods, private goods and the cost of financing the production of public goods state interventions are needed although in few cases other ways can be considered. The challenge of finding the right level of public goods and to find ways to financing the production increases drastically if we move from the national level to an international level. There exists no international institution with the same power as a state. The only way is cooperative solutions and this open for games where non-perfect cooperation or non-cooperation often are be the outcomes. The global warming case is a good example of this, where a successful reduction in emissions can be considered a global pure public good. Another example is human rights across borders. In other cases we have clubs where the participants enjoy goods which have public goods characteristics but for a limited number of users, e.g. EU.

3.4 Externalities

An externality is about the relationship between agents (consumers, firms or organizations) and more specifically how an action of one agent influences the welfare or profit of other agents. More precisely, the definition of externality can in short be as follows: The actions of one agent that make another agent or agents worse off or better off, given that the first party neither bears the cost nor receives the benefit from influencing other agents´ welfare (Corner and Sandler 1996). A negative externality can be related to consumption as well as to production where the other part is not compensated. An example of this is if a firm loses profit due to another firm's production and if the firm is not compensated for the loss. In this case, we have a production-production negative externality. A positive externality can be related to consumption as well as to production where the producer of an externality is not rewarded for improving the well-being of others.

The list of negative externalities is long. All kinds of pollution include externalities. The smoke from a factory, the noise from trucks and cars, odors from pig farms, and pesticides of various kind. There is also a relatively long list of positive externalities. House owners keep their house and garden nice and neighbors can daily enjoy the view, drivers drive carefully, and the very classical one is that a planter's trees improve production of honey. Public provided improvement of a high way is a positive externality for truck companies but might be a negative externality for house owners along the highway. Vaccination programs also produce positive externalities as the spread of a disease decreases as more and more people get the vaccine.

To find the right level of production of goods and services and similarly the right level of positive as well as negative externalities requires regulation. Most common is governmental interventions by use of rules, standards or economic incentives such as fines and subsidies. However, it is also under certain conditions possible to let agents find solutions through negotiations. This normally require well-defined property rights. We will later return to the choice of instruments to correct for negative as well as positive externalities.

The existence of public goods or goods with partly public goods characteristics and of production and consumption implying externalities requires market interventions. These interventions may be direct governmental interventions or a framework set by the government so that private individuals negotiate solutions. In both cases solutions have to found regarding the level of production of a public good or the level of externality, how to finance the production of a public good, the incentives to reach the right level of externalities, and how to monitor and enforce the agents involved. In the following, examples are presented to illustrate some of the challenges.

3.5 Human Rights, Peace and Security

If the world had a set of human rights, broadly speaking, this set of rights could be enjoyed by all, and would be non-rival. If all human beings worldwide have this set of rights with no restrictions, these would also be non-excludable. In this case, we would have a pure global public good. A very serious problem is who is providing the human rights, who is deciding the characteristics of the set of optimal rights, and who has the authority to enforce the right pays for the enforcement.

To focus on human rights as a pure global public good is theoretical interesting but not of practical importance. If we look at peace and security, we get closer to real world politics (Møller 2007; Andersen et al. 2007). The best argument that peace and security is a global public good is that war is a devil that harms. However, some may gain by a war.

As pointed out by Møller (2007) and Andersen et al. (2007), institutions for producing peace and security are in place within the UN system and the Geneva Conventions but not delivered on a global scale, but often in specific, regional context. Why international institutions are not efficient at delivering global public goods is obvious. Firstly, there exists no overall objective as to the effort to avoid a war as some expect gains and some loses by a war. Secondly, it is not straightforward to establish a forum that make consistent choices, and thirdly, the principles for cost sharing are not in place.

This also explain why countries form defense clubs like NATO or free trade clubs like EU. In short, club theory deals with situations where the good is somewhere between a private good and a public good. This means the good to a certain degree is rival or it is possible to exclude agents. This also have the implication that it is possible to charge members of the club and to form rules for a club that partly reveal members' preferences. Some of the key issues are the entry and exit problem, as the club will have entry conditions and perhaps exit conditions, too. Members will have to consider the gains and the cost of a membership. There will very often be the risk that some of the members want to leave the club or at least play the game and threaten to leave the club.

The economic theory of clubs (Buchanan 1965) is linked to game theory developed in the 1940s by John von Neumann and Oskar Morgenstern and made applicable by John Nash, see e.g. Gibbons (1992). The fundamentals in game theory is the strategic behavior among agents (players). If the institutions and rules give the right incentives to cooperate, all agents gain by collaborating but if the institutions and rules are not right, non-cooperative behavior will occur and the overall gain (sum of gains from all players) will be less than the outcome of collaboration. In this case, all or at least some of the players will lose, also known as the Prisoner's dilemma game. If winners compensate the losers, it is possible to turn the case into a win-win situation.

3.6 Climate and Climate Changes

In recent years, climate policy has been intensively discussed and for good reasons. Climate and climate changes can have long-term major impact for people's living conditions around the world. Next, migration is likely to increase and causes conflicts, and the risk of wars increases, too. There is an increasingly political focus on these. At the same time, it also true that the international political capacity to agree on and to implement measures that can effectively curb these threats is insufficient.

Climate changes is an excellent example of a global public good. The impact of a climate change on an agent (a country) is independent of the number of agents (countries) and is non-excludable. The impact will not be equal across borders and over time but the fundamental problems exist. If measures are taken to reduce negative impacts of global warming, all countries will benefit by these initiatives and free riding is very beneficial for most countries. It follows from this that the initiatives will be below what is optimal, and consequently the temperature increase will not be reduced to the optimal level, i.e. where the world marginal cost of reduction equals world marginal benefit of the reduced increase in temperature increase. Even if an agreement could be reached on this fundamental question of the optimal level of temperature increase, the framework for finding the efficient measures to reach the optimal level is not in place. We do not have a world authority to implement and enforce the policy.

Theoretically, the solution is a global tax on CO_2–emission, independent of the source and location of the emission. This is standard knowledge but free riding, the question of fairness across countries and different views on the optimal path of implementation have made efficient international agreements impossible. The Paris

Agreement was a significant step towards a solution but with potential major weaknesses. The Paris Agreement was adopted in 2015 by 195 countries and was proclaimed as a legally binding treaty and with the goal to limit global warming to well below 2 and preferable to 1.5 °C.

Although it is stated that the treaty is binding, it is in fact a declaration of intent. There is no efficient enforcement system in place and the measures different countries take in the years to come will most likely not be cost efficient, countries will leave the agreement and might return like the US. Some developing countries are compensated for participating and other countries will be punished for not participating, most likely by trade restrictions. It is a complicated international game.

3.7 Research-Based Knowledge

A society's welfare depends significantly on productivity and the development in productivity is closely related to research as a base for improving the skill of the labor force and for the efficiency of capital (Andersen 2007). There is an increasing awareness of importance of research-based knowledge for society and the level and structure of research have played a key role in research policy, nationally and internationally (OECD 2003). Pure, basic research is by nature a public good but obstacles exist for finding the optimal level of pure, basic research and applied research, partly due to the time horizon and to different interests among producers of research, including the questions of cost sharing.

If there is open-access to basic research findings across countries and if networks and cooperation among researchers worldwide are without obstacles the right environment for maximizing the gains of pure research exists. The risk of free riding is still present and it is up to research institutions and governments to support international institutions in their effort to agree on rules, securing cooperation among researchers.

Applied research differs from pure, basic research as it is produced to be applied for a specific production and for a specific purpose. This type of research is very often part of private firms' activities and is rival and excludable. Normally, the result of privately organized and paid will be private property and the property right protected via patens rights. If the research results to certain extent have a broader value, society will gain if privately produced research results are spread to a broader group of users. Privately produced research has potential positive externalities. In this case, private production of knowledge is below the optimal level, unless it to a certain extent is publicly subsidized, resulting in more research and more sharing. The very same problem exists in an international context. This is why e.g. EU for many years has been very active in supporting research, including privately produced research under the condition of a high degree of degree open-access to the results.

3.8 Biodiversity and the Noah's Ark Problem

There is an increasing awareness of the importance of a healthy nature as a valuable source for the economy and more broadly for peoples' wellbeing. A high degree of biodiversity indicates a healthy nature. To measure biodiversity and changes in biodiversity is complex and the definition is non-unambiguous and cannot be measured on a simple scale. The definition includes "the number, variety and variability of all living organisms in terrestrial marine and other aquatic ecosystems and the ecological complexes of which they are parts" (see e.g. Perman et al. 2011). The concept thus includes number of populations, distinct species and the diversity and interactions of ecosystems.

In an anthropocentric perspective, the importance of a high degree of biodiversity is the provision of environmental services to improve economic conditions and wellbeing for mankind. This happens in many ways. The direct influence is by improving food production, providing raw materials, avoiding climate changes and improving waste removal. It also plays a major role for recreational activities and may reduce risk of an ecological collapse. These benefits will also apply for future generations and may be essential in a sustainability perspective.

Biodiversity is a pubic good, locally and internationally and the subset of elements and the provision of environmental services gives rise to a number of externalities. We face the classical problem by determining the optimal level and composition of biodiversity, solving free riding problems and deciding who organizes the effort and pays the cost to ensure or improve biodiversity. Presently, UN, EU and other international bodies have strong focus on framing solutions to avoid further degeneration of biodiversity as well as many countries have programs.

To find the right choice of composition of species and number of organisms is complex for many reasons. The knowledge of the important for the provision of environmental services is uncertain, the impact of an effort to save species may not be known, and the cost of an effort for e.g. saving a species differs across species. Environmental economists talk about "the Noah's Ark Problem". This problem illustrates the optimization challenge (Weitzman 1998). We assume that the government has reserved a certain budget biodiversity improvement. Given this budget constraint (the size of the ship), we maximize welfare by protecting those species which give the highest value to society.

A species direct value for human people counts, the uniqueness of each species counts and this depends on the genetic distance between different species. A species might be unique but other species be very close as to importance in providing valuable environmental services, i.e. a species can relatively easily be replaced by other species. Finally, the question is how efficient a certain effort is to save a species. To measure efficiency in saving a species we calculated the increase in the probability of survival per dollar. This gives us a straightforward way to formulate an efficient conservation policy. Firstly, if an effort has no impact on the probability of survival, no resources should be allocated to save this species. Secondly, if the specific species are very costly to save, i.e. it is costly to increase the probability of survival, or the species has low priority, the government should look at species, which relatively easy can replace the species, i.e. the genetic importance counts more or less the same on an index for biodiversity. Thirdly, if a species has no value for a society now or in the future, no costly effort should be allocated to save this species.

3.9 The Commons

Utilization of common resources is rivalry and non-excludable. A society cannot utilize common resources efficiently without regulation as open access results in the tragedy of the commons (Hardin 1968) which means overexploitation of the resource and no or very small resource rent. *Resource rent* measure what is left of economic surplus for the exploitation of a resource after labor and capital have been paid normal salaries and profit. This fundamental insight in how lack of regulation results in a "tragedy" has been known since the Danish economist Jens Warming in 1911 published the paper "On Rent of Fishery Grounds" (Warming 1911; Andersen 1983). The fishery is an excellent example of the economics of commons and the various ways to manage a fish resource gives a broad picture of the policy issues in management of the commons. Other examples are forests, grazing areas and other common areas and natural resources. Open access results in overexploitation as a stock externality occurs.

When fishers catch fish they reduce the size of the fish stock and it becomes more costly for all to catch a pound of fish. At the same time, the individual fisher has no incentive to stop fishing as long as the next pound of fish more than covers the cost. The result is a reduction of the fish stock to a low level where fishers no longer have an incentive to expand their fishing effort. In this equilibrium, all fishers are paid a normal salary, including vessel cost and there is no surplus, i.e. no resource rent. If the cost of catching a pound of fish reduces due to new technology, the equilibrium stock will be reduced. This may result in biological overfishing and a decrease in catches from the specific stock. An identical result will occur as a consequence of subsidies to fishers.

The key to avoid overcapacity and overexploitation is to establish property rights in the fishery. If a single agent or a group of fishers has perfect property right to participate in the fishery, it is possible to manage the fishery and harvest long term maximum resource rent. Perfect property rights have the following characteristics: Exclusivity for an infinite time horizon, transferability and enforceability. Less than full score on all dimensions will reduce, not erode the resource rent. If it is costly to enforce property rights, the pure resource rent will be reduced, as part of the resource rent will cover the enforcement cost. If transferability is not perfect, restrictions in selling and buying fishing rights may reduce efficient fishers to enter the fishery and therefore reduce the resource rent. Exclusivity improves long run planning and investment, given the allocated fishing rights.

The fishing rights can be ownership to exploit a fish stock but it is more common that the government allocate fishing rights as a share of the fixed total quota. If we have such an individual transferable quota system (ITQ system), all conditions for obtaining the maximum long-term resource rent is in place. The question of fairness in such a system is linked to the conditions for obtaining the fishing rights. Such conditions can include a tax on resource rent, tax on landing values or a lump sum tax. Compared to an open-access fishery, an ITQ regulated fishery results in less fishing effort, i.e. fewer fishers, a more healthy fish stock, and higher catches in the case where the stock is biological overfished under open-access. In this case, the activities in the fishing industry will increase as catches increase. A fish stock can be protected by use of other regulatory means such as restrictions in vessels efficiency, a total non-allocated quota or if small-scale, economically inefficient fishers are getting the fishing rights. These measures will reduce resource rent. It is a political question to balance the various objectives, including biodiversity elements in the management of the common natural resources.

An alternative to a government's implementation and enforcement of e.g. an ITQ system is to allocate the property rights to a group, see Ostrom (1990). If a group of fishers take over the fishing right, have a well-functioning organization, efficient implementation, management and enforcement, higher resource rent may be generated compare to the a governmental ITQ system. Management and enforcement cost may be reduced as the incentive to cheat as member of a group may be small as transparency increases. Furthermore, the outcome may be found more fair which also may create a more coherent regulatory system.

3.10 Pollution

Pollution is a typical negative externality and generally considered undesirable. This raises three questions. The first is how to determine the optimal level of pollution? The second question is why the market generates too much pollution. The third is how to reduce pollution to the optimal level? From an economic efficiency point of view, we search for the pollution level where the social damage of the last unit of pollution equals the social cost of avoiding the very same unit of pollution. In other words, optimal pollution is characterized by the rule that the marginal damage cost equals the marginal abatement cost.

A polluting firm or a polluting consumer have incentives to free ride as the social damage caused by the firm and the consumer only marginal harms the very same firm and consumer. Most of the cost comes from the damage on other firms or consumers, affected by the pollution. Polluting firms and polluting consumers produce negative externalities and they do not internalize the externalities in their production and consumption decisions. If consumers react as "political consumers" to firms' polluting behavior, this may, to a certain extent, reduce demand for the polluting firms' products. Generally, this does not happen to an extent where the externality problem is solved.

Many measures can be applied to reduce pollution. Direct control is e.g. implementation of quality standards or a ban of highly polluting production. Indirect regulation includes a tax on polluting emission or use of individually transferable emission quotas. Both economic incentives work through the market system. If the tax on emission is correctly calculated, set equal to social cost of pollution, and results in an optimal level of pollution, each firm will adjust their production to the level, where the firm's marginal abatement cost (the cost of reducing the emission) equals the tax of one unit of emission. Why will this happen? If the firm maximizes profit, the firm gains by reducing the emission to a level where the profit of emitting one more unit equals the unit tax of emission. If the tax is below the marginal profit of emission, the firm gains profit by omitting the reduction of emission. As firms' marginal abatement cost are not constant nor identical, the tax instrument will force firms with the lowest marginal abatement cost to reduce most. This contribute to find efficient solutions compared to e.g. a situation where all firms are forced to reduce emission by the same percentage. An ITQ system works the same way. Market will force the price of tradable emission permits to equal the optimal tax on emission.

Many problems arise in the real world. First, the knowledge of the damage cost, measured in money units, is limited and the estimates found by using the standard methods are uncertain. The precautionary principle will dictate a government to be pessimistic and to use relatively high damage cost. On the other hand, practical politics may go in the opposite direction. If we have to do with international environmental problems and country specific regulation, free riding is most likely and international agreements fail due to the lack of enforcement.

In some cases, it is possible to find a solution by negotiations between private agents and without governmental intervention. If property rights are well defined and enforced by the government, agents have incentives to negotiate a solution. If e.g. a farmer has the right to use fertilizers and pollute to a certain level, the emission of fertilizer lowers the quality of the water in the river. The river water is important for fish farmers, at polluted water reduces the productivity of fish farming. The fish farmer can gain by a reduction of emission but that will reduce the farmer's profit. This situation opens up for a negotiation solution as the fish farmer can compensate the farmer and both can be better off, see Coase (1960). If the property right to the river and water of a certain quality is given to the fish farmer in the first place, a negotiation solution could also be found and be optimal. In this situation, the farmer should compensate the fish farmer for the loss due to the emission of fertilizers. To find an efficient solution by negotiation demands no cost related to negotiation of the deal. This assumption often fails as, if e.g. many agents are part of a pollution problem.

Finally, some comments on the enforcement cost as a complicating factor in controlling pollution. If polluters do not compliance to the rules, the government is facing costly and imperfect enforcement. The consequence is that the optimal level of pollution is higher than if enforcement is costly and imperfect (Becker 1968). If firms' gain by pollute more that the permits allow, the government needs to enforce and punish violators. The optimal level of enforcement will, however, allow for some violation, as the marginal cost of enforcing the pollution rule has to balance the gain by getting a better environment. The optimal level of illegal pollution will depend on the enforcement costs and those are directly linked to the cost of detecting and punishing violation. The incentives for a violator to reduce illegal pollution is directly linked to the expected gain from illegal pollution. The gain is the expected gain if not detected minus the expected loss (fine) if detected and punished. An increase in the probability of detection and an increase in fine level if detected reduce the violation. As it is costly for the government to increase the probability of detection and punishment, the government needs to balance the value of a reduction in pollution and the cost of enforcement to determine the optimal level of illegal pollution.

3.11 Concluding Remarks

Market failures demand regulation and intervention to improve society's overall welfare. The level of and type of regulation are closely linked to the type of market failures we want to correct. A non-regulated market cannot generate acceptable outcomes if severe market failures exist. This is well known and the point of departure for discussing what types of interventions that are needed and efficient under various circumstances to correct for the failures.

When dealing with public goods and externalities it has been shown that public interventions to correct market failures can be property rights, public subsidies, taxes and standards. In some cases, negotiations between private agents can replace public interventions.

It is well known that a free, non-regulated market economy does, generally speaking, fails to allocate good and services efficiently and does not results in a fair distribution between individuals due to market failures. Economics science includes a huge body of literature describing instruments to overcome these problems. Environmental and resource economics provide tools that are very useful for decision makers to deal with these failures.

References

Andersen, P. 1983. 'On the Rent of Fishing Grounds': A Translation of Jens Warming's 1911 Article With an Introduction. *History of Political Economy* 15: 391–396.
———. 2007. Research, Global Public Goods and Welfare. In *Towards New Global Strategies: Public Goods and Human Rights*, ed. E.A. Andersen and B. Lindsnaes, 335–343. Lieden: Martinus Nijhoff Publishers.
Andersen, E.A., P. Andersen, and B. Lindsnaes. 2007. Problems and Potentials in the Application of Global Public Goods. In *Towards New Global Strategies: Public Goods and Human Rights*, ed. E.A. Andersen and B. Lindsnaes, 453–465. Lieden: Martinus Nijhoff Publishers.
Becker, G.S. 1968. Crime and Punishment: An Economic Approach. *Journal of Political Economy* 76: 169–217.
Buchanan, J.M. 1965. An Economic Theory of Clubs. *Economica* 32: 1–14.
Coase, R. 1960. The Problem of Social Costs. *The Journal of Law and Economics* 3: 1–44.

Corner, R., and T. Sandler. 1996. *The Theory of Externalities, Public Goods and Club Goods.* Cambridge: Cambridge University Press.

Gibbons, R. 1992. *Game Theory for Applied Economists.* Princeton: Princeton University Press.

Hardin, G. 1968. The Tragedy of the Commons. *Science* 162: 1243–1248.

Møller, B. 2007. Peace as a Global Public Good. In *Towards New Global Strategies: Public Goods and Human Rights*, ed. E.A. Andersen and B. Lindsnaes, 115–158. Lieden: Martinus Nijhoff Publishers.

OECD. 2003. *The Sources of Economic Growth in OECD Countries.* Paris: OECD.

Ostrom, E. 1990. *Governing the Commons: The Evolution of Institutions for Collective Action.* Cambridge: Cambridge University Press.

Perman, R., Y. Ma, M. Common, D. Maddison, and J. McGilvray. 2011. *Natural Resource and Environmental Economics.* London: Pearson.

Samuelson, P.A. 1954. The Pure Theory of Public Expenditures. *Review of Economics and Statistic* 36: 483–485.

Varian, H.R. 2014. *Intermediate Microeconomics.* New York: Norton and Company.

Warming, Jens. 1911. Om grundrente af fiskegrunde. *Nationaløkonomisk Tidsskrift* 49: 499–505.

Weitzman, M.L. 1998. The Noah's Ark Problem. *Econometrica* 66: 1279–1298.

Peder Andersen born 1952, professor of resource and environmental economics at University of Copenhagen since 2008. Head of the staff at the Danish Board of Economic Advisors 1995–2007. Has been head of the economic departments both at University of Aarhus and Copenhagen. Chairman of the Danish Economic Association 2007–2014

Chapter 4
Unproductive Market Ideology

Hans Aage

Abstract Nothing is wrong with economics. Sometimes, economics is better than its reputation, and in several case it has a lot to offer. What is, however, wrong, is mainstream economists' ideological, liberalist abuse of economics. Simultaneously, economic speculation is being extended to still broader fields, where economists have no insight except an airy "economic way of thinking". For decades we have known that the challenges of our time, global environment and global distribution, desperately require collective action, and also that this is precisely what market governance can not deliver. How market ideology could invade our collective mind so forcefully during these same decades remains a mystery.

Keywords Topics for economics · Market governance · Market failure · Theory and reality · Planning

4.1 Introduction

Economics has transformed itself from a modest scientific tool into an ethical problem. It all began with a scientific discovery, of which there are not many in economics, but there are some. This one, around 1870, provided a theoretical explanation of a centuries old puzzle, namely how market prices come about. It also explained the market economy as a decentralized, efficient and also otherwise attractive solution to the allocation problem, how to optimize economic activity given individual and individualistic preferences, the distribution of initial resources and technology.

This formulation of the allocation problem is highly productive and applicable to many spheres of life, but not to all of them. Neither is the market solution. For one thing, there are widespread market failures, where the market equilibrium is not efficient (monopolies, public goods, externalities, imperfect information,

H. Aage (✉)
Department of Social Sciences and Business, Roskilde University, Roskilde, Denmark
e-mail: hansaa@ruc.dk

non-existing markets, macro-economic disturbances). Then there are distribution issues, which this theory ignores because of their arbitrariness, and so-called merit goods, which represent a "collective inquiry into the value of evaluations" and more (Goodchild 2009 p. 121 and Chap. 9 in this book).

The scientific discovery of the 1870s, known as *the fundamental theorems of welfare theory*, is a strong theoretical result from general and non-arbitrary assumptions. It has been refined and applied during 150 years, but it has not progressed any deeper; little non-trivial or useful for economics is known about future changes of resources, technology or preferences; for example, the assumption of individualistic, insatiable preferences does not solve the problem of the free will (Goodchild 2009 p. 87). Instead economics has become increasingly broad in scope, increasingly speculative and increasingly ideological, as knowledge, beliefs and political preferences are increasingly mixed up. Four elements dominate the economics ideology: imaginary speculation, disregard of distribution and fairness, belief in universal comparability in money terms, and faith in monetary incentives as the only efficient and the only respectable. Market philosophy has become a social philosophy: human relations are regarded as mutually beneficial exchange of goods driven by self-interest, a generalized *quid pro quo*. Everything can be and should be bought and sold. This is an ethical problem (Sandel 2012 p. 8).

But well-functioning market exchange and capitalism have much to their credit: agents enjoy freedom of choice in the market; there are no rules to follow except for the general legal framework and therefore no problem with corruption, power and privilege (Besley 2013 p. 488); no problems with incentives as consumers and producers willingly maximize utility and profits, respectively; market allocations imply a theoretically underpinned efficiency, although in the very weak sense that there is no outright waste; and most importantly: markets and capitalism has demonstrated an enormous potential for prosperity, which very few economists predicted 150 ago; Karl Marx did,[1] but he did not predict the consequences for ideology and workers' standard of living.

And there certainly are cases where new applications of market-clearing prices is an improvement. One example is airline overbooking; the airlines used to move to other flights those in the armed forces and the elderly. The notorious market *cornucopian*, Julian Simon,[2] for many years championed the idea of using an auction process to disclose who are the most prepared to wait, and it is now widely and successfully applied (*The Economist*, 7 March 1998, p 6). Queuing is another solution (Sandel 2012 pp. 30–32) but costly in real terms; in 1981 time wasted *per capita* in queus in the USSR equalled the time wasted *per capita* in unemployment in Denmark.[3] Then simple lottery might well be preferable.

---

[1] Leontief (1938) characterizes Marx as the great *character reader* of capitalism.

[2] Julian Simon won the bet between Paul Ehrlich and himself concerning raw materials prices in the 1980's, but he could have lost if Paul Ehrlich had accepted his offer to go "double or quits" for a future date. (*The Economist*, 6 August 2011, p 58).

[3] The head of the Danish central bank, Erik Hoffmeyer, in the Danish newspaper *Politiken*, 13 December 1981.

But the market is unpopular. Americans in New York are as an example market-unfriendly, as 68% said "no" to market-clearing prices for flowers on Mother's Day (Shiller et al. 1991; Aage 1991). Individual market choices are often critized for being "easily subjected to social manipulation through fashion and advertising" (Goodchild 2009 p. 120). But the market is a powerfull democratic mechanism, although not a perfect one. It allows individual preferences to be expressed with an effect. In the market individual power is effectual, but unequal; in political democracy it is equal, but ineffectual, as the individual voter has no influence, only responsibility for majority decisions. It is also democratic, that privilege does not matter in pure market capitalism, only the depth of your pocket.

Rather than lack of democracy, one real problem among others and the target of pertinent critique of the market economy is, that it evidently results in unacceptable inequality. The Pope dissociates himself from Adam Smith's "invisible hand" (*manus invisibilis*) because of market inequality, "the root of social ills" (Franciscus 2013 pp. 160–161, 46–49). Inequality is also the essence behind much of the critique in Michael Sandel's great and most welcome 2012-book (Sandel 2012; Besley 2013).

Generally, it is not a viable solution to control market exchange directly. It is better to change the initial distribution of resources. Free exchange is beneficial for the parties, and more often than not it is impossible to eliminate. At least since the days of Hammurabi (c. 1810 – c. 1750 B.C.), who introduced maximum grain prices in order to protect the poor, powerful rulers have tried to control market exchange by laws stating maximum prices and maximum rates of interest to prevent usury, only to discover that the laws of supply and demand were stronger than theirs.

But even if free trade is good for individual market agents, it can be damaging for society at large. India's flourishing textile industry was ruined for 200 years by free trade (Fernández-Armesto 1995 pp. 358–363). Between 1839 and 1842 a nasty little war opened Southern China to free trade in opium and subsequently ruined large areas, which is today a founding myth in Chinese historical consciousness. (*The Economist*, 29 October 2011, p 84; Fernández-Armesto (1995 p. 295). The American South suffered from free trade after the civil war 1861–65. German industrialization in the nineteenth century was fostered by protective costums duties for infant industries and by thorough government interventions, as was industrialization in contemporary Asian countries. There is increasing awareness that free movements of capital and "hot money" can be particularly damaging (Stiglitz et al. 2006; *The Economist*, 31 August 2013, p 58).

When it applies, there is nothing wrong with market exchange facilitated by money. Both are highly useful, welfare-augmenting social inventions, but a proper framework and "states, charged with vigilance for the common good, to exercise … control" (Franciscus 2013 p. 47) are badly needed. Vilh. Beck, the renowned helmsman 1861-1901 of The Home Mission, the great Danish revival movement, might have said about market exchange and money, what he said about the knave of clubs: "He never hurt anybody; he just got bad company" (Aage 2002 p. 129).

4.2 Imaginary Speculation

Economic theory is very rich. What is not known about all imaginable structures and equilibrium concepts, is not worth knowing. Theory is not to blame, and there is definitely nothing wrong with mathematics and deductions, as long as it is non-trivial and logically consistent. But problems arise, when theory is mistaken for reality. Its speculative character leaves ample space for ideology, that is the mixing up of what we know, what we conjecture, and what we hope for and believe in.

The speculative nature of economic theory is illustrated by comparing two 2013 Nobel prize laureates, Peter Higgs for physics and Eugene Fama for economics. Fifty years ago Higgs (and others) proposed a theory of the existence of a 17th fundamental particle, *the Higgs boson*, a very good theory, because it fits into *the standard model* and explains why some other particles move around with kinks and thereby acquire their masses. But that is not enough for the Nobel prize in physics; the theoretical prediction must also be experimentally demonstrated, i.e. the theory must be true, which is one characteristic difference between physics and economics, and that took 50 years and the Large Hadron Collider at CERN (Cox and Forshaw 2011: 203–214. This book contains nothing about theory of science, and you will not encounter the word *paradigm* at all).

Eugene Fama also proposed a theory 50 years ago, the *perfect market hypothesis*: The actual price of a security will be a good estimate of its intrinsic value (Eugene Fama 1965 quoted from Frydman and Goldberg 2010 p. 3). But the intrinsic or fundamental value is the sum of the discounted future payments, and nobody knows either the future payments, or the proper rate of discount. This was a fallacy in 1965, and it is still a fallacy (Frydman and Goldberg 2010 p. 3, 2011 pp. 81–102). It was called "the most remarkable error in the history of economic theory" (quoted from Plesner 2015 p. 45) by Robert Shiller, who shared the Nobel Prize for economics in 2013 with Eugene Fama (sic!). However, *the perfect market hypothesis* is better than its reputation, namely in the modified version, expressed by Eugene Fama in 1970: "Prices always 'fully reflect' available information" (quoted from Frydman and Goldberg 2010 p. 3; *The Economist*, 19 October 2013, pp. 12, 69, 2 November 2013 p. 18), which tells us the useful lesson that it is hard to make money from short term trading; you cannot outsmart the market, and salaries for fund managers are wasted.

The problem is twofold, and this is also the problem for economic theory generally: firstly, the relevant information about the future is not available (*The Economist*, 14 January 2012, p. 74); secondly, the parameters of the models are not stable, simply because humans do have a free will, and sometimes they use it. The stable structures, which economics is looking for, are not there. As the great Isaac Newton uttered after having lost a fortune in 1720 by speculating in South Sea Company stocks: "I can calculate the motions of heavenly bodies, but not the madness of people". (Kindleberger and Aliber 2005 p. 41).

This limits scientific progress in economics, but "theoretical speculation is rife" (Cox and Forshaw 2011 p. 197). When Timothy Besley in his essay on Sandel's book mentions "an active research agenda" (Besley 2013 p. 483), it means that large numbers of academic economists imagine situations by making assumptions out of thin air concerning for example how preferences and attitudes are formed endogenously and then deduce the consequences with great speculative ingenuity. An example is Assar Lindbeck's theory of the welfare state mentioned below. In 1982 Wassily Leontief commented:

> ...*economists developed a nearly irresistible predilection for deductive reasoning ... Page after page of professional economic journals are filled with mathematical formulas leading the reader from sets of more or less plausible, but entirely arbitrary assumptions to precisely stated but irrelevant theoretical conclusions* (Leontief 1983 p. 104).

According to the famous Russian mathematician L.S. Pontrjagin "mathematical economics is useless for economists and trivial for mathematicians" (Pontrjagin 1980 p. 104).

Simultaneously, economic speculation is being extended to still broader fields, where economists have no insight except an airy "economic way of thinking" (Aage et al. 2009 p. 309, 313, 317; Sandel 2012 p. 48). An example described by Sandel (Sandel 2012 pp. 151–152) is the *clairvoyance* of the market which allegedly can tell us things which nobody knows about terrorism, weather forecasts, and also future sufficiency of natural resources. This "economic way of thinking" is applied to marriage, psychology, voting behaviour, sports, health care, climate change, criminality, party politics, education, etc. We have got flourishing *health economics, environmental economics, cultural economics, television economics, educational economics,* even an *economics of happiness* heading straight for the meaning of life.[4] Of course economics and bookkeeping have useful things to offer in these fields, but economists inflict their *Weltanschauung* upon the substances. Because of a narrow and distorted perception of human nature, it is largely concerned with economic incentives and economic consistency. Economists pronounce recommendations concerning aspects of migration policy, EU membership, school curricula, social policy, cultural policy, and health care, about which economists have no expert knowledge and no responsibility. Thus, economists never had, and they never will have responsibility for the cure of patients.

In fact, it has been proved by experiment that studying economics degrades morality. A group of students were asked, whether or not they would deliver a wallet found in the street with money and owner's address back to the owner or not. Then one third of students had a microeconomics course taught by an expert on game theory, another third also had a microeconomics course taught by an expert on Marxian economics, and the last third had an astronomy course as a control group. After the courses there was a significant increase of dishonesty among the economics students, especially among those taught by the game theoretician (Frank et al. 1993; Yezer et al. 1996).

---

[4] Layard (2005). But "As for the understanding of life, the philosophy of happiness that's being propagated now, it's simply hard to believe that it's spoken seriously, it's such a ridiculous remnant". Boris Pasternak: Doktor Zhivago, 1955 (1994, 332).

4.3 Social Justice and Distribution

John Rawl's important 1972 book, *A Theory of Justice*, has stimulated large debates on distribution, justice, utility and welfare functions, that is how individual utilities can possibly be combined into a general welfare for society at large, to which several prominent economists have contributed (Rawls 1972; Atkinson 1983; Sen 1987; Konow 2003). Nevertheless, disregard of distribution issues is a common feature of the prevailing free market economics ideology, and many economists go as far as "What is called 'social justice' ... with reference to a society of free men, the phrase has no meaning whatever." (von Hayek 1978 p. 57, cf. Møller and Nielsen 1999 pp. 46, 49).

Apparently, misled by *the fundamental theorems of welfare theory*, which escape arbitrary assumptions on distributional justice, speculation caused Hayek to lose contact with reality, as he neglects compelling empirical evidence, that human beings do care for each other - sometimes and to some extent. Hayek and Marx agree on the irrelevance of distribution policy, although not on the moral and political implications.

> ... *von natürlicher Gerechtigkeit hier zu reden, ist Unsinn. Die Gerechtigkeit der Transaktionen, die zwischen den Produktionsagenten vorgehn, beruht darauf, daß die Transaktionen aus den Produktionsverhältnissen als natürliche Konsekvenz entspringen. ... Dieser Inhalt ist gerecht, sobald er der Produktionsweise entspricht, ihr adäquat ist. Er ist ungerecht, sobald er ihr wiederspricht. Sklaverei, auf Basis der kapitalistischen Produktionsweise, ist ungerecht.* (Karl Marx: Das Kapital III, 1894: Marx and Engels 1962–68, 25:351–352, 23:208).

Then, what about inequality? First of all, nobody likes it. Nobody would argue, at least not in public, that there are *eo ipso* justice reasons for accepting the large inequalities and the very different fates of members of human societies. In fact, equality and justice is more or less the same thing. But there are other economic goods here on earth, notably freedom and prosperity, and inequality is tolerated as a means for obtaining the other two. If it is accepted, that the basic goods in the economic sphere are: (1) *liberté*, (2) *egalité*, (3) *prospérité*, then the empirically well established modern surge in inequality in rich countries becomes a puzzle. Normally, when the total amount of goods increases, when total wealth increases as in rich countries during the same period of time, an increasing amount of all three types of goods would be expected. Is equality an inferior good? Did the marginal rate of transformation between equality and the other two goods alter? Or did relative preference evaluations of the three goods change?[5]

---

[5] Concerning the distribution of wealth as opposed to the distribution of wages, a mechanistic explation is possible: if savings as well as the return on capital are constant and GDP growth rates decline, the share of profits tend to increase at the expense of wages (Piketty 2014; *The Economist* 4 January 2014, p 57).

4.4 Universal Comparability in Money Terms

Money, invented independently in Greece and in China in the first millennium B.C., is an epoch-making social institution which facilitates market exchange and production by making everything commensurable - including the incommensurable. Therefore, as Marx remarked, since Antiquity money was denounced as tending to destroy the economic and moral order, and Marx quotes his favourite authors from Sofokles to Shakespeare:

> ... thou visible god,
> That solder'st close impossibilities,
> And mak'st them kiss! that speak'st with every tongue,
> To every purpose![6]

Money and markets facilitates the making of deals, including the dirty ones. We always had them; it was possible to exchange birthright for "bread and a pottage of lentils" without using money (Gen. 25:31–34).

However, for present day economics ideology it is not a vice, but a virtue to compute money values of everything and compare them, even across long time distances, as a basis for rational choice. Money values define the social value of everything: human lives, global warming, diseases, children, the great grey owl, time saved by fast traffic, unspoiled wilderness etc. etc. The money value of the risk of AIDS from unprotected sex with a random partner is estimated at 0.84 euros (Levitt and Dubner 2005; quoted from the Danish newspaper *Politiken*, 16 December 2005). It is a substitution of simple sums of money values for complicated moral problems of choice in order to achieve seeming consistency and rationality.

Michael Sandel did a great work pointing out, *what money can't buy* and should not buy. More often that not, things are very compound, and when reading Michael Sandel's great and most welcome book, I couldn't help laughing a couple of times: "… one's children are inalienable; it is unthinkable to put them up for sale" (Sandel 2012 p. 2). At least this does not apply to slave owners or royalty. And "*The Nobel Prize is not the kind of thing that money can buy*" (Sandel 2012:94; von Hagen and Welker 2014). But this is precisely what *Sveriges Riksbank*, the central bank of Sweden, did successfully on behalf of the economics profession. Now it is largely forgotten that Alfred Nobel never instituted a prize for economics. In the 1960's Riksbanken stroke a deal with the Nobel Foundation: it donated a handsome amount of money and in return got annual admission for one, two or three economists to this prestigious league of distinguished scientists and authors. What is more, it also got prestige and honour for the economics philosophy of market fundamentalism. Today a scientific stamp is probably more efficient as ideological promotion than even religion.

---

[6] Shakespeare, *Timon of Athens*, Act 4, Scene 3, quoted by Marx (*Paris Manuscripts*, 1844; Marx & Engels Werke, Ergänzungsband:1.564), to whom money was a prime example of alienation, cf. Werke 23:146; Marx 1974:805–806, 823–826.

The economics market triumphalist ideology is more impudent: Everything could and should be compared with money as the universal yardstick in order to obtain rational and consistent decisions and a "gratifying life" (Møller and Nielsen 1999 p. 6, 13), the incarnation of which is cost-benefit analysis, a very useful technique for comparing small, short term projects by means of monetary evaluations, for example whether to build a motorway bridge or a railway tunnel across the Great Belt. In this case cost-benefit analysis unambiguously showed the tunnel to be the most economical solution for any choice of social discount rate, but the bridge was erected. Nothing irrational with that - if you want pyramids, you should build pyramids.

But for big, long term questions cost-benefit calculations invariably end up in paradoxes, because they rest on shaky theoretical foundations beset by insoluble paradoxes concerning interpersonal comparisons of utility, utilitarian welfare, rates of discount, substitutability, money values of human life, uncertainty, and more. For example in health care calculations, money values of human life are used, as did William Petty (1623–1687) ahead of his time; he estimated the value of a person at £60–90, in England £90, in Ireland £70 (*The Economist*, 11 January 2014, p 12; 21 December 2013, p 100). Of course, it makes no sense. If I explained the various methods used, you wouldn't believe it, and values differ wildly. Thus the standard is about three million US dollars in the USA, one million dollars in Denmark, and 150,000 dollars in the Netherlands (Danish Ministry of Finance: Manual for Cost-Benefit Analysis, 1999, p. 63). Just imagine that physical constants, like gravitation or the velocity of light, differed by a factor 20 from one country to another.

A similar paradoxical dilemma arises concerning assessments of costs and benefits for future generations, which are ruined by the discount rate problem. A discount rate of 6% implies that $100 30 years from now only count as $17 and 41 cents today; and $100,100 years from now are reduced to 29 cents. And 6% is, "what most economists think are decent parameter values" (Weitzman 2007 p. 707) for obscure reasons.[7] Still, our great-grandchildren are likely to see things differently. Whether a 100 years is a long time obviously depends upon the point of view: from which of the two extreme points of the time span it is observed. This means, that if the rate of discount is positive, future generations will have no weight; if it is zero, present generations will have no weight. The many attempts to use variable discount rates does not remove the paradox.

We do not know how to handle these ethical problems. We are not getting wiser from chosing some arbitrary numbers for discount rates or for utilities for rich and poor people, as we cannot attribute any genuine meaning to them, neither as moral standard nor as objective knowledge. They are interesting to debate, but this does not simplify anything (which is after all the purpose of the whole exercise), as they are just as complicated as the original problem itself. Probably it is not so that

---

[7] The Stern-report (2007), 45–47, 161–163) uses a rate of 1.4%, including a pure time preference set at 0.1% for the one reason that there is a probability greater than zero that humanity will perish, after which no costs or benefits need to be taken into account.

"the approach has the virtue of clarity and simplicity", but rather the virtue of exposing our fundamental ignorance and bewilderment. Indeed, "such excises should be viewed with some circumspection" (Stern 2007 p. 30, 31; Stern 2013).

4.5 The Spectrum of Incentives

When there is universal comparability in money terms, the obvious next step is to approve of universal exchangeability. Marx shared the traditional disapproval, as he observed the increasing commodification of social life, which has

> ... alle feudalen, patriarchalischen, idyllischen Verhältnisse zerstört. Sie hat die buntscheckigen Feudalbande, die den Menschen an seinen natürlichen Vorgesetzten knüpften, unbarmherzig zerrissen und kein anderes Band zwischen Mensch und Mensch übriggelassen als das nackte Interesse, als die gefühllose "bare Zahlung". Sie hat die heiligen Schauer der frommen Schwärmerei, die ritterlichen Begeisterung, der spießbürgerlichen Wehmut in dem eiskalten Wasser egoistischer Berechnung ertränkt (Manifest der Kommunistischen Partei, 1848; Marx and Engels 1962–68, 4:464–465).

This was not a fallacy, but a prophecy.

The changing attitudes are reflected in Agnar Mykle's novel, *Song of the red ruby*, from 1956. The main character and narrator, Ask Burlefot, a student at the Norwegian School of Economics in Bergen, delivers a speech for the ladies at the annual party for students and professors, in which the joke is to describe the relations between men and especially women in terms of economic theory, supply and demand etc.: "A homo poeticus can *praise* the woman; only a homo oeconomicus can really *price* her" (Mykle 1956 p. 299).[8] In less than 20 years the frivolous dinner speech joke was metamorphosed into academic economics in Gary S. Becker's "theory of marriage" from 1974 (Becker 1973; Michael Svarer in The newspaper *Politiken*, 14 February 2014). This exchange or *quid pro quo* philosophy of life is nothing new, but most likely it has gained increased propagation in recent years. In his *Social Behaviour* from 1961, George C. Homans, an influential sociologist at that time, used *quid pro quo* as the basic principle for understanding society (Homans 1961) and the philosophy permeates economics textbooks.[9]

A further step in this one dimensional perception of society is to apply it to the big question: What motivates human action? And the conclusion is that material, economic incentives are the only efficient, and besides they are also the only respectable. It is curious that the market ideology of economic incentives triumphs right now, simultaneously with numerous recent experiments, which are making even economists aware that there are other significant incentives than economic

---

[8] The novel was banned by court, not because of the dinner speech, but because of pornography, which appear rather innocent by current standards, but finally it was acquitted by Supreme Court in 1958.

[9] See for example the excellent book on *economic organization* by Milgrom and Roberts 1999.

self-interest and other significant ethics than market ethics. For example, participants in experiments are willing to pay money for the pleasure of punishing unfair behavior of others, as demonstrated in the famous *ultimatum game* and many others.

The obsession with economic incentives is a main target of Sandel's criticism, and he worries and demonstrates that economic incentives may crowd out other, more lofty ones, illustrated by the famous example of payment for blood donation, which reduced the willingness to donate blood (Sandel 2012 pp. 43–130, 122–124). However, in economics there are always good arguments in favour of the opposite view (Besley 2013; Bowles and Polanía-Reyes 2012). An example is the theory of the welfare state by Assar Lindbeck, who argues just the other way round, that material incentives create social norms as a superstructure upon the material basis, much in line with Marx (Lindbeck 1997). According to Assar Lindbeck the welfare state destroys itself from within. In the course of some decennia, the economic equality of the welfare state, characterized by high levels of taxation and generous social security and unemployment benefits, evolves into a hammock of abuses and erodes economic work incentives and thereby also - with a time lag - social norms for hard work inherited from the past. The result is an undermining of the economic foundations of the high living standards - the second characteristic of the welfare state. Therefore, work incentives must be strengthened and transfer payments reduced in order so save society.

This theory of incentives implies an almost Marxian prominence of material incentives. In the days of old, social norms (i.e. moral incentives) for hard work emerged as a social superstructure upon the basis of strong economic incentives in families and villages. In the welfare state, "tension easily arises … between economic incentives and an inherited social norm in favor of work", and "social norms like these are likely to adjust to changes in economic incentives" (Lindbeck 1997 p. 371).

However, material incentives is just a segment of a whole spectrum from purely material to purely mental motivating forces: compulsion, inertia, economic rewards, social pressure, conscience, and inherent incentives like pleasure of work. Obviously, other forces than material incentives must be at work too. Which are these forces that keep society together? Assar Lindbeck is navigating in deep social science waters, but he is not the first adventurous explorer, and the problem of solidarity, of collective responsibility, is a major theme in classic as well as modern sociology. The criticism of economics for simple mindedness and obsession with exchange and material incentives is not new. Said Émile Durkheim in 1893:

> *Toute société est une société morale. … Mais si la division du travail produit la solidarité, ce n'est pas seulement parce qu'elle fait de chaque individu un échangiste comme disent les économistes. … Si les économistes ont cru … que les sociétés humaines pouvaient et devaient se résoudre en des associations purement économiques, c'est qu'ils ont cru qu'elle n'affectait que des intérêts individuelles et temporaires* (Durkheim 1960 pp. 207, 402–403).

And in 1928 Charles Gide concluded his investigation into utopian egalitarian societies:

> *... et c'est là assurément une expérience intéressante, car elle prouve que des hommes peuvent vivre en communauté et qu'une entreprise sous cette forme n'est pas nécessairement vouée à l'échec, comme l'affirment tous les économistes* (Gide 1928 p. 103).[10]

According to Durkheim, the problem of material incentives is that they also affects solidarity, which constitutes the basis of social norms, and the two main abnormal forms, where solidarity fails to materialize, are - contrary to Assar Lindbeck's view - those with excessive reliance upon material incentives, either as coercion or as *laissez-faire* individualism. In traditional society norms also originated from solidarity, mainly in family groups, which supported non-working members, even if family life also included exploitation, violence, sexual abuse and intolerance.

How to transform the *mechanical solidarity* of traditional society into *organic solidarity* was a major concern of classic sociological theorists including Durkheim, Tönnies, Weber and Simmel (Lee and Newby 1989), and it recurs in modern theory, again because of the predominance of powerful economic inducements to self-interested behaviour, which penetrate into all spheres of life. In this light solutions to the moral problem of modern society are, indeed, not evident, but the Lindbeck solution – a regression to a more brutal society with potent material incentives – appears particularly dangerous.

4.6 Conclusion: Too Little Planning

Nothing is wrong with economics. What is wrong, is mainstream economists' ideological, ultra-liberalist abuse of economics: "Ultraliberalists are not only morally indecent. They also give poor advice", said the late Paul A. Samuelson in 2008 (*Der Spiegel*, quoted in the newspaper *Politiken*, 29 November 2008). Furthermore, there is something wrong with reality; it is unpredictable, paradoxical and not reducible to one dimension and one type of incentives.

Sometimes, economics is better than its reputation, and in several cases it has something to offer. Tradeable pollution permits used to be considered market friendly by market ideologists and therefore prefered to pollution taxes. But these are exactly as market-friendly as tradable pollution permits, or rather market-unfriendly. Both are instruments for central economic planning. None of them has anything to do with a market economy, which is something entirely different, namely that the market is allowed spontaneously and decentrally to determine how resources are to be allocated. Environmental policy and regulation means central planning: the allocation (the amount of pollution) is fixed politically in advance, before incentives and markets come into play.

The end results of taxation (price regulation) and tradable permits (quantity regulation) are identical, but there are differences in the adjustment process, and therefore tradable permits are normally a poor instrument of regulation. With taxation the

---

[10] Charles Gide was a brother of the author André Gide.

price of pollution is fixed, but with tradable permits prices are often extremely volatile, which impairs enterprises' long-term investment planning concerning abatement equipment and types of plant. The ETS (Emissions Trading System) of the EU for trading CO_2-pollution permits collapsed in April 2013, as the price per tonne had plummeted from 20 euros in 2011 to 5 euros, and these prices are useless for planning purpuses (*The Economist*, 20 April 2013, pp. 61–62; 14 December 2013, p. 58). Now pollution taxes are generally recommended as a necessary means for climate policy.

There are good reasons for using economic incentives in environmental policy. It is difficult to understand the animosity against taxation and tradable permits, also displayed by Sandel, that they imply "an instrumental attitude toward nature" (Sandel 2012 p. 75; Hanley et al. 2001). All economic activity damages the environment, and what is paid for, is a permit to normal production activity that is usually guided by money, markets and profits. We also accept taxing alcohol for health reasons[11] without considering it a vicious instrumental attidude towards human health. Finally the view is gaining ground, that political regulation is imperative and thorough central planning the only hope for not resorting to the traditional mechanisms of adjustment, that is famines, migrations, epidemics and wars (Stern 2007; Arrow et al. 2004; Weitzman 2007).

The fundamental theorems of welfare theory turn out to be an argument for central planning, not for unregulated market allocation, because the conditions for market efficiency are not fulfilled. Whether government allocation will actually work, when the market does not, is no evident question, as market failures are not the only failures – there are also plenty of policy failures. Central planning has got a bad name. Soviet economic policy was as obsessed with GDP growth at the expense of the environment, as was economic policy in western democracies, and the results concerning GDP growth and environmental degradation were very similar. Instruments for environmental policy were in place, but not political will (Aage 1998 pp. 3–15; Ponting 1991 p. 153; Aage 2004). Highly succesful variants of central planning exist, Germany 1933–45 and the war economies in World War II in the UK and notably the USA, where the *Office of Production Management* with planned economy efficiency managed 60–70% of American industry and the avalanche of American war production which proved so decisive for the outcome of the war. Its chairman, William S. Knudsen, became a war hero in the USA and acquired rank of *lieutenant general* (Lund 2018).[12]

---

[11] Although public health never determined alcohol taxation in Denmark; considerations were rather related to provision of grain for food, government coffers and EU internal market policies.

[12] William S. Knudsen – "Mr. Nudsen" or "Big Bill" – was not a socialist, but sympathized with Germany in the early 1930s, and had no military training, as he was not admitted to the military either in Denmark, where he lived until his 20s, or in the USA. But he was a former director of Ford Motor Company, first, and General Motors, later.

Marx conjectured, rightly, that capitalism had an enormous potential for economic growth, and considered material abundance created by capitalism a precondition for socialism (Aage 2004). After 150 years it is time for turning Marx upside down: Increasing abundance is not the means for solving the enigma of history, for achieving socialism, equality and democracy, but the other way about. Rather, socialism, equality and democracy are badly needed means for solving the problems and conflicts arising from the appearance in the horizon of the limits to growth. For decades we have all known very well that the challenges of our time, global environment and global distribution, desperately require collective action, and also that this is precisely what market governance can not deliver. How market ideology could invade our collective mind so forcefully during these same decades, remains a mystery.

References

Aage, H. 1991. Popular Attitudes and Perestroika. *Soviet Studies* 43 (1): 3–25.
———., ed. 1998. *Environmental Transition in Nordic and Baltic Countries*. Cheltenham: Edward Elgar.
———. 2002. Vilhelm Beck – omstridt gennem 133 år. *Kirkehistoriske Samlinger* 2002: 69–97.
———. 2004. *Karl Marx Den proletariske klasses teoretiker*. Copenhagen: Jurist- og Økonomforbundets Forlag.
Aage, H., et al. 2009. Hovedstrømninger i det 21. århundredes økonomi. *Nationaløkonomisk Tidsskrift* 146.3: 301–318.
Arrow, K., P. Dasgupta, L. Goulder, G. Daily, P. Ehrlich, G. Heal, S. Levin, K.-G. Mäler, S. Scheider, D. Starrett, and B. Walker. 2004. Are We Consuming Too Much? *Journal of Economic Perspectives* 18 (3): 147–172.
Atkinson, A.B. 1983. *The Economics of Inequality*. 2nd ed. Oxford: Clarendon.
Becker, G.S. 1973. A Theory of Marriage. Part I. *Journal of Political Economy* 81 (4): 813–846.
Besley, T. 2013. What's the Good of the Market? An Essay on Michael Sandel's What Money Can't Buy. *Journal of Economic Literature* 51 (2): 478–495.
Bowles, S., and S. Polanía-Reyes. 2012. Economic Incentives and Social Preferences: Substitutes or Complements. *Journal of Economic Literature* 50 (2): 368–425.
Cox, B., and J. Forshaw. 2011. *The Quantum Universe: Everything that Can Happen Does Happen*. London: Allen Lane.
Durkheim, É. 1960. *De la division du travail social (1893)*. Paris: Presses Universitaires de France, Paris.
Fernández-Armesto, F. 1995. *Millenium A History of Our Last Thousand Years*. London: Bantam press.
Franciscus, P.P. 2013. *Evangelii gaudium Adhortatio apostolica*. Vatican: English language version, Vatican Press.
Frank, R.H., T. Gilovich, and D.T. Regan. 1993. Does Studying Economics Inhibit Cooperation? *Journal of Economic Perspectives* 7 (2): 159–171.
Frydman, R., M.D. Goldberg 2010. Efficient Markets: Fictions and Reality. Paper presented at the Inaugural Conference of the Institute for New Economic Thinking. King's College, Cambridge, 8–11 Apr 2010.
———. 2011. *Beyond Mechanical Markets*. Princeton: Princeton University Press.

Gide, C. 1928. *Les Colonies communistes et cooperatives*. Paris: Association pour l'enseignement de la cooperation.
Goodchild, P. 2009. *Theology of Money*. Durham: Duke University Press.
Hanley, N., J.F. Shogren, and B. White. 2001. *Introduction to Environmental Economics*. Oxford: Oxford University Press.
Homans, G.C. 1961. *Social Behaviour*. London: Routledge and Kegan Paul.
Kindleberger, C.P., and R.Z. Aliber. 2005. *Manias, Panics and Crashes. A History of Financial Crisis*. 5th ed. New York: Palgrave Macmillan.
Konow, J. 2003. Which Is the Fairest One of All? A Positive Analysis of Justice Theories. *Journal of Economic Literature* 41 (4): 1188–1239.
Layard, R. 2005. *Happiness Lessons from a New Science*. London: Allen Lane.
Lee, D., and H. Newby. 1989. *The Problem of Sociology*. London: Unwin Hyman.
Leontief, W. 1938. The Significance of Marxian Economics for Present-Day Economic Theory. *American Economic Review* 28 (1 Supplement): 1–9.
———. 1983. Academic Economics. *Science* 217 (4555): 104–107, and Vol. 219 No. 4587 pp. 904, 907.
Levitt, S.D., and S.J. Dubner. 2005. *Freakonomics: A Roque Economist Explores the Hidden Side of Everything*. London: Penguin.
Lindbeck, A. 1997. Incentives and Social Norms in Household Behavior. *American Economic Review* 87 (2): 370–377.
Lund, M. 2018. *Big Bill*. Copenhagen: Haase.
Marx, K. 1974. *Grundrisse der Kritik der politischen Ökonomie (Rohentwurf 1857–1858)*. Berlin: Dietz Verlag.
Marx, K., and F. Engels 1962–68. *Werke*. Berlin: Dietz Verlag.
Milgrom, P., and J. Roberts. 1999. *Economics Organization and Management*. Prentice-Hall: Englewoods Cliffs NJ.
Møller, M., and N.C. Nielsen. 1999. *Kunst økonomisk set*. Copenhagen: Gyldendal.
Mykle, A. 1956. *Sangen om den røde rubin*. Oslo: Gyldendal Norsk Forlag.
Pasternak, B. 1994. *Doktor Zhivago (1955)*. Moskva: Izdatel'stvo Trojka.
Piketty, T. 2014. *Le capital au 21e siècle*, Editions du Seuil, Paris 2013. Chambridge: Harvard University Press, Mar 2014.
Plesner, S. 2015. Nobelprisen i økonomi 2013: Efficiente eller inefficiente markeder? *Samfundsøkonomen* 3: 45–50.
Ponting, C. 1991. *A Green History of the World*. Harmondsworth: Penguin.
Pontrjagin, L.S. 1980. O matematike i kachestve ee prepodovanija. *Kommunist*. 1186 September 14: 99–112.
Rawls, J. 1972. *A Theory of Justice*. Oxford: Oxford University Press.
Sandel, M.J. 2012. *What Money Can't Buy the Moral Limits of Markets*. London: Allen Lane.
Sen, A. 1987. *On Ethics and Economics*. Oxford: Blackwell.
Shiller, R.J., M. Boycko, and V. Korobov. 1991. Popular Attitudes Toward Free Markets: The Soviet Union and The United States Compared. *American Economic Review* 81 (3): 385–400.
Stern, N., ed. 2007. *The Economics of Climate Change (The Stern Review, HM Treasury Independent Review)*. Cambridge: Cambridge University Press.
———. 2013. The Structure of Economic Modelling of the Potential Impacts of Climate Change: Grafting Gross Underestimation of Risk onto Already Narrow Science Models. *Journal of Economic Literature* 51 (3): 838–859.
Stiglitz, J.E., J.A. Ocampo, S. Spiegel, R. Ffrench-Davis, and D. Nayyar. 2006. *Stability with Growth. Macroeconomics, Liberalization, and Development*. Oxford: Oxford University Press.
von Hagen, J., and M. Welker, eds. 2014. *Money as God? The Monetisation of the Market and its Impact on Religion Politics, Law and Ethics*. Cambridge: Cambridge University Press.

von Hayek, F.A. 1978. *New Studies in Philosophy, Politics, Economics, and the History of Ideas*. London: Routledge & Kegan Paul.
Weitzman, M.L. 2007. A Review of The Stern Review on the Economics of Climate Change. *Journal of Economic Literature* 45 (3): 703–724.
Yezer, A.M., R.S. Goldfarb, and P.J. Poppen. 1996. Does Studying Economics Discourage Cooperation? Watch What We Do, Not What We Say or How We Play. *Journal of Economic Perspectives* 10 (1): 177–186.

Hans Aage born 1946, professor of economics at Roskilde University since 1994. Has mainly worked with comparative economics. Is known both for scientific contributions and for articles in the Danish newspapers.

Chapter 5
Happiness in the Hands of Empirical Economists

Peder J. Pedersen

Abstract In a discussion of what characterize a good human life the concept of happiness and what determines happiness is important. Since the late twentieth century economists and other social scientists have shown a fast-growing interest in happiness defined as self-reported well-being. Many contributions have analyzed the relationship between happiness and economic factors, especially income, and other relevant background factors. An initial conviction of no relationship between happiness and income – seen as a paradox in economic terms – has changed to a recognition of a dominantly positive relationship. At the same time several studies find a number of other factors such as age, gender, civil status, income distribution, health and education to be equally, or more important. The chapter gives a survey of this literature.

Keywords Happiness · Self-reported well-being · Income · Easterlin paradox · Inequality

5.1 Introduction

In recent decades economists have shown a strongly increasing interest in the area of self reported well-being or happiness. Many contributions have analyzed the eventual relationship between happiness and income along with a battery of other possible explanatory factors. An introduction to the area from the viewpoint of economists can be found in Frey and Stutzer (2002).

An earlier version of the chapter was presented at a workshop held at the Royal Danish Academy of Sciences and Letters in February 2014 on Markets, Ethics and Religion. Comments from participants in the workshop are gratefully acknowledged.

P. J. Pedersen (deceased)
Department of Economics and Business Economics, Aarhus University, Aarhus V, Denmark
e-mail: ppedersen@econ.au.dk

© The Author(s), under exclusive license to Springer Nature Switzerland AG 2023
N. Kærgård (ed.), *Market, Ethics and Religion*, Ethical Economy 62,
https://doi.org/10.1007/978-3-031-08462-1_5

Recent surveys can be found in Clark (2018) and Nikolova and Graham (2020).

The increasing interest among economists has focus on both micro- and macroeconomic aspects. In macroeconomics there has been a long-standing critical attitude to conventional national accounts as an adequate measure of well-being in broader terms. This critical attitude is formulated quite strongly in a book by Wilkinson & Pickett (2010, p. 15) *"In the last chapter we saw that economic growth and increase in average incomes have ceased to contribute much to wellbeing in rich countries"*. The validity of a statement like this is one of the main topics in the present chapter. In 2013 the OECD published a survey of initiatives in the member countries in the area of measurement of a battery of indicators of well-being of the citizens. This has been followed annually, most recently in OECD (2020). One among the broad range of indicators is the topic in the present chapter, i.e. subjective well-being (SWB) or happiness. The OECD (2013) report is a summing up on national initiatives to supplement more traditional economic measures like GDP per capita with a broader range of indicators. A well-known early initiative in this area was the setting up in France of a government commission on quality of life resulting in 2009 in the Stiglitz-Sen-Fitoussi report. Work in this area began in the UK in 2010. Corresponding initiatives are taken up in a number of other countries.[1] Another well-known pioneer example is the setting up of a Gross Happiness Index in the Kingdom of Bhutan. A recent comprehensive discussion of well-being as an important goal for public policy can be found in Frijters et al. (2020).

In microeconomic terms there is a clear interest in going into the eventual relationship between measures of well-being and income. The impact in conventional microeconomics from an increase in individual income is to move the individual to a higher level of utility. The prior expectation is that increasing utility correlates with increasing well-being. In case this is not confirmed in empirical studies there is several possible interpretations. One possibility is that happiness depends on income relative to a reference group more than the absolute level of individual income. Another interpretation is the existence of a fixed individual "set point" for well-being. Temporary deviations from the set-point can occur as a consequence of changes in income – or other determinants – but a gradual return takes place back to the individual set-point. These interpretations are developed further below. In macroeconomic terms, the approach has been studies of time-series of average income and average happiness indicators in a given country or cross-country studies at a specific time.

In the following, Sect. 5.2 presents a brief survey of results in a number of studies mostly based on macro data, i.e. average values of income and subjective well-being (SWB) indicators. Next, Sect. 5.3 presents some results from an analysis based on individual panel data for several EU countries followed over a period of 8 years; the section further summarizes the impact from other factors than income on well-being from a broad range of studies. Focus in Sect. 5.4 is on the eventual

---

[1] In January 2014 the Danish government published an agenda setting up very specific targets for a broad number of indicators 10 years later. Taking one specific indicator as an example, the share of adults with low satisfaction with their life is to be reduced with 10%.

relationship between the average level of happiness in a society and the inequality in the "distribution" of happiness, i.e. the gap between the most and the least happy individuals relative to the average level. Considering the strong increase in income inequality in many countries in recent years, Sect. 5.4 also treats the question whether unequal societies in income terms also tend to have a lower level of average well-being or happiness. Finally, Sect. 5.5 concludes.

5.2 Happiness and Income

A central starting point in the literature discussing the happiness-income relationship is Easterlin (1974, 1995) concluding that average SWB in the USA had been stationary for decades of increasing real GDP per capita. Blanchflower and Oswald (2004) found the same approximately flat level of average SWB in Great Britain from the early 1970s to the late 1990s. After controlling for a number of individual characteristics Blanchflower and Oswald (2004) however found evidence of a significantly upward movement in well-being over these nearly three decades. The original Easterlin (1974, 1995) finding was appropriately termed "the Easterlin paradox". The flat level of average SWB found by Easterlin runs counter to a conventional economic interpretation of SWB as representing utility expected to correlate positively with real GDP per capita An update of the original Easterlin relation taken from Clark et al. (2008) is shown in Fig. 5.1.

A principal solution in utility terms of the Easterlin Paradox is presented in the comprehensive paper by Clark et al. (2008). Studies using micro data on the other hand typically find a positive correlation between SWB and income. This apparent contrast is parallel to findings in consumption studies of a lower marginal propensity to consume in analyses using aggregate time series data compared with studies

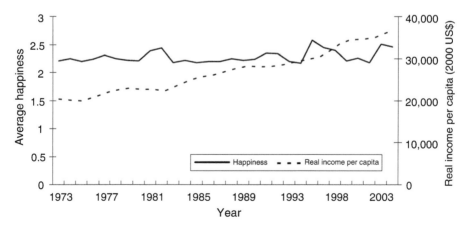

Fig. 5.1 Average values of happiness indicator and real income per capita. USA 1973–2003. (Source: Clark et al. (2008, Fig. 1))

using cross-section micro data finding a steeper relationship between income and consumption. A unified explanation of no or little correlation between SWB and income in time series and positive correlation in cross sections using micro data is presented in Clark et al. (2008) by expanding a utility function with a relative income term. This could be income relative to a reference group at the same point in time or own current income relative to earlier income. If income for an individual rises faster than for a relevant reference group, SWB would increase with income as long as this situation persisted. Over time as income for the reference group catches up, relative income and SWB for the first mover falls back again. Stated in a different way, adaptation to a higher income lasts longer when you are the first – or among the first – to move up in income.

The interpretation of a steeper positive relationship in cross-section studies in contrast to a much flatter long-run time series relationship is illustrated in Fig. 5.2 from Clark et al. (2008) where the analogy with consumption studies appears clearly.

A very special "natural experiment", i.e. the German re-unification, offered an opportunity to study the impact from an unexpected strong increase in income for the population in East Germany. Using data from the German Socioeconomic Panel, Frijters et al. (2004) found a clear positive impact on SWB lasting nearly 10 years until adaptation had occurred to the new higher level of income. The relationship between average values in the former East Germany in the first 10 years after re-unification is shown in Fig. 5.3.

In an analysis using Eurobarometer SWB data for a period of 30 years, Bjørnskov et al. (2008) found evidence that an accelerated growth in real GDP per capita resulted in a significant positive impact on average national SWB. Headey (2006) presents an alternative interpretation of the short run/long run challenge by setting it in the frame of the Set Point Theory from psychology and letting the dynamic

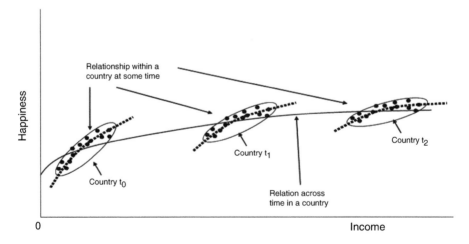

Fig. 5.2 A stylized representation of the relationship between SWB and income in cross-section and time-series analyses. (Source: Clark et al. (2008, Fig. 4))

Fig. 5.3 Average values for life satisfaction and real income per capita. Former East Germany 1991–2001. (Source: Clark et al. (2008, Fig. 3))

equilibrium adaptation consist of a gradual shifting of the individual Set Point as a reaction to changes in income.

Ferrer-i-Carbonell (2005) is also using the German Socioeconomic Panel to study the impact on SWB from own income against the impact from relative income. She finds that the income in the reference group is just as important as own income for SWB. Caporale et al. (2009) working with data from the European Social Survey also find a positive impact from income on happiness and life satisfaction and a negative impact from reference income.

Di Tella and Macculloch (2010) find in a cross-country setting using data from Eurobarometer, the German Socioeconomic Panel and the World Gallup Poll that the cross-section impact from income becomes flat from a certain level, but the adaptation to an increase in income may last longer than 5 years. Ball and Chernova (2008) using data from the World Values Survey find significant impacts on happiness from both absolute and relative income with relative income having the largest effect and with the interesting contribution that the impact from both income measures are small when seen relative to the importance of a number of non-pecuniary factors. Scoppa and Ponzo (2008) confirm this result in a study using Bank of Italy data for 2004 and 2006 finding that several non-economic factors are highly important for SWB. At the same time, they find however a significant effect from own and relative labor income and a highly significant effect from wealth, real as well as financial wealth. The influence from wealth is also one of the topics in Headey et al. (2008). Using national panels from five countries they find a stronger impact on satisfaction from wealth than from income. Further, using the panel property of the data they find that *changes* in income, consumption and wealth have significant effects on changes in the level of satisfaction.

The ambition in Stevenson and Wolfers (2008a) is to evaluate the validity of the original Easterlin puzzle by drawing together several data sets for a number of countries. They find – in contrast to the original puzzle – a clear positive link between average SWB and real GDP per capita in a cross-country setting and find no evidence of an income saturation point beyond which further increases in income is without effect on SWB. Comparing changes in SWB and in income over time in the individual countries they find a clear positive relationship. Stevenson and Wolfers (2008a) conclude that the effect from absolute income dominates the relative income effect. Stevenson and Wolfers (2013) further discuss the question of satiation. A special challenge is taken up by Powdthavee (2009) pointing to the fact that income like SWB might most reasonably be understood as an endogenous variable creating well known problems when regressing endogenous variables on each other. Powdthavee (2009) instruments for income and allows for unobserved heterogeneity and finds a positive impact from income on SWB significantly higher than in the basic specification without correcting for endogeneity.

Summing up the results regarding the SWB-income relationship in a number of studies it seems the original Easterlin Paradox is no longer a puzzle. More datasets covering longer periods and more countries and including more explanatory variables seems without exception to point to a significant positive relationship between SWB and absolute as well as relative income for a reference group. There does not however seem to be consensus regarding the relative importance of the two income measures. Several studies agree on the significance of income, but emphasize that non-economic factors appear to be more important than income.

A study from Eurofound (2013), contains values for average life satisfaction and average income for 26 EU countries where data are collected following the same principles in all the countries.[2] The co-variation between SWB and average purchasing power adjusted income per capita in 2010 is shown in Fig. 5.4. The relationship seems to confirm the overall conclusion in Stevenson and Wolfers (2008a). A final perspective is the topic in Dominko and Verbic (2020) finding important impacts on the relationship between income and wealth and SWB in different welfare state settings. The data are from SHARE, thus containing only observations on individuals 50 years and older in a number of EU countries.

5.3 The Impact on SWB from Other Factors

Several other factors besides income are found in many studies to have a significant impact on SWB. As an example, Table 5.1 summarizes the significant impact found from a number of other factors in a study using data from the European Household Panel (ECHP) where the same battery of questions were given to panels of respondents in EU member countries over a period of 8 years. As expected, the impact from self-assessed health is very clear for all the countries. The same significant impact on SWB is found regarding moves between the states of employment and unemployment. On the other hand, exit from the labor force – to retirement or study

---

[2] Observations for Luxembourg are excluded as the average income is affected by a high level of in-commuting of people living in other EU member states.

5 Happiness in the Hands of Empirical Economists

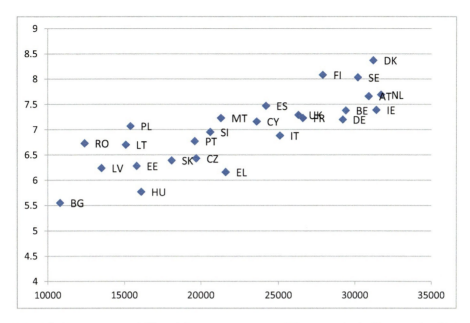

Fig. 5.4 Average value of life satisfaction and average GDP per capita in EU countries, PPS adjusted income, 2010 values. (Source: Eurofound (2013, Fig. 4))

Table 5.1 Impact on SWB from other covariates than income

Country	Explanatory variables – significance indicated by sign				
	Self assessed bad health	From job to unemployed	From being unemployed to job	Exit from the labor force	60+ years
AT	−	−	+		(+)
BE	−	−	+		+
DK	−	−	+		+
ES	−	−	+		+
FI	−	−	+	+	
FR	−	−	+	+	+
EL	−	−	+		+
IE	−	−	+		+
IT	−	−	+	−	+
NL	−	−	+		
PT	−	−	+	−	+

Source: Pedersen and Schmidt (2011)
Note: Results from a cross-country panel study using ECHP data

or family work, is found mostly insignificant and in case of significance no clear impact appears. Finally, Table 5.1 includes the eventual impact from being 60 years or older, which with few exceptions is found to have a significantly positive impact with being younger than 60 as the benchmark.

In many studies the impact on SWB from age is found to follow a U shape over the life cycle.[3] The most recent comprehensive analysis of the impact from age is Blanchflower (2021) who studies the relationship between SWB and age using data for 145 countries. The main conclusion is a clear confirmation of the U shape with the age of minimum SWB around 50. Blanchflower (2021) finds that the age of minimum SWB has been rising over time in Europe and the USA. By gender, Stevenson and Wolfers (2009) find in a survey including data sets over longer periods and across several countries that SWB for women, initially higher than for men, has been falling to a level on average lower than found for men. Eurofound (2013) in the study referred to above, however, finds exactly the same level of self-reported happiness for women and for men. Compared with the general result in the Stevenson and Wolfers (2009) survey this is surprising considering also the big cross-European differences in family patterns, fertility and labor force participation. Finally, a general result in many studies is the finding of a positive SWB gradient in education.

5.4 Happiness, Level and Distribution

In this section we shall look into the eventual relationship between the level of SWB and the distribution, both the distribution of SWB and of income. Clark et al. (2014) find that the inequality in the distribution of SWB has been falling in most of the countries which have experienced a growth in incomes over the most recent 40 years. The falling inequality in the distribution of SWB is typically the result of falling shares of individuals reporting happiness at the highest and at the lowest levels. Stevenson and Wolfers (2008b) find the decline in the inequality in the distribution of SWB in the USA is dominantly a reflection of falling in-group inequality in the US population. The European cross-country study (Eurofound 2013) finds a clear negative relationship between the level of average SWB and the inequality in the distribution of SWB. This is illustrated in Fig. 5.5 showing the co-variation between the average level of SWB and the distribution using the absolute difference between the first and the fifth quintile as distributional indicator (the difference between the index for the 20% most and the 20% least happy). The co-variation appears quite convincing with higher levels of average SWB coinciding with a more equal distribution.

The quite big fall in the inequality in the distribution of SWB is surprising considering the strong increase in the inequality of the distribution of income which has occurred – with different strength – in most OECD countries in recent decades.

---

[3] The same U shaped profile over life is also found in studies of great apes, cf. Weiss et al. (2012).

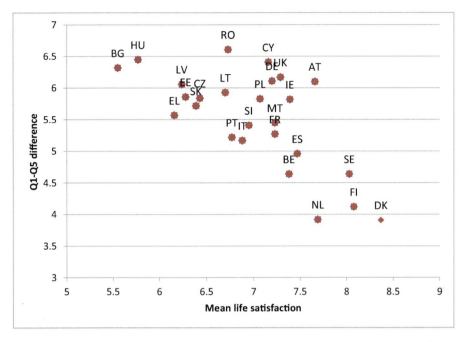

Fig. 5.5 The co-variation between average SWB and an indicator of the distribution of SWB. 26 EU countries. (Source: Calculations from Eurofoundation (2013))

Clark and D'Ambrosia (2015) have collected the evidence on the co-variation between happiness and income inequality in studies from the last decades. The co-variation based on evidence from the available studies is not unambiguous. There is a slight dominance of finding a negative relationship, i.e. higher inequality co-varies with lower SWB. However, these studies differ regarding data, national background etc in a way making it difficult to reach very clear conclusions.

In a study of differences in the co-variation between the USA and European countries Alesina et al. (2004) find a negative relationship, also when many background factors are included in the analysis. At the same time, they find some interesting US-European differences when the results are disaggregated on groups of people. In Europe, people with low incomes and people with sympathies for left wing parties report lower SWB due to inequality. Quite surprising, people who are worried about inequality are found in high income groups.

Graham and Felton (2006) present results for Latin America, a continent with a very high level of inequality. The dominant result is the finding of a negative effect on happiness from income inequality. At the same time the results in Graham and Felton (2006) support that perceptions about status, opportunities and mobility may be at least as important for happiness as income inequality per se.

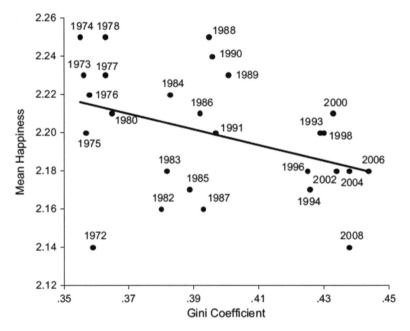

Fig. 5.6 Co-variation between the Gini coefficient and average happiness, USA 1972–2008. (Source: Oishi et al. (2011, Fig. 2))

Oishi et al. (2011) have focus on the co-variation between the Gini coefficient and the average value of the SWB variable for the USA in the period 1972–2008. Figure 5.6 shows the co-variation appearing to be slightly negative in a special way as it seems to consist of three sets of points each referring to 10–12 years without any clear co-variation but where the three sets of points shift downwards to the right. The slight negative co-variation is only found for respondents with lower incomes. Oishi et al. (2011) find that the negative co-variation for this group is not dependent on the incomes in these households but on a perception of lacking fairness and lack of trust increasing with inequality.

Blanchflower and Oswald (2003) present results for the years 1976–1996 using US state data including a variable for earnings inequality for each state among the explanatory variables. The result is the finding of a moderate negative impact on happiness, most pronounced among young people, workers and people with fairly low education.

Berg and Veenhoven (2010) have collected data for average happiness and income inequality in 119 nations. They find a positive but weak effect from inequality. One interpretation of this in Berg and Veenhoven (2010), taken up in some studies referred to below, is that inequality – in some degree or in some countries – could reflect preferences in the population regarding the level of inequality. A recent study by Verme (2011) using a large global sample finds however, in contrast to Berg and Veenhoven (2010), that income inequality has a significant negative impact on life satisfaction. However, as the number of observations of the inequality variable is small, multicollinearity due to the use of country and year fixed effects in the estimations makes the result unstable and less reliable.

Finally, a number of studies, Schneider (2012), Rözer and Kraaykamp (2013), and Bjørnskov et al. (2013), expand on studies of the co-variation between SWB and inequality by including preferences and attitudes regarding trust, income mobility and public sector income redistribution. The main result in Bjørnskov et al. (2013) is that the relationship at the aggregate level is much more ambiguous than the standard micro argument of increasing inequality resulting in a decline in average welfare. The reason for this inconsistency between micro and macro level results is an interaction between perceived and actual fairness of the institutional framework in many countries. An analysis by Eurofound and Bertelsmann Stiftung (2014), combines a study of SWB with a study of social cohesion across the EU countries. The main result in the present context is the finding of higher income inequality reducing the strength of cohesion in a country which then has a negative impact on SWB, i.e. the co-variation is running through an intermediate variable. Finally, a study using pseudo-panel data for Denmark, (Jensen and Pedersen 2020), find a significant negative impact from increasing inequality for the years since 2002.

Summing up, until now data availability has resulted in a number of interesting cross-country studies. The lack of unambiguous results can reflect characteristics with these data, i.e. only one value of the inequality variable for each country, and the potential differences cross-country in the understanding of well-being questions among respondents. In due time, more panels of observations over time in individual countries will reduce both of these problems.

5.5 Concluding Remarks

In recent decades there has been a quite strong increase in economic analyses working with self-assessed quality of life, subjective well-being (SWB) or happiness in relation to economic factors, especially income, and other relevant background factors. An initial conviction of no relationship between happiness and income – seen as a paradox in economic terms – has changed to a recognition of a dominantly positive relationship, with SWB interpreted as utility. The impact from income can be directly from own current income, from relative income and from wealth. At the same time several studies find a number of other factors to be important for reported SWB. This is the case for age, gender, civil status, labor market situation, health and education. Some of these other factors can be more important in quantitative terms than income. Other studies have analyzed the distribution around an average level of SWB typically finding a trend towards falling inequality in the distribution of SWB. A number of studies have looked into the eventual co-variation between happiness and inequality in the distribution of income, an interesting topic in view of the ongoing increase in inequality occurring in different degrees in most OECD countries. The results so far are not unambiguous but have a slight dominance of studies pointing to a fairly small negative impact on happiness from income inequality.

References

Alesina, A., R. Di Tella, and R. MacCulloch. 2004. Inequality and Happiness: Are Europeans and Americans Different. *Journal of Public Economics* 88: 2009–2042.

Ball, R., and K. Chernova. 2008. Absolute Income, Relative Income, and Happiness. *Social Indicators Research* 88: 497–529.

Berg, M., and R. Veenhoven. 2010. Income Inequality and Happiness in 119 Nations. In Search for an Optimum that Does Not Appear to Exist. Ch. 11. In *Social Policy and Happiness in Europe*, ed. B. Greve, 174–194. Cheltenham: Edward Elgar.

Bjørnskov, C., N. Datta Gupta, and P.J. Pedersen. 2008. What Buys Happiness? Analyzing Trends in Subjective Well-Being in 15 European Countries, 1973-2002. *Journal of Happiness Studies* 9: 317–330.

Bjørnskov, C., A. Dreher, J.A.V. Fischer, J. Schnellenbach, and K. Gehring. 2013. Inequality and Happiness: When Perceived Social Mobility and Economic Reality Do Not Match. *Journal of Economic Behavior & Organization* 91: 75–92.

Blanchflower, D.G. 2021. Is Happiness U-Shaped Everywhere? Age and Subjective Well-Being in 145 Countries. *Journal of Population Economics* 34: 575–624.

Blanchflower, D., and A. Oswald. 2003. *Does Inequality Reduce Happiness? Evidence from the States of the USA from the 1970s to the 1990s.* mimeo: Warwick University.

Blanchflower, D.G., and A.J. Oswald. 2004. Well-Being Over Time in Britain and the USA. *Journal of Public Economics* 88: 1359–1386.

Caporale, G.M., Y. Georgellis, N. Tsitsianis, and Y.P. Yin. 2009. Income and Happiness Across Europe: Do Reference Values Matter? *Journal of Economic Psychology* 30 (1): 42–51.

Clark, A.E. 2018. Four Decades of the Economics of Happiness: Where Next? *Review of Income and Wealth* Series 64 (2): 245–269.

Clark, A.E., and C. D'Ambrosia. 2015. Attitudes to Income Inequality: Experimental and Survey Evidence. Ch. 13. In *Handbook of Income Distribution*, ed. A.B. Atkinson and F. Bourguignon, vol. 2, 1147–1208. Amsterdam, New York: North Holland.

Clark, A.E., P. Frijters, and M.A. Shields. 2008. Relative Income, Happiness, and Utility: An Explanation of the Easterlin Paradox and Other Puzzles. *Journal of Economic Literature* XLVI (1): 95–144.

Clark, A.E., S. Flèche, and C. Senik-Leygonie. 2014. The Great Happiness Moderation. In *Happiness and Economic Growth: Lessons from Developing Countries*, ed. A.E. Clark and C. Senik. Oxford: Oxford University Press.

Di Tella, R., and R. Macculloch. 2010. Happiness Adaptation to Income Beyond "Basic Needs". Ch. 8. In *International Differences in Well-Being*, ed. E. Diener, D. Kahneman, and J. Helliwell. Oxford: Oxford University Press.

Dominko, M., and M. Verbic. 2020. The Effect of Income and Wealth on Subjective Well-Being in the Context of Different Welfare State Regimes. *Journal of Happiness Studies*. https://doi.org/10.1007/s10902-020-00225-9.

Easterlin, R.A. 1974. Does Economic Growth Improve the Human Lot? In *Nations and Households in Economic Growth: Essays in Honour of Moses Abramowitz*, ed. P.A. David and M.W. Reder. New York: Academic.

———. 1995. Will Raising the Incomes of All Increase the Happiness of All? *Journal of Economic Behavior and Organisation* 27 (1): 35–47.

Eurofound. 2013. *Third European Quality of Life Survey – Quality of Life in Europe: Subjective Well-Being*. Luxembourg: Publication Office of the European Union.

Eurofound & Bertelsmann Stiftung. 2014. *Social Cohesion and Well-Being in the EU*. Dublin/Gütersloh: Eurofound & Bertelsmann Stiftung.

Ferrer-i-Carbonell, A. 2005. Income and Well-Being: An Empirical Analysis of the Comparison Income Effect. *Journal of Public Economics* 89 (5–6): 997–1019.

Frey, B.S., and A. Stutzer. 2002. What Can Economists Learn from Happiness Research? *Journal of Economic Literature* 40 (2): 402–435.

Frijters, P., J.P. Haisken-De-New, and M.A. Shields. 2004. Money does Matter! Evidence from Increasing Real Income and Life Satisfaction in East Germany Following Reunification. *American Economic Review* 94 (3): 730–740.

Frijters, P., A.E. Clark, C. Krekel, and R. Layard. 2020. A Happy Choice: Wellbeing as the Goal of Government. *Behavioural Public Policy* 4 (2): 126–165.

Graham, C., and A. Felton. 2006. Inequality and Happiness: Insights from Latin America. *Journal of Economic Inequality* 4: 107–122.

Headey, B. 2006. *Happiness: Revising Set Point Theory and Dynamic Equilibrium Theory to Account for Long Term Change.* DIW DP 607. Berlin.

Headey, B., R. Muffels, and M. Wooden. 2008. Money Does Not Buy Happiness: Or Does It? A Reassessment Based on the Combined Effects of Wealth, Income and Consumption. *Social Indicators Research* 87 (1): 65–82.

Jensen, S., and P.J. Pedersen. 2020. *Satisfaction with Life, Happiness, and Inequality – A Pseudo-Panel Study.* IZA Discussion Paper No. 12972.

Nikolova, M., and C. Graham. 2020. The Economics of Happiness. Forthcoming chapter. In *Handbook of Labor, Human Resources and Population Economics,* ed. K. Zimmermann. Cham: Springer.

OECD. 2013. *How's Life? 2013. Measuring Well-Being.* Paris: OECD.

———. 2020. *How's Life? 2020. Measuring Well-Being.* Paris: OECD.

Oishi, S., S. Kesebir, and E. Diener. 2011. Income Inequality and Happiness. *Psychological Science* 22 (9): 1095–1100.

Pedersen, P.J., and T.D. Schmidt. 2011. Happiness in Europe. Cross-country differences in the determinants of satisfaction with main activity. *The Journal of Socio-Economics* 40: 480–489.

Powdthavee, N. 2009. How Much Does Money Really Matter? Estimating the Causal Effects of Income on Happiness. *Empirical Economics* 39 (1): 77–92.

Rözer, J., and G. Kraaykamp. 2013. Income Inequality and Subjective Well-Being: A Cross-National Study on Conditional Effects of Individual and National Characteristics. *Social Indicators Research* 113: 1009–1023.

Schneider, S.M. 2012. Income Inequality and Its Consequences for Life Satisfaction: What Role do Social Cognitions Play? *Social Indicators Research* 106: 419–438.

Scoppa, V., and M. Ponzo. 2008. An Empirical Study of Happiness in Italy. *The B.E. Journal of Economic Analysis & Policy* 8 (1): 1–23.

Stevenson, B., and J. Wolfers. 2008a. Economic Growth and Subjective well-Being: Reasssessing the Easterlin Paradox. *Brookings Papers on Economic Activity* (1): 1–102.

———. 2008b. Happiness Inequality in the United States. *The Journal of Legal Studies* 37 (June): 533–579.

———. 2009. The Paradox of Declining Female Happiness. *American Economic Journal: Economic Policy* 1 (2): 190–225.

———. 2013. Subjective Well-Being and Income: Is There Any Evidence of Satiation? *American Economic Review* 103 (3): 598–604.

Verme, P. 2011. Life Satisfaction and Income Inequality. *Review of Income and Wealth* 57 (1): 111–127.

Weiss, A.S., J.E. King, M. Inoue-Murayama, T. Matsuzawa, and A.J. Oswald. 2012. Evidence for a Midlife Crisis in Great Apes Consistent with the U-Shape in Human Well-Being. *Proceedings of the National Academy of Science.* www.pnas.org/cgi/doi/10.1073/pnas. 1212592109.

Wilkinson, R., and K. Pickett. 2010. *The Spirit Level. Why Equality is Better for Everyone.* London: Penguin Books.

Peder J. Pedersen 1941–2022, professor in economics at Aarhus Business School 1983–1991, since 1991 professor at University of Aarhus mainly working with labor market economics. Chairmanship at the Danish Board of Economic Advisors 1985–1991 and many other commissions and boards. Has the last years published in economics of happiness. Peder J.Pedersen passed away July 2022 after this book was finished.

Chapter 6
Economics, Religion, and Ethics: Economics of Good and Evil

Tomas Sedlacek

Abstract This chapter is an attempt to think about the relationship between economics, ethics, and religion. It tries to approach it from various sides. Both the influence that religion had on economics and the influence that economics had on religion (be it negative or positive). The possible ways to depict the nature of the spirit of economics are debated. Then we turned to analyze the potential good fruits of the spirit of capitalism and the potential evil ones. We compared the fruit of economic ethics compared with Christian ethics in order to encourage a new debate over the spirit (meaning, purpose) of capitalism.

Keywords Spirit of economics · Christianity · Capitalism · Money · Ethics

6.1 Introduction

Economics is presented as a value-free endeavor, but in fact, it is a distinct ethical school and even satisfies many traits of a religious school of thought. Luckman refers to it as "invisible religion" (Luckmann 1967) – well invisible to *us*, since we are so immersed in it. In this regard, one could currently call economic ideology the most ecumenic belief of this planet. It is the most fervent and widespread belief in a non-existent entity (money). This thought appears in academic writing for some time (Benjamin 1921; Wagner 1985; Hörisch 1996; Deutschmann 2001a, b; Nelson 2001; Cox 2002; Paul 2004; Fleischmann 2010); Deutschmann (2012), as well as in popular culture, especially due to the great commitment, sacrifice, and devotion we give to consumerism and in frequent portrayal of supermarkets as temples. One often hears that "consumerism is the new religion."

T. Sedlacek (✉)
Faculty of Social Sciences, Charles University, Praha, Czech Republic

Metropolitan University Prague, Prague, Czech Republic

© The Author(s), under exclusive license to Springer Nature Switzerland AG 2023
N. Kærgård (ed.), *Market, Ethics and Religion*, Ethical Economy 62,
https://doi.org/10.1007/978-3-031-08462-1_6

There are many articles which present the evolution of capitalism as being influenced by Christianity – in particular the protestant movement (Weber 1992; Judaism Sombart 1911; Catholicism Novak 1993), but not so many stressing the differences between the *spirits* of Capitalism to Spirit of Protestantism, Judaism, and Catholicism – of which there are also many. To stress the spiritual aspect of economics (or capitalism), all of the above-mentioned book had a word spirit in their title (additionally see Boltanski, Chiapello 2005, *The new Spirit of Capitalism*). In this chapter, I'd like to elaborate on the distinct spiritual nature of economics and its unique set of economic ethics and offer a comparison with the social ethics of Christianity. This chapter elaborates on the *mutual* influences of Christianity on shaping economics *and vice versa*. The nature of Capitalism in terms of *spirit* and the *fruits of the spirit* will be debated.

6.2 Spirit in Economics

Economics is a partially spiritual discipline, although it doesn't seem like it. But where exactly is this spirituality? To start with, in the frequent usage of the term animal *spirits*. There have been bookshelves written on the topic of animal spirits – and most of them almost exclusively focus on the *animal* part. But animal or not, blue or green, it is *spirits* we are talking about.

Under the term spirit, let us understand as something that moves us, animates us, in perhaps a similar fashion to Hegel's Weltgeist or in a similar way to an even older image of mover: Holy *spirit*.[1] There are – of course – distinct differences between these concepts, but what they share in common is that all of them are *spirits*. They come from the same realm.

It is notoriously hard to describe the spirit. Like a wind, it blows and no-one can see it directly, only by the leaves it affects as it moves (John 3:8[2]). But for purposes here, let's just say that spirit could be the engine of will, the deepest drive, and the core philosophy.

For the purposes here, not just the human person, but also the economy could be somewhat divided into body, soul, and spirit. Body is the physical, material entity (the potato, coal, steal). The soul is the non-tangible structure which organizes us (such as money, law, institutions, democracy, study of economics etc. – the "nervous system," the brain, of the society). And the spirit could be the will, the engine (to power, to profit, to utility, to goodness – the heart, the intent).

---

[1] But the Holy spirit is a personal mover (of whose collective action an individual might not be aware), whereas Zeitgeist is a societal mover (of whom an individual might not be aware). Adam Smith's guidance of the invisible hand seems to be a combination of the two.

[2] "The wind blows wherever it pleases. You hear its sound, but you cannot tell where it comes from or where it is going. So it is with everyone born of the Spirit."

For example, money itself is rather non-material in nature. More precisely, money is the soul of the economy, the nervous system of the body. It is a non-tangible agreement of interpersonal trust, but it organizes us, the whole globe. Prices create an invisible web of contact and information (von Mises 1920) – and exchange. Prices (an aspect of money) can communicate between two parties without them ever meeting or even knowing that they are communicating. "It is no coincidence that in English the root of 'credit' is 'credo,' the Latin for 'I believe'" (Ferguson 2008 p. 30).

6.3 Christianity Based on Economics?

There is a very distinct dialogue going on between Christianity and economics. Of Jesus's thirty parables in the New Testament, nineteen – almost 2/3 – are set in an economic or social context (see Sedlacek (2011, pp. 132–133)). Recall the parable of the lost coin (Luke 15:8–10:); of talents, where Jesus rebukes a servant who did not "put my money on deposit with the bankers" (Matthew 25:27); of the unjust steward (Luke 16:5–12:); of the workers in the vineyard (Matthew 20:8); of the two debtors (Luke 7:41–43); of the rich fool (Luke 12:16–21); Parable of the Hidden Treasure (Matthew 13:44); the Parable of the Pearl (Matthew 13:45), etc.

The second most frequent topics of both the Old and New Testaments are socio economic (after idolatry). As regards the New Testament, economic inquiries are discussed on average every sixteenth verse; in the Gospel of Luke, it is as often as every seventh (see Willis 2006).

In one parable, a man finds out there is a treasure hidden in a field, and he sells everything to buy the land; when a shepherd loses one sheep, he forgets about the remaining 99 and looks for the one, nicely describing the asymmetry of loss and gain; you do not put the light under a bushel, where it would be used inefficiently; when a steward forgives debts of the debtors of his master because it makes sense for him for his own economic benefit (he corruptly seeks personal future favor with the debtors) – the more so your Father in Heaven, etc.

Jesus parables are derived from economic experiences, but building upon it especially using economic terminology and logic to make a point beyond. Jesus takes economics and uses it as clay to build spiritual context. He uses bricks and language of economics to build on and to introduce transcendental logic of his (un) economic salvation.

Example of parable of the workers on the vineyard (Matthew 20:1–16) demonstrates this well: the late coming workers *are* paid unjustly, but they are paid unjustly *much*. They receive *more* than they would fairly deserve as a due fraction of the work-day wage. They are paid unjustly, but *positively unjustly*. Some of them get paid *more*, but none of them less than they signed-up for. It is those who get paid justly (one dinar a day) that complain of the injustice. Jesus is taking an economic principle (the more you work, the more you should be paid) and builds on it the idea of *positive* injustice and in this way *unfair* grace. The economics of Christianity is that one gets more than one deserves. God is unjust, positively unjust. So, from a play on an economic principle, Jesus builds to the core of the key message of the New Testament: salvation by grace (positively unjust justice).

6.3.1 Redemption at a Price

In fact, the whole core engine of Christianity – the very salvation – is portrayed in economic terms. We are redeemed and bought at a price (1 Corinthians 6:20, Revelation 5:9 and many other places). We are ransomed – and not by silver or gold, but something more precious, divine blood (1 Peter 1:18–19). Christ *pays* for our sins, we are *redeemed, bought*. In a similar fashion as the hundreds of over-debted banks were redeemed by the governments in 2008.[3] The whole idea of salvation is depicted in economic terms and portrayed as a divine-earthly trans-action: Christ's blood paid for us, blood being the currency of this divine trans-action, it *ransomed* us from the debt of sin. In fact it's hard to imagine the principle of salvation without these economic terms.

In old times, people could become debt-slaves. Whole families would fall into a debt trap and so lose control over their lives. They could either try to pay the debt back themselves, which was often impossible, wait for the year of jubilee, when debt-slaves were set free, or wait for a redeemer (Lev 25:25). If they were lucky and had relatives with *credit* (in Latin: *belief*), they would pay the debt in their stead, buy them from their previous owners at a price equaling the level of debt, and acquire this slave for himself – and then set them free, letting them go. This is the principle of redemption from debts/sins (opheilo).

In fact, this is exactly this principle which Jesus evokes as He enters public life. He announces and introduces himself publicly so (Luke 4:18–19):

The Spirit of the Lord is on Me,
because He has anointed Me
to preach good news to the poor [...]
to proclaim the year of the Lord's favor [the Year of Jubilee]
[...]
Today this Scripture has been fulfilled in your hearing

He thus combines his role as a redeemer with the Year of Jubilee. During the Year of Jubilee (which occurs once in 49 years), debt-slaves were to be set free, debts forgiven, and fields returned to their original owners. He personalizes the Year of Jubilee and makes this economic principle come alive through him as a person. He personally *becomes* the Year of Jubilee (Bruno 2010), the year of forgiveness of debts, and the year of rest for the fields, which need produce no yield (Leviticus 25).

---

[3] Bailed out banks, CNN money, https://money.cnn.com/news/specials/storysupplement/bankbailout/

6.3.2 Debita Nostra - Our Sins

The economic-Christian parallel continues in the connection between debt and sin. The New Testament Greek used for sin/quilt also means the "debt" (Anderson 2009; Eubank 2013).[4] Instead of "forgive us our sins" Lord's prayer could more literally be translated as "forgive us our debts as we forgive those who are indebted to us" (Luke 11:4). Here is the Latin (Septuaginta) version still understandable to a modern English reader:

et dimítte nobis débita nostra,
sicut et nos dimíttimus debitóribus nostris;

In a parable of an unforgiving servant brings the economic point further: an unjust man was forgiven an enormous debt by the King, but then was unwilling to forgive a small debt to his debtor. The debt-sin (economic-spiritual) parallel is clear.

6.3.3 Old Testament and Judaism

There are many more parallels between economics and religion. The most foundational Old Testament stories can be told in an economic reading, and they have a significant economic side to them.

Take the story of Adam and Eve – the original sin can be read as a sin of (over) consumption, they *ate, consumed* the fruit. To somewhat bring the point home, the word consume appears over a dozen times in the span of this two-pager of Eden story. It was not a sin out of necessity or out of hunger, but it was a sin of overconsumption: they didn't *need* to consume the fruit. They *wanted* to.

This gives us a glimpse into the paradise economy: People here were not happy even in a most ideal context: spiritual, social, *and* economic. They wanted more in all of these areas. Adam and Eve wanted more spiritually (your eyes will be opened to spiritual knowledge, you will be like gods), socially Adam felt alone ("It is not good for man to be alone"), and materially economically: they took something that was not theirs. They ate the fruit, even though there was enough to eat.

Speaking of economics, the curse that followed was also of economic nature. It was the curse of Supply and Demand. Adam was cursed with the curse of supply (you will work in the sweat of your brow, but even with technology of twenty-first century, your labour will not be enough) and Eve got the curse of demand (you will desire, but your desires will not be with you, they will be disjointed and since what

---

[4] In the Greek original the word "opheile͞mata" is used, which means a debt, "opheilo." All English translations of the Bible (save for two) translate it as such. This prayer is also recorded in Luke 11:2–4. Here the Greek "amartias" is used, which at the same time means sin, from the early root "hamart," but it means "to miss the mark, do wrong, sin." These two words are frequently synonyms. (Amartias appears in the New Testament 181 times, hamarant 36 times, opheilo 36 times.) See Sedlacek 2011, p. 134.

you had in the Garden was not enough, nothing never will be enough, nothing will satisfy your demand). (Genesis 2:4–3:24).

Also this story nicely demonstrates the nature of ownership and the nature of the very economy in its most fundamental (spiritual?) level: The first external ownership that Adam and Eve had was something to cover them. Again, they did not dress for biotic reasons, they were not cold, the reason of ownership is here purely psychological in nature: they dressed, they owned, they possessed, because they *felt shame*. Their own skin, which was truly *theirs* to possess, was no longer enough, they needed to own *something else* than themselves to feel/be themselves. They did not "feel in their skin" in their own skin. They no longer felt natural in their natural state. A leaf or goatskin, they needed something *other*, something *not-them* on them, alas around them, to feel more natural, to feel more themselves, not ashamed as when their nature was showing. A human becomes more human when it possesses[5] things that are not naturally theirs. Dressed in clothes and dressed with an (external) stone in hand we rise above the animal kingdom. We have become naturally unnatural. We started possessing things. Economy was born.

6.3.4 Creation Economy

The whole process of creation is in a stark contrast to other beliefs of the day – especially around labor and rest. Compared to violent summerian Enuma Elish (and Egyptian or Greek creation myths), in Genesis creation is a highly structured poem. In Enuma Elish gods fight to blood with the elements and themselves, creation is odd, confusing and almost random. In Genesis, God just speaks and it is so. Reality, as if endowed with responsive and productive intelligence, structures itself around God's wish upon His mere verbal command. Creation – the job of God, God's work, the product of God – is no labour. Genesis centers everything around the seventh day, the day of divine rest and human beings are a crown of this creation.

In Enuma Elish, the Babylonian tablets of creation, not much attention is given to human beings, just a brief mention. But at least a clear reason, meaning is given to humans: Human beings are created to *labour* instead of gods. So that gods no longer have to work and can enjoy leisure.

> *Ea created mankind/On whom he imposed the service of the gods, and set the gods free (Enuma Elish, Tablet VI, v33–34)*

Comparatively in Genesis, human beings were created to rest. The seventh day becomes holy and God rests not because He has to recuperate energy for the work that's ahead next week, but because the work was done, finished. (It was us humans who dis-finished, un-finished the creation.) In the older Sumerian religions, the

---

[5] The double meaning of the word *possess* is also important here. The same word means both to possess something and also in terms of being possessed, say, by a spirit – evil of Holy. When a human being possessed a stone, it possessed it in both meanings.

purpose of human life was clear – to work for gods (or their emissaries: The rulers). In the Old Testament, the *reason* for creating human beings is actually never clearly spelled out.

There are many other examples of economics mingling with religion, some of them we can only touch upon here briefly. The biblical word *awad* literally means "work, worship, and service" and is used till this very day to mean the same three things at once. Joseph's story in Egypt is a fine example of pre-keynesian thought vis-a-vis handling the business cycle: Make surpluses in good years and use them in bad years.

A deep discourse into the economy of good and evil appears in the Book of Job. Here, a strange wager between the forces of good and evil is struck over Job. "Does Job serve the Lord for nothing?" asks the Devil and points out that Job is not a good man, but merely a rational man and a good businessman. One day he sacrifices a bull, and the next day he receives ten new ones. His goodness worked out for him economically. Now deprived of all utility whatsoever, will Job change his core belief? What is the price of his values?

In fact, some level of economic reading can be red into most of biblical stories, and it is not a place here to list them all. This concludes our brief inquiry where I tried to point out the mutual embeddedness of economics, ethics, and religion. Next, we turn to the spirit of economics.

6.4 Economics of Good and Evil

The economy, just like progress, is Janus-faced. It is up to the personal internal infrastructure of the reader whether they lean to a *belief* that positives of economic progress outweigh the negatives. In order to end sunny-side-up, let's start with the negative, the potentially evil side of economics from a Christian perspective.

Jesus solved one of the great riddles of Hebrew economy of ethics: If economic blessing is a sign of God's favour, why do the righteous suffer and wicked rejoice (an empirical fact, observed by many in the Old Testament)? Christianity solved the problem by sending the economic reward to afterlife. This came at a great price: the real world was sacrificed. Life here, our daily reality, became a mere prequel to the really real, eternal, blissful, or accursed spiritual existence which is to follow. In Platonic words: Our world, this existence, is just a shadowland. The real, colorful, spiritual, multidimensional world of supernatural forces and hidden underlying principles – this we yet cannot see.

6.5 Irrelevant to Evil Economy

Even though Jesus often uses economic language, the relationship of Christianity to economics is in the realm of irrelevant at best to borderline radically negative.

First of all, it is not much of a world to care for anyway. In the Old Testament, the Devil barely even appears, but in the New Testament, Devil is suddenly a key character and portrayed as the ruler of this world. Here comes the radically negative: Jesus speaks of the Devil as "the prince of this world" (John 12:31), deducing from it, that this world, including its business, economy, politics, and the like, is Satan's realm. After all, when Satan tempts Jesus in the desert, he offers the kingdoms and riches of the world to Jesus as if they were his to give. The Devil is even called the god of this world (2 Cor 4:3–4). Jesus refers to Satan as the ruler of this world three times (John 12:31, 14:30 and 16:11). In revelation, the Devil is able to seduce *all* the kingdoms of the world (Rev 12:9). Not one nation of the planet will be able to resist, not one. "The whole world is under the control of the evil one" (1 John 5:19).

For Jesus there are either sons of God *or* sons of evil one (in the parable of weed and tares, Math 13:36). In this radicality, there is nothing in between. In the epistle of James, James writes to Christians "You adulterous people, don't you know that friendship with the world means enmity against God? Therefore, anyone who chooses to be a friend of the world becomes an enemy of God" (James 4:4). Jesus is also radical about "no one can serve two masters. Either you will hate the one and love the other, or you will be devoted to the one and despise the other. You cannot serve both God and money" (Matthew 6:24).

There is no other part of New Testament where Jesus gets so angry and physically violent (he even makes a whip) as with the traders in the courtyard of the temple. Surprisingly, no other mischief (prevalent slavery, violent punishments, mistreatment of women, etc.) during his life made him more angry than this form of trade. On the other hand, one must note that Jesus only whipped the money-changers out of the Temple and did not pursue them any further. So as long as money and trade is kept separated from the temple, all seems to be fine. But the rage – vis-a-vis other things that were wrong with the culture of the day – the rage is still hard to understand.

One can find other radical passages. Love of money, for example, is the root of *all* evil (1 Timothy 6:10). Not pride, not hate, not ignorance, nor vengeance, etc. but the love of money. In the book of Apocalypse, those not marked by the sign of the Beast cannot trade, buy, or sell. The payment systems, the blood of the economy, are portrayed as a key function that "the evil one" will have securely under control.

Most of all, this world with all its systems of finance, law, politics... is not only fallen, but bathing in evil, being satan's domain of darkness and unfair suffering. It is systematically and incurably broken, a world that cannot be mended and must be destroyed in pain and suffering of apocalyptic proportions to give way to a completely fresh new world, the New Jerusalem. This stance is in stark contrast to our general current moral efforts: to mend the world through reforms.

In this sense, Christianity is a more radical social critic than Marx. Christianity considers the whole system of the world incurably evil, while Marx sees this world as curable (not by personal revolution – personal repentance, but by a societal revolution).

One last example. The poor man Lazarus seems to get to heaven *solely* on the basis of his low utility levels here on earth, while the rich man (whose only recorded sin was being rich) ends up in hell. As if the earthly utility and heavenly utility were in direct trade-off relationship: "But Abraham replied, 'Son, remember that in your lifetime you received your good things, while Lazarus received bad things, but now he is comforted here and you are in agony" (Luke 16:25).

This is why one can claim early Christianity being borderline radically negative toward any system of the world with all its economy, utility, financial systems, institutions, and philosophies. The following quote sums up this radicality: "Do not love the world or anything in the world. If anyone loves the world, love for the Father is not in them. For everything in the world—the lust of the flesh, the lust of the eyes, and the pride of life—comes not from the Father but from the world" (1 John 2:15–16). There could not have been a more radical social stance than this one: the whole world is in an antithesis to God.

However, there are some soothing quotes vis-a-vis Jesus' negative stance to the system of the world, its economy, and its riches. Jesus' *give to Caesar what is Caesars' and give God what is God's* prevented Christianity from radicalization into a political or economic reform movement. This sentence demarked *a cuius regio, eius religio* in these matters.

Together with the expectation of a very near second coming of Christ (the New Testament is written in the language of living in the last days) led early Christians to a very detached approach to the world, rendering it irrelevant at best. What is broken will remain broken (Mathew 12:20), there is no point to try to unroot the evil in the world (Parable of the Weeds, Matthew 13:24–30). There is no incentive to fight – or reform – the system of the world through revolutions, institutional changes, etc.

More surprisingly, in one latter Paul writes to treat the rulers of this world with respect:

> *Let everyone be subject to the governing authorities, for there is no authority except that which God has established. The authorities that exist have been established by God. Consequently, whoever rebels against the authority is rebelling against what God has instituted, and those who do so will bring judgment on themselves… For the one in authority is God's servant for your good. But if you do wrong, be afraid, for rulers do not bear the sword for no reason. They are God's servants, agents of wrath to bring punishment on the wrongdoer. Therefore, it is necessary to submit to the authorities (Romans 13: 1–5)*

So this gives a counter-weight to the Devil-being-in-charge-of-this-world stance. If the worldly rulers are at the end of the day servants of God, where is this "dark world" (Ephesians 6:2) "lying in evil" (Galatians 1:4)? The system of the world seems to be mixed.

6.6 Fruit of the Spirit of Economics

How to judge a spirit, whether it is good or bad, is a notoriously complicated thing: Perhaps this is why there is an advice – a rule-of-thumb – how to distinguish the spirits. By its fruit:

No good tree bears bad fruit, nor does a bad tree bear good fruit. Each tree is recognized by its own fruit. People do not pick figs from thornbushes, or grapes from briers. A good man brings good things out of the good stored up in his heart, and an evil man brings evil things out of the evil stored up in his heart. For the mouth speaks what the heart is full of. (Luke 6:43).

Can we also judge the spirit of capitalism by this principle, by its fruit?

Economics of capitalism surely bore – in time – good fruit: Even Marx famously admits that it brought more productivity than any other animal ever mounted by humans. It has brought the world to lowest poverty rates in history. Today more people die of obesity than starvation. The ease of living went significantly up since we mounted the spirit of capitalism. Agriculture, once a dominant part of GDP, is now at a level of few percent of it. One example which flies us back all the way to Babylon: cost of one hour of artificial light:

Today it will have cost you less than half a second of your working time if you are on the average wage: half a second of work for an hour of light. In 1950, with a conventional filament lamp and the then wage, you would have had to work for eight seconds to get the same amount of light. Had you been using a kerosene lamp in the 1880s, you would have had to work for about fifteen minutes to get the same amount of light. A tallow candle in the 1800s: over six hours' work. And to get that much light from a sesame-oil lamp in Babylon in 1750 BC would have cost you more than fifty hours' of work. From six hours to half a second – a 43,200-fold improvement – for an hour of lighting: that is how much better off you are than your ancestor was in 1800, using the currency that counts, your time. (Ridley 2011, p. 19)

6.6.1 Kopernikan turn

This amazing process even led Keynes to prophecy that advances in economics will bring about advances in morality (rich people don't have to kill for food, ethics becomes cheap, and vice becomes expensive and unnecessary). In fact, Keynes was so impressed even by the advances of the inter-war economy, and he started talking in religious language about the Old Adam in us and prophecy about "great change in the code of morals" and new mankind, new social order.

When the accumulation of wealth is no longer of high social importance, there will be great changes in the code of morals… I look forward, therefore, in days not so very remote, to the greatest change which has ever occurred in the material environment of life for human beings in the aggregate. (Keynes 1930)

It is not that morality will bring us prosperity (the Hebrew explanation of the morality-related explanation of business cycle), but that prosperity will bring us morality! For Keynes, we will be moral because of affluence (not affluent because being moral). This is a completely original reversal of our traditional fundamental believes about the relationship of morality to economics.

For example, during the Old Testament times, economic and political developments were largely considered as a function of ethics. If a nation behaved well, kept the statues, kept the Sabbaths, did not oppress the widow, orphan, and stranger, it was blessed economically and the land prospered. On the contrary, when these statues were broken, Israel was up for war debacles, slavery, and poverty. Ethics was viewed as a precursor, determinant of history. Economic cycle was a time lagged function of the ethics of the nation and individuals.[6] But now this principle gets reversed in the hands of economists.

I believe that Adam Smith's motive behind the Wealth of Nations was to improve the morality of mankind. That he believed that mankind would become better, less evil, arrogant, selfish, violent if they didn't have to fight and worry for food and shelter on a daily basis. That he believed that economic progress leads to morally improving mankind.

That would definitely mean good fruit, if affluence and trade could truly bring about improvements in morality, in being more human: Keynes writes enthusiastically about this great economy-led moral transformation of mankind:

> *Thus for the first time since his creation man will be faced with his real, his permanent problem – how to use his freedom from pressing economic cares, how to occupy the leisure, which science and compound interest will have won for him, to live wisely and agreeably and well.* (Keynes 1930)

In "hundred years or so" (we should hurry up, in 2030), Keynes predicts the economic problem may be finally solved:

> *Thus we have been expressly evolved by nature – with all our impulses and deepest instincts – for the purpose of solving the economic problem. If the economic problem is solved, mankind will be deprived of its traditional purpose.* (Keynes 1930)

One could argue that Western societies as a whole are collectively much more ethical and caring than even the original church imagined possible (nowhere in the Bible is solidarity through taxes even suggested), see also Rifkin (2010). Today our moral exoskeleton (morality has moved from within our heart to outside, shared, societal institutions) is much more socially ethical than ever in the past. Modern European poor, the widows, the sick, and the elderly are institutionally taken care for much better than at any time in history: Through taxes, insurance, pensions schemes, and extreme rise in welfare, the poor are given a much easier life from a welfare point of view.

---

[6] See for example: "In the twenty-third year of Joash son of Ahaziah king of Judah, Jehoahaz son of Jehu became king of Israel in Samaria, and he reigned seventeen years. He did evil in the eyes of the Lord by following the sins of Jeroboam son of Nebat, which he had caused Israel to commit, and he did not turn away from them. So the Lord's anger burned against Israel, and for a long time he kept them under the power of Hazael king of Aram" (2 Kings 13:1–3).

6.7 Negative Fruit

On the other hand, there are negative fruits as well. Capitalism creates inequalities, it alienates, creating impersonal contact, system of manipulating power, it caters to all our wants, capital gravitates to capital, the rich get richer, but at least the poor are slowly getting richer as well. It maximizes personal utility and legitimizes egoistic stance in life. It makes (over) consumption the center of societal movement.

In economic ideology, through the invisible hand, care for your own utility is the biggest contributor to common good. This is the famous example that Smith gives about the motives of the butcher (Smith 1776), more recently summarized by a famous statement of Milton Friedman "the business of business is business" (Friedman 1970). Capitalism does not lead the obese part of the world to feed the starving poor or to care for them in any way (nor does it prevent it either). Capitalism is often blamed for the ecological disaster.

But one must bear in mind that we should be testing capitalism not against an absolute ideal, but against a different system. The example of ecology could serve us well here. Paradoxically, it was the communist regimes which did far worse when it came to ecological devastation of their own (commonly shared) land. Communist Czechoslovaka ecologically damaged its commonly owned land and air much more than the capitalist, profit-only seeking, uncoordinated egoism of capitalist countries like, for example, the neighboring and culturally close Austria, let alone Finland.

6.7.1 Demonic Capitalism

Even if the majority of the fruits of spirit of capitalism fruits are good, could it still be that we are plowing with the devil (Sedlacek 2011)? The fact that the spirit of Capitalism may run on greed (and hedonistic over-consumption, competition, its models may be based on mathematized ideology of self-interest, which is at the same time the glue and the engine, propeller of economy) seems to hint that way. From this point, the spirit of economics is far from the spirit of Christianity. It goes directly against Kant's moral imperative: It uses other people as means to satisfying one's desires, rather than as goals.

The theologian Paul Tillich went as far as to talk about Demonic capitalism. "The technique of capitalism cannot be isolated from the demonic" (Tillich 1989).

> As Tillich points out, the demonic should not be equated with the satanic, since the demonic – in contrast to the purely negative satanic – combines positive and negative, creative and destructive forces. (Deutschmann 2012)

For example, the amazing creative force, which is commonly summarized by Schumpeter's term *creative destruction*, can also be read as a form of urosborian self-mutilation of the system.

In this respect, some economists seem to agree. Skidelsky writes: "in the language of myth, Western civilization has made its peace with the Devil, in return for which it has been granted hitherto unimaginable resources of knowledge, power and pleasure" (Skidelski and Skidelski 2012 p. 129), and he continues:

> *This is, of course, the grand theme of the Faust legend, immortalized by Goethe. The irony is, however, that now that we have at last achieved abundance, the habits bred into us by capitalism have left us incapable of enjoying it properly. Devil, it seems, has claimed his reward.* (Skidelski and Skidelski 2012)

In fact few a economists would call our economic system – or its spirit – perfect, let alone holy or divine. Michael Novak writes that "Democratic capitalism is by no means the Kingdom of Heaven. It remains in partial bondage to the world, the flesh, the devil" (Novak 1993 p. 338). Keynes complains of our current system of capitalism that "we must still pretend that faul is right and right is faul." Even though Keynes believed that this economic ethics will soon pass away, "avarice and usury and preoccupation must be our gods for little longer still" (Keynes 1930). So, we must still ride these gods, these spirits, plow with them for little longer and then, when the economic problem is solved, the spirit, which will drive us further, will change.

6.7.2 Moral and Moralizing Capitalism

But perhaps it is not so terrible with the spirit of economics after all. The spirit of capitalism has positive values embedded in it as well: It values highly individual freedom and shuns centralized control, let alone force, it exalts the virtue of prudence (see McCloskey 2007), hard work, and not relying on others (government's) help. It thrives much better in peace, when there is law and order, when the community is ethical, caring, and in rich culture and in rich exchange. If the hope of Smith and Keynes is right, economic wealth moralizes the society and makes it more caring (ethics becoming cheap in affluent societies). Of all ideologies, it promotes exchange and peaceful (economic) solutions to things.

6.8 Fruit of the Spirit of Trade: Peace

There is one more very positive fruit of the spirit of economics. Despite the competitive, egoistic and dog-eat-dog nature of current economic ideology, it seems to be the most unifying peaceful ideology of this scope ever to exist on this planet. The previously unexpected side-effect of trade seems to be peace.

This is the very engine that was employed to end a history of violence of war-torn Europe: Economic Integration. An idealistic ("hippie" and perhaps even

Christian) maxim of "make love, not war"[7] was replaced by a more technical (and perhaps cynical) but more realistic and viable version "make trade, not war." It worked. This economic gospel secured more decades of peace than any religious attempt for unity. This is a paradox: Even though Christian religion has the spirit of peace (and love) as one of its core objectives and values, religious piety has never secured such a long lasting lack of hate and violence in European historically Christian nations.

It could also be argued that some Christian social values (care for elderly, widows, poor, orphans, sick) flourished much more once Europe ceased to be Christian and secularized its politics and focused its attention on the economy and growth of prosperity in peaceful times. Instead of religious and political disputes, major European countries started trading steal and coal. Think about it, previous enemies, who blood-bathed each other and wished each other death and destruction mere few years ago, now started trading, thus respecting each other and even helping the defeated initiators of this despicable, cruel war. The enemy, who slapped free countries with a war, got helped by them, after he was defeated (Marshall plan). This is not the exact embodiment of the absolute Christian ethical maxim "show the other cheek," but it is pretty close. It is impressively close. And the logic that led us to enact Marshall plan was primarily and chiefly economic.

And here is another close approach to a Christian maxim: After the war, our enemies were not necessarily treated with love ("Love your enemies"), but they were certainly treated with trade. Trade, which seems to be a better glue of nations than the shared religion once was.

On both these above-mentioned occasions we behaved, and alas: Collectively, in very close reach of the most difficult maxims in Christianity. And in both of these cases, it had a very positive and long-lasting effect on European prosperity and in both cases the key logic (behind the morality of the deed) was economic. That is to say, morality was not the main argument for these unprecedented, highly moral deeds: The economy was.

In short, economic ideology seems to have replaced not just the providence part of theological hope, but also hopes for peaceful co-living of nations. In order to secure peace between nations, nations do not need to *love* each other, but alas: It is enough if they *trade* with each other. Shared Christian faith among European nations was not able to create as peaceful an atmosphere as trade, which started with mere coal and steel.

---

[7] 2 Corinthians 13:11: "Finally, brethren, farewell. Be perfect, be of good comfort, be of one mind, live in peace; and the God of love and peace shall be with you." (KJ21) Psalm 188:1 "How good and pleasant it is when God's people live together in unity!" 1 John 4:20 "Whoever claims to love God yet hates a brother or sister is a liar. For whoever does not love their brother and sister, whom they have seen, cannot love God, whom they have not seen. 21 And he has given us this command: Anyone who loves God must also love their brother and sister." 1 John 2:9–11 "Anyone who claims to be in the light but hates a brother or sister is still in the darkness. Anyone who loves their brother and sister lives in the light, and there is nothing in them to make them stumble. But anyone who hates a brother or sister is in the darkness and walks around in the darkness. They do not know where they are going, because the darkness has blinded them." etc.

6.9 Conclusion

The connection between economics, ethics, and religion is vast and extremely interwoven. This chapter was an attempt to think about the relationship between the spirit of economics, ethics, and religion. It approached the topic from various sides: Both the influence that economics had on religion (be it negative or positive) and vice versa the influence of religion on economics. The possible ways to depict the nature of the spirit of economics were debated. Then we turned to analyze the fruits of the spirit of capitalism with mixed results. We then focused on the effects that trade and welfare have on evolution of morality and on peace. We compared the fruit of economic ethics compared with Christian ethics in order to encourage a new angle to the debate over the spirit of capitalism.

References

Anderson, G.A. 2009. *Sin: A history*. New Haven: Yale University Press.
Benjamin, W. 1921. Capitalism as religion. In *Walter Benjamin: Selected writings 1913–1926*, ed. M. Bullock and M.W. Jennings, vol. 1, 288–289. Cambridge, MA: Harvard University Press. 1996 (German version 1985).
Boltanski, L., and E. Chiapello. 2005. *The new Spirit of capitalism*. New York/London: Verso.
Bruno, C.R. 2010. Jesus is our Jubilee ... but how? The OT background and Lukan fulfillment of the ethics of Jubilee. *Journal of the Evangelical Theological Society* 53 (1): 81–101.
Cox, H. 2002. Mammon and the culture of the market: A socio-theological critique. In *Meaning and modernity: Religion, polity and self*, ed. R. Madsen, W. Sullivan, A. Swidler, and S.M. Tiplan. Berkeley: University of California Press.
Deutschmann, C. 2001a. *Die Verheißung des absoluten Reichtums: Zur religiösen Natur des Kapitalismus*. Frankfurt a.M: Campus.
———. 2001b. The promise of absolute wealth: Capitalism as a religion? *Thesis Eleven* 66 (1): 32–56.
———. 2012. *Capitalism, religion, and the idea of the demonic*, MPIfG Discussion Paper, No. 12/2. Cologne: Max Planck Institute for the Study of Societies.
Eubank, N. 2013. *Wages of cross-bearing and debt of sin: The economy of heaven in Matthew's gospel*. Berlin: De Gruyter.
Ferguson, N. 2008. *The ascent of money: A financial history of the world*. New York: Penguin Press.
Fleischmann, C. 2010. *Gewinn in alle Ewigkeit: Kapitalismus als Religion*. Zürich: Rotpunktverlag.
Friedman, M. 1970. The social responsibility of business is to increase its profits, *New York Times Magasin*, Septermber 13.
Hörisch, J. 1996. *Kopf oder Zahl: Zur Poesie des Geldes*. Frankfurt a.M: Suhrkamp.
Keynes, J.M. 1930. Economic possibilities for our grandchildren. In *Essays in persuasion*, vol. 1963, 358–373. New York: Harcourt Brace.
Luckmann, T. 1967. *The invisible religion: The transformation of symbols in industrial society*. New York: MacMillan. Published in German 1963.
McCloskey, D. 2007. *The bourgeois virtues: Ethics for an age of commerce*. Chicago: University of Chicago Press.
Nelson, R. 2001. *Economics as religion: From Samuelson to Chicago and beyond*. Pennsylvania: Pennsylvania University Press.
Novak, M. 1993. *The Catholic ethic and the Spirit of capitalism*. New York: Free Press.

Paul, A. 2004. *Die Gesellschaft des Geldes: Entwurf einer monetären Theorie der Moderne*. Wiesbaden: VS Verlag.
Ridley, M. 2011. *The rational optimist: How prosperity evolves*. London: Fourth Estate.
Rifkin, J. 2010. *The empathic civilization*. Cambridge: Polity Press.
Sedlacek, T. 2011. *Economics of good and evil: The quest for economic meaning from Gilgamesh to wall street*. Oxford/New York: Oxford University Press.
Skidelski, R., and Edward Skidelski. 2012. *How much is enough? Money and the good life*. New York: Penguin Books.
Smith, A. 1776. *An inquiry into the nature and causes of the wealth of nations*. London: Methuen & co. Several later editions e.g., Penguin, London 1970.
Sombart, W. 1911. Die Juden und das Wirtschaftsleben. New Brunswick, 1997.
Tillich, P. 1989. The demonic: A study in the interpretation of history. In *Paul Tillich on creativity*, ed. J.A.K. Kegley, 63–91. London: University Press of America.
von Mises, L. 1920. *Economic Calculation in the Socialist Commonwealth*. Auburn: Ludwig von Mises Institute 2008, 2012.
Wagner, F. 1985. *Geld oder Gott? Zur Geldbestimmtheit der kulturellen und religiösen Lebenswelt*. Stuttgart: Klett-Cotta.
Weber, Max. 1992. *The Protestant ethic and the Spirit of capitalism*. New York/London: Routledge.
Willis, J. 2006. *God's politics: Why the right gets it wrong and the left doesn't get it*. San Francisco: HarperOne.

Tomas Sedlacek born 1977, Czech economist and university lecturer. Member of the National Economic Council of the Czech Republic and a former advisor for president Vaclav Havel. His book *Economics of Good and Evil: The Quest for Economic Meaning from Gilgamesh to Wall Street* (Oxford University Press, 2011) is an international bestseller.

Part II
Religion and the Market

Chapter 7
Lutheran Social Ethics

Svend Andersen

Abstract What is Lutheran social ethics? In order to answer this question, the chapter takes its point of departure in a classical – or maybe *the* classical – account, namely German theologian Ernst Troeltsch's *Die Soziallehren der christlichen Kirchen und Gruppen* first published in 1912. Troeltsch's perception of the Lutheran social ethics of his time is briefly presented. Next, a picture of Luther's own social and political thinking which differs from Troeltsch's is given, and finally the possibility of formulating a Lutheran social ethics for our time is discussed.

Keyword Lutheran social ethics · Ernst Troeltsch · Luther · Social and political thinking

7.1 Ernst Troeltsch's Perception of Lutheran Social Ethics

In one sense, Troeltsch's book is a history of Christianity, starting with Jesus and ending in the author's own time. But it is also a typology in that Troeltsch, following his friend, sociologist Max Weber, distinguishes between church and sect as two basic social forms of Christianity, adding a third: Mysticism. Troeltsch asks the question: how have the various forms of Christianity through history managed to influence social life? Troeltsch of course asks this question against the background of the social and political reality of his own time. He describes the "social problem of the day" ("[Das] heutige[n] soziale[n] Problem[s]") as follows:

> The problem of the capitalist economic period and the industrial proletariat created by it; and of the growth of militaristic and bureaucratic giant states; of the enormous increase in population which affects colonial and world policy, of the mechanical technique, which produces enormous masses of material and links up and mobilises the whole world for

---

S. Andersen (✉)
School of Culture and Society, Department of Theology, Aarhus University, Aarhus, Denmark
e-mail: teosa@cas.au.dk

© The Author(s), under exclusive license to Springer Nature Switzerland AG 2023
N. Kærgård (ed.), *Market, Ethics and Religion*, Ethical Economy 62,
https://doi.org/10.1007/978-3-031-08462-1_7

*purposes of trade, but which also treats men and labor like machines. (*Troeltsch 1931, p. 1010)[1]

More specifically, Troeltsch asks how Christian religion and its ethics have related to three areas of social life: the family, the state, and economics.

As to his own tradition, Lutheranism, Troeltsch does not express high expectations. In his own time, he regards Lutheranism as a conservative, anti-liberal mode of thought, a patriarchal, agrarian, petty-bourgeois form of ethics communicated by Luther's catechism as "an epitome of the whole of the Lutheran social ethics", and out of touch with modern culture (Troeltsch 1931, p. 543). Lutheran ethics does not possess the force to contribute to the shaping of modern society – its social impact is reduced to the charity of the Inner Mission.

Interestingly, however, Troeltsch sees one exception to the conservative and anti-democratic Lutheran attitude: "In Denmark and Norway a very firmly established peasant democracy is today united most with a sturdy Lutheranism, which is certainly tinged by Pietism". (Troeltsch 1931, p. 574f).[2]

Troeltsch tries to trace the roots of Lutheranism's social impact in the theological and ethical thoughts of Martin Luther himself. His thesis is that Luther does not succeed in really uniting his religious ethics with the reality of social life. Social life is characterised by "law and force, of economic self-interest and of conflict" (Troeltsch 1931, p. 543), which are simply not compatible with the Christian ethics of love. Hence, Luther's social ethics is marked by a dualism:

*On the one hand, it is a pure and radical Christian ethic, a personal ethic which is mainly concerned with the preservation of the Christian spirit and temper; on the other hand, it is "natural" – governed by reason – and therefore only relatively Christian, that is, it is an official morality appointed and permitted by God. (*Troeltsch 1931, p. 499f).[3]

According to Troeltsch, Luther regards Christian faith as an inward feeling or attitude, and accordingly true Christian practice is an expression of faith as brotherly love. As already mentioned, this brotherly love is not compatible with the harsh reality of social and political life. So what is the Christian attitude towards social life? Basically, it involves obedience and passive acceptance of the powers of social life that are essentially foreign to the spirit of Christianity. More precisely, the dualism of social life consists of Christian brotherly love on the one hand, and the ethics of natural law that governs social and political life on the other.

---

[1] As the translation is not quite accurate, I also quote the original:

[D]as Problem der kapitalistischen Wirtschaftsperiode und des von ihm geschaffenen industriellen Proletariats, der militärisch-bureaukratischen Riesenstaaten, der in Welt- und Kolonialpolitik auslaufenden ungeheuren Bevölkerungssteigerung, der unermeßliche Lebensstoffe erzeugenden, im Weltverkehr alles mobilisierenden und verknüpfenden, aber auch Menschen und Arbeit mechanisierenden Technik .. (Troeltsch 1994, p. 983).

[2] "[I]n Dänemark und Norwegen ist eine wurzelfeste bäuerliche Demokratie heute aufs engste mit strammem, allerdings pietistisch gefärbtem Luthertum verbunden"(Troeltsch 1994, p. 602).

[3] eine rein und radikal christliche Ethik der P e r s o n und der Gesinnung einerseits und eine natürlich-vernünftige, nur relativ christliche, d.h. von Gott verordnete und zugelassene Ethik des A m t e s andererseits (Troeltsch 1994, p. 486).

Troeltsch's book is an impressive accomplishment, and I think that he is basically right in his diagnosis of the character of Lutheranism at the beginning of the twentieth century. But, as will become clear, I think he is seriously wrong when it comes to his understanding of Luther's own theological and ethical thinking. Being an ethicist myself, I believe that it is extremely important to keep a clear distinction between on the one hand the facts of real history – including the historical facts constituting the context of Luther's thinking – and on the other hand this thinking itself. In fact, the real development of Lutheranism may rest on a misunderstanding of Luther's own thought. And I think that we – like Troeltsch – should try to interpret Luther's social ethics in such a way that it can be relevant as a foundation for the social thinking and engagement of Lutheran Christians in the world of today – which of course is rather different from the worlds of both Luther and Troeltsch.

7.2 Martin Luther's Social and Political Thinking

Turning now to Luther himself: what characterises the social world in his view?[4] One answer would be to point at his so-called doctrine of the three estates, i.e. the division of social reality into oiconomia, politia and ecclesia, which basically repeats the Aristotelian distinction between household (including the family and private business) and polity, with the addition of the church. However, I can follow Troeltsch when he talks about "the crude Lutheran doctrine of the three classes" (Troeltsch 1931, p. 654) "die grobe lutherische Dreiständelehre" (Troeltsch 1994, p. 731).

Luther's basic premise when talking about social reality is that it is secular in the sense of belonging to the *world*, which is at the same time dominated by sin and evil – as well as being God's good creation. Importantly, the goodness of the world does not reside in individual human beings and their actions, but rather in the offices of society. The structures of society are what have later been called orders of creation, the two basic orders being the above-mentioned oiconomia and politia. What we now call social institutions and social roles respectively are, according to Luther, orders and correlated offices which are constituted not by human activity (such as contract), but rather by divine acts of creation.

In the treatise *Von weltlicher Obrigkeit* (On Secular Authority), Luther gives a more detailed description of social reality:

> To eat and drink and become matrimonial are divine works and decrees. And as they are God's work and creatures, they are good, so good that everybody can use them in a Christian way. - - -
>
> "All God's creatures" not only comprises drinking and eating, clothes and shoes, but also the power of authority and being subject, performing protection and punishment. - - -

---

[4] The following presentation is based on my book Andersen (2010).

> *Therefore you should cherish the sword and official power as highly as matrimony or agriculture or some other handicraft installed by God (WA 11, p. 257).*[5]

What Luther is indicating here is the understanding that social life consists largely of the cultural shaping of basic biological functions (nutrition, sexuality etc.). This cultural shaping takes place in the context of social functions or roles: 'offices'. And according to Luther, these offices are installed by God as part of his creation of human life.

The concept of 'world' and 'worldly' plays a crucial role in Luther's famous doctrine of the Two Kingdoms (Zwei-Reiche-Lehre). I understand the doctrine's distinction between the spiritual and the worldly regiments as being between two divine projects concerning humankind. The spiritual is the project of salvation and of creating faith, and it occurs primarily by way of Gospel proclamation. The spiritual project is power-free, to use Jürgen Habermas' term – remembering that we are talking about human power. In contrast, the worldly is the project of ruling the sinful world by the sword, i.e. by political and legal power. Notice that even if "world" means the domain of sin, the struggle against sin is not the only function of government. Instead, sin must be fought because it is destructive of human life, which is God's creation. In the end, government has a positive, life-supporting aim. Luther makes this point clear in his explanation regarding the first article of the creed in his catechisms: good government is mentioned here as a "corporeal and temporal good" together with "peace and security" (WA 30/I, p.184).

As an order of creation, government or authority has a positive function, and this is true of all the orders that constitute life according to Luther. Hence, in the description of the social orders I quoted above, Luther characterises the function of the orders as follows:

> *As a man in matrimony, in agriculture or handicraft can serve God to the benefit of the other, and as he should so serve, if his neighbour needed it – in the same way [a man] in exercising authorial power can serve God and must serve him therein in so far as the need of his neighbour requires it (WA 11, p. 258).*

In my reading, Luther's idea is that the function of the social orders is to protect and further human life. Actually, at one place Luther summarises this function as keeping the peace. And Christian social ethics basically and essentially involves acting in such a way that one fills the offices or roles in a way that corresponds with the function of the orders, i.e. acting for the benefit of the other. This is what has been named the Lutheran ethics of the calling (Berufsethik). My thesis now is that according to Luther, showing neighbourly love is an adequate way of filling social roles. This means that there is such a thing as social and even political neighbourly love.

The distinction between the two regiments is often presented as a distinction between "religion" and "politics". But this representation is at best a simplification. Luther admittedly seems to support an idea of division when he asks what might happen "if someone would rule the world on the basis of the Gospel" (WA 11,

---

[5] The quotations from Luther are from the Weimar edition of Luther's works: Weimarer Ausgabe (WA). Instead of quoting Luther's Old High German, I give my own translations.

p. 250). But Christianity does not consist only of the Gospel and the faith God creates. Luther's recurring thesis is that the life of a Christian consists of two basic components: faith *and love*. So the question we must ask is: even if the world cannot be ruled by the Gospel, can it be ruled by Christian love?

According to my reading, there is no doubt that Luther's answer to this question is a clear "Yes we can". Whereas the logic of faith cannot be transferred into the world of politics – because it is a logic of powerlessness – the logic of love can. Luther's description of the essential relationship between faith and love goes like this:

> *It is [faith] that performs and drives good works through love. That is to say: He who wants to be a true Christian or to be in the kingdom of Christ must have real faith. He does not truly have faith, however, if love does not follow faith (WA 40/II, p. 37).*

It is clear that love so to speak connects the two distinct regiments, the spiritual and the worldly. To have faith means to belong to the kingdom of Christ, the spiritual regiment. But one cannot have faith without the works of love following from faith. Works of love are also to be performed in the worldly regiment or kingdom. This is one of the distinctive features of a Lutheran understanding of Christianity in contrast to Catholicism: The ideal of Christian life is not to leave the ordinary worldly life – for a monastic life, for example – but to get involved in worldly life, because it is here that one can serve one's neighbour.

How does love follow from faith? Luther answers this question (for instance) in the treatise on the *Freedom of a Christian*: "Therefore, as God has helped us for nothing through Christ, in the same way we should not do otherwise than help our neighbour by our body and its works" (WA 7, p. 36). In Lutheran theology, "God's help for nothing through Christ" is called justification: To have faith means to become just – i.e. to have the right position – before God, which is due to Christ's transferring his justice to the believer.

The faith-love structure is normally called the "happy exchange", but I find it more helpful to name it the "double role exchange". At the moment it is very popular to take the concept of gifts as it is understood in social sciences such as anthropology and use it in theology. Marcel Mauss' *Essay sur le don* is of course a classic in this respect (Mauss 1923–1924). I am not convinced of the fruitfulness of this. Faith not only means receiving the gift that Christ gives, but more specifically letting Christ put himself in your place. In an analogous way, love means putting yourself – out of abundance or plenitude – in the position of the other and doing unto others as you would have them do to you: "[Everybody] should act toward his neighbour with a mind as if the neighbour's weakness, sin and stupidity were his own ..." (*Sermon on Double Justice* WA 2, p. 148f). Following the example of Christ, then, implies putting oneself in the position of the other. Christian neighbourly love is characterised by a *reciprocity of role exchange*.

Does this Christian love have anything to do with politics? Is not Christian love the love Jesus depicts in the Sermon on the Mount, for instance in the recommendation to turn the other cheek and give the other one's cloak? And isn't this practice of love the direct opposite of political action? This is the problem with which Luther opens the argument of *On Secular Authority*.

One important aspect of the solution is to be found in the fact that neighbourly love does not just mean turning the other cheek. In general terms, Christian love is not just one thing, but a complex phenomenon. Basically, the two parts or aspects of neighbourly love are: "love as sacrifice" and "love as beneficence". When Christian neighbourly love is practised in the worldly realm, it takes on the shape of beneficence. Luther makes this clear in *On Secular Authority*:

> But because a true Christian on earth neither lives for nor serves himself but rather his neighbour, therefore he out of the kindness of his spirit does what he does not need, but what is useful and of need for his neighbour. But now the sword is a great necessity for all the world, in that peace is kept, sin punished and evil-doers warded off – therefore [the Christian] most willingly submits to the regiment of the sword, pays tax, honours the authorities, serves, helps and does all he can that furthers power - - - (WA 11, p. 253).

This passage is remarkable because it has the form of a syllogism. I should like to emphasise two arguments that Luther makes: *First*, Christian love has the same aim as the institution of government, namely to meet the needs of people; love as beneficence is (also) political neighbourly love. And *second*, obedience or submission is not an end in itself, but a means of reaching the goal of neighbourly love. It is also important to notice that beneficent neighbourly love is the ethical basis for the politics of Christians, whether they are subjects or rulers.

What has become of the other form of Christian love, the one recommended in Jesus' Sermon on the Mount? Here we need to be aware of another important distinction in the doctrine of the two kingdoms: The distinction between the Christian acting on behalf of the other, and the Christian acting on behalf of him/herself ("für sich selbst"). If a Christian acts on behalf of others, she must show love in the form of beneficence; but if she acts on behalf of herself, she must refrain from claiming her own rights and neighbourly love then resembles self-sacrifice (WA 11, p. 259f.).

According to Luther, a Christian prince is someone who says: "I will not seek my own at the expense of my subjects, but [seek] what is theirs, and in that way I will serve them with my office" (WA 11, p. 273). In short: The Christian ruler is one who – out of neighbourly love as beneficence – uses power for the sake of the citizens. The tyrant, by contrast, uses power for his own interest.

But in Luther's typology of authority there is a third ruler, whom we could call the reasonable and righteous ruler. The normative foundation of this type of rule is given in Luther's theory of natural law, which he introduces in an interesting way in *On Secular Authority*. A Christian ruler must also enforce the law. More precisely, as a judge he must enforce the "Recht der Liebe", the law of love which refrains from punishing evil-doers too rigorously, and which compensates those who have been injured. Not all litigants are willing to accept this kind of adjudication. When confronted with such stubborn parties, the Christian prince-judge should make the following appeal:

> [N]ature teaches as love acts: that I shall do unto others as I want done to me. Therefore I cannot strip somebody in such a way, whatever my right may be, because I myself do not

> *want to be thus stripped; rather, as I want the other to conceal his rights towards me ... likewise I should refrain from my right (WA 11, p. 279).*

The very fact that Luther discusses the case in which some of the parties in a legal quarrel do not accept the law of love is a clear indication that Luther is not advocating a "Christian state". Rather, he presupposes what I call the *split polis*: the world is a place where Christians live together with non-Christians (even though they may be baptised). The normative basis for the possibility of this co-existence is the compatibility between Christian neighbourly love (as beneficence) and action in accordance with the natural law as summarised in the Golden Rule ("Treat others as you would like others to treat yourself"). As is clear from Luther's quotation, the Golden Rule also implies the structure of role exchange. The criterion for the right way of acting towards the other is my own expectation if placed in the situation of the other. Luther emphasises that the law of nature has reason as its source. I therefore characterise the essence of the Golden Rule as rational reciprocity: Reciprocity in the sense of role exchange.

Now one field of social life where governmental power is necessary is economics. I have already mentioned the treatise in which Luther basically deals with two kinds of economic activity, viz. trade and interest charging. Luther's view on economics fits into his overall picture of social life, at least he describes trade in a similar manner as the other social offices:

> *You cannot deny that buying and selling is a necessary thing that you cannot do without and that you can use in a Christian way, particularly in the case of things serving need and honour. In this way the patriarchs have sold and bought cattle, wool, crops, butter, milk and other goods. They are God's gifts that he gives from the earth and distributes among humans (WA 15, pp. 293f).*

But according to Luther, trade is a dangerous thing, almost as dangerous as matrimonial life, which cannot be lived without doing sinful acts. In the case of trade, the danger lies in the temptation to use one's position in a selfish way. As Luther puts it, tradesmen follow the rule: "I will sell my goods as expensively as possible". This does not sound very sinful to us, but for Luther it is the same as taking advantage of the weakness of one's neighbour:

> *It is a rogue and stingy eye that only looks at the need of his neighbour, not to remedy but rather to improve one's own position at his expense, to become rich with the help of one's neighbour's disadvantage. Those are all public thieves, robbers and usurers (WA 15, p. 305).*

According to Luther, there are two positive alternatives to this misuse of the device of trade. One involves being a truly Christian tradesman, i.e. trading in a totally unselfish way, for instance by giving everybody for free what he/she needs. This would be neighbourly love as unselfishness. The other positive alternative involves observing the rule: "I will sell my goods for the price that is right and equitable". This way of acting is in accordance with "Christian love and natural law"; it would be neighbourly love as the kind of beneficence that is compatible with following natural law. And according to Luther, it would be best if the worldly authority instituted this latter form of trade by installing controllers.

Thus, with regard to trade, it is evident that Luther also makes the presupposition that government can exercise its power on the basis of the kind of neighbourly love that corresponds to the Golden Rule. If we now ask whether or not it is possible to formulate a Lutheran ethics of political neighbourly love in our time, it is important to distinguish in Luther between basic theological-ethical thought on the one hand – and time-conditioned beliefs on the other. As to the latter, one important belief of Luther's is that political order necessarily presupposes a clear hierarchical structure of superior and subordinate. Today we know that democracy, and hence equality, actually works. In the field of economics, Luther supposes that if one agent seeks his own advantage, this necessarily means exploitation of the other. Today we know – or at least believe – that if we all act like *homines economici*, each seeking maximum satisfaction, that does not necessarily lead to somebody's ruin.

The basic idea in Luther's social ethics is that political power should be based on Christian neighbourly love in the sense of profane beneficence, so that the political order works to the advantage of all citizens. With regard to economics, Luther's basic idea is that government, on the basis of neighbourly love in the shape of equity, regulates trade and finances in such a way that it does not harm people.[6]

7.3 A Contemporary Lutheran Social Ethics

I now want to conclude with some preliminary remarks about a possible contemporary version of a Lutheran political theology or social ethics. To start this enterprise, we need to reject Troeltsch's picture of a Lutheran ethics, which was influenced by the dominating German Lutheranism of his time, i.e. anti-liberal conservatism. In order to understand the actual ethico-political shape of German Lutheranism, Troeltsch was led, I think, to misrepresent the reformer's conception of the relationship between Christian faith and political action. Presenting an alternative, we naturally have to recognise that we too are to some degree determined by the political and social realities of our time. In short: our effort must be to formulate a Lutheran social ethics on democratic conditions.

As to the basic structure of Luther's own social ethics, I should like to emphasise the following features: *First*, the Two-Kingdoms doctrine means that political action cannot be salvific, and nor can political office be based on the Gospel. *Second*, nevertheless, Christian faith evokes neighbourly action in the political realm. *Third*, this action has the dual character of either unselfishness or beneficence. *Fourth*, under 'pluralistic' conditions, actions of neighbourly love are concordant with observance

---

[6] "Ethics and Economics" (Wirtschaftsethik) is a prominent field of research in Germany, not least within theology, although the same is not true of Denmark. After World War II the German Federal Republic adopted the so-called social market economy (soziale Marktwirtschft), with Christian ideas as an important background. For a recent outline of a Lutheran Wirtschaftsethik", see Koch (2012).

of natural law. And *fifth*, the socio-political order with its offices is created by God with a view to benefiting human beings.

One of the primary tasks involved in reformulating a Lutheran socio-political ethics is to find an appropriate theory about the basic normative structure of society. There is of course more than one possibility, but I would like to defend what I call *Lutheran liberalism*, as I think that the political philosophy of the late American philosopher John Rawls is the best way of reformulating or reconstructing the Lutheran position. According to Rawls, liberalism is defined by a specific conception of political justice which – as is probably well-known – consists of two principles:

1. Each person is to have an equal right to the most extensive basic liberty compatible with a similar liberty for others.
2. Social and economic inequalities are to be arranged so that they are both (a) reasonably expected to be to everyone's advantage [in particular for the worst-off members], and (b) attached to positions and offices open to all.[7]

In my view, these two principles of justice reflect an interpretation of democratic society that is compatible with a Lutheran social ethics. The two principles define, so to speak, the justice counterpart of Christian love, which means, for instance, that neighbours are "translated" into fellow citizens. In order to see this, we need to look at another element in Rawls' theory, viz. his concept of an *overlapping consensus*. This concept can be regarded as Rawls' answer to the question of how there can be consensus and hence stability in a society marked by pluralism in terms of religions and worldviews. Religions are what Rawls calls comprehensive doctrines: They give answers to all basic questions in human life. By comparison, political reality only concerns a limited area of human life, and in order to enter into political consensus adherents of religions or worldviews need to be able to make a distinction between their beliefs as a whole and their participation in political life. And actually, according to Rawls, it is possible to derive the two principles of justice from within a given religion.

The distinction between comprehensive doctrine and the political domain corresponds to Luther's distinction between spiritual and secular. Rawls' distinction constitutes a limitation or relativisation of the political (worldly) that is also crucial to Lutheran Christianity. And from a Lutheran point of view, the possibility that Christians might join a consensus about the basic principles of justice is quite understandable in light of the concept of natural law. According to the Lutheran tradition, Christians expect all citizens – believers or not – to be acquainted with natural law. Naturally, the way in which natural law can substantiate Rawlsian principles of justice is a matter that needs further elaboration.

In closing, I just want to mention two elements in Luther's ethics that need further reflection. First, his idea of offices and roles as "creation ordinances" – i.e. more or less fixed structures – is not tenable in societies in which adaptability seems to have become an inevitable requirement. But in fluctuating conditions, a Lutheran

---

[7] See for instance Rawls (1993, p. 5f).

Christian would also regard it as a fundamental demand to carry out his or her work for the benefit of others. Second, the 'sacrifice' aspect of neighbourly love could have a contemporary meaning in that a Christian in his or her personal life could adhere to a stricter morality than the one permitted by public law.

7.4 Concluding Remarks

What, then, could Lutheran social or political neighbourly love be today? I guess something like this: To be a justified sinner means being able to pay attention to the situation of other people, including their needs – and being prepared or motivated to do what is in one's power to alleviate their hardship. Christian ethics in a Lutheran sense involves to be set free and enabled to showing this fundamental attitude of benevolence. When this attitude is translated into concrete action in the social and political domain, one important intermediate normative idea is a conception of justice. Without going into detail, and as mentioned above, I claim that a convincing conception of justice has been developed by John Rawls under the heading "justice as fairness".

Luther himself does not seem to realise that economic capacity, money, constitutes a kind of power of its own. At one point however, when he criticises the selfish rule of tradesmen, he says: "Selling should not be a work that is free of your power and caprice" (WA 15, p. 295). In our day we have become more conscious about the relationship between economics and power. On this point, the Danish ethicist K.E. Løgstrup makes the following remark:

> It is not acceptable that private persons, thanks to the economic resources and concentrations they have at their disposal, acquire a power over other humans that otherwise only authorities possess, but for which the economic bigwigs – unlike the authorities – are not publicly accountable. (Løgstrup 1972, p. 166).

In a society like Denmark's, the harm caused by capitalism does not really consist in poverty, but rather – to mention one example – in inequality. This raises the question about how to implement the difference principle, Rawls' second principle of justice. But this question leads us away from ethical theory and towards practical politics, which is a different story.

References

Andersen, S. 2010. *Macht aus Liebe. Zur Rekonstruktion einer lutherischen politischen Ethik.* Berlin/New York: De Gruyter.
Koch, Ph. 2012. *Gerechtes Wirtschaften. Das problem der Gerechtigkeit in der Wirtschaft im Lichte lutherischer Ethik.* Göttingen: V & R unipress.
Løgstrup, K.E. 1972. *Norm og spontaneitet. Etik og politik mellem teknokrati og dilettantokrati.* Copenhagen: Gyldendal.

Luther, M. 1883–2009. *D. Martin Luthers Werke. Kritische Gesamtausgabe*. Hermann Böhlau. Weimar.
———. *Von weltlicher Obrigkeit, wie weit man ihr Gehorsam schuldig sei* [WA 11].
———. *Der grosse Katechismus* [WA 30/I].
———. *In epistolum S. Pauli ad Galatas Commentarius* [WA 40/II].
———. *Von der Freiheit eines Christenmenschen* [WA 7].
———. *Sermo de duplici iustitia* [WA 2].
———. *Von Kaufshandlung und Wucher* [WA 15].
Mauss, M. 1923–1924. *Essai sur le don Forme et raison de l'échange dans les sociétés archaïques*, L'Année sociologique, Nouvelle série, 1ère Année (1923-1924), pp. 30–186, Presses Universitaires de France (several translations and reprints).
Rawls, J. 1993. *Political liberalism*. New York: Columbia University Press.
Troeltsch, E. 1931. *The social teaching of the Christian churches*. Vol. II. London/New York: Allen & Unwen, MacMillan.
———. 1994. *Die Soziallehren der christlichen Kirchen und Gruppen*. Neudruck der Ausgabe Tübingen 1912, JC.B. Mohr, Tübingen.

Svend Andersen born 1948, 1989–2019 professor of ethics and religion at University of Aarhus. Member of the Danish Ethical Council 1988–1993. Chairman for the Danish Association of Eccleciastical Law 2014–2020. Has published both in international journals and in Danish newspapers.

Chapter 8
Theology of Money: Rationalisation and Spiritual Goods

Philip Goodchild

Abstract With modern rationalisation we subject life to quantification, generating evidence and models, and the more we subject life to codification, generating systems, regulations and procedures, the less we understand who we are and what we do. We plunge headlong into illusion, blinded by the clarity of our own newly-found rationality and the solidity of the evidence. We experience an eclipse of reason, no longer understanding what it is to formulate concepts and ideals, nor understanding what it is to offer our lives, time and attention in an appropriate ratio or distribution.

Keywords Modern irrationality · Money · Market society · Theology of money · Adam Smith · Søren Kierkegaard

8.1 Introduction

Modernisation involves a process of *rationalisation*: the natural world, social institutions, and individual behaviour are re-ordered to be as efficient and effective as possible. This process is essentially economic: Productive potential is accumulated when wastage is minimised, and economic rationality, which seeks the most efficient use of scarce resources, consists in measuring, calculating and planning their deployment. Progress, then, consists in accumulation, whether of resources, productive capacity, knowledge, skills, systems and procedures, and, from this perspective, whatever has held back progress may be attributable to wastage, idleness, custom, privilege, patronage, ignorance or superstition – in brief, it is irrational. Modern progress may therefore be seen as the advance of economic rationality

---

P. Goodchild (✉)
Department of Philosophy, School of Humanities, University of Nottingham, Nottingham, UK
e-mail: philip.goodchild@nottingham.ac.uk

across culturally differentiated spheres of life: More and more of life is rendered measurable and calculable.

Under such circumstances, a central problem of modern society and a focal issue in its political conflicts has been that of the limits inside which economic rationality is to operate (Gorz 1989 p. 127). For example, which portions of society can be regulated by market mechanisms, and which may more appropriately be left to ethics, politics, and perhaps even religion? Are there goods which money cannot buy (Sandel 2012)? Alongside this, we may ask how economic rationality differs from ethico-political rationality, and question whether there is indeed such a thing as religious rationality.

8.2 Adam Smith and Søren Kierkegaard

One of the principal issues over which this conflict has been staged is over the reasonableness of enlightened self-interest. Adam Smith's famous account of the butcher, brewer and baker is illustrative here of the rationale invoked in favour of extending economic rationality:

> *But man has almost constant occasion for the help of his brethren, and it is in vain for him to expect it from their benevolence only. He will be more likely to prevail if he can interest their self-love in his favour, and show them that it is for their own advantage to do for him what he requires of them. Whoever offers to another a bargain of any kind, proposes to do this. Give me that which I want, and you shall have this which you want, is the meaning of every such offer; and it is in this manner that we obtain from one another the far greater part of those good offices which we stand in need of. It is not from the benevolence of the butcher, the brewer, or the baker that we expect our dinner, but from their regard to their own interest. We address ourselves, not to their humanity but to their self-love, and never talk to them of our own necessities but of their advantages* (Smith 1970 p. 119).

While self-love may tend to dissolve social bonds from the perspective of an ethico-political reason, it does render human behaviour predictable and calculable: then, 'as if by an invisible hand', the private interests of each may be brought to serve the common good, and perhaps do so more effectively than if each sought to subordinate self-love to some ideal of the common good. So the conflict between economic rationality and ethics is staged within political rationality itself: What is most *effective* in realising the common good – subordination to an ideal of society, or the maximisation of individual utility? Which has better consequences – rational regulation or market forces?

To orient the discussion that follows, three brief observations may be pertinent here. *First*, and most significantly, we 'address ourselves' to the butcher, brewer and baker through the offer of money. Money offers a single scale of values in relation to which any 'advantages' may be measured, calculated and planned. The effect of quantification is moral certainty: Measures of 'value for money' and efficiency offer indisputable criteria whereby the more can be preferred to the less. Even an individual's ability and virtue can be measured by how much they earn. André Gorz has explained the revolution in ethico-political reason enacted here:

> *Quantitative measurement as a substitute for rational value judgement confers supreme moral security and intellectual comfort: The Good becomes measurable and calculable; decisions and moral judgements can follow from the implementation of a procedure of impersonal, objective, quantifying calculation and individual subjects do not have to shoulder the burden anxiously and uncertainly (Gorz 1989 p. 121).*

Second, the 'we' of Smith's observation about how we obtain goods applies specifically to individuals who live in a modern, market society. The vast majority of small-scale societies have indeed operated, rather like the modern family, by free and uncalculated distribution where food resources were shared; other, larger societies have operated by appropriation, tithing, and customary redistribution. Negotiated exchange and barter belonged solely to relations between strangers; no local society has ever been discovered that operated by barter (Caroline Humphrey in Graeber 2011 p. 29). So the self-evident appeal to market forces only makes sense as a result of certain effects of modern rationalisation. Outside of a market society with its comparison of prices, there is no way of measuring utility or self-interest.

Third, Smith's alternative between self-love and benevolence is an effect of considering the particular 'good offices' of producing goods for consumption. Perishable goods have to be consumed, given away, or go to waste. The choice of the butcher, brewer and baker is not an arbitrary one: Any meat, beer or bread consumed by me cannot be subsequently consumed by you. Goods for consumption have to be appropriated and possessed, or else wasted. What remains in question is whether it is necessary to generalise from this to the whole of economic, social and political life. Then these three observations raise a possible suspicion: could market-based rationalisation express a moral dogmatism that anxiously represses uncertainty, seeing the world from the perspective of a very limited historical era, and based on the rhetoric of false generalisations?

To demonstrate the existence of an alternative perspective on such matters, one may cite Søren Kierkegaard's moral condemnation of self-interest in his defence of 'the religious' against 'the world':

> *Every earthly or worldly good is in itself selfish, begrudging; its possession is begrudging or is envy and in one way or another must make others poorer – what I have someone else cannot have; the more I have, the less someone else must have - - - Furthermore, all the time and energy, all the mental solicitude and concern that is applied to acquiring or possessing earthly goods is selfish, begrudging, or the person who is occupied in this way is selfish, at every moment has no thought for others; at every such moment he is selfishly working for himself or selfishly for a few others, but not equally for himself and for everyone else (Kierkegaard 1997 pp. 115-6).*

What Kierkegaard set out to challenge was not wealth itself, but the thought of possession, that a rich person possesses and owns this wealth as his (Kierkegaard 1997 p. 26). By contrast, the rich Christian 'bears in mind that he owns nothing except what is given to him and owns what is given to him not for him to keep but only on loan, as a loan, as entrusted property.' (Kierkegaard 1997 p. 29) Of course, one might observe that this Puritan ethic could make for better capitalists than those who are simply motivated by their own advantages. Yet Kierkegaard went on to contrast earthly goods with the 'goods of the spirit', such as faith, love and hope, which can only be possessed insofar as they are shared (Kierkegaard 1997 p. 116). Instead of viewing the world as something to be consumed and possessed, now even consumption goods are viewed as gifts, and hold value insofar as they signify the care of the giver: 'Does not even an otherwise humble gift, an insignificant little something, have infinite worth for the lover when it is from the beloved!' (Kierkegaard 1997 p. 15) What Kierkegaard indicates is that there is more to life than food and drink even when one is eating and drinking.

With Smith and Kierkegaard presented at polar extremes, we can now turn to our main problem: How may we differentiate the spheres of economic, ethico-political, and religious rationality? An initial suggestion would be to distinguish spheres by their respective goods. Some goods are essentially competitive: They can only be mine insofar as they are not yours. Goods such as food, resources, land, lovers, property, patents, rights, prizes, fame, sporting achievements and financial instruments are *objects of appropriation*. Some goods, by contrast, are essentially cooperative: They can only be mine insofar as they are also yours. Goods such as environments, laws, institutions, governments, honour and virtues are *objects of participation*. The underlying distinction here derives from that between the material and the ideal: Public goods such as roads and education, paid for by governments, have both appropriative and participatory dimensions. This distinction between competitive and cooperative goods, or between earthly and spiritual goods, is widely used (MacIntyre 1999, and Tanner 2005), but I believe that Kierkegaard's thought indicates a further category of spiritual goods that pertain solely to the unique individual. These can only be possessed insofar as they are spent: 'All the time and energy, all the mental solicitude and concern'. I only have time insofar as I spend it, and even if I spend it on myself, I no longer have it. Goods such as time, attention, concern, labour, life and love are *objects of offering*.[1] The religious sphere may be considered as the sphere of worship, of offering, of distribution of time and attention, and any disciplined practice for directing attention may be considered a mode of piety (Goodchild 2002). We may therefore set out as a heuristic scheme the following: if distributive objects of offering are regulated by religion, cooperative objects of participation may be regulated by ethics and politics, leaving competitive

---

[1] Thus:

> *If life has taken your riches away from you - - - you will also be freed from wasting your time and your days and your thought on that with which you can occupy yourself only selfishly - - - if life has taken your worldly reputation and influence away from you - - - you are also freed from using your time and your thought on keeping or enjoying that with which one can only occupy oneself only selfishly - - - if you are as if cast out from human society, if no one seeks your company, if no invitations disturb you - - - then you are also freed from wasting your time and your thought on chatter about futility and vanity, emptily engaged in killing time in order to escape boredom or in wasting it in meaningless pastimes. (Kierkegaard 1997 p. 121)*

objects of appropriation to be regulated by the market. Each kind of good would have its own distinctive rationality: Rational offering, rational participation, and rational accumulation may be different activities.[2]

For all its promise, such a scheme is not entirely effective in demarcating separate spheres. In some ways, we can view the progress of modernisation as two distinct secular trends. There is a trend towards the displacement of religious modes of regulation by ethico-political ones such as might realise ideals, for example liberty, equality and fraternity. There is also a trend towards the subsequent displacement of ethico-political modes of regulation by economic ones by rendering further aspects of life measurable and calculable, such as in medicine, psychology and management. 'Rationalisation' is then the progressive analysis of life, first in terms of qualitative concepts, and subsequently in terms of measurable quantities. First one renders explicit for the understanding; subsequently, one measures and monitors. The ultimate progress of rationalisation may be measured in terms of quantitative improvements in indicators of performance. At stake, here, are the immensely complex and contentious questions of whether this rationalisation enhances ends such as those of faith, equality and justice, or whether efficiency and effectiveness as ends of regulation may effectively substitute for them. When is 'rationalisation' itself irrational?

8.3 Modern Irrationality: A Rational Utopia

Modern irrationality may be encountered first of all in certain intrinsic obstacles to the progress of rationalisation. First, in a rational utopia, each individual is free yet each individual wills the good of all. This is only possible when each individual is fully rational, that is, each understands the reasons for coordinating activity for the best.[3] Reason, individual existence and socio-economic life would be coextensive. Yet progress towards such a rational utopia runs into the problem of the finitude of human understanding. Just as most individuals understand little of the events of their bodies, the reasons for their changing health and moods, as well as little of the workings of the machines that surround them and augment their activity and capacities, they also understand little of the complex organisation of social functions in economic life. This central problem, deriving from the division of labour, has been clearly identified by André Gorz:

> As it becomes more complex, the organization of specialized functions, for the purpose of accomplishing a task which exceeds the comprehension of any individual, is increasingly unable to rely on the agents' own motivation for accomplishing this task. Their favourable disposition, personal capacities and goodwill are not enough. Their reliability will only be

---

[2] A Christian philosophy expressed in terms of goods of appropriation, participation and offering has been developed in Goodchild (2020a).
[3] This is the model for Kant's ethics, extended to the social domain through Hegel's idea of the State, and to the economic domain through Marx's idea of communism.

ensured by the formal codification and regulation of their conduct, their duties, and their relationships. (Gorz 1989 p. 32)

Let us note here that the advance of an economic, instrumental rationality and the displacement of religious and ethico-political rationalities is not driven simply by faith, nor by political preference, but by the technical failure of the latter two rationalities to appropriately orient individuals within a complex, modern society. No individual can comprehend the inner workings of a transnational corporation, let alone the workings of a national economy – and even if the broad structural outlines are clear to a few, appropriate quantities and timing are not subject to rational control. Where reason reaches its limits, other motivations must come into play such as those of faith or desire. For example, a worker in a socialist state could not fully grasp the reasons for that which was demanded of them:

They had to desire to be the active instruments by means of which a transcendent will (that of the Plan and the Party) would achieve transcendent aims (those of socialism, history, and the revolution); it was through their devotion to the Party, their faith in the revolution and in socialism that the specialized, abstract, obscure tasks assigned to them by the Party would acquire a meaning. (Gorz 1989 pp. 40-41).

Here we may recall Friedrich Hayek's famous argument that the market is a solution to the problem of rational planning and coordination (Hayek 1944). Where reason and planning reach their limits, there the market laws of supply and demand may come into their own. The interaction of blind market forces can calculate, where no transcendent reason can do so, through the laws of its immanent operation. Yet here reason no longer pertains to the human mind but is the prerogative of the market system. The progress of rationalisation reaches an intrinsic limit: even if we no longer understand our lives, we can have faith in the market to understand our lives for us.

8.4 Modern Irrationality: Organisation and Individual

The introduction of market incentives as an alternative to faith in the Party's vision of progress offers a second intrinsic obstacle to rationalisation identified by Gorz:

Individuals are induced to function in a complementary manner, like the parts of a machine, towards ends that are often unknown to them and different from those offered to them as personal goals. (Gorz 1989 p. 35).

There is a division, here, between two different rationalities: That of the organisation which has its own ultimate objectives, and that of the individual worker whose conduct is motivated either by faith in the organisation (as in socialism) or by compensation (as in a market economy). The odd consequence of compensation, as Gorz notes, is that the objective of work becomes leisure: On the one hand, work has to be adapted to the rationality embedded in the machines, procedures and organisation, where the worker disciplines herself to be more and more productive, more and more heteronomous; on the other hand, compensation is offered in monetary terms to be spent on consumer goods, entertainment and leisure, promoting the hedonistic values of comfort, instant pleasure and minimal effort. Work becomes merely a means to a wage: where production is ascetic, consumption is hedonism. For the worker, there is little role for ethico-political rationality in the workplace, as Gorz explains:

> *Questions about the meaning and goal of life are resolved in advance: since there is no room in a worker's life for anything other than working for money, money is the only possible goal. In the absence of time for living, money is the only compensation for lost time, for a life spoiled by work. Money symbolizes everything that the worker has not, is not, and cannot be because of the constraints of work. This is why work will never pay enough; but also why money earned by working was originally perceived as being worth more than the life one had to sacrifice for it. (Gorz, 1989 p. 118)*

The obstacle to rationalisation lies in this: decisions in the market for consumption goods are based on arbitrary preference or taste. No reason can be given for them.[4] Many purchases are based on status symbols, or symbols of life, which progressively lose their symbolic value the more widely they are distributed: the exotic holiday as a symbol of peak experience, the car as a symbol of freedom and escape, the house as a symbol of sovereignty sheltered from the outside world (Gorz 1989 p. 119). Consumers are encouraged to pursue superfluous luxuries, compensatory goods and services, guided by infantile wishes for gratification or symbolic competition, and the whole edifice of the rational organisation of economic production becomes devoted to entirely irrational ends. In a consumer society, the appetitive part of the soul rules the rational part. Yet at least one may hope that appetites are satisfied and that organisation is effective.

8.5 Modern Irrationality: Do We Know What We Want?

The problem of irrational ends, in turn, produces a third obstacle to rationalisation. Economic rationality is not required when people decide their own levels of needs: human activities are part of the time, movement and rhythm of life (Gorz 1989 p. 111, 109). As soon as one produces for the market, however, counting and calculating are required, as well as organising life according to this calculation. Yet this is precisely what a consumer has difficulty in achieving. On the one hand, consumers may be regarded as unique bearers of preferences who exercise free choice; on the other hand, if the world is to be predictable, then consumers must act together according to determinate laws of economic behaviour. According to this view, the 'wisdom of crowds' is such that estimates of the balance of market forces and future expectations are appropriate for fixing prices at about their true value. The problem

---

[4] Gorz actually makes this point in his discussion of prostitution as a servant-master relationship where one person's work is another person's pleasure – there is no reason behind a client's desire for a particular sexual service apart from preference (Gorz 1989 p 147). It may be generalised more widely to markets for consumption.

for each individual consumer, however, is that they have no better way of estimating the balance of market forces than do economists: the pursuit of rational self-interest, by weighing costs and benefits and assessing marginal utility, is conducted by means of the wild guess. Such wild guesses are informed by the behaviour of others: Market forces, based on numerous such wild guesses that can hardly be considered independent of each other, are together wildly irrational.

The obstacle to rationalisation here is that the inner life of the subject is unknown even to the subjects themselves: We do not know what we want or why we want it; when we get what we asked for we do not know whether we really wanted it; we are not in a position to compare preferences, but simply have to act. The internal cannot easily be made external; it is far easier to make the external internal by copying the behaviour or internalising the demands of others. The clearest indication of preferences is based in action: What people actually decide, how much they actually spend, or what they state on questionnaires. Insofar as economic rationality is a matter of measuring, calculating and planning, then the hard data that constitutes evidence for its calculations is often the externalisation of subjectivity: It is largely arbitrary and inconsistent, subject to innumerable social pressures.

8.6 The Fate of Economic Rationalisation

What, then, are we to conclude about the fate of economic rationalisation in a market society? In the *first* place, reason is divorced from life: We do not have access to the inner lives of things, whether of markets, human bodies, or human minds. It is possible to form complex models, such as those of general equilibrium theory or those of financial markets, and yet the actual behaviour of economies and markets remains inherently unpredictable. It is possible to organise life to satisfy preferences, but the choice of preferences is itself irrational. It is possible to base decisions on evidence, but the data produced by human subjects is arbitrary. Economic rationality makes pragmatic sense within isolated pockets of determinate, consistent behaviour, but these are islands in a wider ocean of chaos. We cannot expect economic rationality to fulfil the ideal of understanding life.

In the *second* place, however, economic rationalisation does not seek understanding, but is essentially a matter of modelling, planning and forecasting. The conduct of an enterprise can only be planned appropriately if all spheres of life, including the natural environment, individuals, and social institutions such as governments behave in a predictable way (Gorz 1989 p. 31). In this respect, the wider ocean of chaos does not really matter – models and plans can be discarded and replaced, assets can be revalued – so long as businesses, individuals and governments behave in a rational, calculable and predictable way. What matters is not whether the plan succeeds, but that there should be a plan so that others can plan. In this respect, economic rationalisation is primarily a form of moral self-discipline rather than a source of knowledge. It is a way of spending time by planning to save time. But as fast as economic rationality plans to save time and money, it actually spends time and money, and neither time nor the value of money are accumulated – since both time and the value of money can only be realised by being spent. Economic rationality, then, does not ultimately concern accumulation but distribution: What matters, above all else, is not whether the plan succeeds but that there should be a plan. Once instrumental reason becomes detached from all ends, then it is entirely irrational.

Let us take stock, then, of the fate of modern progress. Prior to rationalisation, it was faith in the wisdom of ancestors, spirits, customs, traditions and God that regulated human conduct. Monarchy, often claiming divine right, afforded the opportunity to gradually displace elements of these by introducing changes guided by reason. Rationalisation, in the form of the division of labour and the creation of specialised roles and functions, has been so extensive that it has crossed a threshold whereby no individual or government is able to coordinate the progress of history rationally. Just as no individual can wisely safeguard the interests of all, so that the interests of all have to be represented directly in a democracy, and just as no individual can comprehend and manage all the research and teaching conducted within a university, so also no individual can wisely plan for the needs of all. Faith in the rationality of wise governance is fundamentally broken; governance takes on the more modest roles of planning, spending, regulating, modifying and intervening. Ethics takes on the more modest roles of fulfilling one's role and achieving one's codified objectives. For here a traditional ethico-political rationality offers little advice on what is to be done within this newly created world: few contemporary occupations existed a mere two centuries ago, and the rationality governing their conduct and execution has had to be invented. What offers an apparent solution to the limitations of a transcendent, governing reason is the immanent system of the market; what offers an apparent guide to conduct within a market is the measuring, planning and calculating activity of economic rationality.

Yet economic rationality leaves us with a bad conscience. We do not really understand how the world works: If we can make models and machines that work consistently under particular conditions, then we will have to rely on that. We do not have reasons for our preferences and choices; if we can make enough money to buy what we want, then we will have to assume that we will have been content. We do not have evidence for the true needs and interests of others; if we can shape our preferences by copying and serving the expressed preferences of others, then we will have to be content with that. In each case, we may experience anxiety about the limits to reason, but we can soothe our anxiety by more cautious planning. Here it matters less that planning should prove correct than that there should be a market that coordinates human activity. The more that can be measured, calculated and planned, the more that can be codified and regulated, then the more that quantification and evidence can guide decision-making, and the more that moral certainty is achieved. If in doubt, show us the money: when it is merely a matter of implementing an impersonal and objective procedure, then more is always better than less. Faith in the market has displaced confidence in the sovereignty of reason.

8.7 How Successful Is the Market?

Let us return to my initial scheme, where economic rationality was delegated to regulate competitive goods as objects of appropriation. Now we have found that economic rationality is also a form of moral self-discipline, one that seeks to avoid anxiety and achieve certainty, even if it has to marginalise ethical and political considerations by promoting self-interest for the sake of the common good. We have even found that economic rationality expresses a faith in the self-regulating power of markets: it is a way of spending time and money. For independence from ethical and political interference is what a self-regulating market actually means. If the reason governing the ordering of life is not comprehensible within our minds, we may at least have faith that it is in things themselves, in our bodies and environments, in our brains beneath our consciousness, and in our market mechanisms.

We therefore need to reconsider how successful the market is as a solution to the problem of the finitude of human understanding. For out of all the modern plans, systems and procedures that constitute modern rationalisation, it is the 'market' that names the objective mechanism of their interaction. How rational is faith in the market? A market can be considered as a system of free exchange between buyers and sellers where decisions are made by weighing benefits against costs (including opportunity costs) as informed by price signals. As such, it is a collective social practice, and may simply be the expression of a faith. Yet faith in the validity of price signals implies a further element: there must be a mechanism for determining prices, a 'reason' inherent within the market system itself – and it is this mechanism that would be the objective basis for faith. The market mechanism is normally considered to be this: price signals are mainly influenced by the balance of supply and demand and seek to return to equilibrium by affecting the forces of supply and demand. Without such a mechanism, or if the mechanism is itself faulty, then faith in the 'rationality' of markets is misplaced. Now, assumptions built into economic models show that a market only works for optimal resource allocation if certain conditions are met: there should be perfect information available to market participants on alternatives and prices; there should be no transaction costs that would limit trade; there should be constant returns to scale, without undue advantages accruing to larger organisations; and there should be no external restrictions to trade, such as protectionism, subsidies and rationing (Werner 2005 p. 19). None of these assumptions actually hold in the real world. In practice, there are practical limits on access to information – in fact, many people spend most of their working lives gathering, analysing and disseminating information (Werner 2005 p. 25). Similarly, many crucial economic goods are rationed: Real estate, planning allocations, workers' lifetimes, government bonds, insider knowledge and even money are all rationed (Werner 2005 p. 326).

Furthermore, many decisions are not based directly on price signals: For example, if about 40% of GDP is typically generated within the public sector, then most of these decisions are grounded in rational planning; similarly much 'trade' takes place within major corporations, which are hierarchical organisations based on rational planning. Moreover, price signals can be interpreted as indicating future price rises or falls, leading to positive feedback effects rather than negative feedback that returns the price to equilibrium (Keen 2011). Overall, then, there may be 'mechanisms' in the market, but there is little consistency to their operation, little reason to suppose that price stability is anything but local and temporary, and little reason to hope that it should lead to a rational or optimal allocation of resources rather than growing inequality. In a world in which 2153 billionaires own as many assets as the poorer 60% of the global population, then the resources of human potential are clearly being wasted (Oxfam 2020).

It is important to re-describe the nature of market exchange. There are, indeed, many activities of buying and selling, and there is some influence over pricing from availability of alternatives and the laws of large numbers. Yet the 'market mechanism' operates alongside a whole set of other economic forces. Many of these involve beliefs that affect human behaviour, and among these, one of the most crucial is belief in the efficiency and justice of markets themselves: Many people try to generate a market, and behave as though there is a predominating market mechanism. Alongside this, however, economic behaviour is not simply a response to supply and demand: Urgent needs for self-preservation take precedence over personal preferences; information is controlled, withheld, advertised or marketed; planning decisions are made guided by belief, custom, and a sense of 'what ought to be done'; decisions are affected by legal constraints and the exploitation of loopholes; power inequalities can force the renegotiation of contracts; and credit ratings and levels of debt constrain economic behaviour. In many ways, therefore, buyers and sellers interact apart from the mediation of price signals. Supply and demand are never truly independent. If one party can influence the preferences of the other and buying and selling involve a confrontation between parties with unequal resources, needs, capacities and powers, then exchange is often not free but coerced.

In practice, then, faith in the market does not signify a rational commitment to an immanent system of reason, for no such reason exists. Faith in the market is a political belief in the freedom to express one's power as far as possible through exchanges and contracts within the bounds of the law. This faith has positive implications when it enables a division of labour and economic interactions with strangers where these would otherwise not exist – it enhances the possibility for the expression of capacities and the formation of relations. Yet it has more negative consequences when the strong are enabled to dominate and exploit the weak, and when human interests become subordinated to an impersonal market mechanism.

8.8 Money

Overall, then, Adam Smith's paradigmatic visits to his butcher, brewer and baker afford a poor model for economic life. For only a limited portion of economic reality is composed of pure, free, bilateral exchange. Instead, many important economic relations are contracts that endure over time: once a contract has been entered, then it functions as a constraint on activity. Much economic life is composed of regular or repeated payments of bills, rents, wages, interest, dividends, and taxes: these are payments of money, made on a single quantitative scale. So economic decisions are no longer free decisions based on preferences but coerced decisions of those now under obligations: money is owed. Similarly, most bilateral contracts involve activities that affect third parties who were not involved in the original contract, and these often have to bear the cost of 'externalities'. They do not participate in free and rational decisions since they are neither considered nor consulted.

Yet there is a further aspect whereby economic activity differs from a free exchange which I like to dub 'internalities': Most exchanges and contracts are for money, and thus they are supported by the banking and credit infrastructure. Since modern money is created as debt, then what is in fact exchanged is a liability or obligation: the liability of a bank, as recorded in its accounts.[5] But this liability only holds value so long as the bank has assets, which are the liabilities of others.[6] Money, as a bank liability, is only created when a borrower takes on an equal and equivalent debt, a corresponding liability. Such outstanding debts may be guaranteed by asset prices and expectations of future income, in turn tied to the network of ongoing economic relations. In every monetary exchange, a liability or claim on the network of economic relations and its future activity is transferred. The whole of the global financial system is at stake in every single transaction. This simple fact has enormous consequences for the entirety of economic rationality.

Initially, it would seem that economic rationality is concerned with objects of consumption or appropriation, such as meat, beer and bread. Money would appear to be a paradigmatic object of appropriation since it is so easily transferred, and placed in one's pocket, purse, wallet or account. Nevertheless, money holds no intrinsic value in itself: as a piece of paper bearing a promise, or as a figure recorded in an account, it is merely a symbol of value. While the signs can be appropriated, the value of money cannot. Money only holds value insofar as others will accept it in exchange, will treat it as valuable. In this respect, the value of money is essentially social, essentially an object of participation. Money is a collective institution. It belongs to politics, not economics. But we have to go further: When money is created as a liability, a pure obligation, then this obligation pertains to a unique individual or economic entity. I cannot appropriate my liability; my liability appropriates me. Instead of eating it, placing it in my pocket, or using it to build something, my obligation governs the conduct of my life. My undertaking and discharging of liabilities, my conduct in relation to credit and debt, constitutes the way in which I offer my life. When I take out a loan and a bank creates a corresponding liability, then it is my offering that is transferred by others. The sphere of economic life, far from being distinguished from the sphere of religious life, is in reality coextensive

---

[5] The process of money creation has been described erroneously in many economic textbooks. An authoritative account has recently been offered by the Bank of England (2014). This is in accord with the account given by the New Economics Foundation (2011), and Jackson and Dyson (2012).

[6] Every financial asset is balanced by a corresponding liability (Wray 2012 p. 1).

with it. Indeed, if we are to seek out a modern form of religious reason, then we may find it within economic life itself.

8.9 Theology of Money

I call this 'logic' or religious reason embedded in modern economic life a 'theology of money' (Goodchild 2009). It has four principles:

First, the value of money is transcendent: it is a promise, taken on faith, and only realized to the extent that this faith is acted out in practice in contractual exchange.

Second, money is the supreme value because it is both the perspective through which we value the world, in terms of prices, and our means of making what we value real, by purchasing. Since money is the means by which all other social values may be realized, it posits itself as the supreme value.

Third, financial value is essentially a degree of hope, expectation, trust or credibility: it is promised. Yet financial value, measured by money, is our underlying reason, the discipline for our conduct, the pivot around which the world is reconstructed when we seek to make profits and repay debts. Being transcendent to material and social reality, yet also being the pivot around which material and social reality is continually reconstructed, financial value is essentially religious: it only has 'value in motion', when it is offered, spent or invested.

Fourth, the entire monetary system has its own intrinsic logic of growth. This drive for growth is a separate engine of the global economy in addition to the individual acquisition of necessities and the individual pursuit of self-interest.

There are three relevant components here:

- A logic of appropriation: speculative profits can only be made on the basis of profits extracted from production and consumption, and to achieve this, an increasing quantity of the world's physical resources as well as an increasing quantity of the world's moral ends must be appropriated for production, exchange and consumption, in a colonization and commodification of the world that intensifies scarcity.
- A logic of natural selection: wealth brings access to power, so only the powerful and wealthy shape the world. The economy tends towards inequality and oligopoly.
- A logic of intensification: increased production and profits require increased investment, credit and debt. If money is created as debt, then it has to be repaid with interest with more money. Where is this money to come from? Since debts expire, the money to repay them must come from others creating money through debt, so that more and more of the world's resources are governed by mutual liabilities. The entire global economy is driven by a spiral of debt, constrained to seek further profits, and always dependent on future expansion.

In the final analysis, then, it is not a 'market mechanism' that contains the rational ordering principles that regulate economic conduct. Instead, it is simply necessary that there be an obligation to subject more and more of life to measurement, calculation and planning. This obligation is provided by debt, and in an era of 'market failures', debt provides the effective force for economic rationalisation. For one who is in debt, the whole world may be seen as a means to accumulation and appropriation. For maintaining security, holding a place in the world, is no longer regarded as a gift of ancestors, tradition, or God, nor as a right or privilege conferred by ethical or political reason. One's place in the world is achieved by running in order to stay still: by seeking income and profits to repay debts. A world of rational stability is replaced by a world of contingencies and flows. Under such circumstances, salvation is only achieved through quantification. Economic rationalisation, as guided by a theology of money, generates four fundamental illusions.

An illusion of objectivity – Since money is the value through which all other values are measured for the sake of agreement and contract, it becomes the basis for accounting or evaluation. Values are measured in terms of prices, so they are measured in terms of costs of replacement or substitution, even though many things in life cannot be substituted for or replaced. We do not count things themselves, but only money, projecting the shadows of our own collective desires.

An illusion of liberty – Since money is required to repay debts, and meet all other obligations, it becomes that which is most in demand, the supreme value through which all other values may be obtained, the principle guiding practical conduct. Values are measured in terms of money to be spent, so they are measured from the point of view of one who has money to spend, as if he procures whatever he wants or needs by spending, even though the goods and services will in fact be provided by the 'good offices' of others.

An illusion of wealth – Since securities, financial derivatives, and even money itself are created as debts, then each financial asset is someone else's liability. Even investment assets, such as land, commodities, property and shares, are priced by speculation, so that their value is supported by the amount of debt people are willing to undertake for them. Asset values are measured by an anticipated rate of return, an increase in the liabilities of others, even if this involves consuming the basis of material production.

An illusion of reality – Economic behaviour is constrained by competitive selection, so that only those who seek profit prosper and grow. Since money is created as debt, and debt must be repaid in the form of money or more debt, and debt becomes the supreme principle of theoretical knowledge, practical conduct, and mutual trust, then this perspective of evaluation is not chosen but imposes itself as 'the real world'.

8.10 Conclusion

In conclusion, the further we proceed with modern rationalisation, the more we subject life to quantification, generating evidence and models, and the more we subject life to codification, generating systems, regulations and procedures, then the less we understand of who we are and what we do. We plunge headlong into illusion, blinded by the clarity of our own newly-found rationality and the solidity of the evidence. We experience an eclipse of reason, no longer understanding what it is to formulate concepts and ideals, nor understanding what it is to offer our lives, time and attention in an appropriate ratio or distribution. We sleepwalk towards environmental catastrophe, economic collapse, and war when all we can do is make tentative forecasts, draw up systems and procedures, and invent contingency plans. For just as anthropogenic climate change may cross a threshold where positive feedback processes in the earth's systems take the climate beyond human control, the limits to rationality may lead to autonomous social processes, like asset-bubbles and debt-spirals, that exceed the powers of rational human intervention.

Reason may be configured differently when it is no longer subjected to a logic of appropriation but conceives logics of participation and distribution. As Kierkegaard maintained, 'Life can only be understood backwards, but it must be lived forwards' (cited in Pérez-Álvarez 2011 p. 29). As such, individual responsibility cannot be assumed by taking refuge in a system, procedure or idea in relation to which all individuals are indifferent. Reason consists in the individual conduct that makes oneself at the same time as it makes the world. The theological essence of the reason through which we make ourselves and make our world has been explained by Kierkegaard:

> *[The rich Christian] bears in mind that he owns nothing except what is given to him and owns what is given to him not for him to keep but only on loan, as a loan, as entrusted property - - - The rich pagan, however, also has only one thought, riches. All his thoughts revolve around that – yet he is anything but a thinker. Not only is he without God in the world, but wealth is his god, which attracts itself to his every thought. He has only one need, wealth, the one thing needful – therefore he does not even need God. (Kierkegaard 1997: 29, 33)*[7]

References

Bank of England. 2014. Money creation in the modern economy. *Quarterly Bulletin* Q1.
Goodchild, P. 2002. *Capitalism and Religion: The Price of Piety*. London: Routledge.
———. 2009. *Theology of Money*. Durham: Duke University Press.
———. 2020a. *Credit and Faith*. London: Rowman & Littlefield International.
———. 2020b. *Economic Theology: Credit and Faith II*. London: Rowman & Littlefield International.
Gorz, A. 1989. *Critique of Economic Reason*. London: Verso.
Graeber, D. 2011. *Debt: The First 5,000 Years*. New York: Melville.
Hayek, F.V. 1944. *The Road to Serfdom*. London: Routledge & Kegan Paul.
Jackson, A., and B. Dyson. 2012. *Modernising Money*. London: Positive Money.
Keen, S. 2011. *Debunking Economics*. London: Zed Books.
Kierkegaard, S. 1997. *Christian Discourses*, in H V Hong & E H Hong (ed. and trans). Princeton: Princeton University Press.

---

[7] An expanded version of the argument presented in this chapter can be found in Goodchild (2020b).

MacIntyre, A. 1999. *Dependent Rational Animals*. London: Duckworth.
New Economics Foundation. 2011. *Where Does Money Come From?* London: Nef.
Oxfam. 2020. Time to Care. *Oxfam Report* (20 January 2020).
Pérez-Álvarez, E. 2011. *A Vexing Gadfly: The Late Kierkegaard on Economic Matters*. Cambridge: James Clark & Co.
Sandel, M. 2012. *What Money Can't Buy: The Moral Limits of Markets*. London: Allen Lane.
Smith, A. 1970. *The Wealth of Nations*. London: Penguin.
Tanner, K. 2005. *Economy of Grace*. MN: Fortress, Minneapolis.
Werner, R.A. 2005. *A New Paradigm in Macroeconomics*. Basingstoke: Palgrave Macmillan.
Wray, L.R. 2012. *Modern Money Theory: A Primer*. Basingstoke: Palgrave Macmillan.

Philip Goodchild born 1965, professor in religion and philosophy at University of Nottingham since 2008. In periods head of the department. His book "Theology of Money" is an international bestseller.

Chapter 9
Two Bishops on the Ethics of the Market Economy

Niels Kærgård

Abstract A remarkable discussion of the ethics of the capitalistic market economy took place in Denmark in the 1870s. The main contributors were Bishop H.L. Martensen and Bishop D.G. Monrad, two of the most prominent figures in the ecclesiastical history of Denmark. Martensen published a small pamphlet entitled "Socialism and Christianity" in 1874, in which he argued against capitalism, individualism and liberalism. He included the text almost unchanged in his major work "Christian Ethics" of 1878. Bishop Monrad replied in his book "The reply of Liberalism to Bishop Martensen". Even today this debate remains relevant as perhaps the most serious Danish analysis ever of the ethics of the market economy.

Keywords Market economy · Christian attitudes · Social ethics · Welfare state · Poor laws

9.1 Introduction

In the 1870s there was a remarkable debate on the ethics of the market economy, conducted between the most prominent Bishops of the Danish Church, Hans Lassen Martensen (1808–1884) and Ditlev Gothardt Monrad (1811–1887). They were

---

An earlier version of the article has been presented at the 1st European conference of *The Association for the Study of Religion, Economics and Culture*, September, 2014, University of Durham; the participants in this workshop has contributed with many useful comments. The topics of this chapter is also discussed in Danish in Kærgård (2018). The chapter is part of the research project *What money can't buy* supported by The Danish Council for Independent Research, Humanities, FKK. The translation of the Danish quotations and general correction of the language is done carefully by Charles Woollen.

N. Kærgård (✉)
Department of Food and Resource Economics, University of Copenhagen, Frederiksberg C, Denmark
e-mail: nik@ifro.ku.dk

almost the same age, and must have known each other already when studying theology in the early 1830s (Martensen obtained his Master degree in theology in 1832, and Monrad in 1836). Monrad was an opponent at Martensen's Ph.D. defense in 1837.[1]

Both these Bishops rank among the most influential and esteemed figures in the ecclesiastical history of Denmark in the nineteenth century, in which only the religious reformers Søren Kierkegaard and Nikolai Frederik Severin Grundtvig had a more prominent place.

Martensen was Professor in Theology at University of Copenhagen from 1840 to 1854; from 1845 he also served as Pastor to the Royal Family. In 1854 he became Bishop of Zealand (including Copenhagen) and held this post for 30 years. He applied for retirement shortly before the end of this period, but died before it took effect.[2] He made a considerable number of theological contributions, his best known publication being, perhaps, "Den christelige dogmatik" (The Christian Dogmatic) from 1849, reprinted in fifth edition in 1905. He was member of the absolute upper social class of Copenhagen. Denmark's most famous actress of all time, Johanne Luise Heiberg, and her husband, Johan Ludvig Heiberg, Head of the Royal Theatre, were both close friends.[3] Martensen was in many respects (female emancipation, monarchy, universal suffrage etc.) seen as a right-wing conservative.

Whilst Martensen is only known as a theologian, D.G. Monrad is best known as a politician. He continued his studies after obtaining his Master's degree in Theology, now focussing on Middle Eastern languages. He came into contact with young liberals and was active in these circles in the late 1830's but left politics in 1846 to become a priest in the Danish provinces, on the island of Lolland. In the hectic year of 1848, he went back into politics and became Cabinet Minister for Culture, and was the main author of the draft of Denmark's first democratic constitution.[4] He retired from these duties, however, in 1849 due to disagreements within the Government on the subject of internal relations with the German-speaking parts of the Monarchy (i.e. Slesvig), and became Bishop of the Diocese of Lolland-Falster. He simultaneously became a Member of the first Chamber of the Danish Parliament.

He was a rather controversial person and, because of disagreement with the government, was forced to retire as Bishop already in 1854. He became once again

---

[1] There are a lot of literature about both of them, see e. g. Arildsen (1932), Engelstoft (1982), Hauge (1944), Lindhardt (1981), Nyholm (1947), Nørgaard (1918) and Stewart (2012), but very little about their debate about market economi, almost only Svenstrup (2000) and Lein (1980).

[2] The Lutheran-Evangelical church is the official church of Denmark with a place in the constitution and financially supported by the state. There is no Archbishop in this church, but the Bishop of Zealand (later Copenhagen) is in some sense the first among equals in the hierarchy of Danish bishops.

[3] Johanne Luise Heiberg, in common with most other members of the upper class social elite of the time, was very skeptical with regard to the King's Wife, the lower class girl Louise Rasmussen ("Countess Danner"), who had a child before she met the king. This fact, and Martensen's close friendship with Johanne Luise Heiberg, was so well known, that the King opposed his appointment as Bishop in 1854.

[4] Denmark changed from absolutism to a form of democracy in 1848–49.

member of the Government in 1859 and, a few months before war broke out with Prussia and Austria in 1864, became Prime Minister.[5] The war was a disaster and Denmark lost a considerable part of its' territory to Germany. Monrad felt a strong sense of personal responsibility and emigrated to New Zealand with his family in 1865. On his return to Denmark in 1869, he once again took up the priesthood, and in 1871 once again became Bishop of Lolland-Falster, which position he held until his death in 1887.

The debate between Martensen and Monrad about the market economy started in 1874 with the publication by Martensen of a pamphlet of 55 pages entitled "Socialisme og Christendom" (Socialism and Christianity), in which he was positive towards an "ethical socialism".

It was not uncontroversial in 1874 to talk positively of socialism. A small Danish socialist movement was started and had arranged a demonstration in 1872, but the leaders were sent to prison for 4–6 years. The Revolutionary government in Paris 1871 was looked upon with dismay by the established circles also in Denmark and all connections to international socialist movements were forbidden. The socialist leaders were released in 1875 and in 1877 offered a one-way ticket to USA, which they accepted rather than risk new periods of imprisonment.

Martensen did not, however, consider his pamphlet as a political action but as a discussion of Christian ethics, which is demonstrated by his inclusion of all 55 pages almost unchanged in his later major publication "Den Christelige Ethik" (The Christian ethic), completed in 1878. This presented his work on profound Christian ethics in three substantial volumes. The first volume, the general part, was published in 1871. The remaining two volumes came out in 1878, one dealing with social ethics. This volume alone was of 475 pages and included his 1874-pamphlet almost verbatim.

This time Monrad responded. He was, as already mentioned, one of the seven Bishops leading the Danish church. He participated in the public debate publishing inter alia some "political letters". In 1878 he published "Politiske breve Nr. 14–18: Liberalismens Gjenmæle til Biskop Martensen" (Political letters no. 14–18: The reply of Liberalism to Bishop Martensen). It is a book of 165 pages with a commercial publisher as responsible editor, and presented as 5 numbered and dated letters, some of them addressed to an "Old Friend". The book starts without introduction: "You ask me, dear friend, whether I have read the two last parts of Bishop Martensen's Ethics". Monrad is clearly against Martensen's socialism, and for a market economy. He does not like Martensen's mixture of ethics and "individual opinions".

---

[5]This government is sometime called the "Million" because it included nine members, one of a kind (Monrad) and 6 zeros, or "nullities".

9.2 Martensen's Critical View of the Market

As already mentioned, Martensen did not see his contributions to the debate on the market economy as a political point of view separate from his theological studies, but as a part of his Christian belief:[6]

> To claim that Christianity is unrelated to the wealth of nations and to political economy is the same as saying that ethics is unrelated to political economy, that the concepts of wealth and poverty, labour and wages only have physical and not ethical significance, and that the political economics for understanding the measures of the wealth of nations only need examine the natural laws of society without relating these laws to moral laws. On the contrary, subjugating the natural laws to the ethical laws is precisely what must be done. (Martensen 1878, pp. 163–164).

Martensen's point of view is that individualism and liberalism are the curse of modern capitalist society:

> In social relations, in the interrelations between human beings and in the relations between man and man, it is seen in an uncountable number of ways that individuals, instead of considering themselves as connected to one another in solidarity, and as being limbs of the same social body, and instead of using the apostolic words:" When one limb suffers the whole body suffers, too", consider each other as free, "independent" personalities, where "one is closest to one self". Social egoism has in our time, behind the shield of Liberalism, grown strong through the progress of science and the associated control of nature, and through the ever-growing advance of industry and capital. More and more widespread has become that which is, to all higher interests, the destructive mentality that places earthly mammon and earthly pleasures at the top; and people of our time compete for these in restless, anxious and feverish aspiration. They want to be rich and fall into many foolish and hurtful lusts (1 Timothy Ch. 6 v 9). (Translated from Martensen 1878, pp. 127–28)

From this starting point Martensen considered economics, especially Adam Smith, and did not like what he read:

> The common good thus results from the egoism of all. But this shows the problem with this system. Free competition, when it is unrestricted by higher considerations, is actually only a naturalistic and physical principle. It is the right of the strongest which is introduced; an indirect right of the man who is handy with his fists, a war of all against all; as we see in the animal kingdom, where free competition for all resources is found without inhibition, and the weaker creature is suppressed by the stronger. The ethical effect which should be brought about by free competition is the restoration and strengthening of the power of personal moral force. But then it must be restricted. It ought, for instance, only to apply to competition between equals. To let a cripple compete with a sprinter, a poor retailer with a big capitalist, a small landowner with a great one, does not serve to strengthen moral force, but only to let the strong rule and have victory in the name of freedom. Adam Smith's statement that the optimal for social wealth follows from the axiom of "Laissez aller", - that everybody by following their own interests promotes the common interest, that the common good is the result of everybody's egoism, – is not true. It is an untenable opinion that one can construct a just state simply by following one's natural desires, because justice is defined in an entirely different world and must come from a completely different place than

---

[6] All the quotes in the article are original in Danish and translated by the author and Charles Woollen.

from nature or from human beings who are driven purely by nature. (Martensen 1878, pp. 168–169)

Martensen is not blind to the benefits of the market economy in the form of economic growth and international development, but he considered the cost of it to be unacceptable. To him, the poor member of society was more important than the large companies:

> It is not possible to deny that free competition has contributed to developing much power and given wealth to many people; neither is it possible to deny that capital is important for society, for the great companies and a universal economic togetherness, a world economy in contrast to a purely national economy; but neither is it possible to deny that free competition has made many more miserable and poor, that thousands upon thousands of the weak have fought a desperate battle for their daily bread in which they finally succumbed to the strong. (Martensen 1878, pp. 172–173)

Whilst Martensen looked with sympathy on the great masses of poor workers, he was very sceptical concerning the capitalists and the *"nouveau riche"*. Without doubt Martensen himself was a member of the uppermost class in Danish society, but he, and probably many others in his ecclesiastical and aristocratic circles, looked on the modern capitalist with scepticism.

But in political economy it was not only Adam Smith and the market economy that Martensen fought against. Malthus and his followers were another of his targets. Martensen accepted the Malthusian problem according to which it is impossible to give permanent higher wages because the result of higher income is overpopulation and excess supply of labour, but to Martensen it was more of an ethical and social problem, which needed to be addressed and resolved by an ethical society. Many of the Malthusian solutions, where a low wage ("the iron law of wages") and a high death rate among the poor was accepted as unavoidable, were completely unethical and unacceptable to Martensen:

> We do not deny that the Malthusian imbalance between foodstuff and population, between the amount of bread and the number of mouths to be fed, has often been sadly confirmed by experience. But we cannot ignore the assumption that this imbalance is more the fault of mankind than of nature, and that it should be controlled and defeated by moral means, not only by individuals but also by society through better social structures, better use of uncultivated land and better distribution of resources. (Martensen 1878, p. 180)

Martensen describes the miserable living conditions of the poor in modern society, and gives his support to the classical Marxist authors:

> The liberalists and the capitalists on their side claim that the descriptions that can be read in socialist literature (inter alia the one by Engels which, as it dates from 1848, is now rather old, but not obsolete, and which is confirmed and continued by K. Marx, Das Capital, 1872) are one-sided and exaggerated. Nevertheless, the facts presented by these authors have not been disproved, and men (whose moderate and impartial attitude cannot be denied) have declared that no matter how much has been done with the aim of improving the conditions of the working class, how much has been done by noble men and by employers with human feelings, nevertheless the greater evil is still intact and needs to be dispelled in the name of humanity. (Martensen 1878, p. 176)

Martensen was not, however, a classic socialist. Having described the problem of modern capitalism, he also gives a critical description of the socialist movement. He considered himself a kind of socialist, but not a revolutionary socialist of the Marxist persuasion. For him there was a third road, "ethical socialism". Martensen's ethical socialism was not blind to the material living conditions of society. Spirituality and materialism go hand in hand in Martensen's writings:

> One has to go into the material interests of the workers. They must be supported both by spiritual guidance and by material support for the improvement of their circumstances. When our Lord and Saviour fed the 5,000 men in the desert, he fed them not only spiritually by his words, but he satisfied them materially too. It is this double feeding which is needed by the poor. (Martensen 1874 p. 53)

Martensen's contributions were widely debated, both in 1874 in relation to the publishing of "Socialisme og Christendom" and in 1878 when his "Den Christelige Ethik" was published. Martensen himself did not seem to be affected by the criticism of his analysis. As already mentioned, he included in his 1878 book all the parts of his pamphlet that were criticized in 1874, and in a letter to his former mentioned friend, the celebrated Danish actress Johanne Luise Heiberg, he wrote:

> It must not be said, at the end of the day, that the Church has remained silent and neglected to speak out on what Christianity ought to say; for in spite of all contradictions, the Christian truth is that industry must serve mankind, rather than mankind serve industry. (Martensen 1874; see Rahbek 1955, p. 105)

9.3 Monrad's Defence of the Market Economy

As mentioned D.G. Monrad published in 1878 a long "reply from Liberalism to Bishop Martensen". On the surface the reply was very friendly, but the content is never the less highly critical:

> Bishop Martensen has felt himself obliged to comment on a multitude of things and sentiments which have very little relationship to, or are actually completely independent of, the Christian ethic. This makes his work very entertaining; the content leads one somewhat haphazardly through many different passages of human life. One never grows tired of hearing such a spiritual and brilliant man speak, even though he takes us far away from the sphere of ethics. I would much like to see Bishop Martensen divide his "Ethik" into two separate works: one relating to ethics, and the other confined to his personal opinions on a multitude of diverse topics. (Monrad 1878, pp. 6–8).

Monrad is not impressed by Martensen's knowledge of society and of the laws of economics:

> It is with a strange mixture of feelings that one reads Bishop Martensen's opinions on the labour question and on Socialism. Who would not be happy reading of such a brilliant thinker's concerned sympathy for the sufferings of mankind? But for one who knows something about politics, this feeling is combined with displeasure over his unjust and ignorant evaluation of liberalism. And for a person who has some insight into political economy it is accompanied by a sense of grief that such a clear spirit may have such a mistaken conception of the laws of economics. (Monrad 1878, pp. 102–103).

Monrad was of the opinion that the laws inexorably governing economics are just as strong as the laws of nature. Even if one accepts that there are sin and ethics, one must also accept that there are inexorable, God-given, laws of economics:

> It is perfectly true that men, by following their egoism, do not always contribute to the common good. Sin may perturb the God-given natural laws of economics. But God has given his laws not only for the world of physical nature, but also for the world of economics. Science seeks to discover these laws. But it does not in any way follow that mankind unconditionally must be guided by the laws of nature and economics; for God has given us the Ten Commandments, Morality and Ethics as guidelines for the actions of mankind. (Monrad 1878, p. 109).

To Monrad an understanding of the laws of economics is absolutely central, and he devotes considerable space to explaining and elaborating on them:

> From the North and South Poles cold air flows to the Equator where it produces North-easterly and South-easterly trade winds. From the Equator the hot air rises, flows North and South, cools down again and brings the Westerly wind. There is a similar circulation among the powerful economic forces that determine the price. Production costs seem at first to be completely irrelevant. as in reality price is determined by the relation between supply and demand, irrespective of whether production costs are large or small. But then a current flows back from price to production, determining its size and restoring the parameter of production costs to its rightful and dignified place as the provider of equilibrium between supply and demand. If the price had been too low, production is reduced, and if it had been too high, then production is expanded, and such reductions and expansions bringing equilibrium between production costs on the one hand, and supply and demand on the other hand. Should you attempt to stop a speeding train by merely raising your hand, you will not fare well, but you will fare even worse if you believe that your own intervention is enough to stop the powerful forces determined by the laws of economics. (Monrad 1878, pp. 127–128).

This means, according to Monrad, that the interventions proposed by Martensen would not have the desired effect:

> There can be no doubt that wages would have to be very high in the system proposed by the author (i.e. Martensen), for it is the author's charitable intention to raise the working class up to the position and status of the third estate. But then economic power comes into play, including the price law, whose importance we have already analysed. If wages increase the volume of work will be reduced, and the number of those seeking work will increase. Thus arises a mismatch between the numbers of jobs and the number those seeking work. The price law cannot function because the wages are fixed. The wage is high. Excellent! But there will be a large crowd of workers who cannot find employment. (Monrad 1878, p. 138).

Quite contrary to Martensen, it was the opinion of Monrad that the Church and Christianity should not interfere in political and social questions:

> The Church and the State should not in relation to the question of labour behave like Adam and Eve in Paradise, each trying to attach the blame to the other. The Kingdom of Christ is not of this world, and when therefore Christian servants speak, not in their own name as simple individuals, as ordinary citizens, but in the name of Christ, they should not go too far into politics, nor make judgments on governments and constitutions, neither should they try to transform civil society and change it to a new, presumably Christian-ethical, form of state. (Monrad 1878, p. 144).

9.4 Martensen, Monrad, and the Division of Labour

It is a basic point of view in Adam Smith's *Wealth of Nations* that a division of labour is a central element in the achievement of economic growth and increased productivity. A well-known example given in Wealth of Nations is how huge amounts of pins can be produced at low cost by the division of labour amongst different types of workers and with the help of machinery. Such methods will, however, mean that the individual worker no longer can understand the real meaning of what he is doing. This leads according to Karl Marx to "alienation" and "reification". Martensen had certainly read his Smith, but maybe not his Marx. There is no doubt, however, that his views are closer to Marx:

> But even if this is excellent, nevertheless the moral question comes up of whether it is humane to devote your time, nay, even most of your life, to the production of pins. This is the ethical malpractice caused by the over-advanced division of labour, that increased production is achieved at the expense of humanity; for how does it effects the human soul throughout many years to have devoted all waking hours and, perhaps, also some nights, to the performance of an absolutely inane production task, which for the spiritual part of his being is completely futile, and because of which he himself becomes a mere component of the machine? (Martensen 1878, p. 167)

But this view is by no means shared by Monrad. Making pins is of course neither spiritual nor brilliant, but neither is so much else:

> Conceded, that the work is not in itself brilliant, even sometimes soulless. But the same can be said of almost all forms of physical labour. The only exception is when craftsmanship almost reaches the level of fine art: There is nothing spiritual in ploughing, harrowing, digging, sewing pairs of boots and trousers, planeing wood, building, trading etc. In itself such work is as soulless as making pins; in itself all physical labour is soulless. But if the work is carried out in a dignified manner, some happy powers will step in and inspire those without spirit. (Monrad 1878, p. 106)

It is for Monrad something other than the character of the actual work that is crucial:

> He who faithfully herds geese or makes pins shall in the eyes of God stand far above he who preaches well, but without faith. This is the true democratic conception of human life and its multitude of callings and practices. In my opinion, this perception is in accordance with the gracious will of God, as it links all men together in a common brotherhood. It is the faithfulness with which you fulfilled the lot assigned to you by God that will be counted on the final Day of Judgement (Monrad 1878, p. 107).

Monrad does not concern himself with the spiritual welfare of the pin maker. He draws instead a more sentimental picture to illustrate the positive sides of routine work:

> What is to prevent the pin maker, whose hands have become like a piece of the machine, from letting his Soul be uplifted by images of the dear ones at home or the recollection of the smile of his child, from letting his mind revisit the message of last Sunday's sermon, or from silently praying to God? Should one rather believe that the Apostle Paul did not at all times remain in touch with his Soul, even when he sat and sewed tents? (Monrad 1878, p. 115)

9.5 Attitudes to the Nouveau Riche Capitalists and to the Jews

The two Bishops also differed in their views on the nouveau riche class of capitalists. Martensen was very sceptical of the new class of wealthy financiers:

> The liberal state, in its' admiration of the active life and of competing forces, faithfully follows the advice of Adam Smith not to interfere in society, but only to ensure that private property rights and personal safety are not violated. As Lassalle put it, the state need only perform "night watchman duty" and otherwise observe the axiom "laizzez faire and laissez aller". "Anyone may decide to become a millionaire". And a completely new class arises, the millionaires or the moneyed nobility, in which modern Judaism has a significant role. Just like the Midgard Serpent of the fable,[7] they exercise crushing pressure on both the populace and on its' rulers. (Martensen 1874, pp. 22–23, and 1878, p. 172)

This point of view opened two lines of debate, one on "millionaires" and the other on "anti-Judaism". Monrad was less critical on the former of these two, finding the impact of millionaires to be overwhelmingly positive:

> How can a city not rejoice if a millionaire is takes up residence in it! I venture to promise Bishop Martensen that he will be appointed honorary citizen of Nykjøbing Falster (NK: Where Monrad lives), should he just succeed in attracting a couple of those Midgard Serpents to our city. Take the example of a man who is the first in our land to buy grain by weight. By so doing he will bring nurture to crop production, secure the farmers a higher income and he himself become a millionaire. How sad can that be! A second man might begin to sell sweet butter, which initiative will have a positive effect on the dairy sector, secure the milk producers higher profits, and give Danish Butter the place of honour among butters from all countries on the world market. But in doing so he becomes a millionaire; what a misfortune! Another man may improve the brewing of beer; his beer may be sold all over the world, and he himself may become a millionaire. A Midgards Serpent, A Midgards Serpent! (Monrad 1878, pp. 117–118).

Martensen's attitude to "modern Judaism" resulted in a heated debate, including both a long section devoted to this topic in Monrad's book, a separate book by the President of the Mosaic Religious Community, and several other significant written contributions. But before going further into this, it is important to recall that the context of debate at the time of Monrad and Martensen was very different from what it is in modern times. Today, any discussion of anti-Semitism is seen against the background of the Holocaust but, before the era of Nazism and Fascism, religion and race were discussed in a far more outspoken manner in social science. It is widely known that Max Weber found the reason for the success of the rich western market economies in the Calvinistic belief, and that Werner Sombart found it in Jewish religion. It was parts of this scientific debate that later went berserk and degenerated to Nazism and Fascism. It was perhaps also more relevant at that time – as in the quotation by Martensen – to link the financial sector and the Jews together. Jews had historically in many countries not had the right to own land, and thus been forced to keep their assets in cash and securities, whereas their local non-Jewish

---

[7] The Midgard Serpent is a famous monster from the Nordic mythology.

compatriots could invest their fortune in land and property. In the context of the time, many of those who, like Martensen, were critical in respect to the modern monetary economy also took a critical view of the Jews. This is very clearly demonstrated, for instance, by the Danish professor in Economics, L.V Birck, see Kærgård (1997). D.G. Monrad goes to the opposite extreme:

> When you consider the very low number of Jews and compare this with the number that have gained influence and reached important positions in society, one can only admire the superiority of the Jewish nation. It is now more than eighteen centuries since Jerusalem was captured, the Jewish state destroyed and the Jews scattered around the world in a diaspora, but still a Jewish nation exists. Is this not remarkable? When we see it, do we not with our own eyes behold a miracle? How did it come about? – Because the Jews were God's chosen people. When God's only begotten Son took human form, he also took a nationality. Which nationality? The Jewish. Therefore, I esteem the Jewish nation so highly. (Monrad 1878, p. 160)

9.6 Monarchy and Universal Suffrage

Outside the sphere of economics, the two Bishops also collided in their opinions on democracy. They lived at a time when Denmark was in the midst of constitutional struggles. The absolute monarchy had only been abolished for just over two decades and it was still a highly controversial issue whether the King or the Parliament should have the right to appoint the Government. Martensen was inclined to see democracy as another manifestation of the individualism and the liberalism that he regarded with so much scepticism:

> Universal suffrage relies on the assumption that the state is only a collection of atom-like individuals, rather than an organic system composed of interlinked limbs and members. Under such conditions, it is completely random whether their elected representative will be chosen from the ranks of the best qualified and the best informed, or from the ignorants, it will be completely a matter of chance whether all the interests of the people will be taken care of – whether they concern the different classes material well-being, art, science, the Church, or the best interests of the poor and of the unskilled workers. (Martensen 1878, pp. 235–236).

For Martensen, Monarchy is the ideal form of government:

> The position is completely different if one starts from principle of an organism, from a well-coordinated system of a body with limbs and members totally organized and with linkages both upwards and downwards. Here the Monarch represents the final point of unification not belonging to any specific class. But exactly because of his superior and exalted position, he can act and protect all groups of society, and can take care of all the interests of the classes in that society. (Martensen 1878, p. 242)

As the father of Denmark's first democratic and liberal constitution, Monrad is of course a warm advocate of democracy. Monrad's point of view is an early version of the later by the politician Viggo Hørup made famous "Divide yourselves according to your points of view". In the democracy there is for him something more important than rank and class:

The Merchant has disappeared, coffee and sugar are no longer traded, the Councillor of State has become invisible, only political opinions remain. We are uplifted from the world of civic society with all its classes and corporations, businesses and dealings, to the World of politics, which is organized in a completely different way. (Monrad 1878, pp. 91–92)

9.7 Other Participants in the Debate

The two great personalities presented their views profound and clearly, as already discussed, but their elevated position constrained them from engaging in a continuing public debate. Martensen never responded to the objections to his books. Both men were at the end of their careers, so public debate was something they handed over to their students and followers. Nevertheless, an important and interesting debate continued in subsequent years.

Almost all major newspapers and a number of journal and magazines carried reviews and comments. Some of the more profound comments were also published as books and pamphlets. Besides Monrad's book, there were a number of other significant contributions, and Martensen's contributions continued to exert their influence for many years to come.

At that time, there were only two Professors of Economics in Denmark, N.C. Frederiksen (1840–1905) and William Scharling (1837–1911), both at the University of Copenhagen. Both were liberal, market-oriented economists, and both had a political career as Member of the Parliament, representing Liberal or Conservative points of view.

N.C. Frederiksen published already in 1875 a "donner und blitz" review of Martensen's pamphlet in the Danish Economic Journal (*Nationaløkonomisk Tidsskrift*). Frederiksen was the most liberal of all Danish economists of the nineteenth century, so there was nothing surprising in this 20-page article. The arguments are very similar to Monrad's from 1878, and it seems reasonable to assume that Monrad and Frederiksen had discussed the topic. N.C. Frederiksen was Monrad's Son-in-law (Frederiksen, 1875). William Scharling published his review in the Danish Conservative party's main newspaper "Dagbladet"; the newspaper of the upper class in Copenhagen, and was critical, as one might well expect (Scharling, 1875).

More interesting is a review by the young economist Marcus Rubin (1854–1923) (Rubin, 1874). He later became Head of Statistics Denmark (1869–1902), of the Danish tax system (1902–1913) and finally of the Danish Central Bank (1913–1923). He was also the first economist to become a member of the Royal Danish Academy of Science. He was in 1874 a left wing oriented young Jewish economist and his review was rather positive. We still have his exchange of letters with another young Jewish intellectual David Simonsen (1853–1932), Chief Rabbi of Denmark 1892–1902 (Rerup, 1963). They had a very unprejudiced discussion of many things, including Martensen's discussion of the role of the Jews in the economy, and Simonsen suggest that Rubin write a Doctoral dissertation on the Jews in the world economy.[8]

Other reviews worthy of mention include one by Frederik Nielsen (1846–1907) in a Danish Church magazine (*Dansk Kirketidende*). Frederik Nielsen became Professor in Ecclesiastical History at University of Copenhagen a few years later, and subsequently (1900) Bishop of Aalborg. He is rather positive and his research as Professor deals inter alia with the social ethics of the Catholic Church, where attitudes resemble those penned by Martensen.

Other more profound contributions appeared. The theologian Frederik Vilhelm Andersen (1820–1910), priest, External Censor in Theology at the University of Copenhagen, and Ph.D. in Theology, published in 1879 a book of 200 pages on Martensen's social ethics (Andersen, 1879). He was a faithful follower of Martensen and his support was unconditional. Another of Martensen's pupils, Johannes G. E. Kok (1821–1887), priest and linguist, also published a book with 21 letters about Martensen's ethics and replies to his opponents (Petræus, 1878).

The Chief Rabbi of Denmark, A.A. Woeff (1801–1891), published a large volume giving the other side of the debate, with a reply to the latest attack on the Jews and on Judaism.

Some of the other most prominent members of Danish society did also participate in the debate. The politician and poet Carl Ploug (1813–1894) wrote in the main national-liberal newspaper "Fædrelandet" (Ploug, 1874 and 1879). The philosopher Harald Høffding (1843–1931), already a star in his discipline and later a dominating professor with a unique career in Danish science and society, wrote in the magazine "Nær og Fjern" (The same magazine in which Rubin published his review).

There was clearly an intensive debate in connection with the publication of Martensen's 1874-pamphlet and his 1878-epos on social ethics. But there were also long-term effects of the publications. Martensen's contributions were well known to the active participants in the early creation of the Danish welfare state. A person of some importance in these ranks was Fernando Linderberg (1854–1914). He came from a poor family, and was trained as a gardener. In 1880, he read Martensen's "*Socialisme og Christendom*" and this affected him for the rest of his life. He himself became teacher at a Folk High School in 1880, and from 1888 he tried with some success to establish a Christian labour union for farm labourers. Linderberg joined later the Social Democratic Party and his Christian farm labour union became also part of the mainstream labour movement. He worked together with the economist Professor Harald Westergaard to establish an organisation for the dissemination of information about social problems and started in 1901a new organisation with a journal called *Samfundets krav* (The claim of Society), which continued after his death (about Westergaard and this cooperation see Andersen 2012; Kærgård 1997; Kærgård and Davidsen 1998). Linderberg later published a considerable number of books about Christianity and social development.

---

[8] The expression "a donner und blitz review" about Frederiksen's contribution is taken from Rubin.

Perhaps the main architect of the Danish welfare state is K.K Steincke (1880–1963). He was a Minister in the Social Democratic Governments of 1924–26 and 1929–1939, and Speaker of the 2nd Chamber of the Danish Parliament from 1948–50 and again from 1951–52. He is mainly known for the perhaps most important reform of the Danish social system in 1933, when he was Minister of Social Affairs. If one man shall be mentioned as the Father of the modern Danish welfare state he is obvious a serious candidate. And his relation to Christian socialism is clear. He was strongly inspired by Fernando Linderberg, – see Christiansen (1998, pp. 38–42). Some of his typical remarks were: "Had there never been any Christianity in the world, there would never have been any socialism". And he openly said: "I have always said my Lord's Prayer whatever life has been for me and so I intend to continue;" see Bomholt (1963, p. 44).

9.8 Conclusion

H.L. Martensen's and his debate with D.G. Monrad is interesting for at least two reasons. First, it is the most thorough debate in Denmark among Christians about what the attitude to social issues should be. Is it a Christian duty to fight for the weak and poor, or should Christianity leave it to the politicians to address social questions? Never before or since have these questions been so intensively debated among so prominent leaders of the Danish church.

Secondly, there seems to run a causal chain from Martensen to the establishment of the modern welfare state. Not, perhaps, a clear and dominating track, but never the less one of the many threads that were woven together into the fabric that formed the Danish welfare state. The influence brought on this from H.L. Martensen to Fernando Linderberg and from Linderberg to K.K. Steincke is well documented, and if one man has to be named as the Father of the Danish welfare state, then K.K. Steincke must be amongst the absolute favourites.

References

Andersen, F.V. 1879. *Nogle Betragtninger og Studier over og i Sammenhæng med Biskop Martensens "Den Chr. Ethik"*. København: C.A. Reitzels Forlag.
Andersen, L.S. 2012. *Balancekunstneren: Harald Westergaard, kirkesagen og det sociale spørgsmål 1878–1907*. Odense: Syddansk Universitetsforlag.
Arildsen, S. 1932. *H.L. Martensen – Hans Liv, Udvikling og Arbejde*. København: G.E.C. Gads Forlag.
Bomholt, J. 1963. Ekstensialisten. In *K. K. Steincke Socialismens aristokrat*, ed. G. Munch, 36–46. Copenhagen: Stig Vendelkærs Forlag.
Christensen, J. 1998. *K. K. Steincke – Mennesket og politikeren: En biografi*. Copenhagen: Christian Ejlers Forlag.
Engelstoft, P. 1982. Ditlev Gothardt Monrad. *Dansk Biografisk Leksikon* 10: 45–53.

Frederiksen, N.C. 1875. H. Martensen: "Socialisme og Kristendom". *Nationaløkonomisk Tidsskrift* 5: 34–54.
Hauge, S. 1944. *Studier over D.G. Monrad som religiøs Personlighed*. København: G.E.C. Gads Forlag.
Kærgård, N. 1997. Tre økonomiske professorers teologi. *Kirkehistoriske Samlinger* 1997: 129–197.
———. 2018. H L Martensen og D. G. Monrad: To biskoppers økonomi. *Kirkehistoriske Samlinger* 2018: 132–178.
Kærgård, N., and T. Davidsen. 1998. Harald Westergaard: From young pioneer to established authority. In *European economists of early 20th century*, ed. W.J. Samuels, vol. 1, 349–365. Cheltenham: Edward Elgar.
Lein, B.N. 1980. Biskop Martensen og den etisk-kristelige socialisme. *Norsk Teologisk Tidsskrift* 81: 233–247.
Lindhardt, P.G. 1981. Hans Lassen Martensen. *Dansk biografisk Leksikon* 9: 445–450.
Martensen, H.L. 1874. *Socialisme og Christendom*. København: Den Gyldendalske Boghandel.
———. 1878. *Den Sociale Ethik, Den Christelige Ethik, Den Specielle Deel*. Vol. 2. København: Gyldendal.
Monrad, D.G. 1878. *Liberalismens Gjenmæle til Biskop Martensens sociale Ethik, Politiske Breve 14–18*. København: C.A. Reitzel.
Nørgaard, F. 1918. *D.G. Monrad – Et Levnedsløb, Udvalgt for Folkeoplysningens Fremme*. København: G.E.C. Gad.
Nyholm, A. 1947. *Religion og Politik. En Monrad Studie*. København: Nyt nordisk Forlag.
Petræus (J G E Kok). 1878. *Breve om Biskop Martensens kristlige Ethik samt om Dr. Wolffs og Biskop Monrads "Gjenmæler" imod samme*. Vol. 21. København: Gyldendalske Boghandels Forlag.
Ploug, C. (1874). Anmeldelse. *Fædrelandet*, 10. december.
———. (1879). Social og politisk Ethik, *Fædrelandet*, 14.–19. august og 27.–30. august.
Rahbek, J. 1955. *Breve fra og til Johanne Luise Heiberg II*. København: Gyldendal.
Rerup, L. 1963. *Marcus Rubins brevveksling 1870–1922*. Vol. I–IV. København: Rosenkilde og Bagger.
Rubin, M. (1874). Anmeldelse, *Nær og Fjern*, 29. november.
Scharling, W. (1875). "Nationaløkonomi og Socialisme" – Et Forsvarsindlæg imod Biskop, Dr. H. Martensens "Socialisme og Christendom". *Dagbladet*, 10.–11. februar.
Stewart, J., ed. 2012. *Hans Lassen Martensen – theologian, philosopher and social critic*. Copenhagen: Museum Tusculanum Press.
Svenstrup, T. 2000. Den etiske socialisme. Biskop Martensens samfundssyn i 1870'erne. In *Den nordiske protestantisme og velfærdsstaten*, ed. T. Knudsen, 98–123. Århus: Aarhus Universitetsforlag.

Niels Kærgård born 1942, since 1993 professor of agricultural economics and policy at University of Copenhagen. First chairman of the Danish Board of Economic Advisors 1995–2001. In the board of University of Copenhagen 2008–2013, vice-president of The Danish Academy of Science and Letters 2008–2013.

Chapter 10
K.E. Løgstrup's Ethics: Is There a Christian Alternative to Economics?

Niels Kærgård

Abstract There is a fundamental gap between a mainstream economics dealing with rational management of a society with selfish actors and economic incentives, and a Christianity appealing to peoples' virtue and ethics. The Danish theologian K. E. Løgstrup is one of the philosophers who has most thoroughly analysed this basic problem in a market economy. This article describes and discusses both the conflict and Løgstrup's position on it.

Keywords Ethical demand · Selfishness · Christian ethics · Economic incentives

10.1 Introduction: A Fundamental Dilemma

From the very beginning of economics, the discipline has been involved in a fundamental conflict with much of Christianity. Martin Luther writes in 1529 about the seventh commandment in his *Large Catechism*:

> To steal is to signify not only to empty our neighbour's coffer and pockets, but to be grasping in the market, in all stores, booths, wine- and beer-cellars, workshops, and, in short, wherever there is trading or taking and giving of money for merchandise or labour. (Triglot Concordia 1921)

The author thanks Svend Andersen, University of Aarhus, Jakob Wolf, University of Copenhagen, Jørn Henrik Petersen, University of Southern Denmark and Ole Jensen for valuable comments and suggestions in relation to earlier drafts of this chapter. The translation of the Danish quotations and general correction of the language is done carefully by Charles Woollen. A very earlier version has been presented at the Porvoo Seminar "Economics and Ethics" in Bad Boll, November 2014; the participants in this workshop has contributed with many useful comments. The responsibility for error or opinions is of course only the author's.

N. Kærgård (✉)
Department of Food and Resource Economics, University of Copenhagen,
Frederiksberg C, Denmark
e-mail: nik@ifro.ku.dk

Luther's point of view is further developed among other places in the short pamphlet *Von Kaufshandlung und Wucher* from 1524 where he spelled out the sinfulness of greed, of charging interest, of using shortages to inflate prices, and of almost all forms of business, see also Chaps. 16 and 17 in this book.

Adam Smith, the father of economics, had almost the opposite view. He is very positive towards profit maximisation and selfishness:

> It is not from the benevolence of the butcher, the brewer, or the baker that we expect our dinner, but from their regard to their own interest. We address ourselves, not to their humanity but to their self-love, and never talk to them of our own necessities, but of their advantages. (Smith 1776, Book I chapter 2)

If a commodity is scarce, the price goes up, and producers will see profit in producing more of it, whilst the opposite will apply if there is too much of a commodity. Adam Smith described the market mechanism as an invisible guiding hand. Most economists still subscribe to some version of Adam Smith's point of view, see Chap. 1 and 2 in this book.

Many Christians have been very sceptical towards this attitude, whilst others would leave the economy to the economists. In the 1870s in Denmark, there was a very interesting debate about these matters between the two leading bishops Hans L. Martensen and Ditlev G. Monrad, see Kærgård (2018) and Chap. 9 in this book. Martensen is very critical in relation to the market economy while Monrad saw the laws of the market as part of God's creation.

Knud Ejler Løgstrup (1905–1981) has in more recent times participated in this debate from a point of view close to Luther and Martensen. Løgstrup was professor at Aarhus University in ethics and philosophy of religion at the Theological Faculty 1943–1975 and one of the most influential philosophers and theologians in Denmark in the twentieth century. His entire writing is, however, originally written in Danish, only his main contributions are recently translated into German, and even fewer are published in English.[1] Consequently his international reputation has been limited. A number of Løgstrup's contributions and the translations to German and English were published after the death of Løgstrup in 1981.

Both Martensen and Løgstrup had, with their sceptical attitude to an uncontrolled market economy, an important role to play in relation to the Danish welfare state. Martensen was with his writing in the 1870s one of the pioneers in the struggle for better protection of the poor and weak, and has as such a considerable influence on

---

[1] Danish Theology is by tradition oriented towards Germany but some of Løgstrup's contributions are in both German and English. Løgstrup's, *Den Etiske Fordring* (1956) is in German *Die ethische Forderung*, (Tübingen: Mohr-Siebeck, 1968) and in English both *The Ethical Demand*, with introduction by Hans Fink and Alasdair MacIntyre, (Notre Dame: University of Notre Dame Press, 1997) and *Beyond the Ethical Demand*, with introduction by Kees van Kooten Niekerk, (Notre Dame: University of Notre Dame Press, 2007). His *Norm og Spontanitet – etik og politik mellem teknokrati og dilettantokrati* (1972) in German *Norm und Spontaneität*, (Tübingen: Mohr-Siebeck, 1989) and *Solidaritet og Kærlighed – og andre essays* (1972b) in German *Solidarität und Liebe*, in Christlicher Glaube in moderner Gesellschaft. Enzyklopädische Bibliothek Bd.16, (1982), pp. 97–128, Basel.

the very early development of the welfare state, see Kærgård (2018). Løgstrup has no direct influence on the development of the Danish society, but some of his formulations can be seen as perhaps the clearest formulation of the ideas behind the welfare model (Petersen and Petersen 2007). This chapter will summarise his contributions and compare them to modern economics.[2]

10.2 Løgstrup's Attitude and Methods

Løgstrup's method is to observe and interpret the immediate perception of the world; more intuitive than technical and scientific. He is part of the phenomenological tradition, and considers ethics as a pre-scientific consideration of the normative questions:

> Material ethics is a layman's interpretation of the views made by experts on behalf of laymen. Not the views of a dilettante, as the dilettante interferes in matters in which one needs to be expert to be able to comment on - - - The views of the experts are not - - -something we should just uncritically subscribe to. (Løgstrup 1972a/1993, p. 150)

Science is on the contrary seen as a reduction, setting aside feelings and immediate direct interpretations:

> The scientific approach to things is achieved through a reduction. Feelings and interpretations are laid aside – and with them, all the questions that go along with them and fill them out. (Løgstrup 1972a/1993, p. 115)

This description of science is not controversial. It is close to the first Nobel Prize winning economist Ragnar Frisch's description of the science of economics:

> In our minds we create a micro-cosmos for our personal use. A model of the World that is not more complicated than we can encompass within our field of view. And then we proceed to study this micro-cosmos instead of studying the real world. This little trick constitutes the rational approach to research. (Originally Frisch 1928–1929, see Bergh and Hanisch 1984, p.156. Translated from Norwegian)

But Frisch considered the more direct method of observation as "naive". He talked in his Nobel lecture about the historical and institutional economists, who had tried to observe objects in a more unfiltered way:

> These schools, however, had an unfortunate and rather naive belief in something like a "theory-free" observation. "Let the facts speak for themselves". The impact of these schools on the development of economic thought was therefore not very great, at least not directly. Facts that speak for themselves speak a very naive language. (Frisch 1971)

Løgstrup presented a parallel discussion of the relationship between direct observation and science, but he is considerably more positive towards the direct experience, and sees further limitations in the scientific method:

---

[2] Related problems are discussed in Danish in Kærgård (2001).

Selectively applied views of the immediate experience, which differ from scientific discipline to scientific discipline, develop as research progresses into a cohesive set of concepts, which continues to be refined, and which distances scientific research from immediate experience until, at the end of the day, they no longer share a common language of expression. (Translated from Løgstrup 1997, p. 159)

Pre-scientifically Løgstrup observed instead an interaction between different individuals. This observation is the main basis for his ethics:

> Through the trust that a person either shows or asks of another person, he or she surrenders something of his or her life to that person. Therefore, our existence demands of us that we protect the life of the person who has placed his or her trust in us. (Translated from Løgstrup 1997, p. 17)

or

> The demands made by ethics derive from the basic parameters according to which we must live, and which we cannot change, i.e. that the life of any individual is entwined with that of other individuals, in that it requires that we take care of the other's life, to the extent to which that life is delivered into our hands. (Translated from Løgstrup 1971, p. 211).

This entwinement results according to Løgstrup – as illustrated by the quotations – in an ethical demand, the title of his best-known book from 1956 is *Den etiske Fordring* ("The ethical demand"), Løgstrup (1956). This demand is according to Løgstrup silent, one-sided, radical and unrealizable. It is a demand which cannot be fulfilled, and which does not specify any specific action:

> It is self-evident that one person cannot speak to another person on behalf of the silent, radical, and one-sided demand and the claim that it can be fulfilled. We are not able to speak to one another on behalf of existence. (Løgstrup 1997, p. 207)

The ethical demand gives no advice or specification of how one best can take care of our fellow human beings:

> The radical demand arises out of the simple fact that one person is delivered over into the hands of another person. The demand gives no directions whatever on how the life of the person thus delivered is to be taken care of. It specifies nothing in this respect but leaves it entirely up to the individual. (Translated from Løgstrup 1997, p. 56)

Nevertheless, the ethical demand reflects an attitude that stresses interpersonal responsibility, in contrast to pure individualism.

10.3 Løgstrup, Charity, Justice and the Market

In contrast to the economists quoted before, K. E. Løgstrup considered human beings as having a spontaneous tendency to show confidence, mercy and sincerity towards other human beings. These "sovereign expressions of life" have since 1968 formed a main focal point of Løgstrup's philosophy, Løgstrup (1968). We have a spontaneous inclination to speak the truth, to believe in what other say, to help people in need, and to do other similar deeds. Calculation of own interest and more cynical considerations of risk and consequences can suppress these sovereign expressions, but they remain, never the less, a basic part of human nature. We do not consider other people only as competitors and instruments to use in our own interest. It is an important element behind ethics that we do not supress these positive elements in the interaction between people.

The sovereign expressions, and the fact that we have parts of other people's lives in our hands, motivated the ethical demand and the golden rule to "do unto others as you would have them do unto you". These rules introduce a role reversal. If I shall do the right things towards others, I have to be able to imagine myself in the other person's place (Løgstrup 1971/1996, pp. 52–53).

These abstract considerations of the situation seen from another point of view than one's own can be compared to John Rawls' analysis of a just income distribution, Rawls (1971). His discussion of justice has its starting point in the imagination of an abstract discussion of the just distribution of income, under conditions in which information about the participants' own occupation, ethnicity and education is hidden behind a veil of ignorance.

The conclusion of both Løgstrup's idea of role reversal and of Rawls' image of the veil of ignorance is to argue for a rather equal income distribution. If we do not know our own position or imagine ourselves in the others' place, only income differences motivated by unpleasant work, long education, risk full and responsibly work will be seen as acceptable. Such an approach is in contrast to the market mechanism's award of high wages to scarce types of labour, and to selfishness as the dominating motive for matching people and jobs.

Løgstrup does accept that the market mechanism is an effective method of allocation, but, like Luther and Martensen, he is critical to profit maximization, interpersonal competition and selfishness as the basic foundation of the economic system:

> Industrialisation, with its mass production, market expansion, and accumulation of capital as determinants of technical progress, provides a social justification for all the forms of economic manipulation that Luther had branded as unjust, wicked and greedy. They are so to speak ennobled as forms of competition without which the market mechanism cannot function. This does not, however, change the underlying motives of profit seeking, increased power, and the need for security - - - It is unacceptable that we should become so proud of our increased efficiency that we no longer question the mentality which we have enforced on each other in the name of efficiency. (Løgstrup 1972a/1993, pp. 218–219)

These appreciations of the human virtues are in contrast to the values behind the market mechanism, e.g. as formulated by Friedrich Hayek:

> The deliberate striving for the common good would distract you from doing what you are most suited for – using your particular knowledge of time and space – and so decrease the overall effectiveness of the system. Furthermore, with the complex division of labour we have today you cannot have an overview of what the common good is. (Hayek 1988)

It is important to stress that Løgstrup did not consider his conclusions as religious or political. He considered his conclusions as the results of a philosophical analysis of an immediate and direct observation of actual society, in which he found the entwinement between people and the sovereign expressions to be the basic characteristics. Løgstrup was writing in a secular society and at a secular university, so it is important for him to stress that his analyses are based on a philosophical and not a religious foundation. But he is also of the opinion that a religious interpretation of the results could be natural.[3]

It is worth mentioning that where the conflict between Løgstrup and traditional mainstream economics is obvious it is less obvious when the new "behavioural economics" is considered. Behavioural and experimental economics have become a fast growing part of economics in the last couple of decades. This school of economics is as Løgstrup sceptical to the rational calculating selfish homo oeconomicus. The catchphrase of this new part of economics is: "We economists analyses less in homo oeconomicus and more in homo sapiens than one or two decades ago". This is clearly formulated by the Swedish Academy of Science when they awarded the leading spokesman of behavioural economics, Richard Thaler, with the Nobel prize in economics in 2017:

> Economists aim to develop models of human behaviour and interactions in markets and other economic settings. But we humans behave in complex ways. Although we try to make rational decisions, we have limited cognitive abilities and limited willpower. While our decisions are often guided by self-interest, we also care about fairness and equity. Moreover cognitive abilities, self-control, and motivation can vary significantly across different individuals. (Kungl. Akademien 2017)

These ideas are obviously closer to Løgstrup's attitude than mainstream economics at his own time, and behavioural economics is today close to be included as an accepted modification of mainstream economics.

10.4 Løgstrup and the Danish Welfare State

Løgstrup start his discussion of society by a further development of the parable about the good Samaritan. When the Samaritan returned to his home, he began to think about the general problem of all these robberies on the road between Jerusalem and Jericho. What could be done about it? Perhaps a campaign should be started for more police? Now the initial sentiment of charity is transformed into an idea (Løgstrup 1971/1996, p. 53).

If the ethical demands are to be used as an idea, we must force people to act accordingly. If we want to construct a society that takes care of the weak and poor, we cannot base it on people's charitable sentiments:

> A realignment of society towards a more equitable distribution of income will force people to share out consumer goods amongst a greater number of recipients, as if the strong had

---

[3] K.E. Løgstrup and his pupils have sometimes been called "creation theologians" and their characteristic of the entwinement between people and between people and society seen as a result of the "creation", see Chap. 11 in this book. Others had developed a "natural law of justice" on a secular basis. The relation between the theology of creation and a natural law of justice is an interesting question – to what extent shall natural law be interpreted as a result of the creation? But such questions shall not be treated in this chapter.

come to love the weak, and ignores the fact that the strong will gnash their teeth over having a lower income in order to give a higher income to the weak. If we expect to invoke the principal of" Love thy neighbour", we will find that no one actually does, but that some people will be forced to behave as if they actually do. (Løgstrup 1971/1996, p. 54)

This can be considered as the basic idea behind the Danish Welfare State, where the public sector takes care of the poor, the sick and the senior citizens, and where the rich are forced to pay by progressive taxes, see e.g. Petersen (1996, 2004), Petersen and Petersen (2006, 2007), Andersen (2006) and Chap. 18 in this book.

It is important to stress that the welfare state is not an exclusively Christian idea. The Danish Social Democratic party has been a main force behind the development since the 1920's. Many of its members were atheists and the party as such has always been sceptical towards a close relationship between the state and the church. Never the less, there are official statements by the party which sound very similar to Løgstrup's. The Social Democratic economist Erling Olsen[4] writes about the history of his party:

A shared perception that all individuals are part of a community, with a shared responsibility for each other, has all along the line been a fundamental basis for the party. This is the moral message of Social Democracy. We will never leave people to look after themselves if they need help from society. That is why we created our Scandinavian welfare society. My point here is, that the Scandinavian Social Democracy movement has never just been an organisation to secure the economic interests of its member through the political institutions. It has also, and not least important, been a popular movement which sought to realise and implement some of the fundamental principles of Christianity, despite many of its members being atheists. (Translated from Olsen 1983, p. 35)

This welfare model was gradually developed from the late part of the nineteenth Century and until about 1970. Social security benefits were growing and available to bigger and bigger groups of people – and consequently taxation was also increasing. Initially, recipients of public support were subjected to non-economic consequences, such as the loss of voting rights, but all these stigmatizing consequences of support were gradually dropped. Around 1970 the model reached its most complete form where the rich paid high taxes and the poor got high social benefits without being subjected to any negative consequences. There were no limits on the period of entitlement to unemployment benefits etc. This was a "charity-model" where the weak got "something for nothing".

Since the oil crises 1973–74 it has been difficult to get the welfare model funded. The economy, so to say, strikes back and the welfare model has been modified since the 1970s. The period of entitlement to unemployment benefit is now limited to 2 years, and the amount paid in social benefits in relation to actual wage levels has been decreasing since the early 1970s. Income tax rates have also been reduced, and the debate on rights and duties has been reintroduced. Many politicians – including

---

[4]Erling Olsen (1927–2011), professor in economics University of Copenhagen 1970–1972, rector at University of Roskilde 1972–73. Member of the Danish parliament 1964–68, 1971–1973 and 1975–1998. Member of the government 1978–1982 and 1993–1994 and Speaker of the parliament 1994–1998.

some Social Democrats – stress that social benefits are for those who cannot work, and not for those who do not want to work. A stigmatization of social benefit recipients, and especially of immigrants, has reappeared, see Petersen (2014).

It seems likely that Løgstrup would have been very sceptical towards such a debate about "the worthy and the unworthy needy". He strongly stressed what he called a "cosmic equality"

> We can ask two questions of anything that is or of anything that happens: Does it have a purpose, and, if, so, what? – or is it without any purpose? Neither of these questions can be asked in connection with the existence of any human being. Humanity is too superior to become the vehicle of any purpose, and it is too superior to ever be regarded as having no purpose. The either-or concepts of "purposeful" or" with no purpose" cannot be applied to human beings. In short, there is no instrument capable of measuring the importance and value of a human being, and – in the absence of such an instrument – all human beings must be regarded of equal importance and value. This equality also needs to be given a name, and I propose we call it "cosmic equality". (Løgstrup 1997, p. 137)

Or perhaps even more specifically:

> If we allow the importance of a human being to become dependent on the contribution he or she makes to the common good, then contempt for the weak will become the norm by which we organise our society, and we may even go beyond contempt. No external instrument can be brought in from outside to measure the importance of an individual human being. In its essence, the human being exists exclusively for its own sake. It is not possible to regard a human being as the vehicle for a purpose that does not concern it. (Løgstrup 1972b/1993)

In these debates the clash between justice and charity on the one side, and economic efficiency on the other, become very apparent.

Løgstrup is aware that Christianity does not tell us how to organize society, but the Christian ethic gives us a criterion against which we can evaluate and test our society, see Løgstrup (1972b/1993, p. 135).[5]

It may not seem central to the argumentation in Løgstrup's contributions, but it is perhaps never the less worth mentioning, that Løgstrup himself came to the conclusion that the market economy had so many ethical drawbacks that he preferred some sort of a socialist economy.[6]

> If the understanding of democracy is based on equality and the abolition of privilege, then a socialist economy will harmonise better with democracy than a capitalist economy. In a socialist economy, the privileges secured by wealth will be eliminated by an equitable distribution of income and by the abolition of private ownership of the means of production from which incomes derive. (Løgstrup 1972a/1993, p. 267)

---

[5] Løgstrup would surely not have used the word "Christian ethics". He was very sceptical to what Christianity can tell us about more specified acting and saw his ethical demands as a result of the creation of the world, not as specific Christian, see e.g. Andersen (1997) and Jensen et al. (1972).

[6] Bishop Martensen had in the 1870s the same conclusion; also he (as discussed in Chap. 9) supported what he called "an ethical socialism" in contrast to both Marxism and Liberalism. Parts of his social ethics, Martensen (1878), was published in 1874 with the title, *Socialisme og Christendom*.

Such an evaluation should perhaps also be seen as a reflection of attitudes in academic circles in the years after 1968. The contributions of even the most groundbreaking authors are to some extent conditioned by the times in which they write, and this also applies to Løgstrup's works.

10.5 Løgstrup, Nature and the Environment

Another area in which the spontaneous sentiment of good and ethics clashes with economic efficiency is in relationship to nature and environment. Løgstrup does not accept a traditional economic point of view according to which pollution is a "normal" economic cost in all respects other than that it is a social cost not automatically paid for by the private firms, see Kærgård (1996, pp. 42–52) and chap. 2 and 3 in this book. He writes about pollution:

> Take the case of pollution. It is not enough just to ask whether pollution has already become too heavy and too threatening, seen as a social cost of production. Neither will it suffice just to discuss whether the cost of stopping pollution should be borne by the firm causing it or covered by public funds. The whole analysis needs to be turned around. The preservation of nature is a valid goal in itself, and one of the goals behind the need to have an economic system at all. - - - The goal of the economic system must be something other than an economic goal. The purpose of the economic system must be something non-economic. Otherwise economics will lose its meaning. (Translated from Løgstrup 1997, pp. 169–170)[7]

Løgstrup differentiates between economic goods produced for the market with the aim of earning money, and goods produced to satisfy basic needs. To him the satisfaction of basic needs is the only legitimate option whilst the economic system is only an instrument. The idea is that basic human needs are something pre-economic and different from economic goods. It is not trivial to analyse whether the difference this makes to economics is only a matter of formulation, or whether it represents a basic difference in attitude. A mainstream economist will not differentiate between non-economic needs and economics goods; he will see the economic prices only as a way of measuring the power of the needs, and it is uncontroversial to consider economics only as an instrument with which the satisfaction of human needs is maximized.

Løgstrup's point of view seems to be that some needs are so important and necessary for human life that it is meaningless to compare them with other (economic) needs. We cannot consider nature and animals only as economic goods, or as formulated by one of K.E.Løgstrup's pupils, Jakob Wolf:

---

[7] The point of view according to which nature must be taken care of before all economic priorities can be found already in a well-known quotation from the writing of Oluf Chr. Olufsen (1763–1827), one of the very first professors of economics at University of Copenhagen: "Why do a country need to be beautiful can a cattle dealer ask. Just because not all are cattle dealers" Oluf Chr. Olufsen, "Danmarks Brændselsvæsen physikalskt, cameralistiskt og oeconomiskt betragtet". (The Danish system of firewood physical, cameralistic and economic considered), Copenhagen, *BiblDan.II.1014* (1811).

> In our sensory perception of the matter of the world, we do not regard creatures of nature as objects, but rather as beings, and, as such, attach to them ethical standards requiring restraint, recognition, respect, and husbandry - - - It is, however, indisputable that we can behave just as shamelessly and harmfully towards animals and towards nature as we can towards our fellow human being. Precisely because the ethical demand is unspoken, it can also be expressed on behalf of animals without language. (Wolf 1997a, p. 130)

Some of Løgstrup's contributions are very marked by the times in which he lived and wrote. The "Limits to Growth"–debate was seen as actual and important whilst the global climate debate had still not yet really started. But his central message on a non-technical positive experience with nature and an unconditional respect for environment and animal has been followed by and given inspiration to a number of his pupils, especially Ole Jensen and Jakob Wolf see Jensen (1975, 1976/1992, 1980, 1994, 2011), (1997a, b, 2012) and chap. 11 in this book.

Compared to most of the recent debate among economists about bioethics, there are parallels and differences. The economists of today normally formulate responsibility in relation to nature and environment using the concept of "sustainability". Løgstrup stresses our responsibility in direct relation to nature, whereas sustainability stresses our responsibility in relation to future generations of human beings. To some extent the two viewpoints are in almost all practical respects parallel, but what economists call "weak sustainability" (i.e. the future generations' interests are satisfied by the substitution of "natural capital" by "manufactured capital" – the future generations get less nature but are compensate by e.g. more buildings) is in direct contrast to Løgstrup's viewpoint. But in many relations, e.g. in relation to the global climate debate, the interests of the future generation and the interests of nature are parallel, and without doubt the environment, nature and the biodiversity have become a more important part of economics than was the case at Løgstrup's time.

10.6 Summary and Conclusion

Løgstrup has an ethic that stresses respect for weak and poor human beings and for nature; an ethic based on direct observation and immediate experience of the real world. His conclusions are no doubt closely related to the attitude among many left-wing groups, but he was far from a supporter of the progressive and Marxian movements after 1968. He remained very critical of this movement, which he regarded as one of the more dominating revival movements he had come across during his lifetime.

He was also critical of Christians speaking loudly and unsubtly about Christian ideals. He preferred action and trustworthy analysis. He writes about some of the more direct political active Christian movements:

> Its supporters will elevate action to the same status as the Gospel for the work of the Church, and to place the Gospel at the service of the actions organised by the Church, they will begin to thin out the Gospels to such extent, that only the heaviest words will remain - - - The Kingdom of God has already been brought about without our assistance, so we no

longer need to worry at all about what eternity is made up of. Freed from these worries, we should thus even more so be able to remove the obstructions to a happy life on earth for those who today inhabit our planet, and for those who some day will come to inhabit it. But action and Gospel are not one and the same thing. (Løgstrup, 1972b/1993, pp. 65–66)

In his position as university professor he of course worked mostly with principal thoughts and with the clarification of concepts, but he had a pragmatic attitude to practical questions, so no doubt he accepted that politicians and decision makers have to compromise between ethical demands and practical economic considerations. In real life, a balance between economic efficiency and ideals is necessary.

But he would stress that pure pragmatism is far from enough. There are in the created world some basic structures that call for ethical demands which are more than simple rationality. He would never agree with his colleague professor Johannes Sløk, who does not see any alternatives to either a moral code revealed by a religious revelation (and this has according to Sløk become out-dated in a modern secular society) or rules calculated on the basis of pure rationality:

> My point is simply that which is already known, that problems cannot be discussed on a basis of moral-ethical concepts. The real problem is whether it is wise or stupid to do a particular thing, whether doing it will have a desirable or catastrophic outcome, and whether the problem is so acute, that it can be discussed in all due earnest. On this subject the independent human being has shown himself to be a dangerous figure, precisely because no overriding ethical instance can impose a powerful prohibition. Mankind is left to its own devices, with its own creativity and wisdom; it can no longer pass the blame on to outside authorities, but must bear the heavy burden on its own shoulders---In all fields of life, moral norms have been replaced by the rules of wisdom. (Sløk 1993, pp. 138–139)

On the contrary, to Løgstrup it is possible to deduce ethical rules that are well founded in secular philosophical reasoning and on careful observation of the real world. These rules can, however, also easily be interpreted in terms of religion.

References

Andersen, S. 1997. Om der gives en kristelig etik?. In *Kamp må der til – Engagementets brydning mellem åbenhed og tradition*, ed. Niels H. Brønnum, Erling Christiansen, Lars Paludan, and Jakob Wolf, 147–156. Hadsten: Forlaget Mimer.
———. 2006. Religion og social sammenhæng – Kristendommen og den moderne vedfærdsstat – Et teologisk perspektiv. *Religionsvidenskabeligt Tidsskrift* 48: 25–34.
Bergh, T., and T.J. Hanisch. 1984. *Vitenskap og Politik – Linjer i norsk sosialøkonomi gjennom 150 år*. Oslo: Aschehoug.
Frisch, R. 1971. *From utopian theory to practical applications: The case of econometrics*. Oslo: Nobel lecture.
Hayek, F.A. v. 1988. The fatal conceit. In *The collected works of F.A. Hayek*, ed. W.W. Bartley. Chicago: Chicago University Press.

Jensen, O. 1975. *Theologie zwischen Illusion und Restriktion. Analyse und Kritik der existenzkritizistischen Theologie bei Wilhelm Hermann und bei Rudolf Bultmann*. München: Chr Kaiser Verlag.

———. 1976/1992. *I vækstens vold – økologi og religion*. Copenhagen: Gyldendal.

———. 1980. *Frem til naturen og andre essays*. Copenhagen: Fremad.

———. 1994. *Sårbar usårlighed, Løgstrup og religionens genkomst i filosofien* Copenhagen: Gyldendal.

———. 2011. *På kant med klodens klima*. Copenhagen: Anis.

Jensen, O, P. Widmann, and K.E. Løgstrup. 1972. *De store ords teologi*. Copenhagen: Gyldendal.

Kærgård, N. 1996. Økologi, etik og økonomerne. *Økonomi & Politik* 69 (2): 42–52.

———. 2001. Løgstrups etik og økonomiens morale. In *Kritik af den økonomiske fornuft*, eds. C. Fenger-Grøn and J.E. Kristensen. Copenhagen: Hans Reitzels Forlag.

———. 2018. H. L. Martensen og D. G. Monrad: to biskoppers økonomi. *Kirkehistoriske Samlinger* 2018 (2018): 132–178.

Kungl. Akademien. 2017. *Richard Thaler's contribution to behavioural economics*. The Sveriges Riksbank Prize in Economic Sciences in Memory of Alfred Nobel 2017, Advance information. https://www.nobelprize.org/prizes/lists/all-prizes-in-economic-sciences.

Løgstrup, K.E. 1956. *Den Etiske Fordring*, used version. Copenhagen: Gyldendal, 1991.

———. 1968. *Opgør med Kierkegaard*, used version. Copenhagen: Gyldendal, 1994.

———. 1971. Etiske begreber og problemer. In *Etik og Kristen tro*, ed. Gustaf Wingreen. Copenhagen: Gyldendal. The article later published as the book *Etiske begreber og problemer*. Copenhagen: Gyldendal, 1996.

———. 1972a. *Norm og Spontanitet – etik og politik mellem teknokrati og dilettantokrati*; used version. Copenhagen: Gyldendal, 1993.

———. 1972b. *Solidaritet og Kærlighed – og andre essays*. Copenhagen: Gyldendal, 1993.

———. 1997. *System og symbol*. Copenhagen: Gyldendal. The manuscript written but not published before K.E. Løgstrup's death in 1981.

Martensen, H L (1874), *Socialisme og Christendom*. Copenhagen: Den Gyldendalske Boghandel.

Martensen, H.L. 1878. *Den Sociale Ethik*, Den Christelige Ethik, Den Specielle Deel, Vol. 2. Copenhagen: Gyldendal.

Olsen, E. 1983. Den disciplinerede Keynes. *Økonomi & Politik* 57: 1.

Petersen, J.H. 1996. Værdier og interesser i socialpolitikken. *Politica* 28 (4): 440–452.

———. 2004. Velfærdsstatens krav til dig!. In *13 udfordringer til den danske velfærdsstat*, ed. J.H. Petersen and K. Petersen. Odense: Syddansk Universitetsforlag.

———. 2014. *Pligt & Ret – Ret & Pligt: Refleksioner over den socialdemokratiske idéarv*. Odense: Syddansk Universitets Forlag.

Petersen, J.H., and L.H. Petersen. 2006. Næstekærlighed og velfærdsstat. In *13 værdier bag den danske velfærdsstat*, ed. J.H. Petersen, K. Petersen, and L.H. Petersen. Odense: Syddansk Universitetsforlag.

———. 2007. Gensidig eller ensidig? Om Løgstrups etiske fordring og den danske velfærdsstats normative grundlag. In *Livtag med Løgstrup*, ed. D. Bugge and P. Aaboe Sørensen. Aarhus: Forlaget Klim.

Rawls, J. 1971. *A theory of justice*. Chambridge: Harvard University Press.

Sløk, J. 1993. *Moralen der blev væk*. Copenhagen: Forlaget Centrum.
Smith, A. 1776. *An inquiry into the nature and causes of the wealth of nations*. London: Methuen & Co. (a huge number of later reprints).
Triglot Concordia. 1921. *Triglot Concordia: The symbolic books of the Ev. Lutheran church*, 565–773. St. Louis: Concordia Publishing House.
Wolf, J. 1997a. *Etikken og Universet*. Copenhagen: Anis.
———. 1997b. Natur og etik. In *Kamp må der til – Festskrift tilegnet Ole Jensen*, 36–50. Hadsten: Mimer.
———. 2012. *Det ubevæbnede øje – essays om fænomenologi, videnskab, økologi og teologi*. Copenhagen: Anis.

Niels Kærgård born 1942, since 1993 professor of agricultural economics and policy at University of Copenhagen. First chairman of the Danish Board of Economic Advisors 1995–2001. In the board of University of Copenhagen 2008–2013, vice-president of The Danish Academy of Science and Letters 2008–2013.

Chapter 11
Reading Genesis 1.28 with a Plea for Planetary Responsibility

Ole Jensen

Abstract The market economy and economic growth have been important reasons for the sixth mass extinction of species and the climate crisis looming ahead. The fundamental cause of this is the prevalence of an anthropocentric perspective on life, according to which mankind has a right to exploit nature and other species to its own advantage in furtherance of its own development. This perception has its roots in an interpretation of the Judeo-Christian account of the Creation given in Genesis 1:28. This interpretation is, however, one-sided and open to dispute, and this article will propose an alternative, based on a broader, more comprehensive reading including other verses in Genesis.

Keywords Anthropocentrism · Interpretation of genesis · Mass extinction · Climate crisis

11.1 A One-Sided Interpretation of Genesis 1:28, Seen from a History of Ideas Perspective

Mankind has become such a strong factor in the historical development of the Planet that it not only is capable of causing its own extinction as a species – as dinosaurs once were made extinct by the impact of meteors – but seems already well on the way to doing so. Since the onset of the modern industrial era, mankind has been on an ever-increasing collision course with the natural basis for having a life on an inhabitable planet. Hence the term the Anthropocene era.

O. Jensen (deceased)
Hurup Thy, Denmark
e-mail: ojensen@hotmail.com

A veritable – and irreversible – massacre of other life forms than our own is unfolding before our eyes.[1] Large climate-based ecosystems such as the tropical rainforests, the weather, and the atmosphere are encroached upon or violently disturbed likewise irreversibly. The ice will continue to melt at the Poles, and the permafrost will continue to thaw under the tundra for a further half – or even whole – century, even if the most alluring dreams are transformed into reality, such as, for example, the EU's dream of achieving carbon-neutrality by 2050. And who knows what new challenges might be lying in wait on the other side of the Corona pandemic? Perhaps insidious vira are lying in wait in our pork breeding stock, or prehistoric vira might resurface as the tundra thaws? How can we really be sure about anything that might happen once the current "plague" is over? Furthermore, this whole process is evolving at an ever-increasing pace, as demonstrated by the German sociologist Harmut Rosa (2013). The question arises – inter alia – of the role of the element of expansive growth that is intrinsic to a liberal market economy.

The main reason that things have reached this point is a seldom recognised, and even less frequently acknowledged in public, *perception of nature* based on two extremely questionable assumptions: The *first* being that the sole purpose of nature is to serve mankind as a means to our development and growth, and the *second* being that mankind has a right to do with nature whatever it can get away with. This perception is the common denominator for almost everything that society does with an impact on nature, be it in terms of economic activity, means of production, transport, housing, level of consumption, or individual lifestyle aspirations. The common denominator is purely and simply *speciesism* – the egocentricity of human species.

An even less well-known aspect is that this perception of nature has its *roots* in the Bible. Current social functions are reflecting *a very specific and one-sided interpretation* of verse 28 in the first chapter of the Bible. The verse reads: "And God blessed them, and God said unto them, be fruitful, and multiply, and replenish the earth, and subdue it: and have dominion over the fish of the sea, and over the fowl of the air, and over every living thing that moveth upon the earth." (The King James Bible).

The interpretation of verse 28 behind this perception of nature is exclusively focused on the wording "to *subdue* the Earth" and "*have dominion* over" (author's italics) the animals which is taken as a permission, or even as a binding duty (possibly with a humanitarian purpose), theologically called "a mandate to rule", respectively "stewardship". Such interpretation rigidly ignores other elements present in the same Chapter of the Bible, which might have disturbed the overall perception, had they been taken into account.

Our Western cultural norms, which have found favour almost all around the globe, have to a surprising degree kept alive this biblically based concept of permission and/or duty, despite the concept of a transcendent God of Creation as the entity

---

[1] Species death occurs between 10 and 1000 times as fast as what evolutionary ecologists call "natural species death" Pimm et al. (1995). About the sixth mass extinction see also Barnosky et al. (2011).

giving permission or imposing duty having been lost along the way, leaving the two basic assumptions of the perception of nature without legitimacy.

The resulting situation is both peculiar and precarious. Mortal rulers – such as Mao, Stalin, Pol Pot, Hitler, and others – have seized power to fill the vacuum of legitimacy, giving their own very terrestrial, relative and particular interests a status similar to the one that was originally given by a transcendent authority and demanding a similar absolute subjection to them. They became usurpers, demiurges, self legitimating demigods. At the present time – instead of tyrannical dictators – it is our unfettered and potentially suicidal perception of nature and our pillaging of natural resources that has moved in to fill the vacuum and lay claim to legitimacy. Theologians have, as a general rule, shown a shameful lack of awareness of the current situation.

11.2 Selected Milestones Along the Path of the One-Sided Interpretation

The way a statement is interpreted by others will always be conditioned by the obvious but often subliminal background context in which it is received. Society in biblical times was *feudal* with a hierarchical structure based on master and serf/servant/slave relationships. The lord and master had "dominion", i.e., the power of life and death, over his subjects. It was, however, probably implicitly presumed that he also had a duty of care to provide for, as a minimum, their basic needs, both in his own interests and in theirs. Such an idea of a duty of care is introduced in Genesis Chapter 2, verse 15: "And the Lord God took the man and put him into the garden of Eden to dress it and keep it" – in the same way as a gardener would cultivate and care for his garden. This makes it relevant to discuss "a mandate to care" as a counterweight to "the mandate to rule". It does not, however, alter the basic idea that mankind has an unlimited "right to rule" over that which he has been made responsible for, in casu the Planet and its natural resources. And the one-sided interpretation of Genesis 1:28 completely ignores any concept of a duty of care.

On the whole, the Old Testament is pervaded by a sense that life before death is well worth living (Lundager Jensen, 2001, pp. 17–21). God's good, created world is gifted mankind as a place in which it is possible to have a" blessed" life. This is well in tune with the concept of a duty of care. In the Hellenistic Era – from around 300 B.C. to 300 A.D. – however, an opposing ethos was gaining a foothold in the Mediterranean region. These were times of change and brought in a longing for an escape from the misery of the mortal coil.

The Danish historian of religion Vilhelm Grønbech (1873–1948) used the analogy of a pilgrim in progress towards a new destination to depict the new ethos (Grønbech, 1952). The" *myth of the pilgrim"* view was so radically marked by a longing for the life after death that the life before death came to be seen as a preliminary state, in which the soul is trapped in the prison of the mortal flesh and longs for death to release it as a pure unfettered spirit, so that it may return "home" to an apathetic "god", who has neither any relationship to, nor any feeling for, the material world. The spiritual world and the material world – in Latin mundus intelligibilis and mundus sensibilis – are seen as being in opposition to each other (dualism). Various so-called Gnostic sects, some of them "Christian", competed to prescribe how one should behave to reach the promised state. This is also known as "Gnostic dualism".

Theology had to battle to protect the Old Testament's tenet of the goodness of the created and material world. A strong example is the Synod of Nikæa in 325 which formulated the First Article of the Apostles' Creed, in which "the creator of Heaven and Earth is called "God the *Father*"; a further example is that several of the great theologians of the ancient church are known as "the antignostic fathers.""

There is no place for such things in popular religious observance. Instead, prominence is given to the idea that salvation must be earned by doing good deeds, and, not least, by renouncing worldly pleasures. This religious interpretation was predominant in popular religious beliefs throughout the Middle Ages, with Martin Luther as its decisive theological buffer stop. He held that the Grace of God is an undeserved gift. And he praised daily life "in state and calling" as an alternative to the escapism of dualism.

After the Renaissance, however, the religious devaluation of sensuous life was given a materialistic pendant in that nature and natural beings were reduced to being just resources placed at the free disposition of mankind. A prime example is found in the works of the Age of Enlightenment philosopher René Descartes. In his renowned treatise *Discours de la méthode*, published in 1637, he claimed that sciences "can make us the masters and the owners of Nature!"

Descartes´ choice of the words "masters" and "owners" refers without a doubt directly to the words "dominion" and "subdue" used in Genesis 1:28, with all of its force concentrated on the raw mastery of nature, which is understood as an undertaking sanctioned by the Creator, or even imposed by Him as an obligation. As the concept of the "death" of God crept in over the next couple of centuries, it gradually washed away the transcendental legitimacy and the biblical origin of the "mandate to rule" – as discussed above.

This brings us up to the tragic actual end of the history of the one-sided interpretation. The mandate to rule with no regard for those being ruled has quite concrete turned into a "license to kill". The massacre of species in modern times is the clearest possible expression of this (see note 1). Hand in hand with this goes global warming and other catastrophic consequences.

11.3 Reasons Supporting the One-Sided Interpretation

Mankind is *an exception* in the natural world. Mankind is cognisant of its own existence, of the existence of everything else, and of itself as a self/a person. The idea of Man "created in *the image of God*" (Genesis 1:27; author's italics.) is based on these central perceptions.

In addition, the one-sided interpretation of Genesis 1:28 is supported, to a certain extent, by the most fundamental aspect of Genesis 1 – *biblical monotheism*. Ancient Israel was surrounded by neighbouring cultures in which nature was inhabited by divine entities, whom it was extremely important not to offend. They were animists or pantheists. In the biblical account of the Creation, God has "moved out" of nature. In his capacity of the Creator of the Universe differs his own 'being' from that of the universe, he has created. He occupies an Outside, called Heaven or transcendence. And he was 'there' before the Universe created by him came into being. And as an indivisible entity – the one God (Greek: monos theos) – everything holy and divine is assembled within him, and thus not present in the created Universe. In the Babylonian account of the Creation, the Moon and the Stars were deities; in Genesis, they are relegated to just being useful as night-time illumination or as points of reference for a calendar (Genesis 1:14–18).

All this is revolutionary. *Nature becomes secularised*. It can be explored and taken in use without needing the approval of shady dark forces, spirits, or gods, who demands "protection money" in the form of invoking rituals and sacrifices. "Development" has become a possibility. The same chain of thought led to the concept that time is lineal, rather than cyclic as believed by the natural religions – and to the perception of "progress" towards something better. "Humanism", the improvement of the human condition, became a possible aspiration. A reduction of the naturally available resource base to being means only to our (presumably noble) ends becomes an attractive possibility, especially if combined with the one-sided interpretation of verse 28: "to subdue and have dominion over" becoming obligatory in the pursuit of humanism.

An important aspect that should not be neglected is the extent to which the elementary "*fight for survival*", until very recently has been a determining factor in the history of mankind. The power in the relation between Nature and Mankind has, in all previous centuries, overwhelmingly been in favour of Nature, and still is so for the billions of people living under less-favoured conditions than our own.

11.4 The Shift of Power in the Mankind-Nature Relation

Additionally, many centuries had passed before Mankind's use of all its possibilities to exclusively further the sake of its own species became catastrophic. Environmental disaster is not a new phenomenon. The cedar trees in Lebanon, mentioned in the Bible, were felled by the Phoenicians, long time before the writings of The Old

Testament were collected to one book. Forest clearance in ancient times in the Himalayas is a contributory factor to the recurrence of spring floods in Bangladesh; forests, if left to stand, soak up huge amounts of water from the atmosphere which, if not sequestered, would otherwise result in flooding. Such intrusions were, however, only local and with limited impact, so long as the power in the Mankind-Nature relation remained in favour of Nature.

That was the case roughly until the invention of the steam engine some 200 years ago. This invention suddenly made it possible for Mankind to consume more energy each year than Nature could replace by the natural cycle of growth and regeneration. Then came the discovery of the huge reserves of carbon-based energy resources ´waiting´, after millions of years, to be mined or pumped to the surface (Kjærgaard 1991). Mankind is ecstatic, in an almost unbelievably child-like and carefree state of excitement, and proceeds unrestrainedly to retrieve and use these resources, presupposing that "we are fully entitled to do so", and convincing themselves of "what harm can it do, anyway?" – and so demonstrating the self legitimation mentioned above. There is a refusal to face the obvious, that *the balance of power has been tipped over in favour of Mankind* – from then on enabling us to disrupt the large climate-based ecosystems irreversibly. It would take nearly a further two centuries for this obvious conclusion to take root in the minds of men – and, even then, only in a minority some of them understood it – by which time it is far too late to redress the balance, but only still possible to delay the impact of some of the more dramatic outcomes by a few short years. The Artic continue to melt, and the tundra continues to thaw.

As if this was not already enough, yet another powerful factor delays the recognition of the gravity of the situation. Over-intensive exploitation of natural resources is argued to serve a noble purpose: The reduction of *human* suffering. This argument is, for instance, a central justification proffered for the welfare state model. As long as one is able to close ones' eyes to the fact that Nature is bleeding in pace with the rate of improvement in human conditions, there is no reason to feel guilty about continuing to give artificial respiration to this fatal course of events for a while longer. This mindset is made possible by the speciesist concept, humanism, that unchallenged and unacknowledged, is the primus motor behind what appears to pass for a policy on nature and climate in our highly developed Northern countries, see also Jensen (1976, 2011).

The author of this chapter must, at a very personal level, concede that it is this very speciesist humanism, expressed through a toweringly highly developed and extremely cost-effective public health system that keeps him (born in 1937) alive, cost what it will in terms of global resources! Objectively, the most beneficial course of action he could take to benefit the Planet and his descendants would be to just lie down and die – which gesture he has no intention of making.

The same dilemma came into renewed focus during the Corona pandemic, which a couple of health economists had the audacity to classify as a problem of Economics. Strictly speaking, it goes much deeper. It represents the dilemma between Mankind's' self-given species-based state of exemption, legitimated by humanism, contra the preservation of the Planet as a sustainable habitat for Mankind.

11.5 What the One-Sided Interpretation Ignores

The remainder of this article will approach the subject matter from a different angle. It will attempt to open up a new theological perspective by calling attention to other relevant biblical material, that has been ignored so far. The one-sided nature of the interpretation of verse 1:28 as discussed, is beyond dispute. It can only persist if one continues to ignore other disturbing factors, such as the extent to which nature suffers under the yoke of speciesism.

If taken as a way to describe basic existential life conditions, the first chapters of the Bible seem impressively realistic. It begins in Chapter 1 and 2 by describing life's good gifts. In Chapter 3, and with no apparent explanation, the forces of evil suddenly enter the narrative; both the evil in the heart of each and every individual (which is called sin), and the evil to be found in the natural world (suffering, the need to fight for survival, and death). The evil contradicts the good, but does not deny it. Evil only exists spreading destruction. It appears *"after"* the good, drawing succour from its negation of the good. It is a parasite on the good. The "before" and "after", however, is here in the Bible an order of succession rooted in a mythical mindset. Its wisdom reveals if we instead of a succession regard it as a *hierarchy of status or precedence* in which the good outranks the evil. The good is the fundamental element, the evil an inexplicable destructive force which draws its sustenance from the good and is dependent on it as an object for its destructivity. The imagery of a *fall* is telling: Something can be said to fall only if there already is something else present for it to fall down from; in this case, the created goodness of being, as depicted in Genesis 1 and 2, which in mythical time precedes Genesis 3, where evil makes its entrance. This hierarchy of status does not, however, to put it mildly, come through in the one-sided interpretation of verse 1:28.

If we look holistically at Chapter 1, we should not fail to discover other unnoticed and ignored facets of the events which took place in the mythical period preceding the creation of Mankind. These are not just bagatelles but of epic dimensions.

Crucial aspects which have been unnoticed and ignored include even the basic miracle of *being* (Genesis 1:1) and *filling* (1:2): That a 'something' – being – occurs and fills up the former "void". It would be tempting to quote the Danish poet Johannes V. Jensen (1873–1950), who rejected Christian faith but adored Nature. He was awarded the Nobel Prize in Literature in 1944 and delivered his subsequent Speech of Acceptance in the form of an extended poem entitled "Jorden og lyset" (The Earth and the Light), from which the following quote is taken: "An almighty series of *tangible* miracles is the world, a fountain of joy" (1954, p. 323; author's italics.). The poem praises these natural phenomena in their external material filling, and the miraculous in them has nothing to do with any intangible spirituality. You can touch them and find them moveable or immovable. Qua their joyful tangibility, they live up to the Creator's judgement passed on the evening of the Day of Creation, when God looked upon what he had made and "saw that it was good"– almost as if he had been unsure of the outcome of his labours. Take good note of this, as it shows how, in ancient Israel, God is a god receptive to sense impression.

Also unnoticed and ignored is that the creation of Cosmos and Nature takes up the ample time of five "days" – compared to the poor, single, late sixth day (Genesis 1:26 ff.) needed for the creation of Mankind. That which the Creator "saw" and found "good" during the five first, long "days" was the exterior material world, as yet "untouched by the hand of Man". The reader in modern times will be struck by the extent to which the biblical sequence of creation resembles the sequence proposed later on by evolution theorists. Substituting the word *"ages" or "eons" for the word "days"* reveals a new relevance of the biblical account for the contemporary reader. Mankind is a new, young creation; and it would be more appropriate to recognise its relationship with other living beings than to continue to focus exclusively on it being different and having a higher status. So doing might be the birth of a human modesty based on the insight in biological evolution. As corporal beings we share our fate with animals. Both are feeling physical pleasure and pain, and both are mortal. Mankind has a likeness not only to God, but also to other forms of animal life.

11.6 Stewardship

The challenge is thus how to incorporate these overlooked insights into a new interpretation of Genesis 1:28? A first response might be: Certainly not by, yet again, becoming entrapped by the hopelessly outdated perception of Mankind as the "steward" of God's world on behalf of its master. Faced with the threat of the Planet becoming uninhabitable, our perception of Nature must be subjected to a thorough review, starting by a firm rejection of the deeply feudal term "stewardship".

Obviously, as I mentioned above, did "ruling" in feudalism imply an often unspoken "duty of care", as it appears to be expressed in the text of Genesis 2:15. *But the ruling person's hierarchical right to rule remained unchallenged.* Furthermore, we no longer live in a feudal society with a top-down hierarchy, in which the subordinate has the status of a serf or a slave. With the stewardship-model as a representation of Mankind's role and status under God, with a God-given mandate downward over the non-human world, the "world" itself has no intrinsic value other than its upward utility value to its Lord and master.[2] This model is by necessity speciesistic. It is an extension of the concept of overlordship, "the mandate and right to rule".

Even when, in best case, the stewardship does include some degree of taking care (Genesis 2:15), such care is not exercised, per se, for the sake of those being taken care of, but, rather, for the benefit of the master. This applies equally to the appealing modern concept of sustainability – which is sought after only for the sake of Mankind itself.

---

[2] A good example is the title of the German theologian Friedrich Gogarten (1887–1967): *Der Mensch zwischen Gott und Welt* (Gogarten 1956) – Man between God and World.

11.7 Mankind, the Creature Created to Create

The biology based human modesty and self-relativism mentioned above are likely to prompt a rethinking of the verse *preceding* 1:28, i.e., Genesis 1:27 (similarly, 1:26) which describes Mankind as being created in Gods "image", after his "likeness". That Mankind resembles God does not necessarily imply that it differs equally much more from its fellow creatures. It is quite astonishing that it could totally sink in oblivion that we not only resemble God in that we, unlike "animals and trees", are endowed with spirit and language through which we can speak to him and praise him (N.F.S Grundtvig, Danish theologian and poet, 1783–1872; 2020 no. 86). The likeness lies equally in our ability to "see" and "feel" as God did on the evenings of the days of creation, when he "saw that it was good", pleasantly surprised after apparently having been somewhat uncertain of the outcome (Genesis 1:10,12,18,21). At last, as Mankind, which he could talk to, was included, saw he "*everything* that he had made, and behold, it was *very good*" (Genesis 1:31; author's italics.). The overall result was good, Mankind, made in his image with the double gift to "speak" and to "see", could praise him and, at the same time, strive to live in best possible harmony with its fellow creatures in the shared material world. That all this could be forgotten must be due to a dualistic lapse, in which there is more status attached to being able to "speak" than being able to" see" (hear, smell, or touch); in materialistic terms, it is more important to produce more things and to seek constant growth than to enjoy what is given to us and our senses.

However, Mankind's *likeness* to God does not prevent there also being a parallel and decisive *difference* between Mankind and other living beings. Mankind is aware of its own being, and of being as such. This awareness compels it to constantly making choices to avoid possible threats. Caring-for and anxiety, facing Death as the last horizon, seem to be the basic features of Human existence, as the philosopher Martin Heidegger (1889–1976), echoing Søren Kierkegaard, put.

Heidegger's student (and, for a short time, also his mistress) Hannah Arendt (1906–75), who was born into a Jewish family and later forced to flee to the USA, turned everything upside down.[3] She replaced the defensive and resigned attitude presented by Heidegger with a forward-looking perception that Mankind is created with an intrinsic ability to act so, that something new can be brought about. The event of birth, *natality*, the fact that new life is created, is the decisive factor, rather than death, *mortality*. Arendt was an Atheist thinker, but nevertheless inspired from biblical thoughts, such as "a child is born amongst us" (Isaiah 9:5) and "in the image of God created he him; male and female created he them" (Genesis 1:26–27). Arendt also used a quote from the Christian bishop Augustin (ca. 400): "Mankind is created so that beginnings may be made" – Latin creatus, ut initium esset. Mankind has the ability to create. Furthermore, Mankind is a thinking being able to make judgements and endowed with a conscience, so that the new he creates can have a purpose and give meaning. Arendt takes a phenomenological perspective on the factual aspects

---

[3] This section builds on the work of Pahuus (2006), Mortensen (2008) and Schanz (2019).

of being that these biblical thoughts have brought forward. The factual is Mankind's ability to seek out and create new and meaningful beginnings.

In "male and female", the essence is that meaningful beginnings are created by humans *together, in common*. Freedom to act is the freedom to act for the common good. This is exemplified by the free exchange of ideas in a truly political conversation, as demonstrated, according to Arendt, by Socrates in his hometown (polis) Athens. (She does, however, distance herself from the Socrates as presented by Plato). Freedom is the freedom to make the world "a human world", as Arendt puts it. Theologians would tend to add, that God was taking a risk in granting freedom to mankind: Freedom can be used to selfish ends, as happens in the Fall of man.

As far as the author of this article is aware, the work of Arendt does not make any significant contribution to an understanding of *the natural world* as part of the real world. In today's world, however, in which we stand with our backs against the wall and are forced to think anew to find an escape route from the encroaching threat of the Planet becoming uninhabitable, we are now ready to look for answers in the potential for new creation uncovered by the work of Arendt. But the freedom to create new beginnings "together" with others must now include other creatures, with which we have the natural world "in common", who "resemble" us in that they can feel pain and, perhaps, also joy and sorrow, and whom we can sympathise with and share their suffering, and whose case we can and must defend, when necessary, as they cannot speak up for themselves. This must be done with respect, and in thankfulness for the goodness of the Creators six-day work as a whole.

11.8 Re-reading Genesis 1:28 in a Context of Planetary Responsibility

What does the creator, mythically spoken, intend to express in the verse 28 in Genesis chapter 1? Answer: The obligations that follow with Mankind's unique status in the Creation. The way in which this is formulated is unavoidably marked and tempered by the social conditions and ideas held at the time it was written down. When these conditions and ideas change, the formulation as it stands will lose its relevance. It must thus be discarded, and we must look for new ways to express the original intention.

The verse is found in Chapter 1 of the Bible, which describes God's good works of creation, *before* the inexplicable evil of the Fall "made its entrance" on the scene.[4] Hence *a new interpretation based on the context* tells, that God in verse 1:28 expects his new creation, Mankind, to use its unique creative freedom to – taken the actual conditions – take care of and further develop God's intentions in creating the world. The decisive step in the world of today is to consider the feeling side of our likeness to the creator: To see through his eyes, and to recognize what he found "good", and

---

[4] In theological terms "supralapsarian".

the present generations have conveniently forgotten, both that which came *before* the creation of Mankind (the 1.–5. "day") and that which came after (the 6. "Day"). The aim must be to establish the "good" overall outcome of the Sixth Day of Creation, in the form of a home for humans on Earth, including the species and their and our habitats, the miracle of being and the sensory and tangible miracles, allowing human life to unfold with respect for, and as the happy recipient of, these fountains of joy.

However, the history of ideas shows that the text has always, and still in modern times, been read *out of context*, it is" after" the appearance of the evil.[5] Hence we read Genesis 1:28 as parts of the late Anthropocene stage of human development, in which Mankind can choose to continue on its course to the cliff edge *or* choose to take steps to avoid it. Hannah Arendt remarks that the creation of the world is not yet finished; as theologians we can echo her sentiment by concluding that the world has veered dangerously far off course. What is needed now is to make room for, and give political voice to, the feeling of infinite sadness, shame and indignity vis-à-vis the systematic degradation of the work of creation, which is inherent in the ever-increasing reduction of natural resources to become something solely dedicated to benefit Man. In *a new interpretation to Genesis 1:28 on this basis* God expects mankind to use his unique freedom via an open national and global political discourse to take the necessary and drastic steps to create and reinstate the intricate intertwinement between the human and the natural world and, in doing so, recreate the world to what it was intended to be, before it finally is too late. The core implication is to develop *a "non-speciesist" humanism*. In Jensen (1976, p. 104) I argued: "In our times it is only possible to be human by becoming more than human". An updated version alluding to Arendt could be: "In our times, the world can only become 'a human world' by becoming more than just human".

To achieve this will require the dismantling of all beliefs and social structures that currently contribute to the catastrophic race towards the cliff edge. This demands an in-depth reform of the economy, the means of production, transportation, infrastructure, lifestyle aspirations, and much more. It seems obvious that the situation after the current corona pandemic will not only necessitate, but also facilitate, that the need to recalibrate must take precedence over all other considerations, at all levels of society. I recently came across an expression for this *"Planetary responsibility"* (Danish historian Michael Böss).

Concluding in theological terms – the Creators intention when granting Mankind its unique freedom was to get a helper, in Latin a *cooperator Dei*, in the double task of reducing the effects of the Fall of man and in continuing the creation, Latin: *creatio continua*.

Assuming we actually have a future.

---

[5] In theological terms *"infralapsarian"*.

References

Barnosky, A.D., et al. 2011. Has the Earth's sixth mass extinction already arrived? *Nature* 471: 51–57.
Descartes, R. 1637. *Discourse on the method of rightly conducting one's reason and of seeking truth in the sciences.* Trans. J. Veitch. London: Orion Publishing Group.
Gogarten, F. 1956. *Der Mensch zwischen Gott und Welt.* Stuttgart: Vorwerk Verlag.
Grønbech, V. 1952. *Kampen for en ny sjæl.* Copenhagen: Det danske Forlag.
Grundtvig, N.F.S. 2020 [1861]. Menneskelivet er underligt, No. 86 in *Højskolesangbogen* 19. edition. Copenhagen: Forlaget Højskolerne.
Jensen, J.V. 1954. *Digte.* Copenhagen: Gyldendal.
Jensen, O. 1976. *I vækstens vold. Økologi og religion.* Copenhagen: Fremad. German translation (1977): *Unter dem Zwang des Wachstums. Ökologie und Religion,* Chr. Kaiser Verlag, München. Dutch translation (1979): *De natuur in de wurggreep. Notities over ecologie en religie,* Uitgeversmaatschappij J.H. Kok, Campen.
———. 2011. *På kant med klodens klima. Om behovet for et ændret natursyn.* Copenhagen: Anis.
Kjærgaard, T. 1991. *Den danske revolution 1500–1800. En økohistorisk tolkning.* Copenhagen: Gyldendal.
Lundager Jensen, H.J. 2001. Gudsbegrebet i Det Gamle Testamente – med udblik til Det Ny. In *Om Gud,* ed. A. Brink and O. Jensen, 6–21. Copenhagen: Aros.
Mortensen, K.M. 2008. *Skabt til at begynde. Det augustinske spor hos Hannah Arendt.* Copenhagen: Anis.
Pahuus, A.M. 2006. *Hannah Arendt.* Copenhagen: Anis.
Pimm, S.L., et al. 1995. The future of biodiversity. *Science* 269 (5222): 347–350.
Rosa, H. 2013. *Social acceleration: A new theory of modernity.* New York: Columbia University Press.
Schanz, H.-J. 2019. For frihed – introduktion til Hannah Arendts bog Åndens liv. In *Hannah Arendt: Åndens liv,* 9–35. Aarhus: Forlaget Klim.

Ole Jensen born 1937, Dr. Theol 1976 with the dissertation *Theologie zwischen Illusion und Restriction,* 1974–1978 professor of theological dogmatics, University of Copenhagen, 1978–1985 dean of Maribo Cathedral, Head of a Grundtvigian Folk High School 1985–1992 and finally principal of the Danish priests' supplementary education. Member of the Danish Ethical Council 1988–1993. He passed away in December 2021 after the manuscript was finished but before the book was produced. He participated in the whole process except the proofreading.

Chapter 12
Religion, Politics, and Moral in Recent Denmark

Peter Lüchau

Abstract The aim of the article is to investigate the interrelation between religion, politics and moral and their impact on the Danish society. For an investigation of the impact of religion on society it is important to understand religion itself, to examine the relationship between religion and politics and between religion and moral. The influence religion has upon political and moral values in Denmark seem rather limited; the impact is weak and it does not seem to have much potential for changing society as a whole. This is hardly surprising taking the individualisation of Danish religiosity into consideration. Religion may have influenced Danish society in the past but its potential for doing so today and in the foreseeable future is limited.

Keywords Religion · Value · Politics · Moral · Individualisation · Denmark

12.1 Introduction

The interplay of religion, politics, and moral is an interesting topic. Mostly because it may suggest how religion may impact society as a whole. In traditional societies religion may impact society directly. It does this by establishing norms for how society should function. One example could be the caste system of old India or the established church's control of society in medieval Europe. In modern societies, especially democratic ones, a direct impact of religion on society is not possible. Instead religion may influence society indirectly through institutions and values. Here the focus will be the indirect impact of religion on Danish society through values.

The indirect impact of religion on society works through a chain. It is assumed that religion may influence the values of individuals. In the particular case religion means a particular Danish version of Lutheran Christianity. It is also assumed that values may influence how individuals act upon society thereby shaping it. Many different values may influence how individuals act upon society but political and

P. Lüchau (✉)
Frederiksberg, Denmark

© The Author(s), under exclusive license to Springer Nature Switzerland AG 2023
N. Kærgård (ed.), *Market, Ethics and Religion*, Ethical Economy 62,
https://doi.org/10.1007/978-3-031-08462-1_12

moral values both stand out as some of the more influential. The reason for this is that both politics and moral concern what ought to be and hence provide a motivation for changing society. The causal chain starts with Christianity which due to its strong emphasis on the difference between right and wrong may influence the political and moral values of individuals. The causal chain then continues as political and moral values may influence society through how individuals vote and how they act toward each other. The idea is that the laws enacted by parliament and the institutions of society are expressions of the political and moral values of the general population. To make plausible that religion indirectly influence society a relationship must first be established between religion and political and moral values. If such a relationship can be established then the next step would be to establish whether there is a relationship between political and moral values and how society functions. If both connections can be established then it can be claimed that religion indirectly influence society as a whole. Here focus will be on political and moral values but values relating to other areas of life could be important as well, e.g. economics, education, and welfare.

To investigate the impact of religion on present day Danish society the analysis will be done in three steps. The first step will be to examine religion in Denmark today in order to establish a theoretical frame for the rest of analysis. If religion has an impact on society it is important to understand religion itself. The second step will examine the relationship between religion and politics on both the societal and the individual level. This is to establish if religion in a broad as well as a narrow sense has an impact upon politics. The third step will examine the relationship between religion and moral. This is to establish if religion impact the way Danes see right and wrong in a more general sense. Testing whether there is a relationship between political and moral values and society as a whole is beyond the scope of this paper. Political science has already established a connection between political values and voting behaviour in Denmark (e.g. Andersen and Borre 2003) and in that sense political values at least can be said to influence society as a whole through the actions of parliament. Whether moral values influence society as a whole is a different question but if it can be established that religion impacts political and moral values then it should definitely be examined.

12.2 Religion

Within the last three decades religion in Denmark has become individualised. Religion has become a matter of choice (Davie 2000). Individuals must not only choose what religion if any they want to believe in but also the specific content of said religion (Ahlin 2005). This is in contrast to the situation 50 years ago. Before individualisation occurred religion and religiosity in Denmark was collective. It was a social phenomenon. Individuals had the same religion as everyone around them had. Individuals could not pick and choose their religion, it was chosen for them. In other words being religious meant conforming to a specific version of Protestant

Christianity. Since this Christianity was collective and enforced collectively albeit indirectly it was normative. What individuals believed and the consequences of this belief on their values were uniform across the population. Not only was there a relationship between religious and worldly values but the relationship was the same for all Christians in Denmark. And this at a time when more than 90 per cent of the Danes shared the same version of Christianity.

With the coming of individualisation the collective and thereby the normative aspect of religion began to dissolve. Before the functional differentiation of society religion was reinforced in most aspects of life. Regardless of which life sphere the individual was in, be it work, leisure time, family life, medical check-ups etc., religion was there and had an influence. But as the economic, political, scientific, and educational spheres became autonomous and separated so did religion. It became confined to the sphere of the specifically religious and hence only survived in the private lives of individuals. This means that the religious conformity of yesteryears become difficult to uphold and it slowly disappears. The religious impulse of most individuals does not disappear, however, and they stay religious but now there is little to tell them how to be religious and what to believe in.

In Denmark individualisation has led to a change in beliefs and religious activities (Andersen and Lüchau 2011). It did not lead to fewer religious individuals or lower levels of religiosity in general. The change reflected the move from a collective and conformist version of Christianity to a nonconformist and individual centred version of Christianity. It could be argued that in the 1980s the religious beliefs of the Danes were to a larger extend in accordance with the official beliefs of the Danish national church than today. Danes believed in God and a life after death but they also believed in Sin and to a lesser extend Heaven and Hell. In 2008 this had changed. Belief in the more normative aspects of the Christian faith, i.e. beliefs related to sin and punishment, had diminished. The Danes to a much lesser extend believe in Sin and while belief in Heaven and Hell stayed the same it was not widespread to begin with. But at the same time belief in God stayed the same and belief in a life after death rose (Andersen and Lüchau 2011, pp. 82–83). When given the freedom to choose Danes kept believing in the "good" things from the confession of the Danish national church but they rejected the "bad" things. They kept those beliefs that fitted well with a individualistic and individual centred lifestyle and rejected beliefs more appropriate for a collective and group oriented way of life.

Church attendance changed in a similar manner. Focus shifted from regular Sunday service to holiday related services particularly those related to Christmas. While the percentage of Danes who attended Sunday service regularly stayed the same the was a surge in the percentage who primarily attended service at specific holidays particularly Christmas (Andersen and Lüchau 2011, pp. 81–82). This in a sense represents a shift in focus from traditional normative Christianity symbolised by regular Sunday service to an individual centred Christianity symbolised by the freer form of the Christmas service. Christmas services generally employ some sort of variation from the more traditional form of the regular Sunday service. At Christmas services the audience is generally less familiar with the way regular services are conducted which is a fact that the presiding priest accept and take into consideration. It could also be argued that at regular Sunday service the audience come to meet other fellow Christians and hence regular Sunday service is a collective type of religiosity. At Christmas services, on the other hand, the audience come to get a religious experience along with their families but the collective aspect as such is absent.

12.3 Religion and Politics

There are several different aspects of the relationship between religion and politics in Denmark that should be taken into consideration in order to understand religion and politics. On the societal or public level there are at least two important aspects of religion and politics. There is the formal relationship between religion and state and there is the way religion is present and being debated in public discourse. On the individual level there is the question of the consequences of the religiosity of individuals on their political values and viewpoints.

The Danish national church (Den Danske Folkekirke) is a state church in the sense that it is tied to the state through the Danish constitution (Dübeck 2005). The state is obligated to support the Danish national church and in a sense the church reciprocate by lending legitimacy to the state. But the Danish national church is also a state church in the sense that its highest political, economic and religious authority is the Danish parliament (Espersen 1993, p. 68). Legally speaking there is no such thing as inner worldly and outer worldly affairs of the church (ibid. p. 78). Danish parliament, on a day-to-day basis represented by the minister of ecclesiastical affairs, is the leader of the church in all affairs be they secular or religious. Traditionally ministers of ecclesiastical affairs have been careful not to overstep their bounds and have shied away from interfering in matters of theology and religion. A recent example was the case of Thorkild Grosbøll the priest who allegedly did not believe in God. One way to decide whether Grosbøll had neglected his duties would have been to use a legal and theological instrument, an ecclesiastical court (præsteret). But the minister of ecclesiastical affairs chose to avoid interfering with theology by making the case a non-issue by changing the theological oversight of Grosbøll from one bishop to another. This tradition however is being challenged at the moment. The current administration have changed the formal theology of the Danish national church by instituting the marriage of same-sex couples in the church. In this sense there has been a strong link between religion and politics on the legal level and it continues to exist and may even be on the verge of becoming stronger as Danish politicians apparently begin to make their influence felt within the Danish national church.

Within public discourse there are several examples of religion and politics being mixed. All Danish political parties have programmes of principles in which they state their main political views and objectives. Most Danish political parties have statements regarding religion in these programmes of principles. The centre and left wing parties mention religion in conjunction with freedom of religion. The right wing parties are more specific and in addition to mentioning freedom of religion also mention strong support for the Danish national church (Lüchau 2011a, p. 92). Behind this support is the idea that the Danish national church is a national institution. Therefore the right wing parties support the continuation of the privileged position of the Danish national church as stated in the Danish constitution.

This support for the privileged position of the Danish national church can also be found in Danish political discourse. Since September 11, 2001 but also before that religion has been an important topic in Danish politics. Particularly among right wing politicians Christianity has been put forth as an important trait of Danish national identity and of Danish values in general. This has in many ways been a reaction towards Muslim immigrants and their perceived threat to Danish culture. Within the past 20 years the issue of immigration in Danish politics has often been equated with the issue of religion meaning Islam. The main reaction to the presence of Islam has been to accentuate the Christian values supposedly underpinning Danish society. One line of argument supports a strengthening of Christianity in the public space and a tighter symbolic relationship between the state and Christianity. This could express itself in an effort to promote a privileged position for Christian symbols in the public space through Christian chapels in public hospitals and a continued cooperation between local churches and public schools with regard to confirmation lessons. Another line of argument instead supports the almost total removal of religion from public space. The argument is that separating the religious from the secular is at the core of Lutheran Christianity. In that sense the underlying argument is the same: Lutheran Christianity is underpinning Danish society and Danish values albeit indirectly (Lüchau 2011a, p. 93).

While it can be argued that there is a strong relationship or intertwining of religion and politics on the societal level the same cannot be claimed to be the case on the individual level. The relationship between religion and politics on the individual level can be direct as well as indirect. A direct relationship could for instance be support for the idea of Christianity as an essential trait of Danish national identity while an indirect relationship could be a relationship between religiosity and political views in general.

It can be argued that one in five Danes support the idea that Christianity is an integral part of Danish national identity. A study from the 2005 general election showed that around one in five Danes agreed somewhat strongly with the statement that immigrants should come from Christian countries in order to gain entrance to Denmark (Lüchau 2011a, p. 99). This study and several others (see Lüchau 2008b) show that there was a direct relationship between religion and politics among certain groups in the Danish population. These studies also show, however, that these groups did not in any way encompass a majority of the Danish population. Not even among voters of the right wing parties including the Islam critical Danish Peoples Party did a majority claim that it is essential that immigrants to Denmark should come from Christian countries. In this sense there is not much support for a strong relationship between religion and politics on the individual level. Analysing the underlying factors behind mixing religion and politics reveals an interesting picture. The best predictor of agreeing that immigrants ought to come from Christian countries was xenophobia. Religiosity had an impact but it was small and basically insignificant compared to xenophobia (Lüchau 2011a, p. 106). This suggests that on the individual level thinking that Christianity is an essential trait of a Danish national identity was unrelated to actually being a Christian in the sense of going to church. In that sense there is not much support for an indirect relationship between religion and politics on the individual level either.

An ongoing study support this finding and broadens it (Lüchau 2011b). Research shows that the relationship between religiosity and generalised political values has been severely weakened in the past three decades. This means that the weak relationship between religion and politics on the individual level is not confined to the issue of Christianity and national identity, and by extension the issue of immigration, but also extents to politics in general.

Two important observations can be made with regard to the mixing or lack hereof of religion and politics. One, there is a discrepancy between what is the case on the societal level and what is the case on the individual level. Whereas there is an obvious mixing of religion and politics on the societal level this can hardly be said to be the case on the individual level. Or put another way it can be argued that public discourse does not reflect the sentiments of the general population and vice versa. Two, there is no clear nor strong relationship between religion and politics on the individual level. Religion and politics are neither directly nor indirectly related empirically. Individuals may hold views on the relationship of religion and politics or interpret religion in a political way but it is near impossible to predict political viewpoints from religious values.

Both conclusions are consistent with the individualisation of Danish religion. Both it can be argued are the consequences of the lacking collective aspect of religion in modern day Denmark. Because religion is no longer a collective phenomenon there can be little agreement on what Christianity is or on its political consequences. Because each individual is free to choose their own religion and to interpret the content of said religion and the political consequences it should entail there is not one public religion but essentially none. This leads to a discrepancy between how religion, in this case Danish Christianity, is interpreted. Due to the lack of agreement on religious issues politicians do not express widely held sentiments but rather their personal views and probably views formulated for maximum political gain at that. A general consensus simply is not possible. The most that can be hoped for is some kind of consensus among certain groups in the population which seems to be the case. Unfortunately for the argument the groups in question are rather small. But it should also be remembered that the mixing of religion and politics on the societal level is not necessarily a sign of consensus either. The discourse on Danish values being Christian in nature is widespread and very visible in Danish public discourse but it is not universally held. It could be argued that the discourse has been promoted by opinion makers and politicians who have succeeded in making it very visible but it could also be argued that it probably says more about their media prowess than about any consensus among opinion makers. Those who opposed the discourse have had little success in getting in the media but that does not mean that they do not exist. In this sense there is no consensus on religion in the public space either even though it may seem so. If this is indeed the case then the lacking continuity between religion and politics on the societal and individual level stems from the fact that there is no consensus to transfer from one level to another.

The weak relationship between religion and politics on the individual level is also consistent with individualisation. Individuals are now free to choose their religion as well as its exact content. Therefore chances are that they will choose differently from each other. After all they have no social surroundings to get clues from or to follow. Since they can choose their religion and its content then it would be safe to claim that they are also free to choose what they think should be the political consequences of their chosen religion. Even if they may be under indirect pressure toward adopting certain political views they will not be under pressure to adopt the same religious choices as the political peer group. Hence the relationship between religiosity and political views weakens. It can be argue that this state of affairs is also furthered by functional differentiation which removes religion from other spheres of life such as work, economics, education etc.

12.4 Religion and Moral

Moral can be defined as a set of values and attitudes determining the individuals' ideas about right and wrong, The specific issues may be political but in major surveys the moral questions are often articulated so as not to be political. This makes it possible to separate the effect of religion on political and on moral values. Moral can concern anything but in major European values research moral is usually defined as attitudes toward two major areas of life (Halman and de Moor 1994, pp. 56–61). The first area concerns actions that involve more than the moral actor herself. Things such as cheating on your taxes or unlawfully claiming social benefits are all actions that may have consequences for both the moral agent as well as the people around her. This areas therefore can be called public moral since it concerns the rightfulness or wrongfulness of actions that happen in the public sphere and affect the public at large. The second area concerns actions that involve only the moral actor or those very close to her. Things such as homosexuality, abortion, and euthanasia are all actions that in principle can only have consequences for the moral actor and those closest to her. This area can therefore be called private moral since it concerns the rightfulness or wrongfulness of actions that happen in the private sphere and affect the private life of individuals or those close to them.

In Denmark the attitudes toward public and private moral are rather different. Danes generally have very strict views on public moral while they have very permissive views on private moral. Danes seem to think that when one is acting in the public sphere one must behave according to norms but when in private or at home anything goes. This is in sharp contrast to moral attitudes in Southern Europe where views on public moral are permissive but views on private moral are strict. In general this is explained by the Danes' view of the collective. The Danish welfare state is built upon mutual trust between citizens and the state. It has as a prerequisite a high level of collectivism and solidarity. Danes are therefore, indirectly, taught that they and the state are mutually dependent on each other (Gundelach and Riis 1992, p. 215). It could be argued that the end result of this is that the state becomes "ours" in the mind of the Danes. The state and the public sector is seen as something positive, an extension of the collective will, and hence Danes find it very important how one acts toward the state and by extension toward others. With regard to private moral Danes like to think of themselves as liberal and tolerant. What others do within the limits of civil society should be accepted (Gundelach 2002, p. 97). Hence the high level of moral permissiveness with regard to private moral, at least compared to some Southern European nations.

The relationship between religion and moral in Denmark is different depending on the type of moral in question. With regard to private moral individuals who are religious have stricter moral views than non-religious individuals. This is regardless of whether religiosity is measured as Christian beliefs (Andersen et al. 2013, p. 396) or by a statement on whether individuals would consider themselves believers or not (Lüchau 2008a, pp. 269–270). Religiosity leads to a less permissive view of homosexuality and abortion but it is important to remember that Danes are on the whole very permissive. Even religious Danes are still relative morally permissive with regard to private moral when compared to, say, individuals living in Southern Europe.

With regard to public moral the relationship between religiosity and moral differs depending on the way religiosity is measured. If religiosity is measured as Christian beliefs then there is a relationship between religion and moral. The relationship is rather weak, however. In general individuals who believe in central tenets of the Christian faith tend to hold slightly stricter views on public moral than individuals with a weaker Christian faith (Andersen et al. 2013, p. 396). If religiosity is measured as whether individuals would call themselves believers there is no difference in the moral views of believers, non-believers or atheists (Lüchau 2008a, p. 269). All in all it can be argued that it would be safe to ignore what little relationship there may be between religiosity and public moral in Denmark.

If the moral values of individuals affect society at large then all things being equal public moral should have the largest impact since it concerns things that are common for all. Private moral may have an impact but it does not need to. All states regular public behaviour or at least make an effort to do so but not all states regulate their citizens' private lives. Since it is safe to ignore any influence of religion on public moral the possible impact of religion on Danish society as a whole is already somewhat limited. With regard to private moral there may be a societal impact of religion which then could potentially lead to tighter laws on issues like abortion and homosexuality. This would of course require that the political parties in parliament started catering to the religious right which has not really been the case up until now.

The rather weak relationship between religiosity and public moral could be an effect of the individualisation of Danish religion. If individuals can chose their religion and the consequences of said religion then any general relationship between religion and moral should begin to dissolve. An preliminary research project has shown that this has indeed happened (Lüchau 2011b). The relationship between religion and private moral could therefore be considered a survival from the time when Denmark was a traditional society. And like all survivals the relationship will vanish in time. Question is whether individualisation is the best explanation for the relationship or lack hereof between religion and moral or whether the universal Danish welfare system with its emphasis on mutual trust is. If the latter is the case then it suggests that religion may already have lost much of its ability to influence society through moral since it was the Danish welfare system which had the decisive impact. The changing nature of Danish religion cannot impact the relationship between religion and moral as religion was already removed from the equation by the welfare state.

12.5 Conclusion

This paper started with the assumption that religion may impact Danish society indirectly through influencing political and moral values. The analysis has shown that it is difficult to give a straightforward answer as to whether religion impacts politics in Denmark. On one hand religion is visibly an important and decisive issue in Danish politics. Particularly with regard to immigration issues Christian religion and the values it allegedly fosters seem very important for the political suggestions voiced by several high ranking Danish politicians. It should however be noted that there is not a general consensus on the importance of religion and Christianity in particular in public discourse. This heterogeneity undermines the potential impact of religion on politics. For an impact to happen it would normally have to be driven by a majority and this is most likely not the case with regard to religion in politics. Religion and politics are also tightly connected with regard to the Danish national church but here the influence goes from politics to religion as the Danish parliament controls the Danish national church. On the individual level the relationship between religion and political values is rather weak. Those who claim that religion is important for Danish society and Danish values are not themselves Christians in a traditional sense. It can also be suggested that the traditional relationship between religiosity and political conservatism is weakening and may one day disappear altogether.

The analysis also shows that the influence of religion upon moral is relatively weak. The influence of religion on public moral is debatable. This is important since public moral should be the moral dimension that influence society the most. There is however a clear influence of religion upon private moral. This means that religion could potentially influence society through this moral dimension and for instance result in new laws on abortion.

In conclusion what influence religion may have upon political and moral values seem rather limited. What impact there is, is weak and it does not seem to have much potential for changing society as a whole. This is hardly surprising taking the individualisation of Danish religiosity into consideration. As religion becomes a matter for the individual to decide and thereby loses its collective aspect it also loses its social significance. Religion may have influenced Danish society in the past but its potential for doing so today and in the foreseeable future is rather limited.

References

Ahlin, L. 2005. *Pilgrim, turist eller flykting? En studie av individuell religiös rörlighet i senmoderniteten*. Stockholm/Stehag: Brutus Östlings Bokförlag Symposion.

Andersen, J.G., and O. Borre, eds. 2003. *Politisk forandring. Værdipolitik og nye skillelinjer ved folketingsvalget 2001*. Århus: Systime.

Andersen, P.B., and P. Lüchau. 2011. Individualisering og aftraditionalisering af danskernes religiøse værdier. In *Små og store forandringer: Danskernes værdier siden 1981*, ed. P. Gundelach, 76–96. Copenhagen: Hans Reitzel.

Andersen, P.B., P. Gundelach, and P. Lüchau. 2013. A spiritual revolution in Denmark? *Journal of Contemporary Religion* 28 (3): 385–400.

Davie, G. 2000. *Religion in modern Europe. A memory mutates*. Oxford: Oxford University Press.

Dübeck, I. 2005. State and church in Denmark. In *State and church in the European Union*, ed. G. Robbers, 2nd ed., 55–76. Baden-Baden: Nomos Verlagsgesellschaft.

Espersen, P. 1993. *Kirkeret. Almindelig del*. Copenhagen: Jurist- og Økonomforbundets Forlag.

Gundelach, P. 2002. *Det er dansk*. Copenhagen: Hans Reitzels Forlag.

Gundelach, P., and O. Riis. 1992. *Danskernes værdier*. Copenhagen: Forlaget Sociologi.

Halman, L., and R. de Moor. 1994. Religion, churches and moral values. In *The individualizing society: Value change in Europe and North America*, ed. P. Ester, L. Halman, and R. de Moor, 37–65. Tilburg: Tilburg University Press.

Lüchau, P. 2008a. Hvem er bange for de gudløse? In *Gudløs! Religionskritik i dag*, ed. M. Busk and I. Crone, 259–274. Copenhagen: Tiderne Skifter.

———. 2008b. *Religion and societal integration in Denmark. An analysis of civil religion on the individual level*. Copenhagen: Det Humanistiske Fakultet, Københavns Universitet.

———. 2011a. Religiøse politikere og sekulære vælgere? Den religio-nationale dimension i dansk politik. *Politica* 43 (1): 111–134.

———. 2011b. The weakening of Danish religion. Unpublished paper presented at the 2011 ISSR conference, Aix-en-Provence, France.

Peter Lüchau born 1972, has been assistant professor at University of Southern Denmark and post.doc. at the Department of Sociology, University of Copenhagen. Has published in Danish and International journals about sociology of the Dane's religion and attitudes. Since 2020 business intelligence analyst in the public sector.

Chapter 13
Economic Life and the Social Doctrine of the Catholic Church

Else-Britt Nilsen

Abstract Catholic social teaching contains a vast array of moral theories, but not much of applied politics. It does not give final answers but applies Christian principles to actual problems. According to Catholic social teaching, economic activity needs to be guided by clear and fair rules and the actors by fundamental principles of the dignity of the human person, the common good, solidarity and subsidiarity. But the question remains as to how far Catholic theology is equipped to address economic issues. This question is addressed in this chapter by giving a historical outline of the developments that shape Catholic social thought today.

Keywords Catholic social teaching · Option for the poor · Solidarity · Human dignity · Development · Justice · Common good · Market economy

13.1 Introduction: The Early History

The ambiguities in the discipline of economics and the extent of discussions are best captured by an old saying: If all the economists were laid end to end, they would not reach a conclusion. In spite of this, as John Allen comments in the *National Catholic Reporter,* many popes have ventured into this field, "producing a sprawling body of economic analysis that forms the core of what's known as 'Catholic social teaching'." Pope Benedict XVI even describes his social encyclical *Caritas in Veritate*

The author would like to thank two of her Dominican Sisters: Sheeba Jem Irudayam for her very valuable assistance in preparing this article, and Madeleine Fredell for constructive feedback on the manuscript. The language has been revised by Fr. Vivian Boland, O.P.

E.-B. Nilsen (✉)
Faculty of Theology, University of Oslo, Sta. Katarinahjemmet, Oslo, Norway

(2009) as a meditation on "the vast theme of the economy and work." (Allen Jr 2009). But the question remains as to how far Catholic theology is equipped to regulate or address economic issues. This question is addressed here by giving a historical outline of how social thought developed in the Church along with the role and impact of *Rerum Novarum* (1891) and *Populorum Progressio* (1967) in the shaping of Catholic social teaching and the aspects that Catholic social teaching focuses on today.

Although the expression "social doctrine of the Church" is usually understood as modern social teaching, social thought has always been implicit in the Church's teaching (Charles 1998b). From a theological perspective, social thought is as old as the Bible itself. Economic activity considered in the light of divine revelation is a grateful response to the vocation that God extends to each person.[1] Proper administration of the gifts received, both spiritual and material, is a work of justice towards oneself and towards others.

What has been received should not only be put to proper use, taken care of and increased as suggested by the parable of the talents, but also placed at the service of the human being and society.[2] However, as Clement of Alexandria (150-c. 215) asks, "How could we ever do well to our neighbour, if none of us possessed anything?" Therefore, the Church Fathers insist more on the need for the conversion and transformation of the conscience of believers in administering their economy, rather than on the need to change their contemporary social and political structures. They invite those who work in the field of economics and those who possess material goods to consider themselves stewards of these goods that God has entrusted to them. Wealth, explains Basil the Great (c. 330–79), is like water that issues forth from the fountain: The greater the frequency with which it is drawn, the purer it is, while it becomes foul if the fountain remains unused. Gregory the Great (c. 540–604) says that a rich man is only a steward and not an owner of what he possesses, so much so, that he who retains riches for himself is not innocent but rather indebted to those in need. Giving what is required to the needy is therefore a task that is to be performed with humility, as the one who gives is only a steward who distributes what has first been given to him (Pontifical Council for Justice and Peace 2004 § 329).

In the Middle Ages, Francis of Assisi (1182–1226) and Thomas Aquinas (1225–1274) stand out as precursors of modern Catholic social doctrine. Both were religious and members of mendicant orders. Francis is still a source of inspiration with his ecological vision (*Laudato Si'*), his emphasis on a life of simplicity, care for the poor, and his focus on peace and non-violence. The Dominican, Thomas, a giant in the Catholic intellectual tradition and author of *Summa Theologiae*, places virtues and natural law at the center of ethics. Many of the crucial ideas in modern Catholic social doctrine relate to Thomas' understanding of concepts such as «justice», «common good» and «private property» (Heiene 2012 p. 199).

---

[1] Gen 2:16–17; Wis 9:16–17. Cf. Pontifical Council for Justice and Peace 2004 § 323–327.
[2] Mt. 25:14–20; Lk 19:12–27.

According to Thomas, private property was unnecessary before the fall because resources were unlimited, and every need met. Consequently, limitation of resources and insatiable needs are a result of the fall and banishment, which in turn necessitates private property and self-interest. Thomas considered self-interest as a strong urge for production and efficiency that results in private property. However, the individual owns this private property on behalf of the community and is thus obliged to share it with those in need. An unbridled yearning for one's own interest will be destructive to social integration, which would in turn threaten peace and stability. Therefore, Thomas, in line with the Church Fathers, considers profit as morally neutral and legitimate as long as the profit is used for the common good of the society (Massaro 2012 pp. 69–70; Charles 1998b pp. 206 ff.).

Another Dominican worth mentioning is the Spanish historian and missionary Bartolome de las Casas (1484–1566). He converted from being a foreign settler, who exploited Native American Indians, to a defender of the rights of the native population. His efforts paved the way for the modern human rights movement (Parish 1992). In the fifteenth century, papal documents on what we today would call social questions began to appear (Pian 2013). Pius II, in an address to a local ruler of the Canary Islands, condemned the enslavement of newly baptized Christians as a "great crime" (1462).[3] Other popes raised the question of interest on loans.[4] In a letter to the Archbishop of Toledo (1537), Paul III recalls that Amerindians are human beings, who have the right to freedom and property (*Veritas Ipsa*). In the eighteenth century, Benedict XIV wrote on the question of race (*Immena Pastorum Principis*, 1741), and defended the poor and their natural right to daily necessities to remain alive (*Acerbi Plani*, 1742). These are topics that appear repeatedly in *encyclicals* – papal circular letters – and in other official Church documents.[5]

13.2 From Leo XIII to Pope Francis

Economy has as its object the development of wealth and its progressive increase, not only in quantity but also in quality. However, this is morally right only if this progression is directed towards the human being's overall development in solidarity and to the development of the society in which people live and work (Pontifical Council for Justice and Peace 2004 §334). The Church has repeatedly emphasised that an international economic order that condemns large sections of the world population to a permanent state of abject poverty is grossly unjust. One of the first encyclicals that addresses these issues is *Rerum Novarum* (1891). However, it was written from a European perspective and addresses the issues that concerned

---

[3] Noteworthy is the fact that Pius did not condemn the concept of trading in slaves, only the enslavement of those who were recently baptised, who represented a very small minority of those captured and taken to Portugal.
[4] Callistus III in 1455; Leo X in 1515.
[5] For a far more extensive overview see Schuck (1991).

European society at the time. This limitation of *Rerum Novarum* is overcome by *Populorum Progressio* (1967) which lays the foundation for globalisation and concern for the poor everywhere.

The development of Catholic social teaching can thus be discussed by following the influence of these two documents leading into the nature of current social teaching. In light of this, selected papal documents are grouped into three sets and listed below. However, this list is by no means exhaustive.[6] There are numerous other discourses and letters from popes, bishops' synods and bishops' conferences that belong to the fundamental documents of the Church's social teaching, not to mention the new ones that are continually being added.[7]

Papal documents on economic life, 1891–2020

Year	Author	Document	Key themes
1891	**Leo XIII**	***Rerum Novarum***	Private ownership, workers' rights.
1931	Pius XI	*Quadragesimo Anno* (40th)	Reforming capitalism; subsidiarity.
1961	John XXIII	*Mater et Magistra* (70th)	Role of state; criteria for just distribution.
1963	John XXIII	*Pacem in Terris*	Human rights and social responsibilities.
1965	Vatican II	*Gaudium et Spes*	Right of migration; worker participation.
1971	Paul VI	*Octogesima Adveniens* (80th)	Urbanization, industrialization, political action.
1981	John Paul II	*Laborem Exercens* (90th)	Human work; capital and labor.
1991	John Paul II	*Centesimus Annus* (100th)	New forms of property; consumeristic greed.
1967	**Paul VI**	***Populorum Progressio***	Development; economy to serve *all* humankind.
1987	John Paul II	*Sollicitudo Rei Socialis* (20th)	Private property as social debt, structures of sin.
2009	Benedict XVI	*Caritas in Veritate* (40th)	Development; economy of gift, ethical renewal.
2013	**Francis**	***Evangelii Gaudium***	A missionary church; *a poor church for the poor.*
2015	Francis	*Laudato Si*	Ecology; resistance to actual consumer culture.
2020	Francis	*Fratelli Tutti*	Politics centred on human dignity, not on finance.

---

[6] Composed from different sources: Hornsby-Smith (2006 p.185); Crosthwaite (2014) and Massaro (2012 pp. 34–35).

[7] All major documents presented in the following, are freely available on the internet. The same goes for Pontifical Council for Justice and Peace (2004). For readers with Scandinavian language skills, the following edition is highly recommended: Den katolska sociallären. Dokument *1891–2015* (2019). This volume brings together - for the first time in Swedish - the basic texts from Pope Leo XIII's *Rerum Novarum* (1891) to Pope Francis' *Laudato Si* '(2015). Introductions to each document are also included.

The first block builds on the social teachings of *Rerum Novarum* – "of new things" – and applies it to address the social challenges brought about by economic development. On the 40th, 70th, 80th, 90th and 100th anniversaries of *Rerum Novarum*, popes returned to the original document and applied it to address the contemporary social circumstances. Although *Pacem in Terris* and *Gaudium et Spes* were not issued to mark the anniversary of *Rerum Novarum*, they still draw from *Rerum Novarum* and play a role in the development of Catholic social thought and are therefore included in the first block.

The second block contains *Populorum Progressio* and the encyclicals issued on its 20th and 40th anniversary. These were *Sollicitudo Rei Socialis* (1987) issued by John Paul II and *Caritas in Veritate* in 2009 by Benedict XVI, respectively. A common theme for these three encyclicals could be "authentic human development and globalization" (Crosthwaite 2014). John XXIII's *Mater et Magistra* (1961, §157) and Vatican II's *Gaudium et Spes*, although grouped in the first block could be considered as precursors for the second block.

The final block contains the most recent papal documents that also deal with social teaching, economy and justice, but with an emphasis on ecology. This block contains Pope Francis' contributions to social teaching as a continuation and implementation of the earlier teachings presented from an ecological perspective.[8] The development of the Church's social teaching in these three sets are elaborated below.

13.3 Social Teaching as a Formal Discipline

The development of social thought in the Catholic Church as discussed in the introduction has its roots in the Bible. Its implementation both by the Church Fathers and in the Middle Ages, show how it falls within the responsibility of the Church to be involved in social questions, both in formulating moral theories and in practical implementation. However, social teaching as a separate discipline was formally established in 1891 when Pope Leo XIII in his encyclical letter *Rerum Novarum*, addresses the condition of the working classes. The term "social doctrine" came later when Pope Pius XI (1931) refers to the doctrinal collections that deal with issues relevant to society as social doctrine. These were issues that were first addressed in *Rerum Novarum* and further developed through the teachings of the later popes and bishops.[9]

It was no coincidence that the first social encyclical, in its modern sense, appeared at the time when Europe was facing a new situation. The industrial revolution led to an imbalance in a relatively stable society that resulted in serious problems of

---

[8] Protecting the existence and prosperity of "our common home" are examples of themes that can be found in *Populorum Progressio*: The common good and the special care of the poor who suffer most from the abuse of our planet (Fredell 2020).

[9] Included also are bishops' synods and bishops' conferences without forgetting the Second Vatican Council. Pontifical Council for Justice and Peace 2004 § 87 n. 141.

justice. The first "social questions" concerned the gross injustice[10] suffered by wageworkers as a result of the conflict between capital and labour. Events of an economic nature had a dramatic social, political and cultural impact (Pontifical Council for Justice and Peace 2004 § 88). There emerged several social and cultural Catholic movements addressing these issues. Some of these movements developed into trade unions, cooperatives or political parties, such that the Church was blamed by many for being a hindrance to progress and modern culture. Although this was true in some respects, it was not so in the socio-political arena.

In his first encyclical, *Inscrutabili Dei Consilio* (1878),[11] Pope Leo XIII responds to these allegations by referring to the Church's civilizing role in society. By proclaiming the Gospel, the Church has fought against superstition, slavery and human debasement and it has supported the arts and sciences. Now the Church felt the call to go further, to intervene and respond to the new situation. The "new things" represented a challenge to her teaching and motivated her special pastoral concern for masses of people that resulted in *Rerum Novarum*. A new discernment of the situation was required, a discernment capable of finding appropriate solutions to unfamiliar and unexplored problems, that is to say, a systematic theological answer to the questions of the day (Pontifical Council for Justice and Peace 2004 § 88).

Rerum Novarum was drafted by an international team of experts and is the result of several years of social reflection and action. The encyclical marks the beginning of a new path and highlights situations where the dignity and rights of the workers are threatened. Recognizing the poverty of the working class and the Church's responsibility to intervene, Pope Leo XIII states: "We approach this subject with confidence and in the exercise of the rights which manifestly pertain to us ... By keeping silence, we would seem to neglect the duty incumbent on us" (*Rerum Novarum* § 16). Surprisingly enough, his choice of advocate in this encounter with modern times was a man who lived 600 years before, Thomas Aquinas, and his *Summa Theologiae*.

Rerum Novarum focuses on the emerging economic structure. The opposing theories of laissez-faire capitalism (free market capitalism) and orthodox socialism (communism) for governing the progress of industrial societies both regarded human society as subject to inevitable economic law. However, the Catholic Church considers this subordination of human well-being to economic principles as a distorted perception of reality (The Common Good 1996 §§ 25–26). The encyclical outlines an option between these two extremes by asserting the rights of the workers while opposing any notion of class struggle. In addition to addressing the basic economic principles, the encyclical notably affirms: the right of private property,[12] tempered by the duty to use it also for the benefit of others: A fair wage, charity

---

[10] Very meagre income, serious lack of protection, job insecurity etc. (Hervada 1983).

[11] http://www.vatican.va/content/leo-xiii/en/encyclicals/documents/hf_l-xiii_enc_21041878_inscrutabili-dei-consilio.html

[12] Leo XIII developed Thomas' teaching by affirming that the law of nature (natural law) includes the sacred right to acquire property, as one's own and to possess it "by stable and perpetual right". *Rerum Novarum* 11. Here after Benestad (2011 p.322).

towards the poor and freedom of association for workers.[13] This is where the principles of human dignity, the common good, option for the poor and subsidiarity begin to develop. Together with solidarity and human rights, these principles will form the cornerstones of Catholic social doctrine (Pontifical Council for Justice and Peace 2004 §§ 160–208).

Rerum Novarum put the Church in the forefront of social legislation both in Europe and in other continents. It was actually published shortly after Bismarck's Social Laws, – the first social legislation in the world.[14] Although the encyclical only has a limited application in today's society, it laid the methodological foundation that has become "a lasting paradigm" for successive developments in the Church's social doctrine (Pontifical Council for Justice and Peace 2004 § 146, and John Paul II, *Centesimus Annus* § 5). These later documents while still addressing questions related to economic life, like capitalism, the market, just distribution, international debt, poverty and financial crises,[15] do so in response to the changing circumstances. The Church's social doctrine has never stopped highlighting the moral implications of the economy (Pontifical Council for Justice and Peace 2004 § 330). In 1931 Pius XI emphasises that although economics and morality utilise and build on different principles, they continue to influence one another (*Quadragesimo Anno* §§ 190–191). "Every economic decision has a moral consequence," echoes Benedict XVI many decades later (*Caritas in Veritate* § 37). The dignity and complete vocation of the human person and the welfare of society as a whole must be respected and promoted. "The economy exists for the human person, not the other way round" (The Common Good 1996 § 111).

The strength of *Rerum Novarum* is that it does not speculate on theories and visions for society but rather addresses human affairs, as they are in a given society, in light of the Church's teaching about the truth of man (Nguyen 1998 p. ix). This aspect of *Rerum Novarum* is clearly illustrated among others in *Quadragesimo Anno* and in *Pacem in Terris*. In *Quadragesimo Anno* (1931), Pius XI addresses the ethical challenges facing workers, employers, and the state at the end of the industrial revolution and with the onset of the Great Depression. The encyclical expands the Church's response to advocate for Christian morals in challenging economic times. In response to the rise of socialism as an economic system, Pius XI articulates the idea of subsidiarity. According to the principle of subsidiarity, higher order societies, such as institutions run by the government, should not destroy or absorb lower order societies such as private institutions, but instead help and support them to carry out the tasks that serve the common good. In this manner, governments can refrain from wasting resources completing tasks that are best accomplished by individuals or by lower order institutions.

---

[13] https://www.citeco.fr/10000-years-history-economics/industrial-revolutions/rerum-novarum-the-economic-and-social-doctrine-of-the-Catholic-church

[14] These laws were adopted in 1884 and 1889.

[15] Besides economic life, the other actual key domains in Catholic social teaching are the following: the family, work and workers' rights, political life and authorities, the international community and development, care for the earth, the promotion of peace.

Pacem in Terris (1963) was issued by John XXIII around the time that the Berlin Wall had just been erected and the Cuban Missile Crisis threatened millions as nuclear weapons began to proliferate. In this situation, John XXIII appeals to the concern not only of Catholics or other Christians, but also of "all people of good will", recognizing that peace can be built only by appealing to our common responsibility. In addition, the cost and the resources devoted to nuclear proliferation were enormous. He called for a process of disarmament by every nation and appealed to them to assist those nations that were poor and whose economies were just developing. He emphasized that growing economic interdependence requires cooperation in order to progress. This continued integration of the world economy, where no state can pursue its own interests in isolation, is a development and application of the principle of solidarity already presented in *Rerum Novarum*.

13.4 Morality in Economic Life – For All Human Beings and for *All* of the Human Being[16]

Populorum Progressio heads the second block of documents in which Paul VI writes on the topic of the development of peoples and the universal destination of resources and goods. The encyclical is characterized by an openness to going beyond the European nations and extending solidarity to all nations of the world. It calls for structural changes – bold transformations of the structures of the international economic order and touches on a variety of principles of Catholic social teaching. These include changes to international capitalism such that the private initiative and competitive market is not abolished but that it is being guided and monitored by public authorities on a national and global level so as to benefit the poor. This marks the beginning of a process in which the Church gained new allies and new opponents.

Economic relations between countries at very different levels of economic development lie at the center of proposed changes in the structure of international economic relations and the world economy (Benedict XVI *Caritas in Veritate* § 37). All people have a moral obligation to care deeply about world poverty and to do all they can to address this scourge on our common humanity. All are members of a single human family, as John XXIII had already said (*Mater et Magistra* §§ 157–211). Vatican II followed up with these words: "Excessive economic and social inequalities between individuals and between peoples are contrary to social justice - - - God destined the earth and all that it contains for the use of all human beings and all people - - - Furthermore, the right to have a share of earthly goods, sufficient for oneself and one's family belongs to everyone." (*Gaudium et Spes* §§ 29, 69).

A major challenge to Catholic social teaching since Vatican II (1962–65) is the legacy of colonialism and the challenge of economic development in the deprived

---

[16] Benedict XVI *Caritas in Veritate* § 37.

parts of the world.[17] It was urgent to go beyond the level of recommendations (as in *Mater et Magistra*) and the presupposition that the solution to the primary and massive problem of poverty lies in following the Western model of economic development (*Gaudium et Spes*).[18] Paul VI gave high priority to addressing global underdevelopment in a different way (*Populorum Progressio*). Instead of focusing on a fair distribution of wealth from the rich to the poor, the new emphasis was on development that could increase resources, which in turn could be used to elevate those who lived in poverty. However, this development referred to in *Populorum Progressio* differs from the earlier encyclicals in that it points to the notion of integral development that was advocated by Fr. Louis-Joseph Lebret (Lavigne and Puel 2007, and Fredell 2019). Paul VI urged everyone to pool their ideas and their activities for "man's complete development *and* the development of all mankind":

> Today we see men trying to secure a sure food supply, cures for diseases, and steady employment. We see them trying to eliminate every ill, to remove every obstacle, which offends man's dignity. They are continually striving to exercise greater personal responsibility; to do more, learn more, and have more so that they might increase their personal worth. Yet, at the same time, a large number of them live amid conditions that frustrate these legitimate desires. – Moreover, those nations that have recently gained independence find that political freedom is not enough. They must also acquire the social and economic structures and processes that accord with man's nature and activity, if their citizens are to achieve personal growth and if their country is to take its rightful place in the international community. (Populorum Progressio §§ 5–6).

The encyclical calls for reform, not revolution, bold transformations of existing structures of the worldwide economic order (ibid. §§ 30, 32). "Development is the new name for peace", the Pope says (ibid. § 76). Ludovic Bertina describes the original understanding of this integral human development as emphasising a religious goal. This development, although it favours economic growth and technological innovations, is not aimed at creating a secular theory of development but at creating a human family for the reconciliation of humanity and God (Bertina 2013 pp. 115–127). Later, both John Paul II and Benedict XVI marked the anniversaries of *Populorum Progressio* by encyclicals with a continued focus on an integral, full and authentic human development.

John Paul II deplores the huge economic divide between the northern and southern hemispheres. In *Sollicitudo Rei Socialis* he demands – like Paul VI, and John XXIII – a redistribution of resources from arms manufacturing to lifting impoverished people out of poverty (*Sollicitudo Rei Socialis* § 23). By recognizing global interdependence, the Pope emphasizes the need for solidarity, a commitment to the common good not only from men and women of faith, but from everyone. This encyclical offers an extended reflection on the idea of solidarity, beginning from the clear injustices and evils of our globalised economic and political system. Solidarity is seen here as the counterpoint to those 'Structures of Sin' which are embedded in the established order (whether that order be liberal capitalism on the one side or

---
[17] *Mater et Magistra* §§ 157–211; *Caritas in Veritate* §§ 10–33. See also Massaro (2012 p. 98ff).
[18] Dorr (2001 p. 177) and Massaro (2012 pp. 101ff).

then still-functioning state socialism on the other) and which do vast damage to the interests of the poor and the vulnerable (*Sollicitudo Rei Socialis* §§38–40*).*[19]

In the context of solidarity, John Paul II also uses the concept of the "preferential option for the poor",[20] a notion deliberated during Vatican II and first used in 1968 by the superior general of the Jesuits, Pedro Arrupe, in a letter to their members in Latin-America. The term has its origins in the trend one finds in biblical texts where the poor and marginalised are given preference and Jesus associates himself with them, including not only material but also spiritual poverty. The notion attained a higher profile in the 1970s and 1980s when it was widely used by the liberation theology movement and discussed among theologians and bishops of Latin America.[21] This link to "liberation theology" and the demands for governmental or societal action, rather than changes solely in personal morality, raised suspicion about the phrase "preferential option for the poor".[22] Although controversial in the beginning, this phrase has become a theme in more recent encyclicals. It was used by John Paul II not only in *Sollicitudo Rei Socialis*, but also in the encyclical *Centesimus Annus* that marked the 100-year anniversary of *Rerum Novarum* (*Centesimus Annus* § 11). The whole background of the "preferential option for the poor" is important for understanding Pope Francis.[23]

Benedict XVI's *Caritas in Veritate* came out 2 years after the 40th anniversary of *Populorum Progressio*.[24] There were some delays in its preparation, and then came the financial crisis in 2008, which led to a revision. Benedict XVI confirms that globalization and technology offer much that is promising but also something that poses a major threat to full human development. The promise will only be fulfilled through the gift of God and the work of man, a work that is deeply rooted in love and truth, and which is expressed in justice, the common good, and in a consistent ethic for life. Only a community economy, a business ethic linked to individuals and

---

[19] See also. https://www.Catholicsocialteaching.org.uk/themes/solidarity/resources/solidarity-solicitudo-rei-socialis/

[20] *Sollicitudo Rei Socialis* § 42. Cf. Pontifical Council for Justice and Peace (2004 § 449) and Silecchia (2008).

[21] CELAM (General Conference of Latin American Bishops). The themes for CELAM II in Medellin 1968 were radical transformation, solidarity; for CELAM III (Puebla 1979) structural injustice, preferential option. Cf. Charles (1998a pp. 231–330).

[22] John Paul II deliberately avoided using the term "preferential option for the poor" during the early years of his pontificate. "He perceived it as a source of potential divisiveness within the Church and society, and as identified too closely with partisan interests and ideologies such as Marxism.... [F]ear of the development of a "parallel church" emanating from within base communities fuelled concern within certain Vatican circles that the term had been interpreted as a quasi-class alignment, vis-a-vis, pitting the poor against the rich. This led to the standard Vatican practice of substituting the phrases "preferential love" or "love of preference of the poor" in place of "preferential option for the poor" in official documents, deliberately avoiding the latter phrase in writings and allocutions issued during John Paul's early pontificate." Op.cit Silecchia (2008 p. 104, n. 53).

[23] Yes, maybe even for Pope Benedict's thoughts in *Caritas in Veritate*. One should not disregard his personal friendship with Gustavo Gutierrez.

[24] The letter also situates itself in a direct line with John Paul II's *Sollicitudo Rei Socialis.*'

not to profit, can provide an adequate response to the economic and financial crisis (*Caritas in Veritate* §§ 42–46).

Caritas in Veritate goes even further than the previous encyclicals in addressing current economic problems and social injustices and offers a wide range of suggestions.[25] The new suggestions include "the principle of gratuitousness" and "the logic of gift", which go beyond the logic of contracts and calls for a market model that will foster relationships based on gift giving and the expression of gratitude. Benedict XVI suggests this as an option not only for non-profit organizations but appeals for, "the principle of gratuitousness and the logic of gift as an expression of fraternity (which) can and must find their place within normal economic activity" (*Caritas in Veritate* § 36).

This concretizes the call to the market model proposed in *Populorum Progressio*, one based on greater global solidarity, where "all will be able to give and receive" (*Populorum Progressio* § 44). Benedict's model also makes room for motivations other than profit within the markets, such that the market does not become "the place where the strong subdue the weak" (*Caritas in Veritate* § 36). He further emphasizes that economy and finance are instruments, and that the market does not exist in the pure state. "Therefore, it is not the instrument that must be called to account, but individuals, their moral conscience and their personal and social responsibility." (*Caritas in Veritate* § 36).

A section of *Caritas in Veritate* is devoted to the environment (*Caritas in Veritate* §§ 44ff). Integral human development must also be sustainable development. Right relationship with the rest of creation is part of the framework within which integral human development can be achieved. Our relationship with the rest of creation is no longer a secondary issue in Catholic social teaching. According to Benedict XVI, the decisive issue in order to protect nature, "is the overall moral tenor of society" (*Caritas in Veritate* § 51).

Benedict XVI was however not the first pope to address the environmental problem. Paul VI, in *Octogesima Adveniens* (1971),[26] calls Christians and all of humanity, to take on responsible management of material goods so as not to exploit nature and degrade the environment for future generations. In the same year, a statement *Justice in the World*, from the World Synod of Catholic Bishops, addresses the environmental issue from a social justice perspective. The statement stresses the need for richer nations to reduce their material demands, since this results in other nations having to suffer consequences, including environmental ones. These issues were discussed for the first time in a UN-conference on the human environment that was held in Stockholm in 1972. This ecological concern, addressed by popes and bishops, is being amply followed up and brought to central focus by the current pope, Francis.

---

[25] For the presentation of *Caritas in Veritate* in this and the following paragraph cf. Massaro (2012), pp. 136–39.

[26] *Octogesima Adveniens* is not an encyclical but an Apostolic Letter – generally known as a "Call to Action on the Eightieth Anniversary of *Rerum Novarum*",

13.5   An Ecological Dimension to Catholic Social Teaching

Francis, being the first pope from the southern hemisphere and the first from outside Europe since the eighth century, brings with him a new perspective on Catholic social teaching. During his first years as pope, Francis did not publish an encyclical on the anniversary of *Populorum Progressio*, although he often emphasized similar issues in his writings and speeches. Francis' first major document was *Evangelii Gaudium* (2013)[27] followed by *Laudato Si* (2015) and *Fratelli Tutti* (2020). He focuses on climate issues, concern for the poor, evangelisation and ecclesial renewal, and criticises free market economics, consumerism and overdevelopment.[28] Although John Paul II, Benedict XVI and other popes have strongly urged all participants in the global economy to use their influence to fight injustice and reform international structures, there is no pope who has received so much positive attention for their statements on poverty, economy and fair distribution as Francis. In January 2014, he is portrayed to have "turned the Vatican into the spearhead of radical economic thinking".[29]

In *Evangelii Gaudium*, Francis presents the challenges of today's world where technological advances without concern for human consequences has led to extreme economic inequalities. He condemns such an economy and urges Catholics to work towards, "eliminating the structural causes of poverty". These structural causes are, among others, the "absolute autonomy of markets" (*Evangelii Gaudium* § 202), since Francis denounces the idea that "economic growth, encouraged by a free market, will inevitably succeed in bringing about greater justice and inclusiveness in the world" (*Evangelii Gaudium* § 54), and continues that we "can no longer trust in the unseen forces and the invisible hand of the market" (*Evangelii Gaudium* § 204).

Although this appears to contradict the teaching of earlier popes,[30] *Evangelii Gaudium* affirms that "it is through free, creative, participatory and mutually supportive labor that human beings express and enhance the dignity of their lives" (*Evangelii Gaudium* § 192). Francis calls for a new model that can benefit ordinary people in society as a whole and not just a selected few. This ambiguity with regard to a free market is not limited to Pope Francis. Catholic social teaching has been interpreted both as critical of the market economy, by authors like David Schindler, and as promoting free-market economic policies, by authors like Michael Novak, when in fact it adopts neither extreme. As Philip Booth puts it, the Church recog-

---

[27] *Evangelii Gaudium* is not an encyclical but an Apostolic Exhortation on evangelisation. Francis' first encyclical *Lumen Fidei* – published earlier the same year (2013) – was inspired by the draft of an encyclical written by Benedict XVI, which Francis rewrote and published under his own name. As such, he may have wished to signal continuity with Benedict. However, he clearly indicates that he wants *Evangelii Gaudium* to be programmatic of his papacy.

[28] "Pope says he is not a Marxist, but defends criticism of capitalism". *The Guardian*. 15 December 2013.

[29] https://www.afr.com/world/radical-economics-back-at-the-vatican-20140110-iyava

[30] http://www.ncregister.com/daily-news/the-economic-message-of-pope-francis-evangelii-gaudium/#blog

nizes that free market meets consumer preferences and at the same time recognizes that there are human goods that cannot be produced in the market (Booth 2014 p. 221).

In *Laudato Si'* (2015) Pope Francis calls us "to seek new ways of understanding the economy and progress" (*Laudato Si'* § 16) in order to develop a better financial and economic system for the twenty-first century. John Paul II spoke about the need to encourage and support an "ecological conversion"[31] and Francis uses this expression to call for a conversion that will go beyond the personal level: A conversion of society, culture and civilisation. By addressing the challenge of protecting our common home, he urges the whole human family to seek a sustainable and integral development (*Laudato Si'* § 13). Francis unites the fight against poverty and the fight against environmental destruction. He highlights an "ecological debt" that exists between the northern and southern hemispheres that results from commercial imbalances and disproportionate use of natural resources (*Laudato Si'* § 51).

These inequalities go beyond individuals and occur at the level of entire countries that can only be resolved by reforming the ethics of international relations. Paul VI had already addressed the environmental issue in *Octogesima Adveniens*, and Francis calls the world to promote and protect the common good by rearticulating the vision for an economy that is more aligned with Catholic social doctrine and Scripture. It is also an invitation to search together for practical solutions, to concretise a new way of thinking, that will replace an economy that dominates and kills with an economy that serves and promote wellbeing. Francis emphasises this in *Fratelli Tutti* – his third encyclical – where he appeals for a politics centred on human dignity and not subject to the dictates of finance: "the marketplace, by itself, cannot resolve every problem", the social problems caused by financial speculation aimed at quick profit have demonstrated this (*Fratelli Tutti* § 168).

13.6 Conclusions

Critics of papal social teaching often point out that economic models and policies, developed on the basis of values such as solidarity, human dignity and the common good as expressed in these teachings, often ignore concrete economic realities (Woods Jr. 2005). In addition, it is argued that the field of economics is separate from matters of faith and philosopher Étienne Gilson's famous quote is often cited: "Piety is no substitute for technique."[32] However, the Church cannot isolate itself from any arena where human dignity is threatened. The popes do not write these encyclicals alone. Although each pope brings his unique background and experience to address the issues at hand, these doctrines are eventually grounded in the

---

[31] http://www.vatican.va/content/john-paul-ii/en/audiences/2001/documents/hf_jp-ii_aud_20010117.html

[32] https://www.equip.org/article/the-myths-christians-believe-about-wealth-and-poverty/

Bible, in the apostolic tradition, in the experience of the Church and in relevant research from the human and social sciences (Pontifical Council for Justice and Peace 2004 §72–78). These documents have the same authority as the teachings of the Church Fathers and therefore carry great weight in the Catholic tradition. This authority makes these documents relevant for all countries where Catholicism is prevalent and makes the Catholic Church an important observer both at the United Nations and in different international organs (Tomasi 2017). Papal diplomats, also called apostolic nuncios, are posted all around the world to foster diplomatic relations with different countries and cultures. As a result, the Holy See is able to focus on furthering the dignity of man and the inalienable rights of every human person without being obliged to make political alliances. Despite several assertions that the church should not interfere in politics, as John Paul II stated in 1979, "Man's way is the Church's way", and the Church cannot remain indifferent to anything that concerns man.[33]

The purpose of the Church's social teaching is to help the faithful, and potentially everyone else, to make decisions and to ground their actions on a well-formed conscience. Catholic social teaching contains a vast array of moral theories, but not much of applied politics. It does not give final answers; it involves applying Christian principles to actual problems, to changing relationships and needs, by providing the premises for decision making. According to Catholic social teaching, economic activity needs to be guided by clear and fair rules, and the actors need to be guided by fundamental principles of the dignity of the human person, the common good, solidarity and subsidiarity. These principles are put into practice by the virtues of social justice and social love (Pontifical Council for Justice and Peace 2004 §§160, 201, 207 and 208).

Pope John Paul II called for a "strong juridical framework" on which the market economy was to be built *(Centesimus Annus* § 42), and Benedict XVI extends it to include charity as a guiding principle *(Caritas in Veritate* § 37), such that the economic activity could benefit the common good *(Evangelii Gaudium* §§ 56, 203). However, this mission can be accomplished only by the cooperation of all people in the world. The *Compendium of the Social Doctrine of the Church* (2004) affirms this by saying: "The teachings are also addressed to the brethren of other churches and ecclesial communities, to the followers of other religions, as well as to people of goodwill who are committed to serving the common good." (Pontifical Council for Justice and Peace 2004 § 84).[34] Among Catholics, the Church's social teaching

---

[33] Humanity is the 'way of the Church'- https://www.Catholicaustralia.com.au/church-documents/papal-documents/123-redemptor-hominis-1979-pope-john-paul-ii

Man is the way for the Church - a way that, in a sense, is the basis of all the other ways that the Church must walk- because man - every man without any exception whatever - has been redeemed by Christ, and because with man - with each man without any exception whatever - Christ is in a way united, even when man is unaware of it: "Christ, who died and was raised up for all, provides man" - each man and every man - "with the light and the strength to measure up to his supreme calling." (*Redemptor Hominis* § 14).

[34] Beginning with the Encyclical *Pacem in Terris* of John XXIII, the recipients are expressly identified in this manner – usually in the initial address of such documents.

has a mixed reception. Some consider it to be the Church's "best-kept secret," and strive to promote it, while others criticize it as an example of clergymen exceeding their competence. A glance through the different encyclicals and other documents quickly reveals how different the approach of each pope is to a given issue. At times it might seem as if popes contradict each other but, in reality, this serves to indicate the capacity of the Church to extend itself to address the vast themes of economic life, at different historical moments.

References

Allen, J.L. Jr. 2009. *Economic encyclical expands on church's 'best-kept secret*. National Catholic Raporter 06.22.2009 https://www.ncronline.org/news/economic-encyclical-expands-churchs-best-kept-secret

Benestad, J.B. 2011. *Church, State, and Society*. Washington, DC: Catholic University of America Press.

Bertina, L. 2013. The Catholic Doctrine of 'Integral Human Development' and its Influence on the International Development Community. *International Development Policy: Religion and Development* 4: 115–127.

Booth, P. 2014. *Catholic social teaching and the market economy* (Rev. 2nd Edn.). London: Institute of Economic Affairs Monographs

Charles, R. 1998a. *Christian social witness and teaching. The modern social teaching*. Vol. II. Gracewing, Herefordshire.

———. 1998b. *Christian social witness and teaching from biblical times to the late nineteenth century*. Vol. I. Gracewing, Herefordshire.

Crosthwaite, A. 2014. *Caritas in Veritate. Pope Benedict XVI's Blueprint for Development*. Roma: Lecture.

Den katolska sociallären. Dokument 1891–2015. 2019. Veritas Förlag, Stockholm.

Dorr, D. 2001. *Option for the poor: A hundred years of Vatican social teaching*. New York: Orbis Books.

Fredell, M. 2019. Introduktion till Populorum Progressio. In *Den katolska sociallären. Dokument 1891–2015*, 397–401.

———. 2020. *Catholic social doctrine*. Lecture for the bishops of the Church of Sweden 20 October 2020. https://www.dominikansystrarna.se/katolsk-sociallara/

Heiene, G. 2012. Kirkens sosiallære – et kritisk blikk. In *Hellig uro*, ed. P. Kværne and A.H. Utgaard. Oslo: Emilia forlag.

Hervada, J. 1983. *The principles of the social doctrine of the Church*. https://www.coursehero.com/file/36908281/THE-PRINCIPLES-OF-THE-SOCIAL-DOCTRINE-OF-THE-CHURCHdoc/

Hornsby-Smith, M.P. 2006. *An introduction to Catholic social thought*. Cambridge: Cambridge University Press.

Lavigne, J.-C., and H. Puel. 2007. For a human-centred economy: Louis Joseph Lebret (1897–1966). In *Preaching justice – Dominican contributions to social ethics in the. Twentieth Century*, ed. F. Compagnoni and H. Alford, 100–125. Dublin: Dominican Publications.

Massaro, T. 2012. *Living justice – Catholic social teaching in action*. 2nd ed. Maryland: Rowman & Littlefield Pub.

Nguyen, V.T. 1998. Preface. In *Centesimus Annus. Assessment and Perspectives for the Future of Catholic Social Doctrine*. Città del Vaticano: Libreria Editricie Vaticana.

Parish, H.R., ed. 1992. *Bartolomé de Las Casas, the only way, Paulist press*. New Jersey: Mahwah.

Pian, C. 2013. *La pensée sociale de l'Église racontée à ceux qui n'en savent rien*. Paris: Les Éditions de l'Atelier/Éditions ouvrières.

Pontifical Council for Justice and Peace. 2004. *Compendium of the social doctrine of the church*. Città del Vaticano: Libreria Editrice Vaticana.

Schuck, M. 1991. *That they may be one: The social teaching of the papal encyclicals 1740–1989*. Washington, DC: Georgetown University Press.

Silecchia, L.A. 2008. *The "Preferential Option for the Poor": An opportunity and a challenge for environmental decision-making*, 5 U. St. Thomas L.J. 87 (2008). https://scholarship.law.edu/scholar/85/

The Common Good. 1996. *The common good and the Catholic Church's social teaching*. A statement by the Catholic Bishops' Conference of England & Wales 1996.

Tomasi, S.M. 2017. *The Vatican in the family of nations. – Diplomatic actions of the Holy See at the UN and other international organizations in Geneva*. Cambridge University Press, Cambridge.

Woods, T.E., Jr. 2005. *The church and the market. Studies in ethics and economics*. New York/London: Lexington Books.

Else-Britt Nilsen born 1946, has a Ph.D. in sociology and a doctorate in theology. Government grant holder 2001–2013. Adjunct Professor at MF-Norwegian School of Theology 2010–2016. In periods also connected to University of Oslo. She is a Dominican Sister of Notre-Dame de Grâce, and prioress of this French-Norwegian congregation 2003–2022.

Chapter 14
On Muslim Attitudes to Modern Capitalism and to What It Brought Along

Jakob Skovgaard-Petersen

Abstract If many Muslim states are economic laggards, it is not enough to note that they are Muslim; it is rather more important to note that they are states, and to scrutinize the financial and economic policies of these states. These policies have, in retrospect, often been misguided and unsuccessful. But this has generally little connection to Islam. The Muslim countries were placed on the receiving end of an already advanced Capitalism, which obviously made it more difficult to compete.

Keywords Islam · Capitalism · Market · Secularization · Economic development · History of Middle East

14.1 Introduction

Western visitors to classical Muslim cities always marvel at the *suq*, or market. Narrow streets, overflowing with goods, charts, donkeys, insisting sellers and haggling buyers. Chaotic, and yet clearly organized, with streets dedicated to particular crafts and goods. And right in the middle the major mosque, the *jami'a*, with gates on every side opening up to the markets, and minarets calling to prayer and thus structuring the trading day.

If ever there was a religion connected to the market, it was Islam. Its weekly holiday, Friday, was not a day of rest, but a day of congregation, with markets open. Its founder, Muhammad, was a merchant himself, and its holy book, the Qur'an, is replete with terms and norms of trade. The religion matured in the major trading entrepôts of the world, and for hundreds of years its law covered vast stretches of land, thus providing a standardized legal framework and an encouragement to

---

J. Skovgaard-Petersen (✉)
Department of Cross-Cultural and Regional Studies, University of Copenhagen, Copenhagen S, Denmark
e-mail: jsp@hum.ku.dk

long-distance travel and trade. The caravan, that historical forerunner to the truck train, is a quintessentially Muslim phenomenon.

And yet, if today there is a religion accused of being antagonistic to Capitalism and modern markets, it is Islam. Contemporary critics consider Islam as an impediment to development: Muslims sit and pray, or even fast, instead of making money. Muslim states tend to be rich on oil, not on inventions, or not rich at all. The ban of interest is seen as an indicator of a general anti-Capitalist attitude. The image of the airplanes crashing into the World Trade Center in 2001 seems to be an apt metaphor for the relationship between Islam and Capitalism.

What went wrong? Not so much, really. In the nineteenth century, Capitalism made its way into a fairly receptive Muslim culture. But, like everywhere else, it was a mixed blessing, good for some and bad for others. In society, and between societies. Capitalism had its Muslim supporters and detractors. And that goes for Western scholars of the Muslim World, as well. More than simply investigating and establishing *the* relationship between Islam and Capitalism, we are, in short, entering a marketplace. Namely that of ideas. This chapter will briefly outline the scholarly debate on Islam and Capitalism and place it in an historical context.

14.2 Max Weber and the Sociology of Islam

On the subject of religious impact on social and economic behavior, Max Weber's sociology of religion forms an established point of departure. Instead of seeing religion, like Marx, as just a superstructure, or, like Comte, relegating it to a pre-modern era, Max Weber considered religion a significant sociological variable and a driving force in human development. Moreover, he emphasized the changeable nature of religion itself: instead of studying basic religious scriptures, Weber turned the attention to dominant carrier groups who developed a particular ethos which informed their social norms and behavior. With Weber, then, a dynamic sociology of religion was born.

Apart from his famous study on "The Protestant Ethic and the Spirit of Capitalism" (1904–05), Weber wrote substantively on "The Economic Ethics of the World Religions" (1920) investigating the developing ethos of the major world religions. Here, however, he omitted Islam. This omission is all the more remarkable as Islam seems to pose a very specific problem to Weber, namely in its similarity to Protestant Calvinism, the variety of religion that, under particular historical circumstances, had created an ethos favorable to the emergence of a spirit of Capitalism. Max Weber appears to have been well aware of these similarities: an "inner-worldly asceticism", a drive for salvation, a belief in Godly pre-destination. And he was working, or perhaps struggling, to formulate his response. A partial study on the differences between Christianity and Islam that might resolve this matter was written, but later omitted, from his posthumous work on "Economy and Society" 1920–21 (Schluchter 1987 pp. 22–23). It is, however, possible to collect Weber's many notes and remarks on Islam into a broader synthesis.

This work has been undertaken by an eminent Max Weber scholar and editor of the collected works, Wolfgang Schluchter. According to Schluchter, Weber identified several "material conditions" in Islamic culture that would have worked against the rationalization of economic production that is Capitalism. In the field of law, Weber pointed to the limitation of legal subjects to human persons, and what he called Qadi-justice, meaning the unhampered subjectivity of the judge and hence the overly arbitrary rulings of the courts. In the field of economics proper, Weber noted the ban on interest but made a more specific point about the prevalence of pious foundations (*awqaf*) which cannot be used as collateral and thus hamper the mobilization of capital for enterprises. And in the political field he pointed to the predominance of absolute and arbitrary rule ("Sultanism") which again would work against the predictability that would enable entrepreneurs to take long-term risks (Schluchter 1987 pp. 27–29).

More than these material preconditions, Weber was concerned about the religious roots of an ethos of social action. As mentioned, Weber had some problems with the *ethos* of Islam, as it bore many similarities with Protestantism. Like Protestantism, Islam was oriented towards active involvement in this world, under a supreme single God who is all-knowing and will reward or punish us for our deeds. Nevertheless, according to Weber, irrespective of these similarities, Islam did not provide the psychological basis for a capitalist personality. Unintentionally, Calvinism gave rise to a character who was never certain of salvation and, as a consequence, developed a method of self-control which engaged in earthly enterprises with a restless and feverish activity. Islam, by contrast, provided a self-assurance of salvation. Its engagement in this world resulted in military conquest, not in the formation of a hyperactive entrepreneurial personality (Schluchter 1987, 43–44).

14.3 The Spread of Capitalism and Inter-War Industrialization

Writing in the 1910s, Max Weber's project was a kind of "heuristic Eurocentrism", as Schluchter points out (Schluchter 1987 p. 25); it was about explaining the rise of Capitalism in Europe, not about understanding what was going in other parts of the world of which he had neither a particular expertise, nor a particular interest. Of course, he knew that the Muslim World was undergoing huge transformations. By the 1910s, most of it had been colonized by the British, the French, the Dutch, the Spanish, the Italians, and even his own German Empire. But even those parts that had not been colonized – the Ottoman Empire, Persia – were dramatically modernizing. European Capitalism had arrived in the port cities and was transforming the hinterlands. Slavery had been outlawed, and wage labor was taking hold. Banks, insurance, postal services, industrial companies and even stock exchanges had been introduced. Whatever factors Weber had identified as hindrances for the first development of Capitalism had not been capable of thwarting it when it finally arrived.

Nor was Capitalism simply seen as a European tool of dominance. Nationalists in Egypt and India did not oppose it but founded their own companies and banks to combat British economic dominance and exploitation and bolster their demand for political independence (Davis 1983). Moreover, this embrace of Capitalism was not limited to secular nationalists; even the Muslim Brotherhood did in fact invest in and set up businesses such as cotton mills (Beinin 1988 p. 219). And in his most famous speech in 1939, the founder of the Brotherhood, Hassan al-Banna, described it as an economic enterprise. The Brotherhood provided small-scale loans to set up enterprises, but it also called for the establishment of a ministry of social affairs to support the needy (Lia 1998 pp. 207–11). On the issue of support to workers, however, the Islamists were up against a formidable rival: unionized labor. And in independent or semi-independent countries such as Iran, Egypt, Syria and Iraq, a Communist movement emerged which considered Capitalism the enemy and effectively spread its message through pamphlets, evening schools and agitation among the workers.

14.4 Decolonization, the Cold War and the Rise of Modern Islamic Economic Thought

In the history of the Middle East, Asia and Africa, the 25 years from 1945 to 1970 are generally labeled de-colonization, as the most important development was the attainment of national independence and sovereignty. The period label in the Northern hemisphere – the cold war – was, however, also of great significance. What was of fairly minor significance was Islam.

The newly independent states set out on ambitious nation-building, including developmental targets such as universal schooling and healthcare. These were costly goals - often reached temporarily through nationalizations - and the states' expenses and size in the economy grew markedly. Most of the states were now republics, and many tilted towards some sort of Socialism. Some were allies of the Soviet Union, but others wanted to pursue a more independent course, allying with other third world states. Practically all were stridently nationalist and secularist.

On the other hand, their Secularism was not of an atheist variety. Rather, they tried to interpret Islam in a more socialist and materialist direction that would make it an instrument for mobilization of a generally believing citizenry. Muslim scholars went along with this new interpretation, either out of conviction, or because they saw it as the only way of maintaining some space and influence for religion. Islam, according to the new interpretation, was an ideology of the collective, and solidarity; it opposed all forms the hoarding of wealth, and let the state dispose over the collective fortune, collect taxes and redistribute them to the poor and pensioners. Some even went so far as to call Islam the blueprint of a Socialist welfare state (Skovgaard-Petersen 1997 pp. 370–71). The new ideology of "Islamic Socialism" was popular with so-called revolutionary republics such as Egypt, Tunisia and Iraq. On the other hand, it was opposed by their rivals, in particular Saudi Arabia, Morocco and Jordan. These monarchies were allied with the United States of

America and promoted a more Capitalist version of Islam, stressing the sanctity of private ownership, moral and propriety, rather than solidarity and redistribution.

Islamic Socialism was initially also adopted by Islamist opposition thinkers such as Mustafa al-Sibai in Syria, Sayyed Qutb in Egypt and Muhammad Baqer al-Sadr in Iraq. The latter introduced a state-centered, redistributive Islamism also within Shia Islam (Mallat 1993). Later in the 1960s, when Islamist thinkers and activists were forced to seek refuge in Saudi Arabia and the Gulf Emirates, the Socialism part of their Islamism was toned down.

Scholarship on the subject of Islam and economy also went into a kind of cold war period. In the Soviet Union and Eastern Europe, the subject was treated according to the doctrines of materialist history as it evolved. The West, in turn, was dominated by modernization theory, a kind of vulgarization of Weberianism that tried to identify drivers towards (Western) modernity, in terms of consumption, choice, individualism and capital accumulation. Muslim societies were seen as undifferentiated "tradition" which would have to move, or be moved, in the direction of rational Western modernity. Weber's thesis of a Protestant ethos that was both irrational and unintended was ignored. Instead, there were tangible, even measurable, markers of modernity that could be registered and counted. As Salvatore has formulated, in Talcott Parson's version, Weber's heuristic eurocentrism was transformed into a normative eurocentrism in an objectivist American social science (Salvatore 1996 p. 473).

One example of modernization theory as applied to economic orientations in the Muslim World would be Bernard Lewis' *Communism and Islam* from 1954. In this article Lewis discusses the attraction of Communism to the Muslim World and predicts that Muslim countries will adopt Communism with ease. After pointing to some "accidental factors" such as the popularity of anti-Imperialism and widespread poverty, he moves on to what he calls the "essential factors", namely the congruence between Communism and Islam. Both are totalitarian, have a mission and a clergy, and believe in their inevitable victory. They are anti-individualist and egalitarian: brothers can easily become comrades. (Lewis 1954).

A kind of counter-narrative is provided in Maxime Rodinson's book *Islam et capitalisme* from 1966. Like Lewis, Rodinson was a specialist in Middle Eastern languages whose interest were in contemporary politics. But while Lewis was a representative of British Conservatism, and a supporter of Zionism and Turkish Kemalism, Rodinson was a Marxist who had broken with Soviet Communism. In the book Rodinson rebuts Weber's attempts at demonstrating Islam's incompatibility with Capitalism. Population density in major urban centers, artisan excellence and long-distance trade were the material conditions for a proto capitalism, with a standardized currency and a unified legal framework (Rodinson 1966 p. 5). Moreover, Rodinson demonstrates that credit was readily available, and that the ban on interest was habitually circumvented. Pointing out that there was a great variety of social modes of production in the vast Muslim expanse, Rodinson maintains that, like in early modern Europe, a capitalist sector was in place. Disregarding Weber's emphasis on the irrational Calvinist *ethos*, Rodinson stresses a rationalism in Islam. At the end he states that, in modern Muslim states, Islam will not be decisive for the development of a modern humanist society with social justice (Rodinson 1966 pp. 241–43).

There is some irony in the conservative Lewis seeing that Islam will lead to Communism, while the socialist Marxist Rodinson considers Islam as a proto-Capitalist religion. All the while the parties in the "Arab cold war", especially Nasser's Egypt and Faisal's Saudi Arabia were busy harnessing their respective scholars to redefine Islam as a modern economic doctrine. What none of them seems to have anticipated was the huge religious awakening that swept over much of the Muslim World (and, indeed, Israel, India and other countries, as well) from the 1970s.

14.5 The Islamic Awakening and the Rise of Islamic Banking: The Period 1970–2000

Many factors seem to have converged to provide a fertile ground for a Muslim religious awakening: the 1967 defeat to Israel and the ensuing demise of Nasserism and secular nationalism, the oil boom and the rise of Saudi Arabia, the Vietnam war and a new culture of political protestation. That need not concern us here. What matters is the emergence of a broad religious awakening across the Muslim World, after generations of secularization. Political Islamism was a benefactor of the awakening, as became clear in the 1979 Iranian revolution, the 1977 Zia ul-Haqq coup d'état in Pakistan and a general rise of Islamist movements. But politics did not exhaust the phenomenon of the awakening, and many believers did not channel their new-found religiosity into political engagement. The awakening took many forms, but it could be subsumed under the slogan of the "Islamic solution", or the "Islamic alternative." It was a period of experimentation, also economically, and the cold war competition between Capitalism and Communism was increasingly irrelevant.

Islamic solutions had to be found – also in the field of economics. The earlier period's rivalry between Capitalism and Communism gave way to more "third-way" initiatives. The most conspicuous was Islamic banking. First set up in the countryside of Egypt to attract small savings, in the 1970s Islamic banking was re-established in Saudi Arabia and the Gulf as part of a huge financial build-up in the wake of the skyrocketing oil revenues after 1973. Since then, other Islamic financial instruments have been introduced, such as bonds (*sukuk*) and mutual insurance (*takaful*). Today, Islamic finance has spread to practically all Muslim countries, with new centers in Malaysia and South Asia, and indeed to Europe and the US, and is a multi-billion-dollar business. Western banks, too, have opened specific Islamic branches to cater to Muslim customers. Even so, it is important to stress that, despite their use of classical Islamic legal terms, these are novel products and institutions, and they remain a minor fraction of banking and finance in the Muslim World.

The "Islamicness" of these modern financial institutions rests in their criticism of ordinary commercial banking and finance, and their ostensible ban on a fixed interest. Instead, they have developed a number of alternative lending and savings instruments – called *mudaraba or murabaha* - based on a principle of risk-sharing between the bank and its customer (Kuran 2004 pp. 8–15). Investigating these instruments,

Western scholars have generally concluded that, at the end of the day, they operate very closely to ordinary interest-based products and that there are elements of obfuscation which make these products less transparent (Kuran 2018 p.1308).

14.6 Scholarship and Modern Muslim Financial Norms

Scholarship, too, has moved on from the cold war. There is no longer a discussion about whether Islam "in its nature" is Communist or Capitalist, or whether it will lend itself to one system or the other. The reason why the Muslim World did not provide the ground for modern Capitalism, or modernity in general, can still be discussed. But there is little discussion that the Muslim World adapted to Capitalism fairly fast when the latter finally arrived. An early study on the subject by Peter Gran established that the Middle East increased its trade with Europe and began to import industrial products already in the eighteenth century (Gran 1979). Imports from Europe undermined traditional local production, and the rulers of the Middle East realized the need to establish their own factories. To achieve this, they had to export crops to Europe to raise money. And to do that, they need to build infrastructure, including commercial laws and registers to enable to establishment of banks and companies. By 1900, markets had been transformed and capitalist structures were in place in the major cities and states.

So if Islam did not initiate the emergence of Capitalism, nor the introduction of it, how did Muslims respond to the new mode of production and to all the developments that came in its wake? This has been the more rewarding question in scholarship since the 1970s.

The most comprehensive overview of Muslim responses to Capitalism is probably provided by Charles Tripp in *Islam and the Moral Economy: The Challenge of Capitalism* (Tripp 2006). Beginning with Napoleon's invasion in Egypt in 1798, the book follows the struggle of Muslim scholars and intellectuals to come to grips with the new European order and its overwhelming economic powers. This, again, is a marketplace of ideas, from incomprehension to appreciation to criticism, to innovation. Tripp considers Capitalism not just an economic system but a way of turning everything into objects of value, and thus items on a market, hereby challenging the moral system already in place. Muslim responses are thus not seen as feeble attempts at comprehension, but as a perfectly sensible struggle to rise to the challenges to a moral lifeworld (Tripp 2006 pp. 3–4), parallel to what believers in Europa, and indeed all over the world, have been facing.

This struggle, while perhaps commendable, has not been able to alter the course of Capitalism very significantly. Contemporary Islamic financial institutions, also in Tripp's view, do not amount to an islamization of modern finance. Rather, they amount to a further Capitalization of Islam. Islamic finance is yet another example of modern Capitalism's capacity to market itself to new customers and tastes:

> *Islamic banking may alert people to the ethical implications of their financial transactions, but, despite the hyperbole that attended the inauguration of Islamic banking in the 1970s, this is now seen as a means of engaging successfully with the forces of global capital, rather than the first step on the road to the undermining and overthrow of the capitalist system.*
> (Tripp 2006 p. 199).

To illustrate the development Tripp outlines, I myself made a more narrow study of Muslim scholars' fatwas on insurance. This was not so much to establish whether the Muslim scholars were pro or against insurance, but to investigate their understanding on the phenomenon. To sum it up, they move from incomprehension of the phenomenon (and the insurance contract) in the early 1800s, over understanding the need and use of insurance (if not its technicalities) in the early 1900s, towards a distinction between (bad) capitalist insurance and (good) social insurance in the 1950s (to the point where Islam itself is characterized as a mutual insurance system) (Skovgaard-Petersen 1997 pp. 335–73). From the 1970s, so-called Islamic Insurance Companies have been set up, catering to worried Muslims and stressing their basis in solidarity (*takaful*) and claiming to be competitive on capitalist grounds.

A different approach to modern Islam and economy can be detected in books on Islam and economic development which seek to demonstrate that Islam is hampering economic development even today. This type of book has proliferated especially since the Jihadist attack on World Trade Center in 2001. With titles such as "How Islamic Law Held Back the Middle East", "Why the West Got Rich and the Middle East Did Not", and "Das Verfallene Haus des Islams" they make no secret of their point of view and organize their studies as a case-building (Kuran 2011; Rubin 2017; Koopmans 2020). Here Islam is seen as a force in itself, and economic development is considered the ultimate good.

Some of the books focus on Max Weber's old question: why Capitalism took off in Europe and not in the Muslim World. Considered as a method, looking at the Muslim World to identify "deficiencies" in connection to developments in Europe is certainly heuristic Eurocentrism. Still, it may not be utterly futile. To live up to Weber, though, at least we should look at actual history, and not normative teaching. Muslims' actual observance of the ban of interest, the interactions with non-Muslim minorities, or women's work, seem to have varied a lot and cannot simply be inferred by referencing a sacred text. To take another example that is seminal to these works, Islamic hereditary laws do divide estates into numerous small allotments and may thus have hampered the accumulation, or continuity, of merchant capital (Kuran, 2017 p. 1333). But here, too, there were ways to pass on estates before death that would work against this division. And in modern times states have reformed their inheritance laws, allowing for a greater undivided part to be passed on through a will.

One issue in Islamic law and actual practice which may well have hampered the emergence of Capitalism, is the predominance of *awqaf*, or pious foundations. These foundations do not date back to the time of the prophet, and they are not mentioned in the Qur'an, but they become an important institution in Muslim societies in the middle ages. Serving as a means to avoid confiscation or harsh taxation, they proved popular with many rich families who would maintain some control of their assets through the supervision of the foundation. The incomes of the foundations were, however, tied to their stated pious purpose, and the asset could no longer be traded or used as collateral. Following Weber, Timur Kuran argues that the widespread and accumulated use of *awqaf* took many assets out of the market and minimized the capital available for enterprises. Moreover, considered against the European corporations, the stipulations that governed the Muslim *awqaf* could not be altered with the changing of the times and thus became increasingly cumbersome (Kuran 2011 pp. 97–142). No wonder, then, that in the twentieth century they were considered an economic impediment and often nationalized. All the same, like charities in the West, in pre-modern times the *awqaf* were an indispensable social good, funding hospitals, schools and other social services.

While in this heuristic sense it may be relevant to look for impediments to the emergence of Capitalism in social and economic practices related to Islam in the pre-modern Muslim World, it is also a speculative endeavour. As Patricia Crone har commented, perhaps the real question is not an Islamic culture that held back, but the "oddity of Europe" that pushed on (Crone 2003 p. 147). After all, history is not teleology, and industrial Capitalism is not its logical outcome. Even more dubious is these books' proclivity to take these "deficiencies" and project them up to modern times as the (Islamic) reason why many Muslim countries remain economic laggards. This is where, once again, Weber's heuristic eurocentrism is transformed into a normative eurocentrism in an objectivist American social science.

The fact is that, in modern Muslim states, Capitalism rules, and the characteristics that may once have impeded its emergence are long gone. The *awqaf* are either abolished or insignificant. The ban on interest – never fully upheld – was abandoned long ago, and Islamic financial institutions are no less capitalist than ordinary banks. Corporations as legal entities were introduced along with European commercial laws in the nineteenth century, and companies are as common as in the West, many of them stable for generations.

What these studies tend to explain away, is Colonialism, the very result of the rise of Europe. It was, after all, colonial powers that allotted to the African and Asian territories a role as suppliers of raw materials and consumers of expensive industrial goods. The Muslim countries were placed on the receiving end of an already advanced Capitalism, which obviously made it more difficult to compete. Even more so, these studies tend to ignore the significance of the modern state. If many Muslim states are economic laggards, it is not enough to note that they are Muslim; it is rather more important to note that they are states, and to scrutinize the financial and economic policies of these states. These policies have, in retrospect, often been misguided and unsuccessful. But they have little connection to Islam.

An example of the projection of the old Weberian "deficiency" claims upon contemporary Muslim states, is Ruud Koopmans' popular *The Decayed House of Islam* (Das Verfallene Haus des Islams, 2020) (Koopmans 2020), a general indictment of Muslim practices, norms and mores, in Muslim states and among immigrants in Europa. While there may indeed be many things to criticize, the characterization of Muslim economic practices and thinking seem to be more about the middle ages than about today. Using UN statistics, Koopmans points to a general underdevelopment in Muslim countries, except for those rich in oil. This he attributes largely to characteristics of the classical period, such as the prevalence of *awqaf*, the ban on interest and the hostility towards to printing press (Koopmans 2020 pp. 135–44). None of this is of any relevance today. Conversely, Colonialism was, in his view, beneficial to the Muslim countries, in that it introduced statecraft and rule of law. (Koopmans 2020 pp. 62–69). That is true, albeit one should remember that it also introduced its opposite: dual legal systems, racial segregation, emergency rule and many other features which have had a more lasting impact on the modern independent states than medieval Muslim norms. Comparing Egypt to South Korea – in 1970 at the same level, today South Korea many times richer – Koopmans concludes that this is due to Islam's hold on Egypt's economic policies through its religious university, al-Azhar, and the political prominence of Islamists (Koopmans 2020 pp. 145–47). This is incorrect; neither Islamists nor al-Azhar have had any significant influence on Egypt's economic policies which have indeed been disastrous.

A recurring argument in these books is the significance of trust, or the lack of it, for economic development, combined with statistics that show high level of trust in Western Europe and other advanced economies, whereas it is lower in Muslim countries and in the Third World in general. In these countries, people have little trust in each other, or in companies or governments, something that may well complicate economic transactions (Kuran 2018 p. 1312). Once again, this may in part be due to a strong in-group attitude which again may be reminiscent of earlier Islamic norms. But it seems fair also to point to actual experiences with sequestrations and nationalizations, inequality, the significance of connections, corruption and other features of weak and authoritarian states. Under these conditions, a lack of trust seems to be a sensible and self-preserving response. If people in much of the Muslim World invest their surplus money in gold, this may again be a fairly sensible investment, even from a capitalist point of view, and not simply an expression of "traditional Islam". Not only is gold portable, protectable and easily exchangeable; it may also have protected them from inflation, red-tape, or even sequestration.

Even though they are common in many Muslim countries, authoritarianism, corruption and mismanagement are not a monopoly of the Muslim World. And to Muslims, they are certainly far from ideal. In fact, these authoritarian features and economic failures are often singled out as being among the reasons for the religious resurgence from the 1970s onwards. Rather than being a product of a vaguely defined "Islam", part of the attraction of Islam may well be a – possibly naïve – moral and religious reaction to them. This latter interpretation is more in line with Charles Tripp's investigation into Muslim responses to Capitalism and other economic realities of modern life.

14.7 Conclusion

Historically, Islam has been intricately related to trade and the market. This is clear in its scripture, in the trade of its founder, and in the detailed regulations and interest bestowed on trade in the classical Islamic legal tradition. It is also evidenced in the introduction of its universal currency, the dinar, and in the urban architecture on its major historical cities. This may all have prepared the ground for industrial Capitalism which gradually made its impact from the eighteenth century, and came to dominate Middle Eastern and other Muslim economies from the beginning of the twentieth century, whether they were colonized or not.

Industrial Capitalism, however, had its roots in Europe. Since Max Weber, the issue of its religious roots has been intensely debated, and Weber also opened the discussion about reasons for Capitalism's non-emergence in non-Christian civilizations. Weber's study of Islam was never completed, but in his works are numerous observations as to why Muslim societies did not develop modern Capitalism before it was imposed upon them. These are partly deficiencies, in that Muslim civilization lacked certain features, such as the corporation or the municipality. But while Weber importantly attributed great significance to certain rational features, e.g. double book-keeping, his special emphasis was on irrational, psychological drivers which formed a spirit of Capitalism with its own personality, the methodical but ultimately also irrational capitalist entrepreneur. Weber had, it should be noted, no problems with the fact that the Muslim World had later adapted to Capitalism. His was a project about the preconditions, not the later developments.

By the 1950s, Weber's tentative explorations and conclusions had been frozen stiff in cold war ideologies. The Muslim World was dominated by nationalists and secularists, but also divided between those who leaned towards the United States and those who leaned towards the Soviet Union. In the Western World, modernization theory dominated, with a vulgarized Weberianism identifying drivers of modernization, and bastions of tradition, with claims to scientific objectivity. Non-Christian religions were seen to embody "tradition" and hence to be obstacles to development. The discussion was therefore about the adaptability of Islam to Capitalism (or Socialism), based on its institutions and teaching, not on Weber's idea of an ethos, which might even be irrational.

From the 1970s onwards, an Islamic awakening has taken place in many Muslim countries. The secular ideologies that dominated most of the twentieth century went into a decline, but secularization as a process does not seem to have been reversed, or only marginally. Islamic branding has certainly become commonplace, but this is largely within the market and has even created its own consumption of Islamic products (Haenni 2005). This includes banks, insurance companies and financial instruments. Among researchers, this new Muslim interest in Islamic solutions has revived an interest in the relationship between Islam and economics. This chapter has pursued two tendencies: one is to study Muslim responses to Capitalism and the regulation and consumption that is brought with it. This literature considers Capitalism a social and historical fact in the Muslim World, but also a perennial challenge to Muslims, and indeed to everyone else. The other tendency is to re-open the modernization theory and discuss the overall question of Islam's compatibility, if not with Capitalism as such, then with successful economic development. While not denying that Islamic norms can influence social and economic behavior, this chapter points to their context and historicity. In doing so, it considers some of the arguments in this literature unconvincing, due to its method of isolating Islamic features and privileging them as factors, and its relative disregard of other factors, including the whole setting of Colonialism, as well as the establishment, growth and economic policies of the modern Muslim states.

References

Beinin, J. 1988. Islam, Marxism and the Shubra textile workers. In *Islam, politics and social movements*, ed. Burke and Lapidus, 207–227. Los Angeles: UCLA Press.

Crone, P. 2003. *Pre-industrial societies*. New York: Simon & Schuster.

Davis, E. 1983. *Challenging colonialism. Bank Misr and Egyptian Industrialization, 1920–1941*. Princeton: Princeton University Press.

Gran, P. 1979. *Islamic roots of capitalism*. Austin: University of Texas Press.

Haenni, P. 2005. *L'islam de marché*. Paris: Seuil.

Koopmans, R. 2020. *Das Verfallene Haus des Islams*. C.H. Beck, München. Here quoted from the Danish translation, *Islams forfaldne hus,* Presto, Copenhagen 2020.

Kuran, T. 2004. *Islam and mammon: The economic predicaments of Islamism*. Princeton: Princeton University Press.

———. 2011. *The long divergence: How Islamic law held Back the Middle East*. Princeton: Princeton University Press.

———. 2018. Islam and economic performance. Historical and contemporary links. *Journal of Economic Literature* 56.4: 1292–1359.

Lewis, B. 1954. Islam and communism. *International Affairs* 30 (1): 1–12.

Lia, B. 1998. *The society of the Muslim Brothers in Egypt. The rise of an Islamic mass movement*, 1928–42. Ithaca Press, Reading.

Mallat, C. 1993. *The renewal of Islamic law*. Muhammad Baqer al-Sadr, Najaf, and the Shia International, Cambridge University Press, Cambridge.

Rodinson, M. 1966. *Islam et capitalisme*. Paris: Seuil.

Rubin, J. 2017. *Rulers, religion, and riches: Why the west got rich and the Middle East did not*. Cambridge: Cambridge University Press.

Salvatore, A. 1996. Beyond orientalism? Max Weber and the Displancements of 'Esseentialism' in the study of Islam. *Arabica* 43: 457–485.

Schluchter, W. 1987. Zwischen Welteroberung und Weltanpassung. Max Weber's Sicht des Islams. In *Max Webers Sicht des Islams*, ed. W. Schluchter. Frankfurt a.M: Suhrkamp.

Skovgaard-Petersen, J. 1997. *Defining Islam for the Egyptian State*. Brill/Leiden: Muftis and Fatwas of the Dar al-Ifta.

Tripp, C. 2006. *Islam and the moral economy: The challenge of capitalism*. Cambridge: Cambridge University Press.

Jakob Skovgaard-Petersen born 1963, since 2008 professor of Islam and the Arabic world at Department of Cross-Cultural and Regional Studies, University of Copenhagen. Director of Danish-Egyptian Dialogue Institute 2005–2008. 2020 he published the book *Muslimernes Muhammad – og alle andres (The Muslims Muhammad – and all others')*

Part III
The Limitation of the Market: Some Cases

Chapter 15
Markets for Human Body Parts: The Case of Commercial Surrogacy

Kirsten Halsnæs and Thomas Ploug

Abstract The trade in human body parts can be understood as a solution to key challenges for both buyers and suppliers, as well as being a manifestation of individual property rights over one's own body. However, it can be argued that there are serious ethical issues involved in commercializing the body in this way, despite which there has recently been a large increase in the international trade in human body parts. The most extensive transactions have concerned the trade in kidneys and the services of the fertility industry. An important driver of this is the fact that the medical profession is increasingly able to facilitate exchanges of human body parts relatively smoothly. The chapter focuses on commercial surrogacy as an example of the ethical aspects of the trade in human body parts and addresses the potential interplay between markets and ethical issues.

Keywords Trade in human body parts · Commercial surrogacy · Economics · Ethics · Dignity and exploitation of people

15.1 Introduction

The trade in human body parts can be understood as a solution to key challenges for the health and economic opportunities of both buyers and sellers, as well as manifesting individual property rights over one's own body. However, it can also be argued that there are serious ethical issues related to commercializing the body in

---

K. Halsnæs (✉)
Department of Technology, Management and Economics, Technical University of Denmark, Lyngby, Denmark
e-mail: khal@dtu.dk

T. Ploug
Department of Communication and Psychology, Aalborg University, Aalborg, Denmark
e-mail: ploug@hum.aau.dk

this way, with implications for human dignity and the exploitation of individuals with low capacities and opportunities through such market mechanisms.

One very early debate in this regard revolved around the practice of paying for blood taken from donors. Richard Titmuss (1971b) analysed blood donor systems in the UK and USA, in which no payment is made for blood in the former, unlike in parts of the latter. He found great disadvantages in forms of payment, both ethical (with large quantities blood being transferred from the poor to the rich) and practical (some volunteers pull out, or the blood proves to be of inferior quality because the poor 'blood-sellers' hide the diseases they have). Titmuss's book attracted a great deal of attention and was intensely discussed within the medical profession (Titmus himself wrote an article for *The Lancet*; Titmuss 1971a) and by ethicists (see, e.g., Singer 1973, Archard 2002, Hausman and McPherson 1993) and economists (where the Nobel laureates Kenneth Arrow and Robert Solow participated with lengthy contributions to the debate; see Arrow 1972, and Solow 1971).

Despite this, there has recently been a large increase in the international trade in human body parts, an important driver for which is that the medical profession is increasingly able to facilitate exchanges of human body parts relatively smoothly. Large differences in intergenerational wealth also provide a strong basis for the market. The commercial exchange of human body parts ranges from trading in them, especially kidneys and in the fertility industry, to surrogacy. In the following we focus on surrogacy as an example of the ethical aspects of the trade in human body parts, in which the requisite services are offered by low-income mothers to well-off buyers in, for example, OECD countries. We also address the potential interplay between markets and ethical issues seen from the perspectives of economic theory and philosophy respectively. Our aim is to contest claims that markets are the ultimate instruments in facilitating freedom for those actors who resort to them.

In this paper we contrast what might be called the libertarian approach, in which markets are seen as a means to facilitate a process characterized by freedom for both the surrogate mothers and the buyers of their services, with approaches in which the capabilities and opportunities of individuals are treated as important aspects of their freedom to choose from among the alternatives they have reasons to value (Sen 2002). Approaches stressing dignity and human autonomy inspired by Kantian philosophy will also be considered in this context before we offer conclusions about the role of moral and cultural values in market transactions like commercial surrogacy.

Commercial surrogacy was legal in India until 2015, including both arrangements with foreigners and domestic services, and other Asian countries were also extensively involved previously, like Thailand until 2015, when a ban was also imposed there. The markets for surrogate mothers have now been taken over by other countries, including Ukraine and Poland. We will provide examples of official government arguments for allowing surrogate motherhood before and after India and Thailand banned the practice and provide empirical evidence of surrogate mothers and their stated reasons for deciding to offer surrogacy. Based on this, we will compare the norms and business of the now closed surrogacy markets and those emerging in countries like Ukraine.

15.2 Assessment of Surrogacy Markets

It is very difficult to assess the scale of the commercial market for surrogacy due to the lack of official statistics on exchanges and the fact that private clinics have no obligation to report their activities.

An overview of the legislation on surrogate motherhood country by country is provided by Wikipedia 2021 (see Fig. 15.1), which shows that remunerative and altruistic forms of surrogacy are only allowed in parts of eastern Europe, including Greece, Ukraine and Russia, parts of the US and certain other previous Soviet republics. During the last decade there has been a large shift in the geographical locations of surrogate clinics. Before 2015, countries like India and Thailand played a dominant role in the market, but remunerative surrogacy with buyers from abroad is now forbidden in India, where only Indian citizens are now permitted to be involved.

Nonetheless India was formerly one of the largest hosts of surrogate motherhood due to its very favourable legal conditions and low prices. Furthermore, the perceived risk of surrogate mothers insisting on keeping babies from the buyers had been very low because most surrogate mothers could not afford not to be paid (Centre for Social Research 2010). The conditions offered to Indian surrogate mothers were nonetheless poor, the women suffering from a lack of freedom, being kept in crowded hostels under the control of others, and their contacts with their families being highly restricted during their pregnancy. Furthermore, high numbers of eggs were often implanted in the women, with potential consequences for their health.

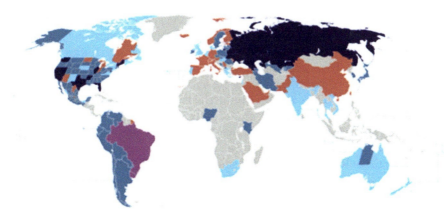

Fig. 15.1 Legal regulation of surrogacy in the world
■ Both remunerative and altruistic forms are legal
■ No legal regulation
□ Only altruistic surrogacy is legal
■ Allowed between relatives up to second degree of consanguinity
■ Banned
□ Uncertain

The Centre for Social Research (2010) has collected very extensive information about the conditions and social statuses of surrogate mothers in India, concluding that the mothers' primary reasons for engaging in surrogacy were the poverty of their families and the wish to be able to pay for the education of their own children.

According to Shetty (2012), before 2002 about 25,000 children were born in India, 50% involving biological parents from the West. Due to concerns about the very low payments to the surrogate mothers, the Indian government banned such services with the exception of domestic Indian citizens (Timms 2018). To our knowledge there are no public data available about the extent of the commercial services supplying surrogate mothers in India after 2015.

In 2015, Thailand, like India, started a process forbidding surrogate motherhood with foreigners, one of the main drivers behind this being a case which raised widespread international attention: a surrogate mother gave birth to a handicapped baby, which the biological commissioning parent refused to accept. However, the evidence now suggests that the business of providing the services of surrogate mothers is still going on in Thailand involving cross-border collaboration in the provision of clinics.[1] Ukraine and Poland are now both rapidly emerging markets for surrogate mothers.[2] Providing such services to foreign clients is legal and is endorsed by both governments, this being a relatively low-cost alternative to similar services offered in, for example, the USA.

15.3 Alternative Economic Perspectives on Surrogacy

Considering the ethical aspects of surrogacy from the perspective of economic theory is directly related to basic theoretical differences between ethical and libertarian paradigms (Hausman and McPherson 1993). The ethical paradigm draws on ideas in moral philosophy, but it adds the efficient allocation of resources as a major criterion of the level of efficiency within the boundaries of ethical issues. On the other hand, libertarian approaches emphasize the rights of individuals to engage in the actions they want and find useful according to their preferences.

In economics the market is generally understood as a central mechanism governing exchanges of goods and services due to its role in facilitating efficiency and thereby optimizing welfare. Markets for surrogacy can therefore be discussed in the context of whether there are reasons to make specific moral claims in relation to the exchange of such services. The notion of individual freedom is often used in arguments claiming that the market system makes people "free to choose" and thereby optimizes social welfare (Hausman and McPherson 1993), thus ensuring that individuals have the freedom to engage in surrogacy.

---

[1] https://www.bbc.com/news/world-asia-43169974

[2] https://neweasterneurope.eu/2020/12/24/lack-of-regulation-and-covid-19-leaves-ukrainian-surrogate-mothers-and-babies-in-limbo/

The concept of the market was introduced by Adam Smith in his *Wealth of Nations* in 1776 (Adam Smith 1981). The argument here is that individuals should be responsible for their own choices and the consequences of those choices, which could be interpreted as endorsing the idea of a free market in surrogate motherhood. In his *The Theory of Moral Sentiments* (Smith 1759), however, Smith claimed that 'Man was capable of forming moral judgements beyond a limited sphere of activity, again centred around his own self-interest', and he continued that 'The administration of the great system of the universe … the care of the universal happiness of all rational and sensible beings, is the business of God and not of man'.

This suggests that the role of the market should be seen in its historical and cultural contexts. In the case of Smith, the freedom and role of individuals were framed by a Christian moral philosophy that extended to related aspects of human dignity and autonomy. This also implies that, when applying the framework suggested by Smith for assessing the ethical aspects of markets for surrogacy, the fact that transactions may take place between humans from different cultural and religious backgrounds makes the assessment more complicated. The buyer of the service is then involved in a transaction with a surrogate mother, for whom different moral rules and traditions apply.. Even though it can be argued that surrogacy is permitted by law in some countries, it can still be questioned whether it is morally acceptable in society generally.

The Indian economist and Nobel Laureate Amartya Sen argues that the view that markets are a mechanism providing freedom has two important components, namely opportunity and the processual aspects of freedom (Sen 2002). He argues that, just as freedom gives us the opportunity to achieve our objectives, things we have reason to value, so opportunities are concerned with our ability to achieve. The process component can be related to the notion of autonomous choice, that is, having the lever of control in one's own hands. The concern is over the procedure for taking free decisions by oneself.

Key aspects of Sen's categories of freedom as they might relate to surrogacy are how the fact of a surrogate mother entering into such a transaction can influence her opportunity to achieve her aspirations as an individual, with full autonomy of decision-making and full immunity from encroachment by others. We will now address these issues in a discussion about the dignity of individuals from the point of view of Kantian philosophy.

In focusing on the ethical consequences of an exchange involving a surrogate mother, from a libertarian perspective the transaction might be justified provided both the supplier and the client are aware of the consequences and these are in accordance with their respective ethical values. Both agents can then maximize their utility by undertaking the transaction. Blazier and Janssens (2020) support this argument in their review of surrogacy markets in India and the Netherlands. Surrogacy is considered a labour market issue, it being suggested that fair-trade principles should apply in respect of payment for the services and information about the implications of entering into a surrogacy arrangement. The authors conclude that exploitation is not particularly an issue of surrogacy, but rather a consequence of unequal societies with low returns for labour. The role of full information is emphasized in order to avoid manipulation woman being treated as disposable resources for the benefit of the fertility industry.

Several questions can be asked in relation to this conclusion. In exchanges involving human body parts, it is obviously highly uncertain whether the supplier and buyer are able to ignore all the consequences of their engagement with each other. These consequences include various physical, psychological and other outcomes from both short- and long-term perspectives, including the arrangements made for the exchange with regard to, for example, the role of clinics, which may have a vested interest in not supplying full information about the risks involved.

Even in the ideal case, where all the consequences are fully understood and agreed by the individuals involved, there is still a question whether individuals' preferences can be understood as well-defined standards of measurement for what creates utility. Mainstream economics indulge in rich discussions about what constitutes the preferences of individuals, ranging from views that only understand preferences as self-centred to views that, in addition to self-interest, also make reference to more altruistic values and have more diverse reasons for making the necessary choices (Sen 2002).

Seen in the context of surrogate mothers, to the extent that preferences are understood as merely being self-centred, it is easier to argue that, if an individual engages in a practice like surrogate mothership, then she is just following her own self-interest, this being ethically acceptable to the extent that she understands the possible consequences and receives a fair price for her services. However, if we understand preferences in a more complex way, where there is a broader set of values underpinning the reasons and choices involved, then it is more difficult to assess the ethical consequences of being a surrogate mother.

15.4 Dignity, Autonomy and Consent: A Perspective from Kantian Philosophy

There are many similarities in how economics and philosophy have addressed the existence of market activities like commercial surrogacy. A key concept in the philosophical perspective on commercial surrogate motherhood is the principle of human dignity in the work of Emmanuel Kant, who provides a defence of human dignity. He writes:

> But man regarded as a person, that is, as the subject of morally practical reason is exalted above any price. For as a person (homo noumenon) he is not to be esteemed as a mere means to the ends of others or even to his own ends, but rather as an end in himself, that is, as possessing a dignity (an absolute inner value), through which all other rational beings in the world are required to have respect for him ... (Kant 1998)

Accordingly, commercial surrogacy may be regarded as violating the dignity of the surrogate mother and the child she bears. If so, and if the principle of dignity can be justified, this principle may present a restriction on allowing the market allocation of goods and opportunities to apply to surrogacy.

Kant sees human dignity as closely interwoven with the requirement always to treat others as ends in themselves, thus linking respect for dignity with respect for autonomy. Kant's reasoning is as follows: We are as human beings endowed with reason in the sense that we have the capacity to generate ideas that may help regulate our lives. We are rational beings who, through the exercise of reason, may impose binding goals on ourselves. In short, we have the capacity for autonomy. Treating others and oneself as an end is a requirement if the human capacity to legislate for or govern oneself is not to be violated, thus respecting his or her autonomy. Treating someone merely as a means to one's own ends happens when we intervene in the lives of others in ways that undercut their ability to exercise their powers of reason in formulating their own goals and in their ability to pursue these goals in action.

In the Kantian view, protection of the principles of autonomy and dignity is not simply a matter of preserving freedom of choice in the sense of ensuring that an intervention leaves the individual with alternative, possible choices of action or an unaltered or relevantly similar set of choices. Protecting autonomy is also not simply a matter of respecting an individual's expressed preferences. Protecting an individual's freedom of choice and expressed preferences are necessary to protect that individual's autonomy, but they are not sufficient. To treat others as an end indeed means providing them with room to make choices from among the variety of options they find relevant and valuable, and to refrain from violating their declared preferences. The Kantian conception, however, is more substantial than that: it ties autonomy to a rational procedure in which, on the basis of reflection, an individual formulates goals, values and life-plans, and it also considers by what means they may be implemented in action in a given situation. Protecting autonomy is matter of protecting this rational procedure and the choices made on this basis.

The Kantian conception lays down a strong foundation for discussing whether the dignity of individuals is being respected in cases where surrogate mothers are kept fully informed and are aware of the consequences of their actions. This, for example, could form the basis of support for a libertarian approach to surrogate mothership, on the assumption that the surrogate mother is well informed and can monitor what she is engaged in, which could be referred to as informed consent (Faden and Beauchap 1986).

Clearly, seeking consent, in particular informed consent, may not protect individual autonomy in the Kantian sense. An individual may be unable to understand, reflect or make a choice on the basis of the information provided, and the choice the individual makes may be manipulated to his or her disadvantage. In all these cases the provision of consent will fail to protect the rationality of the end-setting activity that constitutes autonomy in the Kantian sense. In modern bioethics giving valid informed consent is typically also assumed to require deliberative and decisional competence, understanding, and the absence of undue influence (Beauchamp and Childress, 2001). In this context we can ask whether the limited opportunities available to a surrogate mother living in a condition of poverty really enables her to make a decision that is not influenced by her family or her own failure to fulfil the wish, for example, to provide educational opportunities for her own children.

In relation to the arguments previously discussed that are based on the approach of economic libertarianism, Kant's emphasis on autonomy seems to posit a strong right grounded in the individual's body, which might be considered to extend to the right to engage in commercial surrogacy. However, two problems present themselves here.

First, the Kantian imperative of non-instrumentalization requires not only that one avoids treating others as a mere means to one's own ends, but also that one does not treat oneself as a mere means to an end either. In short, we are also required to protect our own capacity to engage in the rational formulation and pursuit of our own goals. For Kant this implies limitations on the use of the body. Mutilations of the body, whether temporary or permanent (e.g. suicide), are thus, for Kant, violations of this requirement. The body can only to be put to uses that are consistent with maintaining the ability to exercise autonomy. Selling certain organs, such as the heart, would obviously undermine this capacity as well. However, the precise restrictions placed on the potential uses of the body on the basis of this argument are unclear.

Second, and more importantly, the Kantian conception of autonomy places constraints on the formulation and pursuit of goals, values and life-plans that may be difficult to honour in many de facto situations of commercial surrogacy. Assuming informed consent to constitute an adequate protection of autonomy in the Kantian sense, it follows that surrogate mothers, for instance, must be adequately informed about the consequences of engaging in the transaction they are being asked to provide, must understand all the relevant information and must provide consent without being forced or manipulated into doing so. In commercial surrogacy large sums of money typically change hands. From a fairness perspective this seems justified because of the invasive character and the risks involved, and it may be inevitable simply because of the global demand. However, the large amounts of compensation offered clearly transform these services into an industry with many stakeholders. This potential introduces a financial interest into the transaction from a multitude of actors apart from the surrogate mother, such as the owners of clinics, the health-care professionals that work in them, middlemen of various kinds, politicians, families and relatives etc. Interests are therefore created that threaten to bias information in various ways. Given so many actors with a vested financial interest in the transaction, there is reason to suspect that the surrogate mother will be exposed to different kinds of pressure to engage in the transaction, not least from her own family members, who may benefit significantly from it. However, the strongest threat to the voluntary nature of the consent may come from the impact of the financial offer on the surrogate mother's own attitude to surrogacy and its potential risks and side-effects. The financial offer associated with surrogacy may thus be seductive in the sense that it alters and distorts the surrogate mother's *ex ante* beliefs about the legitimacy of surrogacy, her evaluation of the harms and risks associated with it and her assessment of what it is in her own long-term interests that favours her agreeing to the surrogacy. If financial incentives impact on the voluntary nature of one's choices and actions in any way, it seems particularly likely to happen in the case of surrogacy given the relatively large sums of money involved when compared to the general socio-economic conditions of the surrogate mother in countries like India.

Note that the protection of dignity so conceived becomes a prerequisite for protecting a person's welfare and autonomy. It is by ascribing equal moral worth to others – and thus respecting their dignity – that the requirements of protecting welfare and autonomy become relevant.

15.5 Recapturing the Economic and Philosophical Perspective on Commercial Surrogate Motherhood

Based on economic theories about the market as an efficient allocation mechanism and the rights of individuals to pursue their individual preferences, including offering the services of a surrogate mother, it can be argued that these services are legitimate and should be facilitated by the implementation of regulations and information that can support fair process and protect woman's rights. There are, however, certain moral implications involved in using markets as a tool for commercial surrogacy services, as they can harm the possibilities, opportunities and freedom of individuals to choose from among the alternatives they might value (cf. again Sen 2002). Kant's philosophical perspective similarly focuses on the dignity of individuals, a central question here being whether commercial surrogacy involves an attitude of respect for others and whether such practices underpin our perceptions of others as persons of absolute value that must be treated as ends in themselves?

The answer to these moral questions, raised in the context of this comparison between economics and philosophy, depends on the moral norms that predominate in a given cultural context. From our perspective, however, it does seem that commercial surrogacy is a degrading practice in many cases and contexts. We base this evaluation on three features of these practices. First, they are *exploitative* in that they often involve people in advantageous socio-economic conditions buying these services at a relatively low price from others living in extreme poverty, who are desperate to accommodate the needs of their children and their family as a whole, and who are ill-informed about the consequences of entering into the transaction. That is, surrogacy takes advantage of very significant asymmetries in socio-economic conditions in order to obtain a service at an unfair price from others who are kept ill-informed and are under pressure from their disadvantageous conditions to enter the transaction.

Secondly, these contracts involve *irreversible invasions* of bodily integrity, as well as significant costs and risks of harm both physical and psychological in character. Thirdly, they are *commercializing* in that they put a price on a significant invasion of bodily and psychological integrity. That is, they treat bodily and psychological integrity – and ultimately human life – on a par with other commodities.

15.6 Conclusion

Surrogacy is an example of the trade in human body parts, which, we have argued, can be understood as violating human dignity, just as can be argued in relation to other parts of the market for human body parts, such as the trade in kidneys. On top of the human dignity aspects, the trade in kidneys also poses serious health risks to the donors from having only one kidney, risks associated with the surgery and physical weakening afterwards, which often leave the donor in declining health.

References

Archard, D. 2002. Selling yourself: Titmuss's argument against a market in blood. *Journal of Ethics* 6: 87–103.
Arrow, K.J. 1972. Gifts and exchanges. *Philosophy & Public Affairs* 1 (4): 343–362.
Blazier, J., and R. Janssens. 2020. Regulating the international surrogacy markets: The ethics of commercial surrogacy in the Netherlands and India. *Medicine Health Care and Philosophy* 23: 621–630.
Centre for Social Research, CSR. 2010. *Surrogate motherhood – Ethical or commercial*. Vasant Kunj: Centre for Social Research.
Faden, R.R., and T.L. Beauchap. 1986. *A history and theory of informed consent*. Oxford: Oxford University Press.
Hausman, D.M., and M.S. McPherson. 1993. Taking ethics seriously: Economics and contemporary moral philosophy. *Journal of Economic Literature* XXXI (June 93): 671–731.
Kant, I. 1998. *Kant: Groundwork of the metaphysics of morals*. Edited by Mary J. Gregor. Cambridge: Cambridge University Press (first published 1785).
Sen, A. 2002. *Rationality and freedom*. Cambridge: Belknap Press of Harvard University Press.
Shetty, P. 2012. India's unregulated surrogacy industry. *The Lancet* 380 (9854): 1633–1634.
Singer, P. 1973. Althruism and commerce: A defence of Titmuss against Arrow. *Philosophy and Public Affairs* 2 (3): 312–320.
Smith, A. 1759. *Theory of moral sentiments* (2 ed.). A Millar, A Kincaid & J Bell, Strand & Edinburgh, retrieved 26 May 2014 from google books.
———. 1981. *An inquiry into the nature and wealth of nations*. Edited by R. H. Campbell and R. S. Skinner. I–II Vols. Indianapolis: Liberty Press.
Solow, R.M. 1971. Blood and thunder: Review of the gift relationship: From human blood to social policy by Richard M. Titmuss. *The Yale Law Journal* 80 (8): 1696–1711.
Timms, O. 2018. Ending commercial surrogacy in India: Significance of the surrogacy (regulation) bill, 2016. *Indian Journal of Medical Ethics* 3 (2): 99–102.
Titmuss, R.M. 1971a. Why give to strangers. *The Lancet* 297 (7690): 123–125.
———. 1971b. *The gift relationship: From human blood to social policy*. New York: Random House.
Wikipedia. 2021. https://en.wikipedia.org/wiki/Surrogacy_laws_by_country

Kirsten Halsnæs born 1956, professor of climate change and economics at Technical University of Denmark. Member of the Danish Ethical Council of Denmark 2013–2019 and author of a number of rapports for United Nations Panel of Climate, IPCC. Intergovernmental Panel on Climate Change, IPCC.

Thomas Ploug born 1973, professor of ethics of information and communications technology at Aalborg University since 2017. His research includes different types of applied ethics, ICT ethics, medical ethics and bioethics. Member of the Danish Ethical Council 2010–2016.

Chapter 16
Gender, Sex and Market – "Can Sex Be a Service Like Any Other?"

Hanne Petersen

Abstract This article links historical and religious views of morality with representations of gender and sex on the market. The intention has been to understand the trends towards commercialization of sex and intimate life in a late modernity where neoliberal economic theories could be in the process of losing the power they have had for several decades. Religious morality (understanding sex as sin), human rights (rejection of human slavery) and modernist feminism (claiming equality) clash with a neo-liberal discourse which legitimizes commercial sex as an outcome of individual choice and free will. The market for sex is highly lucrative and often still most often only quasi legal, which is perhaps why it has often been described in fiction as much as in theoretical treatises.

Keywords Sexual services · Commercialization · Gender equality · Morality · Sacred sex

16.1 Introduction

*"Male sexuality is a bit like air – you breathe it in all the time, but you aren't much aware of it.", (*Dyer *(1985) here quoted from* Hirdman *(2004))*

In 2012 the young Swedish economist and journalist, Katrine Kielos, published a book with a title which in translation would be *"The only Gender"*. Having worked as a journalist during and after the financial crisis, she was intrigued by the complete lack of gender perspectives in the economic analyses of the crisis. The

---

The quotation and question in the title is from Bernstein (2001).

H. Petersen (✉)
Centre for European and Comparative Legal Studies, University of Copenhagen, Copenhagen S, Denmark
e-mail: Hanne.Petersen@jur.ku.dk

© The Author(s), under exclusive license to Springer Nature Switzerland AG 2023
N. Kærgård (ed.), *Market, Ethics and Religion*, Ethical Economy 62, https://doi.org/10.1007/978-3-031-08462-1_16

book was later translated into several languages, among them English under her married name Katrine Marcal, (Marcal 2015).

When she was analyzing (neo)liberal economic theorists, especially the work of Adam Smith, she found out that he hardly mentions gender issues, and that the 'invisible hand' which put the food on his table on a daily basis was that of his mother, with whom he lived together until her death, when she was over 90 (Kielos 2013). Other authors have commented on the remarkable absence of concern with gender and women in Smith's work (Harkin 2013). The issue of commercialization of sex is seemingly not something liberal economic theory has historically dealt with. Neither does it seem to have been addressed during the last decades of the promotion of neo-liberal economic theory.

This article seeks to link historical and religious views of morality with representations of gender, sex and market in popular culture. The intention has been to understand the trends towards commercialization of sex and intimate life in late modernity at a period of time, where neoliberal economic theories could be in the process of losing the powerful status they have had for several decades.[1]

16.2 Sexual Power, Sacred Prostitution and Commercialized Sex

"None of the daughters of Israel shall be a cult prostitute, nor shall any of the sons of Israel be a cult prostitute." (Deuteronomy, Ch.23, v.18) – New American Standard Version (1995).[2]

Sexuality is power, and sexuality is a resource of utmost importance for living beings. It is thus not surprising, that sexuality has been celebrated (religiously and socially) for millennia. The Bible and especially the Old Testament has a well-known negative view of prostitution and prostitutes – or whores, as they are also called. Adultery has been considered a sin, a transgression of social norms, and until recently also of state norms especially in the form of family and criminal law. As the quote above indicates, this may to some extent be a reaction to earlier celebrations of sexual power and sexual rituals performed in the context of pre-monotheistic religious worship perhaps as fertility rites and divine marriage – also called *Hieros Gamos*. The existence of 'sacred sex' or 'cult prostitution' points out that the social

---

[1] This presentation was first held at a workshop on "Market, Ethics and Religion" at the Academy of Sciences in Copenhagen in the beginning of February 2014. It has only been revised superficially for publication at the end of 2020, where the Epilogue was added.

[2] I am grateful to Marianne Aagaard Skovmand, priest and Ph.D. in theology, for providing me with references to prostitution including sacred prostitutes from the Bible – especially the Old Testament. The Danish present translation uses the term 'helligskøge', and the new American Standard Version used here speaks of cult prostitutes, whereas the King James Bible uses the term prostitute.

stigma attached to sexuality – and especially women's sexuality – has not existed forever (see for instance S. Bell 1994).

In Greek mythology and religion the (sexual) interrelationship between humans and animals was also of considerable importance. Zeus would constantly change form in order to copulate with the women, he desired. Robert Graves writes about the story of Leda and the Swan, where Zeus changes form to a swan that

> *it was Leda herself with whom Zeus companied in the form of a swan beside the river Eurotas; - - - she laid an egg from which were hatched Helen, Castor and Polyceuces; and ... she was consequently deified as the goddess Nemesis - - - Nemesis was the Moon-goddess as Nymph and, in the earliest form of the love-chase myth, she pursued the sacred king through his seasonal changes of hare, fish, bee, and mouse – or hare, fish, bird, and grain of wheat – and finally devoured him. With the victory of the patriarchal system, the chase was reversed: the goddess now fled from Zeus - - - (Graves 1958, p. 206 & 207).*

Nymphs were minor deities, typically associated with a particular location or landform. They were generally regarded as divine spirits who animated nature, and are usually depicted as beautiful young maidens. Their sexuality is supposed to be more unrestricted, probably related to the celebration of female sexuality before the victory of the patriarchal system, Graves describes.

Historically norms about sexuality have been policed, and sexual 'services' have been criminalized not only in Western societies. The rise of commercialized sex at the end of the twentieth century seems to have gone together with the combination of especially economic globalization and the collapse of state socialism and the Soviet Union. In 1991 the Council of Europe organized a seminar in Strasbourg with the title *"Action against traffic in women and forced prostitution as violations of human rights and human dignity"*. As a participant and speaker at this conference I witnessed the ideological contests about terminologies. The term trafficking was just beginning to be used, and in the neoliberal spirit it was important to distinguish between 'forced' and 'voluntary' prostitution, which has later increasingly come to be termed 'sex-work'. These terminological and ideological shifts have allowed several countries – in Europe especially the Netherlands – historically known for its liberal trade regimes – and perhaps more surprisingly also Germany to make it easier to legalize certain forms of commercialization of sex. The market is not self-regulating, and state regulation often supports the commercialization of sex and the sex trade and benefits from it economically.

Commercialization of sex during the period of globalization has meant that the economic gain related to sexual 'services' has made commercial sex morally much more acceptable generally both in traditional religious societies, such as Buddhist Thailand (Peach 2006) and secular/Christian Germany. The market appears to be an institution in contemporary societies, which is both male dominated, patriarchal and gender conservative and which seems to continue securing gender hierarchies (Connell 2008, p.326). But/and the trend of sexualization also "implies a shift in tendency from morals and ethics to taste and aesthetics as well as the apparent breakdown of norms and regulations, supposed to keep obscenity as a distance" (Mühleisen 2007, p.174).

The supply and demand of commercial sex is highly gendered and the market for commercial sex is overwhelmingly addressing male needs on a global scale. Figures are difficult to get at. In my first search for information around 2013, I found a website on overseas investment, listing the Top 10 countries in the world with the most prostitutes. At that time Venezuela, South Korea, Peru, Philippines and Nigeria were in the Top 5 followed by China, Brazil, Malaysia, Germany and Thailand.[3] In 2020 this website no longer exists, but it is possible to find websites on "10 sex tourism destination around the world",[4] and Wikipedia has a long article on "Prostitution statistics by country". Figures are only available for a limited number of countries, and figures are conflicting and contested, not least in countries, where prostitution is not legal.[5] In relation to Nigeria, the 2013 website informed that *"a sex tourism market for divorced older western women is on the rise in the country"*, indicating that the rest of the market is for non-identified men. Elizabeth Bernstein has similar observations about the 'supply-side' in the sex commerce, but she also emphasizes a late-modern shift from 'sex-as-romance' to 'sex-as-recreation' (Bernstein 2001, p. 393). She quotes Monica Prasad, who claims, "the prostitution exchange contains within itself a form of morality specific to mass-market societies." (Bernstein 2001, p. 396). Prasad notes that her interviewees 'praise "market exchange" of sex for lacking the ambiguity, status-dependence and potential hypocrisy that they see in the "gift exchange" of sex characteristic of romantic relationships' (Bernstein 2001, p.397, quoting Prasad). Thus cultural aestheticized sexualization seems to produce a kind of mass-market morality which has legitimized commercialization of 'recreational sex', some of which may go back to the Vietnam War, where American soldiers were sent to Thailand for "rest and recreation".

Monotheistic or other religious norms and practices have not offered protection of women against sexual exploitation. The rhetoric of human rights and the demand for actions against human trafficking have to some extent taken over the role of moral/legal concern and have been used as arguments for criminalization of 'new forms of slavery' or white slavery, which national criminal legal systems are often unable and unmotivated to go against.

One example is the 2004 "Agreed conclusions of the UN Commission on the Status of Women on the role of men and boys in achieving gender equality", which urges governments, and amongst others also international financial institutions, civil society, the private sector and other stakeholders to take actions such as:

Take effective measures, to the extent consistent with freedom of expression, to combat the growing sexualization of, and use of pornography in media content and in the rapid development of information and communications technology, encourage men in the media to

---

[3] http://news.liveandinvestoverseas.com/Lifestyle/the-countries-with-the-most-prostitutes1.html (last accessed March 17, 2013 – this website is no longer available)

[4] Germany, Dominican Republic, Spain, Malaysia, Kenya, The Netherlands, The Philippines, Brazil, Colombia, Thailand. Prostitutions is legal in most of these countries. https://www.deccanchronicle.com/lifestyle/travel/080817/10-sex-tourism-destinations-around-the-world.html (last accessed December 7, 2020)

[5] See Wikipedia, Prostitution statistics by country (last accessed December 7, 2012).

refrain from presenting women as inferior beings and exploiting them as sexual objects and commodities, combat information and communications technology- and media-based violence against women, including criminal misuse of information and communications technology for sexual harassment, sexual exploitation and trafficking in women and girls, and support the development and use of such technology as a resource for the empowerment of women and girls, including those affected by violence, abuse and other forms of sexual exploitation (Agreed conclusions of the UN Commission on the Status of Women on the role of men and boys in achieving gender equality, 2004/11).[6]

A more economic view on the supply side is presented in an ILO discussion paper, stating that

there exists a statistical relationship between the number of victims trafficked out of a country and the level of female youth unemployment in that country. The results also support the hypothesis that countries which are more opened to the forces of globalization and have more prostitution are more likely to be destination places for victims of trafficking. (See for instance Danailova-Trainor and Belser 2007*)*

The economic and social collapse of amongst others the so-called socialist states and increasing globalization has contributed considerably to the supply of young women in the sex trade.

The hegemony of neoliberalism is according to Connell not only an economic ideology, praising the free market, it is also a program for social change that includes a reorganization of institution, a move towards 'flexible' employment practices, outsourcing and reinstallation of privileges for leadership. His interviews on masculinity in finance describe a macho-culture with high alcohol consumption as another aspect of this reorganization, but not one which claims an aggressive masculinity (Connell 2010).

16.3 Money, Market and Commercialized Sex in Fiction, Film and Popular Culture

The market for sex is highly lucrative and often still most often only quasi legal, which is perhaps why it has often been described in fiction as much – and as convincing – as in theoretical treatises.

Another reason may also be the value confusion related to the processes of commercialization. Religious morality (understanding sex as sin in monotheistic religions), human rights history (of rejection of human slavery) and modernist feminism (claiming equality) clash with a neo-liberal discourse which legitimizes commercial sex as a an outcome of individual choice and free will, and 'sex-positive' feminists claiming that 'sexualization of culture' (Attwood 2006) also may have a subversive potential (for some women) as it coexists with a "representational and political

---

[6] http://www.un.org/womenwatch/daw/public/agreedconclusions/Agreed-Conclusions-English.pdf p.133 (last accessed December 2020). Connell (2005) describes the preparation and process of the drafting of these conclusions.

vitalized feminist context" (Mühleisen 2007, p.179). These ambiguities may be more easily portrayed in art than within in the different discourses of economy politicy or other fields of science.

Especially the situation of young women, who had difficulties finding paid jobs in their home communities, and who have been attracted by the temptation and promise of fast and easy money of pimps and brothel owners (including female pimps and owners) have increasingly been described in novels and films, which may have a stronger resonance among a non-academic audience than theories of liberal economy and working papers and academic reports on these subjects.

Swedish crime fiction writer, Arne Dahl – a pen name – has published a novel called *Europa Blues* (Dahl 2003), dealing with the work of the Swedish national special police entity for international violent crime, the A-group. In *Europa Blues* the group investigates the crimes of a group which finally describes itself as the *Erinyies* – the Greek goddesses of revenge, who punish those who have sworn false oaths. In the novel these goddesses of revenge and justice punish the transnational traffickers of eight (or more) Southern and Eastern European women working as prostitutes. Only 2 years earlier in 1999 the Red-Green Swedish government had criminalized clients buying sex by enacting a legislation, which did not follow the liberal trend.

The Russian female author, Ljudmila Ulitskaja tells in her book *Women's Lies. Tales* a story of the protagonist and academic Zjenja, who "betrays her incomplete Ph.D. dissertation"' and starts working with television (Ulitskaja 2007, originally 2002). She is hired for a 'delicate job' – to do research for a film describing the situation of Russian prostitutes in Switzerland (where prostitution is forbidden), whom she is going to interview – for the same amount of money as the prostitutes will receive for their job. It turns out that most of the prostitutes tell an almost identical paradigmatic story of loss in childhood as a reason for entering the sex trade. They also expect only to work for a short period before getting out of the sex business, because very many of them claim to have fiancés, who are almost all bankers.

The novel by Estonian-Finnish author Sofi Oksanen, *Purge* (Oksanen 2010) has received a large number of literary prizes, including the Literature prize from the Nordic Council and the 4th European Book Award – both in 2010. The novel describes the young woman, Zara, of Estonian origin, whose mother and grandmother fled to the far east of the Soviet Union after World War 2. Zara has been lured to work in a German brothel (where brothels are legal). After a longer period of abuse she manages to flee from her pimps, who are traveling with her through Estonia, and to find her grandmother's sister, who has her own long and complicated history of being abused and herself abusing others. Before *Purge* was published as a book, it was a theatre play performed in both Finland and Sweden, and the book *Puhdistus* (the Finnish name) has been published in 30 editions. In 2011 it had been printed in 210.000 copies in Finland since it was first launched in April 2008. It is translated into several languages, and is an example of the strength of fiction to describe and criticize contemporary and historical social and economic conditions of abuse and authoritarianism.

Martin Scorcese's film "The Wolf of Wall Street" was released in 2013 – based upon an auto fiction by a Wall Street banker, Belfort. The film gives an image of the world of finance – and financial speculation – as basically populated by only one gender. The few women present serve as increasingly expensive prostitutes or highly sexualized wives, and constantly increasing abuse of drugs, alcohol and sex seems to be the most important factor keeping men going under conditions of frantic financial speculations. The goal and the orientation seem to be that more is better, whether it be money, drugs, alcohol and sex. The film portrays an almost completely male dominant and misogynist business. Both scoundrels and heros – if there are any – are male. The male extrovert, almost pathologically over-consuming protagonist, Belfort, really seems to be the hero of finance capitalism as is indirectly acknowledged in a comment on the film from one of the main online websites about finance:

Belfort is an attractive, charismatic, sociopath with incredible natural sales and leadership skills. An over the top, testosterone loaded, greed fueled, relentlessly driven, self-promoting, completely unscrupulous personality, Wall Street is just made for him. In few other venues could he have risen so far so fast while irrevocably damaging so many lives… If there is a hero in the story, it's the FBI agent that finally nails Belfort. Unfortunately and ironically, his reward for defending all of us from dirt bags like Belfort is to continue his lifetime of dreary subway rides and cheap suits.[7]

Research on gender and transportation demonstrates that it is primarily women – from the working and middle classes – who utilize public transportation (see Swedberg 2013). Men drive fancy impressive cars as is strongly underlined in a comical scene in the film illustrating the beginning of the downfall of Belfort through a fantasy car ride, which completely ruins the auto mobile – symbol per se of masculine status especially in modernity. A subway driving agent – dependent on public service – can seemingly not be a real hero in the world of global financial capitalism.

The ambivalent contemporary status of and public evaluation of female sexuality in late modernity is exposed in another film *"Nymphomaniac"* by Lars von Trier, also released at the end of 2013. The film shows a woman, who as a young girl – perhaps a nymph – becomes aware of her sexual desire when she is lying in a meadow, where she has an almost religious experience. After that she chases men in order to have sex – neither for money nor only for pleasure according to the 4 hour version of the film, but because her desire is overwhelmingly strong. The film is extremely complex and open for very many interpretations, but in this context it is interesting to note, how the female protagonist in the film refuses to be called – or diagnosed – as a 'sex addict', when she is at some point part of a circle of women, with similar 'maladies'. She claims that she is in fact a 'nymphomaniac', a term, which is seemingly no longer used for her 'condition', as it has been taken over by the term and diagnosis of 'sex addict'.

Where "The Wolf of Wall Street" depicts the 'charismatic' male 'addiction' for money, power and sex, the "Nymphomaniac" – with the telling subtitle "Forget

---
[7] www.forbes.com, Frank Armstrong, Lower Than Pond Scum: The Wolf of Wall Street, (last accessed December 3, 2020)

about Love" – depicts female desire for sex combined with sexual agency ambiguously describing it as bordering on the obsessive and leading to self-exploitation.

The male 'addictions' seem clearly to be related to market society and market economy. The female 'sexual desire' is much more ambivalently described. Both forms seem self-destructive, and also highly gendered. It would be impossible to reverse the gender of the protagonists in the two films. The almost asexual male 'conversation partner' Seligman (meaning the lucky) in Nymphomaniac remarks to Joe, the 'heroine' that what she has done would have been evaluated very differently (probably also by herself) if she had been a man. In that case it might have been told as a repetition of the story of a Don Juan. This is one among many films, where Lars von Trier investigates the complex interrelation between female sexuality, depression and the challenge of religion(s) (in this film Eastern and Western Christianity), as well as the relation of the child to distant parents. The film is set in an unidentified probably central European anonymized city – thus probably also underlining the transnational and supranational aspects of the topic(s) of the film.

To the extent there exists a contemporary moral, ethical or religious uneasiness with the character of commercialized sexual relations in globalized market societies, popular fiction and film seem perhaps as insecure about how to handle this unease, as do politicians, economic theorists and religious believers.

16.4 "Commercialization of Intimate Life"[8] – Trends and Counter Trends

In her book, *The Commercialization of Intimate Life,* Arlie Hochschild uses a 2001 internet advertisement from somebody, whom she calls 'the shy millionaire'. (Hochschild 2003). This man describes himself and his demand in the following way:

> *Beautiful, smart, hostess, good masseuse – $ 400/week*
> *Hi there,*
> *This is a strange job opening, and I feel silly posting it, but this is San Fransisco, and I do have the need! This is a very confidential search process.*
> *I'm a mild-mannered millionaire businessman, intelligent, traveled but shy, who is new to the area, and extremely inundated with invitation to parties, gatherings and social events. I'm looking to find a "personal assistant" of sorts. The job description would include, but not be limited to*

1. *Being hostess to parties at my home ($40/hour)*
2. *Providing me with a soothing and sensual massage ($140/hour)*
3. *Coming to certain social events with me ($40/hour)*
4. *Traveling with me ($300 per day + all travel expenses)*
5. *Managing some of my home affairs (utilities, bill-paying etc.) ($30/hour)*

---

[8] This heading is borrowed from Hochschild (2003), see especially Chapter 2, The Commodity Frontier, pp.30–45)

You must be between 22 and 32, in shape, good-looking, articulate, sensual, attentive, bright and able to keep confidences. I don't expect more than 3–4 events a month, and up to 10 hours a week on massage, chores and other miscellaneous items, at the most. You must be unmarried, unattached or have a very understanding partner... (Hochschild 2003, p. 30)

Hochschild describes the ambivalent and disturbing reactions to the advertisement by her students. Some reject it, others find it appealing. Some also consider applying. I found similar ambivalent attitudes amongst my own students in courses in 2013 and 2014 on both "Gender and Legal Culture" and Family law. There is insecurity about the nature of the relationship and the status of the woman. Is this a 'substitute' love relationship, or is it a work relationship – including sexualized services. The Danish students tended towards the latter evaluation, and they did not find it strongly morally reprehensible as a job provided it was an expression of "free choice". At the end of the decade this position became even more prevalent.

Gender sociologist Raewyn Connell writes in her article about "The Rise of the Global-Private" that in the post-communist 'countries in transition', the result of neo-liberalism has been "a sharp deterioration in the status of women, accompanied by an ideological resurgence of archaic models of masculinity" (Connell 2008, p. 324).[9]

According to Connell, neo-liberalism and the expansion of what she calls 'the global-private' is also a new environment for the making of 'elite masculinity'. This masculinity is not necessarily characterized by *personal* misogynist attitudes, but perhaps rather by what she describes a mediated 'gender ruthlessness'. Managers of transnational corporation have "limited need for the capacity to dominate face-to-face confrontation and do not need hands-on experience with the industries they control" (Connell 2008, p. 325). – As in the case of 'the mild-mannered shy millionaire'.

> *Universal commodification means that the global-private can supply all necessary services itself, buying in the food, the accommodation, the sexual services, the education. The result will be alienated, prefabricated and soulless and perhaps therefore emotionally unbearable for many. (Connell 2008, p. 325)*

Bernstein, who has studied mainly white middle class American clients/consumers of commercial sex claims, however, that for them 'one of the chief virtues of commercial sexual exchange is the clear and bounded nature of the encounter' (Bernstein 2001, p.398). She links this to demographic transitions, declines in marriage rates, doubling of divorce rates (in the US but not only there), and a 60% increase in single-person households (Bernstein 2001, p.399). This leads to a move from 'relational' to 'recreational' – and commercial – sex. She indicates that there may be a class and race bias in her findings.

---

[9] The world famous gender sociologist, Robert Connell, who was (and is) a consultant to international bodies on issues of especially masculine gender, began publishing under the first name Raewyn from 2006, and has later written on her transsexual experiences.

In Europe today (again) a certain movement against the 'commercialization of intimate life' is observable –linked to a confusion about standards and ethics.

When the Red-Green German government in 2002 legalized commercial sex it also created conditions for and protected an expanding market for sex, which led to a situation, where Germany became home to very large brothels. The Pascha in Cologne was the largest brothel in Europe until it was closed in 2020 due to corona. The Pascha filed for bankruptcy in early September 2020. Prostitution was outlawed in the state of North Rhine-Westphalia from the beginning of the pandemic, which led to authorities repeatedly renewing fortnightly closure orders.[10] The brothel was formerly housed in a 12-storey building 'employing' about 120 prostitutes and receiving up to 1000 customers per day.[11]

According to the presently accessible Wikipedia site, which still reads almost like an advertisement cum information site, rooms in the building were rented to

> *the prostitutes for a fee of 180 Euros per day, which includes meals, medical care, and the 20 Euros of tax that authorities collect per prostitute per day (including Cologne's "pleasure tax" of 6 Euros). The women come from many countries; about 30% of them are German. They typically sit outside of their rooms and negotiate with customers who wander the hallways. Some of the women live in their rooms, others rent a second room to stay in, while still others stay in their own apartments in Cologne. The house is open 24 hours a day; customers of the prostitutes pay an entrance fee of 5 Euros and then negotiate directly with the women, who work independently and keep all of the money. One floor is reserved for low-cost service and another one for transgender prostitutes. The house also contains a regular hotel, a table dance nightclub with separate entrance, several bars, and a separate club-style brothel on the top floor."*[12]

These large scale German brothels clearly do not cater to the demand of 'elite masculinity', and they seem to supply a transnational group of customers, who are arriving in busloads from different parts of Europe with low cost sexual services offered by women, who are paying a high percentage of their income for very expensive rooms and other 'services' including taxes. This has seemingly to some extent had as a consequence that the sex trade has continued to be a part of the 'black economy' to avoid costly taxation in order to be paying off also to the women who perform the sexual services, and not only to the middlemen, who earn very lucrative profits. Europol has assessed that trafficking thrives because it "remains a low risk – high reward enterprise for organized crime."[13]

Nonetheless the 'purchasing power of the population in the countries of destination' of trafficking of women for sexual services matters for the 'demand'. "In high-income countries, customers typically pay higher prices for non-tradable services, including sexual service," write Danailova-Trainor & Belser (2007, p.5), who also write that

---

[10] https://en.wikipedia.org/wiki/Pascha_(brothel) (last accessed December 3, 2020)
[11] Ibid
[12] This text is completely identical with the text I visited in March 2014. The only change being that transsexual has been replaced by 'transgender'
[13] Here quoted from Danailova-Trainor and Patrick Belser (2007, p. 4).

> There are reasons to expect that the rapid expansion and diversification of a market such as the sex industry that is poorly regulated, widely stigmatized and partially criminalized will be associated with an increased incidence of abusive labor practices and fuel trafficking. This may be especially true in countries that are high destinations for sex tourism" (Danailova-Trainor & Belser, 2007, p. 6).

The controversial German feminist Alice Schwarzer has edited and published a book called in translation *"Prostitution. A German Scandal. How could we become the paradise of traffickers of women?"* (Schwarzer 2013). She and the group of people with whom she cooperated also launched a campaign against prostitution in Germany. This seems to have given rise to tensions and conflicts between the 'old style' feminists in favor of a policy of abolition of prostitution, and a 'prostitution lobby' in favor of a liberalized sex trade.[14]

There are a number of different legal regimes – or legislation typologies – used to regulate prostitution in the EU member states, which have in a 2005 report been categorized as *abolitionism, new abolitionism, prohibitionism, regulationism*. The last category of 'regulationism' was in 2005 consisting of 7 countries: Austria, Germany, Greece, Hungary, Latvia, The Netherlands and United Kingdom. The 'opposite' regime of 'prohibitionism' comprised Ireland, Lithuania, Malta and Sweden. Under both these models trafficked prostitution is more frequently exercised indoors (Di Nicola et al. 2005, viii & x). Denmark is in the category of 'new abolitionism', where prostitution is not criminalized, but brothels are.

In a "Communication from the Commission to the European Parliament, the Council, the European Economic and Social Committee and the Committee of the Regions" on "The EU Strategy towards the Eradication of Trafficking in Human Beings 2012–2016", trafficking is described as 'the slavery of our times" and as "a lucrative form of crime" (European Commission, COM 2012). The role of neoliberal economy and market theory is not addressed in a description and explanation of the phenomenon:

> *Trafficking in human beings is a complex transnational phenomenon rooted in vulnerability to poverty, lack of democratic cultures, gender inequality and violence against women, conflict and post-conflict situations, lack of social integration, lack of opportunities and employment, lack of access to education, child labour and discrimination. (*(European Commission, COM 2012*), p. 3).*

The communication underlines the difficulty of developing an efficient policy and the need for a much broader approach than normally:

> *A multi-disciplinary, coherent policy against trafficking in human beings requires the involvement of a more diverse group of actors than before in policy-making. These should involve police officers, border guards, immigration and asylum officials, public prosecutors, lawyers, members of the judiciary and court officials, housing, labour, health, social and safety inspectors, civil society organisations, social and youth workers, consumer organisations, trade unions, employers organisations, temporary job agencies, recruitment agencies and consular and diplomatic staff as well as those more difficult to reach, such as*

---

[14] http://www.spiegel.de/panorama/emma-kampagne-prominente-unterzeichnen-brief-gegen-prostitution-a-930377.html (last visited December 3, 2020)

legal guardians and legal representatives, child and victim support services. Volunteers and people who work in conflict situations could also be involved. ((European Commission, COM 2012), p. 5–6).

In the context of a workshop on "Market, Ethics and Religion" in which this article was originally presented, the absence of any reference to religious institutions in this very long list may seem somewhat surprising.

A press release by the EU Committee on Women's Rights and Gender Equality called *"Punish the client not the prostitute"* from February 26, 2014 addresses the difficulties of legislative action:

"Rather than blanket legalisation – which has been a disaster in Holland and Germany – we need a more nuanced approach to prostitution, which punishes men who treat women's bodies as a commodity, without criminalising those who are driven into sex work," said Mary Honeyball (S & D, U.K), who drafted the resolution. "We send a strong signal that the European Parliament is ambitious enough to tackle prostitution head on rather than accepting it as a fact of life.""[15]

A number of Danish researchers working with issues of prostitution, sex work, human trafficking and gender and sexuality have criticized the non-binding EU-resolution for following the Swedish model, which punishes buying sex, but not selling it. According to these Danish researchers the Swedish legislation has decreased the trust of 'sex sellers' (which is the term used) in public authorities, which makes them work under more hidden and dangerous conditions than before the enactment of the law. (Gaihede 2014).

It is well known that Denmark in many fields has a tradition of a more (neo) liberal legal culture than the other Nordic countries. It is not as strong as that of the Netherlands, but in no way as state interventionist and restrictive as that of Sweden, and to some extent also Norway. General policies also often influence the views of researchers and participants in public debates. Given the different traditions and moral, legal and economic cultures in the world, the need for nuanced approaches as well as for global perspectives on the local and national markets for sexual services seem important.

For Connell the only viable response to the fact that everything is for sale in the global-private lies

> *in the spaces of the public left by the expansion of the global-private and in the arenas of the global-private itself. This means contesting the corruption, reasserting a concept of the public interest and finding democratic ways of ordering gender relations and the economic life of society. Neoliberal ideology attempts to rule out these ideas in advance, to present the global-private as the only possible world. This is mystification. Though the rise of the global-private has been remarkable, it has never been unopposed. (Connell 2008, p.329).*

Perhaps the reactions against corrupted gender orders have to go hand in hand with reactions against the 'vices' of other forms of social life both inside and outside the important social and economic institutions of state, market, family, military and

---

[15] https://www.europarl.europa.eu/news/en/press-room/20140221IPR36644/punish-the-client-not-the-prostitute (last accessed December 3, 2020)

media as well as with the expansion of economic theory to also include gender – in order not to be seduced by "economic man" who according to the subtitle of Katrine Kielos' book risks to ruin your life and the world economy.

The rise of commercial sex with its offer of "bounded authenticity" (Bernstein 2001) in temporary, intimate relations perhaps signified a shift from an era dominated by state intervention and one dominated by market forces – linked perhaps by religious insecurity. Will the aftermath of the economic crises (Castells et al. 2012) and 'new' challenges (climate change, global inequalities and pandemics amongst other) contest the hegemonic position neo-liberal economic theory has achieved during the last decades? We have recently observed the publicity about work of a younger generation of European economists (most notably Thomas Piketty 2020) pointing in this direction and perhaps leading to a certain diversity of theories on economy and sexuality.[16] The market is not the only way to organize relations amongst human beings, and perhaps sexuality is after all not "a service like any other" but something to be cultivated and celebrated not only before modernity but also beyond markets.

16.5 Epilogue: #MeToo and Corona

The oral presentation on which this article is based took place in a workshop on "Market, Ethics and Religion" at the beginning of the second decade of the twenty-first century, relatively few years after the financial crisis which was followed by the EURO-crisis. During this decade the general awareness increased about the impact of a neoliberal economy in general but perhaps somewhat less in relation to its gendered implications. Wendy Brown's book *Undoing the Demos. Neoliberalism's Stealth Revolution* was an exception first published in 2015. In neoliberalism, Homo Oeconomicus of the market replaces or even extinguishes Homo Politicus – the citizen in democracy. Both were predominantly male, and as Brown remarks, "when homo oeconomicus becomes the governing truth, when it organizes law, conduct, policy, and everyday arrangements, the burdens upon and the invisibility of those excluded persons and practices are intensified", (Brown 2017 p. 107). As most countries are based upon a gendered division of labour both in the market and in families, this means an extra burden not least on women. Women perform the glue in contemporary market societies under conditions of gender stereotyping, which requires them to bear the double burden of being carers and (weak) competitors at once. The consequences of this are amongst others stress and exhaustion, which again affect those, they care for, (Petersen 2019). Globalization and commercialization including of sexuality and bodies has continued during the second decade of the

---

[16] Although Thomas Piketty in the Danish translation of his most recent book "Capital and Ideology" only uses very few pages on specific gender issues, for instance 2½ page on "Gender, social quotas and conditions for their transformation" (pp 330–332) and almost 4 pages on "The continued existence of patriarchy in the twenty-first Century" (pp 604–608)

twenty-first century, where Europe has experienced neoconservative Anti-gender policies in many countries, (Kováts and Pöim 2015). A forerunner of the #MeToo movement took place in Germany in 2013 where legislative reactions were discussed, which were then coopted by racist reactions to the 2015/2016 events of mass sexual harassment at New Years Eve in Cologne (Lembke 2020). Tarana Burke coined a *Me Too* slogan already in 2006 more than a decade before the movement took off in the 'dream factory' of Hollywood, see also Olsen (2019). With the election in 2016 of an openly sexist and racist president in the US, it dawned on many Americans, not least women that they had to mobilize to protect themselves against neoliberal and neoconservative forces and (gender) policies. January 2017 saw the largest single day protest in US history by millions of women – and some men – against the incoming president and policy. In October 2017 the digitally conveyed #MeToo movement went viral and gradually global, with unprecedented consequences for a sexually and economically exploitative entertainment industry relying on young, beautiful, ambitious women in very precarious positions – particularly but not only in the USA. A political mobilization followed in 2018 and brought a number of young left-wing women into the US congress. As we know, in 2020 a presidential team was elected – with the first ever female vicepresident in the US – only with a rather narrow margin and only because it was supported by women of all colours, particularly black women.

The Nordic countries have had female presidents and prime ministers since 1980, where first Iceland elected the world's first female president, and 1986 where Norway got its first female prime minister. In 2011 Denmark finally got its first female prime minister, a Social Democrat and since 2019 has the second one. Finland got a coalition government of parties all led by women and all in their 30s in 2019. Slowly politics is changing its face, which may have an impact also on the market. In 2016, 2018 and again in 2020 very big strikes by women and men took place in especially Poland primarily against a reactionary abortion policy backed up by the Catholic Church, but also with a broader intention of supporting democracy. Many Christian (and Muslim) religious forces and institutions have so far sided with the market (and market economy) in its dubious alliances with more or less autocratic states, probably leading to a loss of faith of many women around the world in these institutions. The corona pandemic has called into question certain key premises of the neoliberal ideology – including individualism and the (in)ability of the market mechanism to maintain economic redistribution, fairness and health. With women constituting not only the bulk of the sex market but also of care work, the pandemic means increased burdens and vulnerability, increased uncertainty and increasing domestic violence. But it probably also has increased the political awareness of many women. Denmark experienced a surprisingly strong second #MeToo wave from August 2020, which in my interpretation can also be interpreted as an indirect criticism of neo-liberal living and working conditions. The market clearly cannot solve problems and challenges related to health, care of the young and the elderly and respect and protection of life. Marketized sex does not secure the lives of future generations in a world challenged by climate change.

The exploitation of gender and sex by the market (and sometimes also by the state) has not stopped and will not stop without a considerable and continuous mobilization of women of all ages and colours around the world. – Hopefully supported by a growing number of men who will show solidarity – also with themselves.

References

Agreed conclusions of the UN Commission on the Status of Women on the role of men and boys in achieving gender equality, 2004/11., http://www.un.org/womenwatch/daw/public/agreedconclusions/Agreed-Conclusions-English.pdf

Attwood, F. 2006. Sexed up: Theorizing the Sexualization of culture. *Sexualities* 9: 77–94.

Bell, S. 1994. *Reading, writing & rewriting the prostitute body*. Indiana University Pres, Bloomington.

Bernstein, E. 2001. The meaning of the purchase: Desire, demand and the commerce of sex. *Ethnography* 2001: 389–420.

Brown, W. 2017. *Undoing the demos. Neoliberalism's stealth revolution*. New York: Zone Books, Near Futures.

Castells, M., J. Caraca, and G. Cardoso, eds. 2012. *Aftermath. The cultures of the economic crisis*. Oxford: Oxford University Press.

Connell, R.W. 2005. Change among the gatekeepers: Men, masculinities, and gender equality in the global arena. *Signs* 30 (3): 1801–1825.

Connell, R. 2008. The rise of the global-private. Power, masculinities and the neo-liberal world order. In *Das Private neu denken. Erosionen, Ambivalenzen, Leistungen*, ed. L. Jurczyk and M. Oechsle, 315–330. Münster: Westfälisches Dampfboot.

———. 2010. Im Innern des gläsernen Turms: die Konstruktion von Männlichkeiten im Finanzkapital. *Feministische studien,* (2010) Special issue: Organisation, Geschlecht, soziale Ungleichheiten, pp. 8–24.

Dahl, A. 2003. Europa Blues, Forlaget Modtryk, Aarhus (Translated from Swedish).

Danailova-Trainor, G., and P. Belser. 2007. *Globalization and the illicit market for human trafficking: An empirical analysis of supply and demand*, Working Paper No. 78. Geneva: Policy Integration Department, International Labour Office.

Di Nicola, A., I. Orfano, A. Cauduro, and N. Conci. 2005. Study on National Legislation on prostitution and trafficking in woman and children. *Zurich Open Repository Archive*. https://doi.org/10.5167/uzh-80851. (last visited March 18, 2014).

Dyer, R. 1985. Male gay porn. *Jump Cut – A Review of Contemporary Media* 30: 27–29.

European Commission, COM. 2012. 286 final, Communication from the Commission to the European Parliament, the Council, the European Economic and Social Committee and the Committee of the Regions. The EU Strategy towards the Eradication of Trafficking in Human Beings 2012–2016 (English version).

Gaihede, G.B. 2014. Forskere advarer mod forbud mod købesex. Universitetsavisen, 5.3.2014. http://universitetsavisen.dk/politik/forskere-advarer-mod-forbud-mod-kobesex

Graves, R. 1958. *Greek myths*. London: Cassell & Company Ltd.

Harkin, M. 2013. Adam Smith on Women. In *Oxford Handbooks Online*. Oxford: (Print Publication Date 2013).

Hirdman, A. 2004. Mirrored masculinity? Turning the perspective of sexualization and representation around. *NIKK Magasin*, Special Issue: Sexualization of Public Space, pp. 8–11.

Hochschild, A. 2003. *The commercialization of intimate life. Notes from Home and Work*. Berkeley: University of California Press.

Kielos, K. 2013. *Det eneste køn. Om hvorfor du er blevet forført af den økonomiske mand, og hvordan det ødelægger dit liv og verdensøkonomien*. Copenhagen: Forlaget Pressto.

Kováts, E., and M. Pöim, eds. 2015. *Gender as symbolic glue. The position and role of conservative and far right parties in the anti-gender mobilizations in Europe*. France, Germany, Hungary, Poland, Slovakia: Published by the Foundation for European Progressive Studies in cooperation with the Friedrich Ebert-Stiftung.

Lembke, U. 2020. Early start, slow progress, racist takeover, but destined not to yield: The #MeToo movement in Germany. In *The global #MeToo movement*, ed. A.M. Noel and D.B. Oppenheimer, 197–213. Berkley: Full Court Press.

Marcal, K. 2015. *Who cooked Adam Smith's dinner*. London: Portobello Books.

Mühleisen, W. 2007. Mainstream Sexualization and the potential for Nordic new feminism. *NORA-Nordic Journal of Women's Studies* 15 (2–3): 172–189.

Oksanen, S. 2010. *Purge*. New York: Black Cat.

Olsen, F. 2019. Sex in Hollywood. In *Dette brenner jeg for.: Festskrift til Hege Brækhus 70 år*, ed. T. Haugli, S. Gerrard, A. Hellum, and E.-M. Svensson, 323–344. Bergen: Fagbokforlaget.

Peach, L. 2006. Sex or Sangha? Non-normative gender roles for women in Thai law and religion. In *Mixed blessings: Laws, religions and Women's rights in the Asia-Pacific region*, ed. A. Whiting and C. Evans, 25–60. Leiden: Martinus Nijhoff Publishers.

Petersen, H. 2019. "Beyond gender"? – Strategies for (sociolegal) transformations? In *Dette brenner jeg for.: Festskrift til Hege Brækhus 70 år*, ed. T. Haugli, S. Gerrard, A. Hellum, and E.-M. Svensson, 345–364. Bergen: Fagbokforlaget.

Piketty, T. 2020. *Kapital og Ideologi* (Danish edition), Copenhagen: Information & DJØFs Forlag.

Schwarzer, A., ed. 2013. *Prostitution. Ein deutscher Skandal. Wie konnten wir zum Paradies der Frauenhändler warden?* Köln: Kiepenheuer & Witsch.

Swedberg, W. 2013. *Ett (o)jämställt transportsystem i gränslandet mellan politik och rätt*. Malmö: Bokbox Förlag.

Ulitskaja, L. 2007. *Kvinders løgne. Fortællinger (Women's lies. Tales)* (See especially the story "Et lykketræf" (A piece of good luck). Copenhagen: Gyldendal.

Hanne Petersen born 1951, since 2001 professor of law at University of Copenhagen. 1995–1999 professor at University of Greenland. Among other things member of the European Research Council 2008–2013.

Chapter 17
The Problem of Interest for Luther and the Danish Reformers

Martin Schwarz Lausten

Abstract A heated debate about interest took place in both Germany and Denmark in the sixteenth century, but this was nothing new and came as no surprise to Lutheran reformers. The topic had already been the subject of intensively discussion in the Middle Ages and even if interest charges were unlawful the church itself was frequently engaged in lending out at interest. The debate was a complicated mixture of economics and moral theology and the demarcation between the Catholic Middle Ages and the Lutheran Reformation was fluid and blurred. Luther (and the Danish reformers) did not want to be a politician or an economist; he was a theologian and a spiritual adviser also in this debate and both he and the Danish reformers was profoundly religious.

Keywords Luther · Danish Lutheran reformers · Ban of interest · Theology of economics · Social ethics

17.1 Martin Luther

In order to understand the heated debate about loan interest that took place in both Germany and Denmark in the sixteenth century, several things need to be borne in mind. *First*, the question of interest charges was nothing new and came as no surprise to Lutheran reformers. It had already been the subject of lively discussion in the Middle Ages despite the fact that both interest charges and payment were unlawful, even if the church itself frequently engaged in lending money out at interest. *Second*, what is at issue here is a mixture of economics and moral theology. *Third*,

---

The manuscript is translated from Danish by Bodil Sampson, M.A.

M. S. Lausten (✉)
Faculty of Theology, Department of Church History, University of Copenhagen, Copenhagen S, Denmark
e-mail: msl@teol.ku.dk

the demarcation between the Catholic Middle Ages and the Lutheran Reformation is far more fluid and blurred than is often stated. *Fourthly*, Martin Luther did not want to be – nor indeed was he – a politician or an economist. He was a theologian through and through, one could say a spiritual adviser on the question of interest charges. *Finally*, the life that Martin Luther and the Danish reformers lived was profoundly religious. At all times they endeavoured to act according to the will of God, in a constant struggle against the Devil and his practices. We may find it difficult nowadays to comprehend such a mindset, but even though it may be a challenge, we have to try to understand people living at that time and avoid the mistake, indeed the 'sin', of ridiculing earlier generations and their behaviour.

It would not be an exaggeration to say that Luther found it very difficult to understand the modern, growing capitalism of his time, the expansion of commerce and industry, the emergence of large businesses with their policies of creating monopolies, and the transition from barter to a money-based economy. Luther's ideal was still the tilling of the land, i.e. agriculture. The Bible had taught him that that was what God had intended for mankind. Now he realised that money was not just a means of exchange enabling labour and commodities to be bought. He saw that people could use money to enjoy a life of plenty and live in luxury without having to toil in the fields. He also realised that the loving care for one's fellow human beings, which God demanded, could disappear to be replaced by the exploitation of people for cheap labour. For him that was simply unchristian, a negation of the Christian faith and trust in God. As a preacher of the Word he had to oppose this, see Christensen (1964, pp. 358–367) and Strohm (1983, pp. 206 and 210).

Luther wrote no fewer than four separate works on the problem of interest charges. In addition, he dealt with this question in chapters appearing in other works, and he also raised it in several sermons. The first of the published writings addressing this issue appeared in 1519, the last in 1540, but over the years his views never changed. He was deeply concerned about the problem of interest charges, as may be deduced from the fact that he dealt with it in one of his very last sermons, namely the one delivered in Eisleben on 15 February 1546 just 3 days before he died. In this sermon he levelled violent accusations at the Pope, heretics, mediocrities in positions of authority, and Jews, maintaining that the last of these schemed to kill Christians whenever the opportunity arose. Some of them, he said, claimed to be doctors but only did so in order to be able to poison Christians. The Jews should stop charging interest when lending money and embrace Christianity. Otherwise we Christians would no longer tolerate them (Luther 1519, 1520, 1524, 1540, 1546). Luther's views on interest and usurers can be summarised in the following:

The major publication on usury is introduced by a long chapter in which Luther sets out his dissatisfaction and indignation at the monetary policy of the time and the way in which he saw commerce operating, and also the threat which the new capitalism and trading practices posed for what God had decreed for man. Luther makes a distinction between true Christians and non-Christians, the latter being people who are Christian in name only. He paints a rather crude picture in which businessmen are simply evil and avaricious and where it is therefore necessary for secular authorities to regulate, govern and possibly punish them. In a sermon delivered in

1539 based on Matthew chapter 24, he lists all the calamities that will happen prior to doomsday. Devilish lies and murder will be widespread; false prophets, Turks and Jews will become prominent; fanatical movements will break out; and sections of the population will initiate wars between the social classes. Farmers as well as the nobility will deliberately create inflation. As an example of this Luther draws on his own experience: up until now he has been able to pay for household necessities out of his fixed income of 200 Guilders. Now he needs 300 Guilders to cover these expenses. Some of the inflation may be due to bad weather or poor harvests, but inflation created by man is caused by avarice and affects poor people in particular. Usurers and the avaricious are no more than murderers (Luther 1539).

Luther's central contention is that any levying of interest is usury. If money, goods or equipment are lent out and more is required in return than what was originally lent, then that is usury. He writes:

> Those people are usurers who lend out wine, grain, money or anything else to another person on condition that he pays back interest after a year or some other agreed timespan, or accepts the onerous liability of having to give back more or something better than what was borrowed. (Luther 1520, p. 48)

By totally banning interest charges, Luther is in complete agreement with Canon Law, which had recently been renewed at the Lateran Synod in 1515. In that same year, at a debate in Bologna, the well-known Catholic theologian Johann Eck – who shortly afterwards became one of Luther's fiercest opponents – had defended an interest rate of 5% (Strohm 1983, p. 214).

Luther's reasoning is based on the bible, Leviticus 25:36, Deuteronomy 23:19–20 and Luke 6:35 where Jesus says: 'lend, hoping for nothing again', and also in natural law as expressed in Matthew 7:12: 'Therefore all things whatsoever ye would that men should do to you, do ye even so to them.' Thus, those charging interest act against the commandment of charity. Usurers love themselves, not their neighbour. In their avarice, they are thinking of themselves rather than what would benefit their fellow man.

Luther's ideal therefore is that we should use our possessions for the benefit of others. Accordingly, loans should be made free of charge and considered as a gift. This is the way of true Christians and not like the children of this world, he points out.

Luther also rejects so-called 'interest purchase', of which the Catholic Church had made widespread use.[1] By calling it 'interest purchase', it was thought that the ban on interest charges by Canon Law could be circumvented. Luther condemns this as hypocrisy in the strongest terms, saying that it is the same as usury. The

---

[1] A landowner or capitalist could lease a piece of land to a tenant for life for an annual sum ('interest') or he could invest in farming using a contract that stipulated what the borrower had to give as security. This was called 'interest purchase', because the lender was considered to be the person who had bought the right to the income while the borrower sold the income that was derived from the property or capital he had received, cf. Christensen (1964, p. 152) and Strohm (1983, p. 217). In other words, 'interest purchase' is seen to be a loan camouflaged as a sale, often of a piece of land which has right of purchase, and it is expected that more than the original price is paid back. In reality, therefore, interest is being paid.

practice is for one's own benefit, not that of one's neighbour, he insists. Moreover, it leads many into economic difficulties. He demands that the authorities outlaw the practice.

Finally, it is noteworthy that Luther shows some realism in recognising that interest charges may be necessary in certain circumstances. He therefore appeals to the secular authorities to operate on occasions on the basis of what is *reasonable*, 5% being reasonable although this rate should be reduced if the borrower cannot manage it. However, he insists that elderly people, impoverished widows, and orphans should not pay any interest when they are forced to take out a loan.

17.2 The Problem of Loan Interest for the Danish Monarchs and Theologians During the Reformation

The treatment of the problem of loan interest charges in Denmark during the Reformation reflects very clearly the way in which economic, theological and socio-ethical issues are involved. The sources used for our investigation are drawn from Royal Acts and ordinances as well as publications by leading theologians.

In the late Middle Ages while the country was still Catholic, the prohibition of interest charges was stressed on several occasions, last of all by Archbishop Birger Gunnarson in 1524 just a few years before the unrest at the start of the Reformation. However, as in other parts of Europe, the Church itself was a very prolific lender. Looking at a number of church accounts, the historian Troels Dahlerup has shown that interest rate charges around 1400 could be as high as 10%, with 8% as the norm. At the beginning of sixteenth century, it was lowered to 6¼ %.[2] How did the pious King Christian III react to this charge when he introduced the Lutheran Reformation in Denmark-Norway? The tradition of interest charges was strong here too, but no act or ordinance was issued in the first 10 years. However, the question was raised in the Church Ordinance of 1537, in which it was stated that usurers must be banned from the pulpit just like heretics, lunatics, adulterers and violent criminals. This had already been put in the draft version of the Church Ordinance and it was carried over without change into the revised Danish Ordinance of 1539. No distinction was made between interest charge and usury, and no reason was given for the punishment meted out. It is useful to recall here that a ban affected the person in question not only in his relationship with the Church and its sacrament, but that it also had serious consequences for him at a social level (Lausten 1989, pp. 63, 111 and 187).

However, the Danish King was not to get away with things so easily. Time and again the leading Danish theologians wrote on the question of interest charges,

---

[2] Dahlerup (1963). The following account of the period up to the king Frederik II and the theologian professor Niels Hemmingsen (Nicolaus Hemmingius) builds in part on Lausten (1985, 1989, pp. 140–153). The common use of 6¼ %. is caused by the monetary system at that time where one mark was equal to 16 skilling. Consequently 6¼ % means an interest rate of one skilling per mark.

indeed they fairly bombarded the King and the authorities with their attacks on interest charges and usury. There was an exchange of letters between the King and some leading politicising landowners, while Mads Lang of Aarhus, one of the new Lutheran bishops, sent a letter to the King (16 April 1547) earnestly entreating him to *improve the salvation of his poor subjects*. He wanted the King to intervene in the legislation concerning religious holidays (points 1–6), adulterers (point 7) and usurers, and moreover he wanted more emphasis on the teaching of the Catechism. Mads Lang complains about the *unchristian and undisciplined usurer* and encourages the King to take the wise decision of issuing a new ordinance stating that a person who charges higher interest than that laid down *in the old Empire and Church Act*, i.e. 5%, should be punished. However, he cautiously adds that the King may decide on a different rate.

His plea is undated but was evidently sent prior to the Royal Act on interest charges and usury, which was issued on 18 February 1547. The King mentions that he has received many complaints about unchristian usury, which many people engage in and which harms the poor. To combat such an unchristian practice, which goes against the righteousness of God, he and his Council have now fixed a maximum interest rate of 6¼%. If more than that is demanded, the lender will be punished for usury.[3] He legitimises interest charges and even sets the rate higher than that stipulated in Canon Law. He thus does not follow Luther's vision here.

It is very interesting to note that leading theologians in the reformed Church felt free to protest vehemently against this policy. The first known denunciation came from the Bishop of Lund, Frands Vormordsen, who quite openly protested against the Royal Act. This occurred in July 1548 at the meeting of the diocese. It is noteworthy that while arguing his case, he referred not only to the Bible but also to Canon Law and the Church Father Jerome, using the phrase *the church canon of the orthodox holy fathers*. He knew perfectly well that Canon Law had been abolished in Denmark-Norway with the implementation of the Lutheran Reformation, but he obviously thought that references to Canon Law gave more weight to his arguments. Just like Luther, he stated that there is no greater crime than *the charging of interest and usury* (foenus sive usura). Characteristically, Vormordsen does not distinguish between interest and usury. His biblical references come from classic sections of the Old Testament (Leviticus and Ezekiel) and the words of Jesus in the New Testament (Luke 6:35 and John 3:17). Vormordsen's definition of usury is similar to that of Canon Law, namely that it is usury whenever more is demanded in return than was originally lent. He stresses that usury exists not only where money is concerned but whenever anything at all which has been lent involves a fee.[4] Those who commit this sin go against God's command and must be expelled from the church. He appeals directly to the clergy of the diocese and 'earnestly entreats and implores in the name of our Lord Jesus Christ and His glorious coming' that they be aware that

---

[3] On Mads Lang see Rørdam (1860–1862) and on the Royal Act see Clemmensen (1940, p. 123).

[4] Liber Extra c. 3 X de usuris lib. V Tit XIX, c. 3 and Canon. usura, cavsa 14, qvæstio 3.

they are just as duty bound to combat usury as adultery, drunkenness, lust and avarice. In addition, they should publicly excommunicate usurers.

Three years later (1551), he repeats his vehement protests against any form of interest charge. Again it happens at a meeting of the diocese, where he complains that this evil practice has spread amongst all social classes, the nobility, the middle classes and farmers, and indeed even amongst the clergy. He threatens members of the clergy who do not intervene locally when they learn of interest being charged. The threat is that God's punishment will strike both them and the whole country, for if they stay silent, they are accessories to this sin, and they must consider how terrible it would be to fall from the grace of the living God (Lausten 1987, pp. 142–144).

The King took note of the protest. He evidently ordered a report to be made by the two university professors he usually consulted in such cases, namely Peder Palladius and Johannes Macchabaeus. Their report has since been lost, but its conclusions can clearly be seen from the King's next step when he asked for advice from the greatest Lutheran authorities in this field, Philipp Melanchthon in Wittenberg and the jurist Hieronymus Schürff in Frankfurt an der Oder. The two Danish theologians had concluded that *all* forms of interest charges were usury, and they had referred to the scriptures, especially the command to 'love thy neighbour'. Christian III's pangs of conscience can clearly be seen from his letter to Schürff. He knew from the scriptures that all interest charges were a sin, and he mentioned that his own theologians had written the same thing – in the report that is now lost – and the King did not want to burden his conscience with evil ordinances, but on the other hand, he also had a duty to look after the common good, and as things stood then (*wie die Welt ist*), it would harm commerce if no interest charges were to be allowed. He asked if an interest limit could be allowed – just so that major damage could be avoided.

Schürff was sorry that this evil – usury – had spread throughout Denmark-Norway, and he applauded the Danish theologians while stating that all interest charging was a sin. It would not help the King's conscience if he fixed a maximum interest rate, because that would only make it look as if some form of interest charging was acceptable and legal. He advised the King against this and encouraged him to punish all usurers by denying them the sacrament and, if they died before they had repented, excluding them from burial in Christian soil in accordance with Canon Law. They would have to be buried in a field.

Melanchthon sent in a fuller report where various points are raised.

(a) One had to distinguish between rightful income and usury, which is interest on a loan.
(b) God's command of equality. It is stated in Leviticus that a loan is cancelled by repayment of no more than the capital that was originally lent.
(c) In response to the question raised by Christian III as to whether it was right to punish the charging of extortionate rates of interest but not lesser rates, Melanchthon reminded the King of Emperor Charles V's renewal of Justinian's arrangement by which no more than 12% interest could be charged. But this did *not* mean that Emperor Charles V thereby actually accepted usury of less than

12%, which could be seen from the fact that the Emperor ordered the clergy to preach against *all* form of usury. However, the secular authorities could not punish all sin, only the most serious. It was the King's duty, he went on, to preach the will of God to his people. This included banning adultery within marriage and also eschewing ingratitude. Such things were sinful, but clearly the King could not punish everything. This whole question had been discussed by Martin Bucer, Melanchthon, Johannes Gropper and others at the Regensburg Reichtag (parliament) in 1541.

(d) Despite the ban on loan interest charges as expressed in the scriptures, the King was obliged to consider the interests of commerce. Melanchthon advised the King that he might allow an interest rate of up to 5%. A higher rate should be punishable by loss of the original capital or worse.

(e) The relevance of laws on usury in Antiquity.

(f) Melanchthon also recommended that the King's edict should contain the demand that all priests and servants of God should state in their sermons that any form of usury, major or minor, would be punished. However, they should consult informed sources to gain knowledge of different types of business contract. In other words, they should carry out detailed investigations before making a concrete statement about anything.

(g) Melanchthon had written this report hurriedly because the messenger to Denmark was in a rush, but even so he did manage to get the endorsement of the Wittenberg jurists.[5]

However, the resistance of the theologians on this issue continued. The Primate of Denmark, Peder Palladius, did not share the view of his teacher Philipp Melanchthon whom he otherwise greatly admired, and in various works he fought against all forms of interest charges. During the plague in Copenhagen, Palladius published a spiritual guide while, at the same time, Peter Capiteyn, the Professor of Medicine, produced a medical one. People should repent and desist from sin. Usurers, male and female, as well as hoarders of grain, should give back all that they had unjustly and fraudulently acquired from others (1553). In the publication *De mest bemærkelsesværdige steder I den hellige skrift, som forbyder åger* [*The Most Remarkable and Memorable Passages in the Holy Scriptures Prohibiting Usury*] he quoted and commented on a number of texts. He had no scruples in cutting and adapting these texts to serve his purpose. An example of this appears with Deuteronomy 23:20 where it is written that interest may not be charged on loans to one's brother, for Palladius here omits what follows which states that strangers may indeed be charged interest! The publication was a fiery admonition to Denmark's clergy. Usury was theft, it went against the Bible, and Palladius noted the social aspect of the practice, namely that it harmed the poor. God would punish usurers, and he illustrated this with a grim story of the fate of a usurer from his childhood

---

[5] Melanchthon to Christian III, Wittenberg 8th of May 1553, see Scheible (2006, No. 6824). For Melanchthon's position on commercial ethics and especially his views on the problem of interest, see Bauer (1958) and Clemmensen (1940, pp. 128–129).

town of Ribe. In his special edition of Psalm 73, the same subject was referred to. The psalmist was tempted to feel bitter and full of doubt when witnessing the success, happiness and security of the rich and godless. But then he realised that their happiness was nothing but an illusion because, in the end, God would destroy the godless, whereas the psalmist would find happiness with God. In his work of exegesis, Palladius is full of social indignation and resentment at the success of the rich and at the harm that they were doing to the poor. However, he is comforted by the conviction that in the end the Devil will carry off the rich while he himself, the true Christian believer, will enjoy security and happiness with God who will bring him to heaven.

The same vision is present in his preface to one of the Devil writings of Andreas Musculus, the well-known German moralist. In the poem 'On this final and brief time and on this wicked world' with which he ends the translation of Musculus's work, he sets the Devil of usury on a par with the trouser Devil, the Devil of drunkenness and the Devil of cursing. His depiction of the fate of usurers is stark and forthright:

> who of them imagines that the agonies can be everlasting? Even if the gates of Hell are open right in front of a person's door, he will not cease engaging in usury until the Devil carries him off through the gates and down into the pit of Hell, there to burn in the mire, flames, sulphur, tar, smoke and steam of Hell - - -. (Peter Paladius: Om Hosedjævelen, Jacobsen 1911–1926, Vol. 4, p. 64)

Seemingly depiction of the fate of usurers can be found many places.[6]

Notwithstanding the vehement protests of theologians, Christian III yielded to commercial pressures. After a meeting of the Rigsråd (State council), an edict was passed on 20 May 1557 in Copenhagen setting the maximal rate of interest at 5%. The reasoning behind the King's decision was that he had learnt that unchristian business transactions were taking place across the country with not only nobles, burghers and farmers but also priests asking up to 6%, 8% and even 10% interest on loans. But while it was undoubtedly distasteful and against God's will to charge any interest at all, as was conceded in the edict, the King acknowledged that 'such a thing cannot be completely avoided'. Accordingly, charging up to a stipulated maximal interest rate was now permitted. If anybody demanded more than this, it would amount to usury and would be severely punished. Characteristically, the King advised people to behave in such a way that they had clear consciences and did not act against God's will. A few months later, the King communicated the decree to the Council for the town and surrounding administrative area of Flensborg, stressing even more strongly that it was unchristian to practise usury. If anyone was caught charging more that 5% interest, then priests were bound by their office to publicly excommunicate them and exclude them from church. The seriousness with which this obligation was taken is borne out by the fact that the King refers to it on two

---

[6] Peder Palladius: En Præservativ mod Pestilens, in Jacobsen (1911–1926, Vol. 2, pp. 339–348); Peder Palladius: Om Hosedjævelen (Andreas Musculus), 1556, in Jacobsen (1911–1926, Vol. 4, pp. 55–56, 62–67); Peder Palladius: Den LXXIII. Psalme. Quam bonus Israel Deus, 1554, Jacobsen (1911–1926, Vol. 4, pp. 373–377).

occasions. It was repeated once more in the Kolding decree of 13 December 1558, in which the King added that though interest charges and usury were against God's will, they were unavoidable. The King also stated that he had debated the issue with the Rigsråd and with 'some of the most learned of the land' (Lausten 1987, p. 152; Rørdam 1881–1883, p. 500). The provisions of the edict stood until 1683 (Clemmensen 1940, p. 133).

How could it be that theologians took it upon themselves to oppose the policies of the government and the King so vehemently on the question of interest charges? It happened because they were interpreting the Bible literally and following Martin Luther's views. Also, they knew that the King was actually in agreement with them although commercial and business considerations meant that he was unable to follow his conscience or religious convictions.

However, the 1557 edict did not silence the theologians. Bishop Hans Tausen noted the difference between in the way that the Bible and a royal edict interpreted usury (December 1557).[7] Foremost amongst the theologians in Denmark was Niels Hemmingsen (Nicolaus Hemmingius), one of Europe's leading Protestants, who discussed the question on a number of occasions (Lausten 2013, pp. 246–251). In his manual of dogmatics *Enchiridion theologicum* (1557), he declares that the basic rule is to be found in Luke 6:34–35 where Jesus says that one should lend without expecting to receive anything in return. Any agreement (Latin *contractus*) that contravenes this principle is forbidden. Consequently, usury can never be excused because usury is an income over and above the capital that was lent out. Interest and usury are thus one and the same.

Christian III's measure allowing interest rates of 5% to be charged was, as already mentioned, issued on 20 May 1557. The preface to Hemmingsen's manual, which was dated 1 October of that same year, was directly aimed at the King. Was it not courageous of Hemmingsen to condemn all forms of interest charges? The probable explanation for his condemnation is that he knew that the King himself was averse to all forms of loan charges for religious reasons but had felt forced to take the step that he did. Hemmingsen was in line with the other Danish theologians on this point. He returned to the subject in later writings. In his work on natural law [*De lege naturae*, 1562], he modified his views writing that one had to distinguish between general and special necessity.[8] The prohibition against charging interest was a general necessity but, as a *special* necessity, it was permissible to demand up to 5%. The great uncertainty about the sanctioning of interest charges, combined with the King's attitude, the position adopted by his advisers and the criticism of the theologians prompted the Chancellor Johan Friis, the leading man in the King's close circle, to ask Hemmingsen for an opinion on the question. While working on his *Commentary to the Jacob Epistle* (1563), which among other things contains a fierce condemnation of the rich, Hemmingsen had the opportunity of expressing his

---

[7] Hans Tausen: Judicium de excommunicatione, in Rørdam (1870, p. 325).
[8] Bl. Rr-Rr 4.

own views. These did not run to just a few pages as in his manual of dogmatics. The chapter on contracts, loans and interest charges runs to no fewer than 238 pages.

In the introduction, where once again Luke 6:34 and Psalm 112:5 are cited, he states *that everything that is paid back over and above what was originally lent is usury*. Thus he does not distinguish between interest and usury. He then divides his deliberations into five long chapters. These may be summarised:

First, Hemmingsen notes historical bans on usury and shows that these were pronounced by both classical and Christians writers. He cites a quotation from Aristotle whom he calls the Prince of Philosophers. He does not mention Melanchthon but there is little doubt that the quotation was taken from Melanchthon's handbook on Christian ethics which also provides the inspiration for other passages of the book (Melanchthon 1538). Apart from the quotation from Aristotle, he cites similar pronouncements from Plato, Plutarch, Cicero and others. He then quotes the well-known texts form the Old Testament forbidding usury before pointing out that people in ancient Rome also took a negative view of usury, although in Imperial times modest interest charges were permitted. He then goes on to present numerous quotations which show opposition to interest charges. These are taken from synods and the writings of scholars such as Gratian, Jerome, Ambrose, Augustine, John Chrysostom, Lactantius and Bernard of Clairvaux. He completes the list with Luther, adding 'but as his works are well known to most people, I will not quote from them'. It can be concluded, he writes, that interest charges and usury are forbidden so that people will not harm their neighbour, undermine the giving of charity, cause social unrest or possibly even ruin families and social order.

Secondly, follows a summary of the punishments that can be meted out to usurers. First, there are the punishments that society can impose. These are physical in nature and even though they are harsh in themselves for the usurer, he should be aware that his children will also receive punishment. Hemmingsen recalls two infamous usurers from his childhood in Denmark, one of whom, a man from Jutland, had become rich. However, his children suffered a pitiful fate. He said that he saw the daughter in Copenhagen wearing ragged and dirty clothing that scarcely covered her body. The children of the other usurer fared equally badly. But in addition to the secular punishments there are the spiritual ones, a fact which seems to affect Hemmingsen greatly. In this connection, he becomes passionate and hostile in his condemnations and warnings. The spiritual punishments are the worst, he says, even though many people consider them laughable, for usurers no longer belong to *the family of God*. They are the servants of Satan and no longer members of the Church, for it is clear that they consider the will of God as a matter of trifling importance. 'What, I ask you', he writes, 'if you enjoy all the riches that you have obtained through usury but lose your soul? Oh, what a dreadful sentence that will be for you!'. Such people end up in Hell. Finally he indicates the punishment meted out by the Church: gifts from a usurer to the poor or to the Church will be rejected since money obtained in that way is an abomination in the eyes of God. Usurers are the slaves of Satan, excluded from the sacrament and unable to receive a Christian burial.

In his *third* chapter, Hemmingsen abandons his uncompromising stance and questions whether there are certain forms of loan interest or usury that are not forbidden according to God's law and which even a pious person is allowed to charge with a clear conscience. In this chapter, which covers nearly 50 pages, it is interesting to observe that he divides people into a number of groups in order to assess their position within society. This was necessary when considering the question of interest charges. The poor, the sick and those unable to work could not be asked to pay any interest; indeed, they should be given alms. Artisans and those living by the sweat of their brow must be given interest free loans in accordance with the words of Jesus. Here, Hemmingsen is probably thinking of Luke 6:34–35. The third group consists of farmers, especially those with smallholdings. They should not be charged any interest either. However, they are urged to live modestly at all times: 'I would like these people to be forbidden luxurious clothing and unnecessary spending on weddings and for confinements'. The young also make up a special group, particularly the children of the rich. If money is lent to them, it is right and proper to demand interest, but in reality one should not be lending money to frivolous young people of this sort. And Hemmingsen then inserts a long section on the appropriate way to bring up children. Finally, there are the merchants. In this group too, further subdivisions are required. The principle of social equality [Lat. *aequalitas*] means that interest can be charged on a loan to a rich merchant but not to a poor and modest grocer. It is also permissible to lend to a merchant and then demand a certain part of the subsequent profits. In this as well as in other examples cited here, Hemmingsen operates with a maximum interest rate of 5%, and he positively extols Christian III because he was the one who 'introduced an act stating that nobody was allowed to receive more than 5% per annum. That is the upper limit, and the person who exceeds it abandons the principle of *aequalitas*'. In this connection, Hemmingsen quotes directly from Melanchthon's above-mentioned writings.

In the *fourth* substantial chapter, warnings of various types are given, arranged under eight headings. Most of these are elaborations on texts drawn from the New Testament where there are warnings against evil and the love of money, while at the same time we are encouraged to embrace charity and a life that can offend neither Turks nor heathens. Children of decent folk can achieve great dignity by honest work, ability and prudence without any money behind them. 'I could mention examples from home, but as they are already well-known I will refrain', he remarks modestly.

The *final* chapter continues in the same admonitory vein and concentrates on the duties of the priests in this connection. They must condemn any 'unfair contract', though naturally not what has been ordained or approved by the authorities. When necessary, they must excommunicate a person, but only after attempting counselling. One has to be careful when admonishing the rich, although the priest might perhaps tell them that Christ intended society to include poor people because He wanted to see if the rich followed His commandment of charity (Hemmingsen 1563, pp. 181–319).

In his 1592 commentary on 21 psalms, Hemmingsen again touches on the question of loan interest and usury in the interpretation he offers for psalm 15:5: *He that putteth not out his money to usury* (shall abide in thy tabernacle and dwell in thy holy hill, psalm 15:1). Even in his introductory remarks, it is clear that his principal concern now is to defend the charging of interest. However, he explains that there should be a balance between, on the one hand, the needs of trade and commerce and, on the other, indefensible greed. One has to steer between Scylla and Charybdis, as it were. Matthew 7:12 must always be the point of departure, meaning that charity should be the guide to everything that one does. In addition, the measures approved by the authorities should apply but only as long as they do not contravene the will of God. Hemmingsen divides loans into interest-free loans and loans with interest. For either of these, the borrower's circumstances and living conditions always have to be considered. If a borrower merely wishes to increase his possessions, loan interest can be charged without committing sin, but only up to the maximum interest rate of 5% as determined by the authorities. Again, Hemmingsen refers to the principle of *aequalitas*. Thereafter he rejects the arguments put forward by the opponents of *any* form of interest charge. Augustine's rule of interpretation has to be adhered to, namely that every single case should be examined carefully and its background and purpose taken into account. He also rejects those who advocate Aristotle's claim that loan interest charges go against nature. Money does not belong to nature, says Hemmingsen, so money is not something *natural*. Hence, Aristotle's objection can be ignored. Hemmingsen has thus abandoned his original opposition (1557) against interest charges. In that work, it was *inter alia* Aristotle and the cited passages from the scriptures that he used to support his position but now these are rejected. He can now argue that it is legitimate for trade and business to charge interest on loans, see Hemmingsen (1592), Madsen (1946, pp. 331–332), Glebe-Møller (1979) and Lausten (2013, pp. 246–251).

References

Bauer, C. 1958. Melanchthons Wirtschaftsethik. *Archiv für Reformationsgeschichte* 49: 115–160.
Christensen, T., ed. 1964. *Luthers skrifter i Udvalg*. Vol. IV. Copenhagen: Gads Forlag.
Clemmensen, V. 1940. *De religiøse Systemers Indflydelse paa de erhvervsetiske Princippers Udvikling i Danmark*. Copenhagen: Nyt Nordisk Forlag.
Dahlerup, T. 1963. *Bidrag til Rentespørgsmålets Historie i dansk Senmiddelalder og Reformationstid, Festskrift til Astrid Friis*, 47–64. Copenhagen: Rosenkilde og Bagger.
Glebe-Møller, J. 1979. Socialetiske aspekter af Niels Hemmingsens forfatterskab. *Kirkehistoriske Samlinger* 1979: 7–56.
Hemmingsen, N. 1563. *In Epistolam Divi Iacobi Apostoli Commentarivs*. Copenhagen: Johannes Xylander.
———. 1592. *Enarratio viginti et unius psalmorum*. Genéve: Apud Petrum Santandreanum.
Jacobsen, L., ed. 1911–1926. *Peder Palladius' Danske Skrifter*. Copenhsagen: Universitets-Jubilæets danske Samfund.
Lausten, M.S. 1985. Rentespørgsmålet hos teologer i den danske reformationskirke. In *Festskrift til Troels Dahlerup*, ed. Aa Andersen, 91–104. Århus: Arusia.
———. 1987. *Christian den 3. og kirken 1537–1559*. Copenhagen: Akademisk Forlag.
———., ed. 1989. *Kirkeordinansen 1537/1539*. Copenhagen: Akademisk Forlag.
———. 2013. *Niels Hemmingsen. Storhed og fald*. Frederiksberg: Forlaget Anis.
Luther, M. 1519. *Sermon von dem Wucher*, WA, Bd. 6, pp. 3–8.
———. 1520. *Sermon von dem Wucher*, WA Bind 6, pp. 36–60.

———. 1524. *Von Kaufshandlung und Wucher*, WA Bind 15, pp. 293–322.
———. 1539. Sermon, the 13 of April 1539, WA bind 47, pp. 558–559.
———. 1540. *An die Pfarrherrn wider dem Wucher zu predigen*, WA Bind 15, pp. 331–242.
———. 1546. Sermon the 15 of February 1546, Eisleben, WA Bind 15, pp. 187–196.
———. 1883–2009. *D. Martin Luthers Werke. Kritische Gesamtausgabe (Weimarer Ausgabe, WA)*. Weimar: Hermann Böhlau.
Madsen, E.M. 1946. *Niels Hemmingsens Etik: en idehistorisk studie*. Dr. Thesis, University of Copenhagen, Copenhagen.
Melanchthon, Ph. 1538. *Philosophia Moralis Epitomes Libri Duo*. Wittenberg.
Rørdam, H.F. 1860–1862. Bidrag til den danske Reformationshistorie, *Kirkehistoriske Samlinger* 2. Række, II.
———., ed. 1870. *Smaaskrifter af Hans Tausen*. Copenhagen: Det kongelige Danske Selskab for Fædrelandets Historie.
———. 1881–1883. *Danske Kirkelove*. Vol. 1. Copenhagen: Selskabet for Danmarks kirkehistorie.
Scheible, H., ed. 2006. *Melanchthons Briefwechsel, Regesten 6691-8071*, Band 7. Stuttgart-Bad Cannstatt: frommann-holzboog.
Strohm, T. 1983. Luthers Wirtschafts- und Sozialethik. In *Leben und Werk Martin Luthers von 1526 bis 1546*, ed. H. Junghans, 205–223. Göttingen: Vandenhoeck & Ruprecht.

Martin Schwarz Lausten born 1938, professor in ecclesiastical history at University of Copenhagen 1996–2008, since professor emeritus. Has written a lot of scientific and popular books about ecclesiastical history.

Chapter 18
Poverty, Income Distribution, Lutheran Christianity and the Danish Welfare State

Jørn Henrik Petersen

Abstract The preface of Gabriel et al. (Religion und Wohlfahrtsstaatlichkeit in Europa. Mohr Siebeck, Tübingen, 2013) states that the normative 'in depth grammar' of the modern welfare state is significantly, but diffusely influenced by religiously procured values and initiatives. This chapter analyses relations between the social attitudes, Christianity and the welfare state in a Danish context. The social attitudes of Luther and contemporary Christianity are presented, and the moral and religious background underlying the Danish welfare state is discussed.

Keywords Social ethics · Evangelical and Catholic ethics · Luther · The welfare state

18.1 Some Indicative Figures

This chapter is about income distribution, poverty, Christianity, and the welfare state. The reasoning rests on the idea that societal responses to inequality and poverty are related to the electorate's and the political actors' conception about what constitutes "good" social policies, and it is hypothesized that Christian values and norms do play a role in forming the conception. Those who argue that the welfare state is a purely secular invention based on secular actors' secular views neglect that historical antecedents are important in shaping contemporary conceptions about the "good society". Religious legacies are important because they may have been transposed into current societal values. Gabriel et al. (2013) rightly state that the

---

J. H. Petersen (✉)
Department of Political Science, Danish Centre for Welfare Studies, University of Southern Denmark, Odense M, Denmark
e-mail: jhp@sam.sdu.dk

© The Author(s), under exclusive license to Springer Nature Switzerland AG 2023
N. Kærgård (ed.), *Market, Ethics and Religion*, Ethical Economy 62,
https://doi.org/10.1007/978-3-031-08462-1_18

normative 'in depth grammar' of the welfare state is significantly, but diffusely influenced by religiously procured values.

Sigrun Kahl has attempted to develop a link between the modern welfare state and the content of religion – the "social doctrines" of the various Christian creeds (Kahl 2009, see also Kahl 2006). Religion is seen as a key concept in understanding the different configurations of welfare states. During a process of secularization religiosity is transposed into ethics, and part of the religious doctrines become associated with secular value sets. By shaping the historical antecedents, religion outlines societal values even if they have ceased to be identified as religious.[1] These values constitute the core of a civil or secularized religion.

Historically Catholicism and Reformed Protestantism have had a strained relationship with the state, whereas Lutheran Protestantism has endorsed state activity. If religious legacies are important, one expects the most intense governmental activity in policies of redistribution and poverty abatement in the Lutheran countries and the least in countries characterized by a Reformist Protestant legacy with the Catholic countries placed in an intermediate position. In a "soft" sense this is confirmed by the figures of the table.

A few indicative figures							
	Denmark	Sweden	Germany	France	Italy	United Kingdom	United States
Gini coefficient of household disposable income[a]	0.261	0.275	0.289	0.292	0.334	0.366	0.39
S80/S20[b]	3.7	4.1	4.5	4.4	6.1	6.5	8.4
Relative income poverty rates[c]	5.8	8.9	10.4	8.1	13.9	11.7	17.8
Households making ends meet with difficulty[d]	6.0	4.1	4.0	14.0	19.5	9.9	–
Index for interpersonal trust[e]	131.9	134.5	75.8	37.9	60.8	61.7	78.8

[a]http://www.oecd.org/social/income-distribution-database.htm. "Key indicators on the distribution of household disposable income". Data are based on equivalized household disposable income, i.e. income after taxes and transfers adjusted for household size. Inequality is measured by the Gini-coefficient. A Gini-coefficient of zero indicates perfect equality and a coefficient of one indicates complete inequality. The data on Gini coefficients, S80/S20 and the relative poverty rates refer to 2017 except Sweden and the United Kingdom (2018) and Denmark (2016)
[b]Ibid. The S80/S20 income share refers to the ratio of average income of the top 20% to the average income of the bottom 20% of the income distribution
[c]Ibid. The poverty threshold is set at 50% of median disposable income in each country
[d]Eurostat ilc_mdes09
[e]Jaime Diez Medrano, "Interpersonal Trust", http://www.jdsurvey.net/jds/jdsurveyActualidad.jsp?Idioma=I & SeccionTexto=0404 & NOID=104. His data are in the Danish case taken from "Values Surveys EVS/WWS Waves 1–4 (1981–2004) and in the remaining cases from World Values Survey Wave 5 (2005–2008). The data are based on the respondents' answer to the ques-

---

[1] "Differences between Catholicism and Protestantism as well as differences between various forms of Protestantism are important if one is to understand why different countries chose different paths of socio-political development", (van Keesbergen and Manow 2009, pp. 210–235).

tion: Generally speaking, would you say that most people can be trusted or that you need to be very careful in dealing with people? The index is based on a formula according to which trust equals 100 + the percentage responding that most people can be trusted – the percentage responding that "you can never be too careful when dealing with other". It means that an index above 100 corresponds to countries where a majority of people trust others, while an index below 100 corresponds to countries where a majority of people think one can never be too careful when dealing with others.

The table shows some indicative numbers on income inequality, poverty and personal trust. The seven countries included are one undisputed Catholic (Italy), one Reformed Protestant (USA) and two genuine Lutheran (Denmark and Sweden). Germany mirrors a Lutheran country with an influential Catholic minority and France exemplifies a Catholic country in which the state claims supremacy over the church. Finally, the United Kingdom represents a country with a church being a hybrid between Catholicism and Reformed Protestantism.

One observes that the two genuine Lutheran countries attribute greater emphasis to equality as measured by the Gini coefficient as well as the quintile share ratio than do the other countries. They also score high when relative income poverty rates and the share of population making ends meet only with difficulty are concerned. It looks as if France compared to Germany has attributed relatively greater emphasis to poverty abatement than to redistribution.

The two Lutheran countries are the only ones in which a majority trust other people. This is important, because interpersonal trust disposes for the establishment of a society in which individuals care for each other. The remarkable high indices of trust suggest either the willingness of the population to build "a strong society" or the acceptance of the societal institutions as they have developed.

In the following I shall first make a few remarks on the place of inequality in Scripture. Second, I shall give a presentation of Luther's social teaching and some brief observations on the "social doctrines" of the Catholic, the German Evangelical and the Presbyterian Church. Finally, the attention is turned towards income distribution, poverty abatement, Lutheran Christianity and the Danish welfare state.

18.2 Inequality and Scripture

Christians are called to seek justice and to care for the poor. It is important, therefore, for Christians to understand where income inequality is natural, and to challenge the status quo where it is unjust.

Income inequality is a fact of economic life. People are born with different gifts and choose to pursue them differently. The market rewards contributions to satisfy consumer demand through profit and punishes those who do not successfully satiate consumer demand through losses. Profits and losses serve as critical feedback mechanisms which alter behaviour and give incentives to creativity and innovation.

To accept in a biblical sense the mechanisms giving rise to inequality we may imagine that all human beings are equally loved by God, but that they are also created with different gifts and will, therefore, be rewarded differently by the market in compliance with how they apply these gifts.

Markets allocate scarce resources most productively. They help to determine the ends to which the scarce resources are allocated by bringing together demanders and suppliers. By this procedure everyone is better off than they would be without this resource allocation mechanism.

Since humans are created with different gifts and individually decide how to utilize these gifts some will earn higher incomes than others, because diversity of gifts opens for specialization.

The Parable of the Talents (Mt 25:14–30) is illustrative. The servant who hid his master's one talent in the ground was received by the Master by the words: "… Then you ought to have invested my money with the bankers, and at my coming I should have received what was my own with interest. So, take the talent from him, and give it to him who has the ten talents …".

Matthew tells that the three servants were given different amounts, "each according to his ability" suggesting that each servant had a level of ability different from the others and implying different productivity across the three servants. The master understood the idea of comparative advantages.

The two of them invested the money allocated to them so that they collected a rate of return equal to 100%, whereas the third achieved a rate of return equal to zero. It is obvious, that if the Master had been an egalitarian giving each of the servants the same amount, he would have come into a position inferior to the one realized.

The master could alternatively have given the servant who received five talents all eight talents distributed to the three servants. But by giving different amounts to the three, he simultaneously spread his risk. It is a story about comparative advantages and risk spreading – not far from a market approach.

This, however, is not the end of Scripture's story. In Deut. 10:18 we are told that God "executes justice for the fatherless and the widow, and loves the sojourner, giving him food and clothing". It is a thought frequently presented in Scripture. The widow, the fatherless, the sojourner are terms describing society's weak and vulnerable members. If due to their gifts they are handicapped, justice must replace efficiency as the dominant criterion. Transfer payments might be called for – even at the cost of reduced incentives and decreased efficiency.

That the relation to God follows from the single man's relations to his fellow human beings is clearly seen from the description of the Day of Judgment (Mt 25:31–46) in which Jesus uses the phrase 'eternal punishment' for anyone and everyone who allows humans to go hungry:

> When the Son of Man comes in his glory, and all the angels with him, then he will sit on his glorious throne. Before him will be gathered all the nations, and he will separate people one from another as a shepherd separates the sheep from the goats. And he will place the sheep on his right, but the goats on the left. Then the King will say to those on his right, 'Come, you who are blessed by my Father, inherit the kingdom prepared for you from the foundation of the world. For I was hungry and you gave me food, I was thirsty and you gave me drink, I was a stranger and you welcomed me, I was naked and you clothed me, I was sick and you visited me, I was in prison and you came to me.' Then the righteous will answer

him, saying, 'Lord, when did we see you hungry and feed you, or thirsty and give you drink? And when did we see you a stranger and welcome you, or naked and clothe you? And when did we see you sick or in prison and visit you?' And the King will answer them, 'Truly, I say to you, as you did it to one of the least of these my brothers, you did it to me.' Then he will say to those on his left, 'Depart from me, you cursed, into the eternal fire prepared for the devil and his angels. For I was hungry and you gave me no food, I was thirsty and you gave me no drink, I was a stranger and you did not welcome me, naked and you did not clothe me, sick and in prison and you did not visit me.' Then they also will answer, saying, 'Lord, when did we see you hungry or thirsty or a stranger or naked or sick or in prison, and did not minister to you?' Then he will answer them, saying, 'Truly, I say to you, as you did not do it to one of the least of these, you did not do it to me.' And these will go away into eternal punishment, but the righteous into eternal life.[2]

Scripture primarily pays attention to the obligation to provide for 'the least of these my brothers', i.e. poverty abatement and redistribution is only affected by the claim of equality of all men in the view of God.

18.3 Luther's Teaching on Poverty and Beggary

Christians are to be taught that he who gives to the poor or lends to the needy does a better deed than he who buys indulgences.[3] From the release of the 95 Theses (1517) theology and social ethics are inseparable. What is implicit in the Theses became increasingly explicit up to the publication of the Wittenberg Order.[4]

Prior to the Reformation, Europe was a feudal system with strict class lines. Luther revolutionized the social classes by claiming that

> a cobbler, a smith, a peasant – each has the work and office of his trade, and yet they are all alike consecrated priests and bishops and every one by means of his own work or office must benefit and serve every other, that in this way many kinds of work may be done for the bodily and spiritual welfare of the community, even as all the members of the body serve one another. (Luther, 1520, WA vol. 6, p. 409. 1–10)[5]

Everybody was important to society, every man was equal to and was to serve his neighbour. This mirrors a belief in social equality foreign to the sixteenth century. Luther believed that the wealth distribution of the day characterized by the few rich and the thousands of poor must be equalized. The desire for economic equality was born through the ideas of Martin Luther.

---

[2] "The passage in Matthew about the Day of Judgment graphically describes the connection between God's option for the poor and the just action of human beings. ... The reconciling encounter with the poor, in solidarity with them, becomes a place to encounter God", see Evangelischen Kirche Deutschland (1997, § 106).

[3] Luther, "Disputatio pro declaratione virtutis indulgentiarum", 1517, WA, vol. 1, 229–238.

[4] *Ordnung des gemeinen Beutels zu Wittenberg 1521* and *Kastenordnung der Stadt Wittenberg 1522* (Strohm and Klein 2004, pp. 15–17 and 17–19).

[5] Luther, M. (1520), "An den christlichen Adel deutscher Nation von der christlichen Standes Besserung", WA vol. 6, pp. 409. 1–10.

Luther also wanted to outlaw begging in Christendom since it was detrimental to society and culture in total:

> It is one of the most urgent necessities to abolish all begging in Christendom. No one should go about begging among Christians. It would not be hard to do this, if we attempted it with good heart and courage: each town should support its own poor and should not allow strange beggars to come in, whatever they may call themselves, pilgrims or mendicant monks. Every town could feed its own poor; and if it were too small, the people in the neighbouring villages should be called upon to contribute. As it is, they must support many knaves and vagabonds under the name of beggars. If they did what I propose, they would at least know who were really poor or not. (Luther, 1520, WA, vol. 6, pp. 450.22–31)

He added:

> If a man will be poor he should not be rich; if he will be rich, let him put his hand to the plough, and get wealth himself out of the earth. It is enough to provide decently for the poor, that they may not die of cold and hunger. It is not right that one should work that another may be idle, and live ill that another may live well, as is now the perverse abuse, for St. Paul says, "If any would not work, neither should he eat" (2 Thess. 3:10). God has not ordained that anyone should live of the goods of others - - -. (Luther, 1520, WA, vol. 6, pp. 451.9–17)

This is a medieval argument in favour of an incentive system.

The social implications were revolutionary. Luther advocated that all men should be socially equal because they were equal before God. Human beings are made in the image of God and so endowed with a unique, inalienable dignity. The medieval concept of a stratified society could not fathom this new idea. He went on to discuss doing good works for one's neighbours as well as providing welfare for the poor in one's community. He advocated that each man should give from his abundance to help the poor. Every person should be socially equal, and the discrimination between helping a friend or an enemy should be superfluous.

Traces of the "protestant work ethic" idea are spread throughout *The Freedom of a Christian*.[6] Luther argued that "man cannot be idle, for the need of his body drives him and he is compelled to do many good works to reduce it to subjection".[7] By proclaiming that all men were equal, Luther said that all vocations were equal before God and therefore holy. Man was created to work as the birds were born to fly.[8]

Luther assisted to develop the so-called Beutelordnung in Wittenberg run by four stewards. They were to be "honest, prosperous, and faithful citizens", "who are well acquainted with the towns and with the poor as to their property, character, status,

---

[6] This work exists in two versions, the shorter one in German, and the longer one in Latin. "Von den Freyheit einitz Christen menschen", 1520, WA, vol. 7, 12–38 and "Epistula Lutherana ad Leonem Decimum summum pontificem. Tractatus de libertate christiana", 1520, WA, vol. 7, 39–73.

[7] "Epistula Lutherana ...", WA, vol. 7, 60.25–27.

[8] "Eine Predigt vom Ehestand, getan durch D. Martinum Lutherum seliger. Anno 1525", WA, vol. 17.1:12–29, 23.39–40. The comparison with the birds is used earlier, see "Decem praccepta Wittenbergensi praedicate populo" 1518, WA, vol. 1, 394–521, 505.20–21.

origin, and integrity, and who are capable of discerning those willing to work from the idle ones, judging conditions and making decisions" (Lindberg 1977, p. 327).

In his 1520-work *On Usury*[9] Luther discussed the issues of "social care" and "helping the weakest". His point of departure was the words of Jesus (Mt 5, 42): "He who asks of thee, to him give." What Luther terms "the second degree of dealing with temporal goods" amounts to the demand "that we give our goods freely to everyone who needs them or asks for them" – a demand "hard and bitter for those who have more taste for the temporal than for the eternal goods" (41.17–20).

Arguing for social care Luther referred to Deut 15, 4: "There will always be poor people in the land, therefore I command thee that thou open thy hand to thy poor and needy brother and give to him." "There shall be no beggar or indigent man among you" (41.35–42.3).

He condemned men who "give and present things to their friends, the rich and powerful who do not need them, and forget the needy". It would be much better if they did these things to the needy. Of such men Christ says (Luke 14: 12–14),

> If thou make a midday or an evening meal, thou shalt not invite thy friends or thy brethren, or thy relatives, or thy neighbours, or the rich, so that they may invite thee again, and thus take thy reward; but when thou makes a meal, invite the poor, the sick, the lame, the blind; so art thou blessed, for they cannot recompense it to thee; but it shall be recompensed to thee among the righteous, when they rise from the dead. (42.22–28)

To summarize: In Luther's view every man was important to society, every man was equal to his neighbour, and every man was to serve his neighbour. The distribution of wealth should be narrowed. Each town should support its own poor and beggary be prohibited, but in such a manner that incentives were to be effective. The instrument was a distinction between deserving and non-deserving poor. Remembering that his views are coloured by his medieval time it is fair to say that the desire for economic equality was born through the ideas of Martin Luther. Even though redistribution of wealth is emphasized, the weight is given to poverty abatement.

According to Luther justification by God's unconditional grace sets man free to serve his fellow human beings.[10] God and fellow human men are separate aiming points. It is impossible, therefore, to separate works from faith.[11] Good deeds are those that serve the neighbour's welfare and spring from faith.[12] To serve the neighbour is to serve God and to serve God is to serve the neighbour. Encountering God and serving society are inseparable for Christians. Since men are redeemed in Christ, they are liberated to act without care for themselves but can respond to the needs of their fellow human beings. This links faith and ethics insoluble together. To

---

[9] "Eyn Sermon von dem Wucher. Doctoris Martini Luther Augustiner zu Wittenberg" (Großer Sermon von dem Wucher, 1520), WA, vol. 6, 36–60.

[10] Only a small part of Luther's social ethics is presented here. For an in-depth analysis of the relation between Luther's thinking and the development of the welfare state in the Danish configuration and its later move towards a so-called competitive state, see Petersen (2016, 2018a).

[11] See Martin Luther, "Das neue Testament Deutzsch" 1522/15/1546, in WA, vol. 6, 9–10.

[12] See Martin Luther, "Von den guten wercken" 1520, WA, vol. 6, 202–276.

love God without loving and taking care for one's neighbour remains abstract and ultimately unreal.

To love thy neighbour, however, does also have a collective dimension because man is curved into himself.[13] 'Incurvatus in se' means that despite our best efforts to get beyond ourselves, to love and serve others to the best of our ability, human beings find it impossible to escape the gravity well of self-interest, and we are often unconscious of this fact, even as it in fact drives our behaviour. The world, therefore, cannot in a societal sense rely on the gospel and Christian love. The world accepts neither gospel nor love but acts according to its own will unless compelled by force.[14] 'Ordnungen'/regulations, i.e. decisions governing the community, are necessary – in Luther's days set up by the benevolent prince, in our days to be determined in a collective process.

This is part of the reason why the Danish welfare state in my interpretation is an "as if -institution", a surrogate for love of the neighbour, institutionalized love. Some might think this interpretation of the welfare state is a bit romantic and unrealistic. But it is not.

Obviously, it demands that love of the neighbour in Luther's sense corresponds with reality. That correspondence, however, is to be found in the concept of secularized religion developed by a process by which hitherto religious doctrines and concepts are turned into ethics and embedded into secularized values. I urge that such a process has characterized Danish Social Democracy. (Petersen 2018a, pp. 1–27).

18.4 Current Social Doctrine of the Catholic Church

"Compendium of the Social Doctrine of the Church" offers a complete overview of the fundamental doctrinal corpus of Catholic social teaching (Pontifical Council for Justice and Peace 2006). The obligations to the poor and the strangers are strongly emphasized (§23). The poor, the marginalized and in all cases those whose living conditions interfere with their proper growth should be the focus of particular concern (§182). The Church, however, is cautious regarding ideological positions and Messianic beliefs that sustain the illusion that it is possible to eliminate the problem of poverty completely from this world (§183). Nevertheless, the poor remain entrusted to us and it is this responsibility upon which we shall be judged at the end of time (cf. Mt. 25:31–46). Giving alms to the poor, therefore, is one of the chief witnesses to fraternal charity, but charity implies also addressing the social and political dimensions of the problem of poverty (§184).

The Church does not only stress the obligation to care for the poor in an absolute manner but also underlines the importance of the distribution of income. In addition

---

[13] See for example Martin Luther, *Diui Pauli apostoli ad Romanos epistula* (Römervorlesung) 1515/16, WA, vol. 56, 304.23–30.

[14] Martin Luther, "Von Kaufshandlung und Wucher" 1524, WA, vol. 15, 279–322, 306.28–36

to the quantity of goods produced in a country, its economic well-being also depends on equity in the distribution of income to be pursued inter alia by means of suitable social policies for the redistribution of income which, taking general conditions into account, look at merit as well as at the need of each citizen (§303).

Public taxation and spending are important in helping to increase the credibility of the State as the guarantor of systems of social insurance and protection that are designed above all to protect the weakest members of society (§355). The stress attributed to 'the weakest' mirrors some scepticism towards universal measures.

The Church, however, puts some distance towards the idea of a "welfare state". "Solidarity without subsidiarity can easily degenerate into a 'Welfare State'" (§351). The compendium refers to John Paul II's Encyclical Letter *Centesimus Annus* (John Paul 1991, § 48). John Paul wrote about the State's substitute function replacing the principle of subsidiarity and stressed that such intervention had expanded, to the point of creating a new type of State, the so-called "Welfare State". Its malfunctions and defects are the result of an inadequate understanding of the tasks proper to the State restricted by the principle of subsidiarity. By intervening directly and depriving society of its responsibility, the Welfare State leads to a loss of human energies and an inordinate increase of public agencies, which are dominated more by bureaucratic ways of thinking than by concern for serving their clients, and which are accompanied by an enormous increase in spending.

The catholic church claims that the free market is an institution of social importance because of its capacity to guarantee effective results in the production of goods and services (Pontifical Council for Justice and Peace 2006, §347). In some cases, however, the market is not able to ensure efficiency and to guarantee an equitable distribution of the goods and services that is essential for the human growth of citizens. In such cases complementarities of state and market are needed (§353). For a discussion of the social doctrine of the Catholic Church see also Chap. 13 above.

18.5 The Evangelical Church in Germany

In 1997 the Council of the Evangelical Church in Germany and the German Bishops' Conference on the economic and social situation in Germany released a statement on a future founded on solidarity and justice (Evangelischen Kirche Deutschland 1997).[15] Guided and encouraged by the Christian understanding of the human being, the biblical message and Christian social ethics, the churches wanted to make their contribution to the necessary reorientation of society and renewal of the Social Market Economy. The aim was not to give detailed political or economic recommendations, but to advocate what served the cause of more social equality and the common good. Like the Catholic Church the Evangelical Church also uses the term

---

[15] The numbers in the subsequent text refer to the numbering in the statement.

Christian social doctrine conveying perspectives, values, and criteria for judgment and action.[16]

The biblical point of departure is the dual command to love God and the neighbour (Mk 12:28–31). It is the basic norm crystallizing the biblical ethic into a community ethic. The unity of love for God and the neighbour expresses the connection between relationship with God and responsibility for the world.

Christian love of the neighbour is primarily directed to the poor, the weak and the disadvantaged. All social, political, and economic action and decision-making should be gauged by the extent to which it concerns, benefits, and empowers the poor:

> Searching for justice means moving towards those who as the poor and powerless are marginalized in social and economic life and who cannot improve their share and participation in society in their own strength. (§112)

The Christian tradition of justice and mercy calls for fairer structures in society for the prevention of poverty.

Even though poverty is strongly emphasized the discussion paper also points to income distributional issues noting that the German economic success is to be ascribed to market efficiency along with redistribution between social groups and strata (§143). In view of genuinely different starting conditions, it is fair to remove existing discrimination in terms of inequality and to enable all members of society to enjoy equal opportunities and equivalent conditions of life. The logic of economic acting, however, is different from the acts of the welfare state (sozialstaatlicher Aktivitäten), which means that economic efficiency and social security must go hand in hand – it is not only a question of redistribution. If the economy is put under strain from a disproportionate rise in governmental redistribution, then the financial foundations of social security will be undermined.

The statement attributes greater weight to a more balanced and fairer distribution of wealth than to income distribution. The eligibility to show financial solidarity should also be assessed based on assets, not just of current income (§ 215–220):

> Wealth, not just poverty, must become a theme of political debate. Redistribution is frequently the redistribution of scarcity nowadays because the abundance on the other side is hardly touched. (§220)

The welfare state has been the decisive precondition for social peace. The institutions of the welfare state have thus developed into a constitutive element of western social systems. They are ascribed a moral value of their own as they incorporate the commitment to a socially just sharing in all life opportunities.

The evangelical churches, however, do – as does the Catholic Church – urge the principle of subsidiarity meaning that the state must not be turned into a welfare state that paternalistically provides for its citizens from the cradle to the grave.

---

[16] "The doctrine is not an abstract system of norms but stems from continued reflection on human experience in the past and present in the light of the Christian understanding of humanity", § 102.

Personal responsibility and initiative must be encouraged.[17] Subsidiarity is on the other hand not intended to be understood in isolation, merely as a restriction of state responsibility. It is precisely the weaker ones who need to be helped to help themselves. Subsidiarity and solidarity are two sides of the same coin, together providing criteria for the organization of society along the lines of social justice (§121).

The German Evangelical Church argues to some extent along the same lines as does the Catholic Church. Christian love of the neighbour has primarily to be directed to the poor, the weak and the disadvantaged (§ 37, 41, 105, 107, 135), and it is considered fair to remove existing discrimination in terms of inequality. Redistribution must not be carried too far, however, because it might undermine the financial foundations of social security.

The German Lutheran Churches consider the social market economy as the most suitable setting for sustainable economic and social policy. In order to endure, however, the structures of the market economy must be embedded in a supportive culture. Individual self-interest, a crucial structural component of a market economy, may deteriorate into destructive egotism. The most visible consequence is bribery, tax evasion or the abuse of subsidies and social benefits. It is a cultural task to give self-interest a form compatible with the common good (§12).[18]

18.6 The Presbyterian Church in the United States

In its Confession of 1967, the Presbyterian Church urges that the reconciliation of humankind through Jesus Christ makes it plain that enslaving poverty in a world of abundance is an intolerable violation of God's good creation (Presbyterian Church, U.S.A. 2002, § 9.46 c). Because Jesus identified himself with the needy and exploited, the cause of the world's poor is the cause of his disciples. The church cannot condone poverty, whether it is the product of unjust social structures, exploitation of the defenceless, lack of national resources, absence of technological understanding, or rapid expansion of populations. The church calls all people to use their abilities, their possessions, and the fruits of technology as gifts entrusted to them by God for the maintenance of their families and the advancement of the common welfare. The Presbyterians urge poverty abatement, whereas distribution and redistribution are not mentioned.

---

[17] Subsidiarity means empowerment for personal responsibility. It does not mean leaving individuals to provide for their social security on their own. "So, subsidiarity and solidarity, subsidiarity and the welfare state belong together. Subsidiarity means empowerment for personal responsibility. It does not mean leaving individuals to provide for their social security on their own" (§ 27. See also §§ 119–121).

[18] § 91 adds: "The Social Market Economy is … founded on anthropological and ethical preconceptions. It starts from a human image involving freedom and personal responsibility, solidarity, and social commitment. The Social Market Economy is based on preconditions that it cannot create or guarantee itself, but without which it will not be viable in the long run".

18.7 The Danish Context

There is no Danish, nor for that sake Swedish, Christian "social doctrine". The Danish church does not have any synodic institution able to formulate or approve "statements of principle". In the absence of a social doctrine one may fall back on Kahl's idea of religiosity's transformation into ethics, or one may study the relative emphasis given to respectively the first and the second part of Luther's teaching on justification, i.e. the relation to the Creator and the relation to all other creatures.

Many forces have been engaged in developing the Danish welfare state, but the primary mover has been the Social Democratic Party. Therefore, it is of interest to look at the secularized religion of that party.

One of the party's predecessors, Frederik Dreier (1827–1853), rejected the Christian faith but the objective of his program was to realize "the loving and fraternal living together that Christ preached, whereas it is presently only hollow words spoken on Sundays" (Dreier 1853, p. 11). This represents a godless secularized religion – the one track found in the party's reasoning.

The other track is represented by twice chairman of the Danish Parliament (1945–50; 1964–68), minister of education (1953–57), social affairs (1957–61) and the first minister of cultural affairs (1961–64), Julius Bomholt (1896–1969). He was educated as a theologian but early he ascertained that he was not to become priest. Even though he is very modest and shy when it comes to his religious views I have no doubts that he represents a view in which God is a living reality, but his unwillingness to become preacher for instead of engaging himself as educator, politician and author mirrors a view similar to Dreier's: The risk of preaching only hollow words on Sundays and a scepticism towards the church as an institution, but contrary to Dreier he never denies the reality of God (Petersen 2021).

These are the two tracks of secularized religion found in the Social Democratic Party. The one is godless, the other is not. They can be found from the early days of the party and up to the present time (Petersen 2018b).

In my opinion Swedish sociologist Hans Zetterberg (1927–2014) has given a precise description of the origin of the Swedish (and Danish) welfare state:

> The most elaborate manifestation of the welfare state—the one we find in Sweden—is a product of Leftists in a rather secular state, often working in opposition to church officials. The welfare state may be unlikely to flourish except in a civilization in which values of neighbourly love and charity have been preached for generations: Yet its establishment in Scandinavia is mostly the work of a generation of atheists or lukewarm believers. It is the product of a political struggle over the distribution of income and privilege, not a gift from heaven. (Zetterberg 1984, pp. 89–90; see also Petersen and Petersen 2010a)

It is true that Scandinavian welfare states emerged from a struggle between political parties and interests, that they have met with some scepticism from church officials, but the institutional set-up can be understood only with the Christian message in general and Social Democratic secular religion in particular as back-drops.

18.8 Luther and the Normative Basis of the Danish Welfare State[19]

The *first* principle upon which the Danish welfare state is founded is that the life of the single individual is entangled with the lives of all other individuals. Life itself, therefore, dictates a responsibility for taking care of the other. The corresponding element in Luther's teaching is the sacramental community. Partaking in the sacrament is, Luther argued, meaningless if it does not change men so that they seek community with others. Those seeking community with God are obliged to seek community with all others. Community means our basic dependence on others, the entanglement with the lives of others.[20]

The *second* basic principle of the Danish welfare state is the idea of "something for nothing," i.e. the decoupling of former, present, and future behaviour as well as contributory payments from the right to benefits. Similar to neighbours in distress and in need of our works, we have, Luther argues, ourselves been in distress in relation to God and in need of God's grace.[21] As God in Christ has helped us without any quid-pro-quo relation we are obliged to help the neighbour. Luther's point is that love of the neighbour gives something for nothing because of God's grace given to us for nothing. The tax-transfer mechanism void of quid-pro-quo-relations disposes for redistribution of income.

A *third* basic idea is "role reversal" based on imagination in the sense that one empathetically places oneself in another's position and imagines what would be appreciated in the other's place; then one does to the other precisely that. The Lutheran correspondence is his frequent use of the golden rule as voiced by Matthew (Mt 7:12).[22] The individual's everyday life teaches him or her to act towards the neighbour in the same way as she or he would like to be treated had they been in the neighbour's place (495.29–496.2). This is the very idea of role reversal.

A *fourth* basic element in understanding the Danish welfare state is the equal value of all individuals irrespective of their place in society, the value of "equal dignity in hut and palace" as phrased by the Danish theologian and poet Grundtvig (1783–1872). Other related concepts are universalism, egalitarianism, and family. Universalism means that everybody is covered by social provisions. Access to benefits and services is based on citizenship. Egalitarianism means that people in principle consider each other as equal citizens irrespective of their social status.

The parallels in Luther's teaching is first the equality of all human beings because we are all created in God's image and second the equality of status following from

---

[19] The normative basis of the Danish welfare state is developed in Petersen and Petersen (2007a, b, 2010b) and Kærgård (2013).

[20] Martin Luther, "Ein Sermon von dem hochwürdigen Sakrament des heiligen wahren Leichnams Christi und von den Brüderschaften" 1519, WA, vol. 2, 742–758.

[21] Martin Luther, "Von der Freiheit eines Christenmenschen" 1520, WA, vol. 7, 12–39.

[22] Martin Luther, "Wochenpredigt über Matt. 5–7. Das fünfte, sechste und siebend Capitel S. Matthei gepredigt und ausgelegt" 1532, WA, vol. 32, 299–555.

the idea of the general priesthood. These relations to God are in Danish cultural thinking transferred to the relation between individual and state. Let it be added that the Lutheran emphasis on the household as the key estate of society, and marriage as the best way of life, complies with the importance of family and home in the welfare state. It was not accidental that the Swedes years ago talked about the welfare state as "Folkehjemmet" [the home of the people], a phrase frequently used also by Danish social democrats.

The very idea of the welfare state as the surrogate of loving the neighbour has as a *fifth* point a parallel in Luther's vision of the good society as a country-wide hospital.[23] Both images mirror the thought of the good society as an "as-if-institution."

A *sixth* point is concerned with the view on work versus idleness. As already mentioned, humanity was created to work, not to idleness. Work is a service to God, because it represents a service to the commonality and the neighbour as part of God's continued Creation. There is no bridge, therefore, between this and the dawn of early capitalism. The fruits of work were God's gift and were not to be attributed to the working man himself. That would lead only to greediness. Work was to be seen in close connection with the obligation to love the neighbour and with God's vocation. Norwegian theologian Dag Thorkildsen therefore considers the welfare state's objective of full employment as a secularization of the Lutheran view of daily work as the fulfilment of God's vocation (Thorkildsen 1997). This might be right, but it must be added that it was also an important objective of the welfare state to weaken the individuals' dependence on the labour market's cash nexus.

There are, of course, also differences between the Danish welfare state developed since the 1950s and Luther's 500 years old thinking. The most important difference is that the idea of abolishing all elements of worth and the punitive legal effects of collecting benefits was outside the conceptual world of Luther and his time.

18.9 The Fundamental Tension of the Danish Welfare State

Each one of us is to contribute to the community. We must pay the taxes demanded of us and help to ensure a suitably high level of work on offer. At the same time, we must refrain from elbowing our way to the trough to siphon off as much as possible from the large public coffers.

Obviously, there is a fundamental dilemma between, on the one hand, the (ethical) demands made by the welfare state, ones which it cannot guarantee itself, and, on the other hand, the private-economic, rational impulses we learn at our mother's knee. In fact, a functional welfare state that lives up to its normative standards requires people to behave in a private-economically irrational way. If we see the

---

[23] Martin Luther 1530, "Der 82. Psalm ausgelegt", WA, vol. 31.1, 183–218; 201.5–12.

welfare state as an attempt to realise a Christian universe of values in a secularized, the fundamental dilemma of the welfare state comes sharply into focus.

For the Christian, there is an instance outside the world and outside history to refer to. When you are told to lay aside your own interests, God's acts are your model. The ideological (godless) basis of the welfare state, on the other hand, can only be justified by referring to itself. If the individual asks why he or she must display solidarity and act non-selfishly when this is not going to benefit the individual in question, this is precisely the question for which the welfare state can find no answer. It is, in a certain sense, dependent on a religious foundation that it has put behind it in the process of secularisation. It is vulnerable, because no ideology can make absolute demands if it only can refer to itself.

The question is whether morality can control part of society while the other part is given over to being controlled by self-interest.

18.10 Instead of a Conclusion

It is impossible to "prove" that the Danish welfare state and its comprehensive redistribution, abatement of poverty and high degree of trust is a child of Lutheran Christianity. At most one might indicate that there may be a connection, but a criterion on which to falsify the thesis is not available. There is no doubt that a monocausal explanation is meaningless. The channels of causality are numerous.

I have, however, no doubts that Lutheran Christianity proclaimed during centuries has become part of Danish secular religion and, therefore, influenced the structure of the Danish welfare state. Despite this 'creed' I must acknowledge that the main characteristics of the classical welfare state are under erosion, i.e. that the unconditional care of the other is toned down to the advantage of a quid-pro-quo-view. The view of human beings as economic men seem to crowd out the view of humans as solidary creatures – and – if I am right – this runs counter to the religious legacies as explanatory. I have no explanation why.

References

Dreier, F. 1853. Forord [Preface]. In *Samfundets Reform, Et Ugeskrift* no. 1, 1–24. Copenhagen: J.D. Quist. http://runeberg.org/samfundets/0021.html.

Evangelischen Kirche Deutschland. 1997. *Für eine Zukunft in Solidarität und Gerechtigkeit*, Wort des Rates der Evangelischen Kirche in Deutschland und der Deutschen Bischofskonferenz zur wirtschaftlichen und sozialen Lage in Deutschland. https://archiv.ekd.de/1729-justice_1997_social4.html.

Gabriel, K., H.-R. Reuter, A. Kurschat, and S. Leibold, eds. 2013. *Religion und Wohlfahrtsstaatlichkeit in Europa*. Tübingen: Mohr Siebeck.

John Paul II. 1991. *Encyclical Letter Centesimus Annus 1991*. http://www.vatican.va/content/john-paul-ii/en/encyclicals/documents/hf_jp-ii_enc_01051991_centesimus-annus.html.

Kærgård, N. 2013. Religion und wohlfahrtstaatlichkeit in Dänemark. Der wohlfahrtstaat als Product gottesfürchtige Christen oder mächtige Politiker? In *Religion und Wohlfahrtsstaatlichkeit in Europa*, ed. K. Gabriel, H.-R. Reuter, A. Kurschat, and S. Leibold, 57–91. Tübingen: Mohr Siebeck.

Kahl, S. 2006. *The religious foundations of the welfare state: Poverty regimes, unemployment, and welfare-to-work in Europe and the United States.* PhD dissertation, Humboldt-Universität, Berlin.

———. 2009. Religious doctrines and poor relief: A different causal pathway. In *Religion, class coalitions and welfare states*, ed. K. van Keesbergen and P. Manow, 267–298. Cambridge: Cambridge University Press.

Lindberg, C. 1977. There should be no beggars among Christians: Karlstadt, Luther, and the origins of Protestant poor relief. *Church History* 46 (3): 313–334.

Luther, M. 1883–2009. *D. Martin Luthers Werke. Kritische Gesamtausgabe (Weimarer Ausgabe, WA)*. Weimar: Hermann Böhlau.

Petersen, J.H. 2016. *Fra Luther til konkurrencestaten*. Odense: Syddansk Universitetsforlag.

———. 2018a. *Den glemte Luther*. Odense: Syddansk Universitetsforlag.

———. 2018b. Martin Luther and the Danish Welfare State. *Lutheran Quarterly* 12: 1–27.

———. 2021. *Julius Bomholt – Fra idé til handling*. Copenhagen: Gads Forlag.

Petersen, J.H., and L.H. Petersen. 2007a. Næstekærlighed og velfærdsstat. In *13 værdier bag den danske velfærdsstat*, ed. J.H. Petersen, K. Petersen, and L.H. Petersen, 113–134. Odense: Syddansk Universitetsforlag.

———. 2007b. Gensidig eller ensidig? Om Løgstrups etiske fordring og den danske velfærdsstats normative grundlag. In *Livtag med den etiske fordring*, ed. D. Bugge and P.A. Sørensen. Århus: Klim.

———. 2010a. Manden der blev sin egen – Løgstrup og velfærdsstaten. In *I himlen således også på jorden? Danske kirkefolk om velfærdsstaten og det moderne samfund*, ed. N.G. Hansen, J.H. Petersen, and K. Petersen, 155–176. Odense: Syddansk Universitetsforlag.

Petersen, J.H., and K. Petersen. 2010b. Kirkefolk og velfærdsstat i Danmark 1945–1965 – med udblik til Storbritannien og Norge. In *Som i himlen således også på jorden? Danske kirkefolk om velfærdsstaten og det moderne samfund*, ed. J.H. Petersen, N.G. Hansen, and K. Petersen, 201–242. Odense: Syddansk Universitetsforlag.

Pontifical Council for Justice and Peace. 2006. *Compendium of the social doctrine of the church*. http://www.vatican.va/roman_curia/pontifical_councils/justpeace/documents/rc_pc_justpeace_doc_20060526_compendio-dott-soc_en.html.

Presbyterian Church (USA). 2002. *The confession of 1967 – Inclusive language version 2002*. https://www.pcusa.org/site_media/media/uploads/theologyandworship/pdfs/confess67.pdf.

Strohm, T., and M. Klein. 2004. *Die Entstehung einer sozialen Ordnung Europas, Bd. 2, Europäische Ordnungen zur Reform der Armenpflege im 16. Jahrhundert*. Heidelberg: Universitätsverlag Winter.

Thorkildsen, D. 1997. Religious identity and nordic identity. In *The cultural construction of Norden*, ed. Ø. Sørensen and B. Stråth, 138–160. Oslo: Scandinavian University Press.

van Keesbergen, K., and P. Manow, eds. 2009. *Religion, class coalitions and welfare states*. Cambridge: Cambridge University Press.

Zetterberg, H. 1984. The nordic enigma. *Daedalus* 113 (1): 75–92.

Jørn Henrik Petersen born 1944, since 1974 professor in welfare economics and social policy at University of Southern Denmark. Has been Chairman of the board both for Danish television TV2 and for a newspaper and has been member of a lots of commissions and boards for the Danish government and parliament.

Chapter 19
The Company as a Good Citizen: Institutional Responsibility and Cosmopolitanism

Jacob Dahl Rendtorff

Abstract The market requires more focus on responsibility and business ethics. This article discusses the vision of the business company as a responsible company with focus on good corporate citizenship as an expression of the limits of the market with regard to social responsibility and values of business organizations. This includes discussion of the challenges of business legitimacy in a global society. These must also be seen in the relation between economics and religion. Social, spiritual and cultural values lie behind the search for business legitimacy and the republican conception of corporate citizenship, and this is also an expression of ethical values at the limits of economic rationality. But cosmopolitan business ethics can be criticized for moralizing the market so we move from economic religion to moral economy forgetting the importance of economic rationality.

Keywords Corporate citizenship · Social responsibility · Business legitimacy · Cosmopolitan business ethics

19.1 Introduction

In the current debate on the philosophy and business ethics, the legitimacy of the business corporation which has created good relations with its social, economic and legal environment is defined by the concept of "Good Corporate Citizenship" (Scherer and Palazzo 2007, 2008). This notion has a long history and is defined by public or private organizations and institutions which contribute to the integration of human beings and society to develop a free society (Drucker 1946, pp. 23–24 and 114). Moreover, many authors see a close connection between trust, legitimacy and good corporate citizenship (Govier 1997; Matten et al. 2003; Mirvis and Googins 2006; Waddock 2005). From this, one could say that the notion of corporate

---

J. D. Rendtorff (✉)
Department of Social Sciences and Business, Roskilde University, Roskilde, Denmark
e-mail: jacrendt@ruc.dk

© The Author(s), under exclusive license to Springer Nature Switzerland AG 2023
N. Kærgård (ed.), *Market, Ethics and Religion*, Ethical Economy 62,
https://doi.org/10.1007/978-3-031-08462-1_19

citizenship very early on was considered as a holistic concept that defined an ideal concept of legitimacy of the business corporation as a responsible participant in processes of society. Accordingly, this is a political turn of the classical concept of corporate social responsibility (Carroll 1999).

Thus, we could conceive of the notion of corporate citizenship as fundamental in a democratic theory of Republican political philosophy which concerns democratic legitimacy of business in society. The problem of republican democracy has been discussed in the great tradition of political philosophy from Rousseau and Kant to Arendt, Habermas and Rawls (Rawls 1971). The idea is that the legitimate political community is considered as a democratic and deliberative political system in which the citizen engages for the values of the constitution as the foundation of society. Being a responsible citizen includes this commitment to the common values and to human rights and citizen rights of every member of society. The following analysis is based on the concept of business legitimacy as a framework for cosmopolitan business ethics (Rendtorff 2020a, b, c, d, e).

Thus, we will discuss this vision of the company as a good corporate citizen with focus on the most important aspects of good corporate citizenship as an expression of the limits of the market regarding corporate social responsibility. Section 19.2 discusses the challenge of business legitimacy in a global society and Sect. 19.3 analyzes the relation between economics and religion and the values behind the ideal of business legitimacy. Section 19.4 deals with the Republican conception of corporate citizenship and Sect. 19.5 elaborates the concepts of corporate citizenship and cosmopolitan business ethics. Finally, the critique of cosmopolitan business ethics and the transformation from economic religion to moral economy is discussed in Sect. 19.6.

19.2 The Challenge of Business Legitimacy in Global Society

Thus, the values and business ethics that companies currently implement may seem surprising but should in reality be considered as a logical consequence of the connection that has always been between economics, values and religion. We will now analyze the legitimacy of the cosmopolitan business ethics in this framework, that is how the emphasis on the ethical economy conceptions of two of the twentieth century's most important economic theories, respectively the Chicago School and the Cambridge School can provide deeper explanations for companies' current needs for ethical and moral legitimacy (Nelson 2001).

The firm's activities in the tension between ethics and economics is a characteristic feature of the postmodern industrial society. The boundaries between public and private, between social, political and economic values are fluid as never before (Axelrod 1984). Values-driven management, business ethics, ethical, social and environmental accounting in the private business sector, but also in public organizations and institutions are a sign of this increasing accountability of companies (Rendtorff 2017a, b, c, d). With its focus on corporate social responsibility with the emphasis on making the European Union the most competitive, dynamic and innovative economy, EU has insisted on the need for Europe's companies to take responsibility in the environmental and social field of their own free will to ensure ecological sustainability and to avoid social exclusion. The firm's Good Corporate Citizenship and care for the common good in society's institutions are encouraged as an essential dimension of business ethics and corporate social responsibility.

In this context, the vision of values and ethics as ideological and political concepts have come into focus. Companies are considered not only as neutral and independent economic entities, but also as organizations in "turbulent and dynamic environments" and as "systems of interacting individuals with interests and preferences" (Rendtorff 2017a, b, c, d). Economic activity is determined by conflicts between individuals struggling for the distribution of goods and resources. As social systems embedded in social interactions, businesses express a confrontation between different types of values, which to a greater or lesser degree are prioritized by the different stakeholders and members of the company. When businesses are searching for cosmopolitan values, this idea of doing good in social relations is the basis for a vision of ethics and CSR of the corporation, as suggested by research in values-driven management (Pedersen and Rendtorff 2004; Mattsson and Rendtorff 2006; Rendtorff and Mattsson 2012; Rendtorff 2015b, 2016, 2017b, 2019a, b, c).

The new dimension of the trend towards corporate moralization and politization of business is here that we can observe a shift from a perception of politics as power to conceive business politics as a vision of responsible management and ethical leadership (good corporate governance), where the organization's contribution to society is essential for its values and visions of doing business (license to operate). In addition to the requirement of firms to live up to being economically profitable and to have a good and solid business base without red numbers on the bottom line, it is now required that they have a politically correct business base that can achieve broad legitimacy in a democratic public evaluation, as suggested by business ethics research and theory of business legitimacy (Rendtorff 2009a, b, 2010a, b, 2011a, b, 2012, 2014b, 2017a, b, c).

The international consulting industry, PR agencies, accountants and corporate lawyers have therefore turned their eyes to business ethics and to the theory and practice of corporate social responsibility including philanthropic sponsorships and donations (corporate philanthropy) of business as elements to improve corporate policy (Rendtorff 2017a, b, c, d). This focus on business legitimacy is also oriented towards ethical leadership and responsible management as well as to improvement of the ethical profile of the company in the public sphere.

Today, many international companies have written down their visions and values in mission statements, established mechanisms to strengthen these values in the organization, and they have set up training programs to whip up the ethical values of employees and improve ethical branding of the company (Rendtorff 2017a, b, c, d). Communication and human resources departments, but also special public relations and ethics officer's staff are put to work to strengthen the company's reputation in the sphere of public political participation.

In the Western world, emergence of increasingly well-educated, enlightened, and fundamentally democratically minded citizens mean that the political consumer has become an inevitable factor in the company's formulation of sales strategy and appearance in the public sphere. Without being particularly systematic, consumers' critical attitudes typically manifest themselves in areas such as engagement for social issues, environmental and human rights (criticism of poor working conditions, environmental degradation, child labor, animal testing or oil pollution), and consumers are therefore strongly influenced by the company's reputation in public. In these cases, there is a need to find a harmony between political and ethical values, where ethical notions of corporate social responsibility become a political requirement for companies. This new horizon for philosophy of management and ethical leadership includes a focus on economic transitions towards sustainable development (Rendtorff 2010a, 2013a, b, c, d, 2014a, 2015a, 2017c, 2019d).

When it comes to shareholders 'and investors' demands for ethical, social and environmental investments in companies in order to achieve sustainability, there is not only an increased awareness of the need to demonstrate ethical values of governance to shareholders and investors, but also an increased understanding of how political issues in the public influence economic markets, which can no longer be neutral on political issues, but must relate to the social and political norms of society. This is the case with the increased focus on ESG-criteria in investments, where corporations are measured on their ESG, i.e., environmental, social and governance impact on society. Although it is unclear whether pension funds and other investment funds, with stated ethical considerations, also fully meet their objectives, ethical investments are an expression of a far greater public and political interest in the use of financial resources for socially responsible purposes than ever before. The differentiation of investment funds into companies that respect human rights or are ecologically sustainable and the emergence of international ESG and sustainability indexes of companies that meet these objectives also express this value turn in investment strategies moving towards concern for cosmopolitan business ethics.

19.3 Economics and Religion: Values Behind the Search for Business Legitimacy

Actually, the tension between ethics and economics and the moralization of society is not new, but has its background in the Western European discussion of political economy. Already in Max Weber's famous book *The Protestant Ethics and the Spirit of Capitalism* there was a focus on the spiritual value-basis of the economy (Weber 1987). In fact, it can be argued that there are a number of religious views of life that have influenced economic thinking, that lie behind the major ideological conceptions of economics as an economic science (Nelson 2001). Economy is thus not ethically and religiously neutral, but economics as a practical ideology is determined by the basic ethical and religious views of life. Thus, one can mention two basic approaches to economics that reflect the Christian religion and cultural tradition of the west: Namely, the optimistic "Catholic" economists who believe in human community and the possibility of a common welfare on the one hand, and the "Protestant" pessimistic economists who reject community and prioritizes the individual's freedom and right to self-determination on the other hand.

In the book *Economics as Religion* the American economist Robert H. Nelson addresses these two value traditions in economic science (Nelson 2001). The optimistic Catholic tradition and the pessimistic Protestant tradition. The optimistic approach to political economy includes names like Aristotle, Aquinas, Claude Saint Simon, who are all philosophers who believe in the common good of the good and justice state, where people are together in a community to create unity. The same can be said of economist John Maynard Keynes, who believed in the economic potentiality of the welfare state by emphasizing that good economic policy consists in creating a strong state that pumps money out into society. The pessimistic view of political economy in contrast to this includes philosophers such as Plato, Luther, Calvin, the Puritans, and Social Darwinists, who claim that humanity is sinful, egoistic and without an orientation towards the common good of community. They do not believe in the state and are skeptical of the possibility of justice (Nelson 2001). Plato perceives justice as ideal that is far from the reality of the human life in the cave of poor representations of an ideal world that can never be reached. Luther and Calvin distinguish between worldly and religious state, and they emphasize that economic behavior is the result of the individual's own choice at the expense of community norms and values. This also applies to the Puritans, who prioritized the individual's search for salvation through a righteous life. Moreover, pessimists often see economics as a kind of social Darwinism, which puts the individual's egoism above the altruism of the community. Nelson argues that these two perceptions have shaped Western culture and that they still influence the ideology behind contemporary economic sciences (Nelson 2001).

Nelson argues that even though economists perceive themselves as scientists, they cannot avoid being influenced by morality, ethics, and religion. In fact, they function as some kind of priests or prophets who preach moral views rather than objective science, and they want these views to determine the political and economic organization of society. The idea of economic efficiency, which is one of the most important ideas in modern capitalist societies, is not value-neutral, but depends on a religious view of the world. This relationship can be explained by using the so-called market paradox, where economic action is not located in mathematically perfect markets, but in a situation where cultural and social conditions determine economic behavior (Nelson 2001). The market paradox deals with the relationship between economic values and the other social values. Economics as a science contributes to the best organization of society. It can be said that political economy comes with proposals for organizing human happiness on earth, in Nelson's words "how to reach heaven on earth". Therefore, economists can be described as the philosophers of worldliness who will determine what morality and ethics should govern the society that human beings should live in.

This means that the modern economy of the twentieth century is a response to the problems of the confrontation between Protestant ethics and spirit of community. The question is how to promote self-interest and at the same time serve society. Two prominent directions in modern economics, the Chicago School and the Cambridge School, represent two opposing answers to this problem (Nelson 2001).

The optimistic tradition, the Cambridge school is represented by the famous Nobel Prize winner, Paul A. Samuelson, who wrote an important *Foundations of Economic Analysis*, which sold over 5 million copies in more than 15 editions (Nelson 2001). Samuelson inscribes himself in the optimistic tradition from Aquinas to Keynes. This was the project of the post-war welfare economy.

The Chicago School represents a sharp reaction to the Cambridge School's progressive economic project. They protested against the view of state, individual and market in Samuelson. It was an ultra-liberal critique of the welfare state, based on a very cynical view of human nature. The Chicago school includes people like Richard Knight, Gary Becker, Milton Friedman and Richard Posner.

Samuelson's economic theory can be considered as a Catholic economic thinking that criticizes the Protestant ethics of the individualist capitalist. It was an optimistic economic thinking after World War II. The project can be seen as a secularization of the Catholic economic project, where the constant investment in market development and the common good is prioritized as the most important for economic development in society. Against this background, Samuelson formulated the progressive view of the economy as the science of the welfare state. This was based on a combination of Keynesian ideas, a belief in the market economy and in the principles of scientific management. Markets were important for economic development, but at the same time it was important to have a government that had a strong social function. However, the market was still central to the scientific economy, based on mathematical analysis (Nelson 2001).

One could say that Samuelson would use the scientific economy to realize a moral and ethical ideal of the heavenly paradise on earth. Scientific management of modern business organizations as well as of the economic market should be a way of constructing the best society. It can be said that Samuelson introduced economic reason as a basis for the good society. Economic rationality prioritized scientific management in a society with a mixed economy that combined the state and the private market. Unlike the Protestants, however, Samuelson wanted to realize Utopia in this world, not in the afterlife. The instruments for this were the rational science og economics and the utilitarian view of moral life as based on the idea of the greatest happiness to the greatest number. The economy should contribute to the common good, solve the problems of collective action and fight egoists (free riders) (Nelson 2001). The economy is a scientific tool to generally create a better standard of living and improve the conditions of the most disadvantaged in society while making businesses prosper at economic markets.

The Chicago school, on the other hand, represents an individualistic and ultraliberal critique of the optimist welfare state project. This approach to economics perceived Samuelson's arguments for a mixed economic system as ideological and without a scientific basis. The Chicago School highlights the superiority of the market combined with a defense of social Darwinism and a defense of natural property rights of individuals.

We can mention an early twentieth century economist, Frank Knight, as a major founder of the Chicago school. He had a very negative view of human nature. Economy was based on self-interest and freedom. He represented a classical Christian view of human beings as possessed by original sin. Knight was a realist and he argued that economic markets and private property were the result of the presence of evil in the world, not in a community or opportunity for a common good. Knight highlighted the sinful nature of humanity in continuation of Calvinism and Puritanism (Nelson 2001). The market is present as the basis of community not because of human virtues but because of the evil nature of man. The market has the social function of bringing people together, even though they have different values and perceptions of life. The reason is that the market is without power relations, and therefore it is the real basis for a radical pluralism of a society of free relations between human beings. This means that at the market, the Christian can exchange goods with other religious groups without compromising their faith, because the exchange in the market is a matter of exchange, self-interest and profit. This expresses a revival of Calvinism and Puritanism in contemporary economic thinking.

Knight was the teacher of a number of very important economists such as Milton Friedman and George Stigler, who represented a later generation of Chicago economists. Friedman was also influenced by the notion of sinful humanity. He presented himself as an economic technician who argued for the free market as a basis for progress. But his works are characterized by the emphasis on self-interest and freedom and his critique of corporate social responsibility "The social responsibility of business is to increase its profits" shows how marked he is by the ideal of market efficiency. The state must not intervene in the free market, which is central to economic activity. This generalization of the economic method was followed by, for example, Gary Becker and Richard Posner, who used the economic method in other areas of the social sciences, respectively. Sociology and anthropology. This was based on a generalization of a secular version of the Christian concept of the sinful man. They emphasized that social agents are only determined by self-interest and utility maximization. Economic motives were considered the real basis of social behavior.

Individuals act according to this view in order to maximize their personal well-being and Becker believes that this economic behavior is everywhere. In social life the family was analyzed as an economic unit, discrimination and robbery were analyzed strictly financially. Becker, who received the Nobel Prize in 1992, believed that polygamy had a rational justification under certain circumstances because the value of women would increase in the market when men could have more than one woman. Marriage was analyzed as based on implicit calculations of financial gain. Becker believed so much in the selfish dimensions of human nature that he would explain altruism as a form of selfishness based on the so-called "Rotten kid Theorem", the nice child, where one realizes that the altruistic act will have the greatest economic benefit in the long run for the individual.

We could say that the Chicago school continues the Protestant ethics and the notion of a rational economy, while abandoning notions of belief in a calling from the Christian religion. The Chicago school conflicts with Webers' Protestant ethics because it considers individualism and profit maximization as values. Values of efficiency and economic progress have taken the place of respect for the divine commandments. One could say that the notion of the sinful humanity is generalized in a secular perspective. One retains the Calvinistic view of human nature without maintaining Calvinism's belief in revelation and in the power of the divine.

19.4 The Republican Conception of Corporate Citizenship

View in this economic perspective, the notion of corporate citizenship goes beyond the conception of citizenship in the liberal political tradition which defines citizenship only through the political rights of citizens. The notion of corporate citizenship is also broader than the traditional socialist notion which defines it on the basis of economic equality. The notion of corporate citizenship does not only refer to the responsibility of individuals but implies an institutional conception of the responsibility of organizations and institutions (Birch and Littlewood 2004). In this view, which is different from the liberal notion of citizenship, business as globally responsible citizens, as public and private actors, act to create a good and just society in the cosmopolitan perspective. When companies must legitimize themselves as good citizens, their role in society is not only economic but also social and political and this implies a challenge to the neoclassical and liberal model of the company which conceives firms only as economic actors who must not have political legitimacy in society (Rendtorff 2007, 2009a, 2017a, b, c, d, 2019a, b, c, d).

Here the communitarian position of business ethics goes further, because in addition to economic value, it emphasizes personal and organizational integrity as important for legitimacy within the framework of the political community of local and national culture (Logsdon and Wood 2003, p. 161). It is in this context that the Kantian and cosmopolitan conception represents an attempt to overcome the confrontation between the Catholic and Protestant view that goes even further than liberal and communitarian conceptions of the enterprise. Here, Kantian business ethics is oriented towards the common good while still preserving the value of the individual in community. Business legitimation is not only about creating economic value, but this must be integrated into creating value for society at national and international level (Rendtorff 2009a, 2017a, b, c, d, 2019a, b, c, d). Nationally, the communitarian approach implies that legitimacy is created by integrating the business for the cohesive work of society. On the international and universal level, represented by the Kantian approach, universal legitimacy implies respect for the company as a citizen of the world who is committed to the defense of human rights and universal ethical principles at the same time as there is a free moral space for each culture to form its own rules of corporate ethics.

This democratic and republican conception of legitimacy can be conceived according to a tradition of "civil republicanism" following Rousseau and Kant congratulating the citizen's commitment to the community. Thus, the notion of corporate citizenship is a metaphor for corporate engagement in society (Moon et al. 2005, p. 433). As a metaphor the notion of citizenship describes the ethical responsibility of the company that has received good acceptance in society (Morgan 1997). At the highest level it also implies a deliberative ideal of the company that finds its identity and ethical integrity in its commitment to the good development of the company in the context of the common good of community (Moon et al. 2005, p. 435). The republican democratic conception of the company is based on a deliberative ideal involving an open communicational dialogue with the stakeholders of the organization as a regulative ideal. Thus, as a regulatory ideal, the deliberative model of politics implies an adherence to the principle of discourse of communication without domination, of mutual understanding and of openness to the arguments of others (Rendtorff 2009a).

This conception of deliberative and civil republicanism is based on the conception of companies and the market as a mediating institution which contributes to social integration between the State and civil society with an intimate connection between market economy, democracy and economic growth and social of society. (Rendtorff 2009a). This is expressed with Paul Ricoeur's vision of the "good life with and for others in just institutions" (Ricoeur 1992, p. 202; Rendtorff 2009b, 2017a, b, c, d, 2019a, b, c, d). Corporate citizenship implies a "process of identification, analysis, and response to the social, political and economic responsibilities of the company as they are defined in law and in public policy and through the expectations of stakeholders as well as in company values and strategy" (Thompson 2005). This constitutes a concrete definition which opens towards an ethical commitment of the company at the national and international level in the globalized society.

The republican conception implies a holistic integration of the aspects of the liberal, communitarian, Kantian and universalist conception in a republican, democratic and deliberative conception of society according to which the legitimacy of the company is based on the values of the constitution of the republic (res publica). This is inspired by Habermas's description of democratic rule of law in *Faktizität und Geltung* (Habermas 1992) and the theory was developed by Peter Ulrich (1998, 2008), who works with the notion of 'ethical' integrative economy, which integrates the economic, social and political aspects of societal action. According to "integrative economic ethics" it is the object of the economic market and of economic action in companies to contribute to achieving the good life between free and responsible citizens in a democratic state (Rendtorff 2009a). We can say that the enterprise becomes a legitimate citizen in society (Ulrich 1998, p. 235). Contracts and agreements are only legitimate if they contribute to the creation of value for the common good and for the economic, social, political and economic well-being. Environment. The company must see itself as a unit that serves the interests of society (Rendtorff 2009a, 2017a, b, c, d, 2019a, b, c, d). According to this conception of the firm, communication with stakeholders is mediated through dialogue and critical application of rationality. In this context, the foundation of social responsibility is defined as responsibility for stakeholders according to R. Edward Freemans who speaks of "Corporate stakeholder responsibility" (Freeman et al. 2010). Thus, communication must fit into the debate of democratic advertising in dialogue with stakeholders (Ulrich 1998, p. 304) according to the ideal regulation of discourse through a community of communication and argumentation (Ulrich 1998).

With the American economist Alan Buchanan this interaction between economic market, political system and civil society can be conceived as a "new constitutional economy" which goes beyond the separation between state, society and market of the liberal tradition of political philosophy. In the republican and constitutional conception, economy and economic action are based on the ethical stakeholder management (Buchanan 1990). This implies a democratization of the company with an ongoing dialogue on the legitimacy of privileges and conceptions of property, governance and wages (Rendtorff 2009a, 2017a, b, c, d, 2019a, b, c, d). Economic inequality is based in this context of considerations of effectiveness, based on the principle of difference of John Rawls which implies that economic inequality can only be justified if it is to the advantage of all and to the weakest (Rendtorff 2009a). Thus, in this constitutional economy, the legitimate strategy must pursue the democratic objectives of the society (Crane and Matten 2004). This includes in particular the national and international vision of sustainable development, integrating the concern for the economy, for the well-being social and human rights and for the protection of the environment in the management of the business corporation (Rendtorff 2006).

19.5 Corporate Citizenship and Cosmopolitan Ethics in Globalization

The vision of corporate citizenship goes beyond the national state and relates to the global scale. It is important to conceive the business corporation as a good citizen within the framework of a global and cosmopolitan ethics. (Scherer and Palazzo 2007, 2008). When the World Economic Forum in Davos defines corporate citizenship, it is emphasized that this is not only an additional conception of CSR but that the notion of the cosmopolitan corporate citizenship is much more fundamental, because it must be integrated into the strategy and the daily practice of the company, if it is to be possible to legitimize the activities of the company in the globalized society (Rendtorff 2009a). At the same time, the concept of corporate citizenship viewed in a republican and democratic basis implies an effort to conceive the company in a global and cosmopolitan society where different cultures and states live together as a common transnational reality.

The ethics of the democratic and republican business firm here becomes an ethics of the cosmopolitan enterprise which with the starting point in the universal standards (Rendtorff 2009a, 2017a, b, c, d, 2019a, b, c, d) for human beings and for companies at the same time is able to recognize the importance of national and cultural difference as long as it does not violate human rights and fundamental ethical standards (Scherer and Palazzo 2007; Rendtorff 2009a, b, c). In practice it is important in a cosmopolitan business ethics to recognize the importance of cultural variation and the creative dynamics of different practices of corporate citizenship according to local and national need (Katz et al. 2001, p. 149).

So being a good citizen as a business corporation does not only mean that you follow the ethics and rules of the national state. Rather, the effort to legitimize oneself as a good citizen goes beyond belonging to the nation state and asks the company to become a "citizen of the world" who participates in global society and who relates to problems of world society and acts according to its universal obligations as a member of world society. The United Nations Global Compact Principles concerning the environment, human rights and corruption in the perspective of the United Nations international policy for sustainable development realized in the sustainable development goals (SDGs) from 2015 is an indication of how companies have obligations that go beyond concern for the nation state. Because more than 12,000 companies now have signed the principles of Global Compact one could argue that there is a greater international understanding for the need for this cosmopolitan legitimization of good corporate citizenship (Rendtorff 2009a, 2017a, b, c, d, 2019a, b, c, d).

It can be emphasized that companies that want to be good citizens are forced to be able to deal with and meet the expectations of global society and to be able to take responsibility for the societies where they operate, for example by paying taxes and not doing business with corrupt regimes that do not respect human rights. The efforts of companies to gain legitimacy on the international level become more and more urgent, as they act more and more at a high level at the global level beyond the formal expectation of national legislation (Rendtorff 2009a, 2017a, b, c, d, 2019a, b, c, d). Not less because critical media like high degree international watchdogs chase corporations and report it to the global public if corporations only pursue their own interests and profit without being able to legitimize their actions as important to the international community. They are more and more obliged to demonstrate the positive consequences of their activities for the world society, in particular their efforts to help solve problems concerning climate, environment, poverty etc.

Internationally, corporate citizenship is about overcoming the challenge of balancing economic growth, poverty and environmental destruction by trying to create a connection between economics, happiness and social wealth. Internationally, corporate citizenship also implies an intimate connection between "Fair trade" and other ethical initiatives concerning trade beyond nation state borders (Zadek 2001, p. 40). We should try to overcome the inequality between Western countries and developing countries (Zadek 2001). The cosmopolitan corporate citizenship is realized in working for greater national and international justice in the world.

American researchers Jeanne M. Logsdon and Donna J. Wood developed the notion of global corporate citizenship "Global business citizenship", which expresses the need for the legitimization of global corporate engagement (Logsdon and Wood 2005). Scherer and Palazzo also speak of "Global corporate citizenship" (Scherer and Palazzo 2008). Theoreticians argue that global corporate citizenship, say corporate cosmopolitan citizenship has a strong bearing on corporate efforts to legitimize themselves to be cosmopolitan by incorporating universal values into their mission catalogs and of values to show that they follow international standards for business activities. The cosmopolitan visions of the business firm as "Global corporate citizenship" are proposed as efforts to build a corporate ethic on a global level which can justify the responsibility of companies as responsible international agents. Logsdon and Wood define global corporate citizenship as follows:

> "A global business citizen is a multinational enterprise that responsibly implements its duties to individuals and to societies within and across national and cultural boarders" or "A global citizen enterprise is a multinational enterprise which responsibly implements its duties to individuals within and beyond national and cultural boundaries." (Logsdon and Wood 2005)

Thus, the vision of cosmopolitan citizenship is precisely to assume this global ethical responsibility which goes beyond the national and cultural responsibility.

To be a citizen of the world in cosmopolitan business ethics means for a company which should develop universal standards, norms and values for its actions and which it must have global principles for its management and action strategy which it pursues everywhere in the world. This is especially necessary in a world with great cultural differences. The company must be aware of cultural differences and respect these cultural differences as long as these differences do not violate universal and international human rights standards. In addition, global corporate citizenship implies that companies engage in a learning process regarding the development of international norms and values with a view to respecting human wealth in global development and growth.

James E. Post also defined the notion of "Global corporate citizenship". This definition lies behind the definition we have proposed of cosmopolitan corporate responsibility. Post emphasizes the importance of the company's overall engagement as a business for the Stakeholder Corporation integrating all stakeholders in management decision-making. At the same time global corporate responsibility implies that companies are actively engaged in developing democratic values in global society (Post 2002, pp. 143–153). It also implies that companies relate critically to countries that do not respect human rights and democratic values. Companies that respect their own cosmopolitan citizenship do not accept that governments do not respect human and citizen rights.

Then it becomes particularly clear that the legitimization of the enterprise through the cosmopolitan citizenship of the enterprise is not only about the economic value, but also about the public activities of the enterprise as a contributor to the common good in a democratic society. It is a commitment to common democratic and civic values as well as to human rights and political and economic citizens, which form the basis of the notion of cosmopolitan corporate citizenship. This notion of corporate citizenship implies an intimate connection between citizenship and democratic engagement for stakeholders with a concern for human rights and the environment in sustainable development. Here cosmopolitan business ethics is integrated in the global efforts to realize the sustainable development goals (SDGs) (Rendtorff 2017a, b, c, d, 2019a, b, c, d).

19.6 Critique of Cosmopolitan Business Ethics: From Economic Religion to Moral Economy

This moralization of business corporations with cosmopolitan business is not without connection to the basic economic discussions of economic religion and values. Many people perceive the moral enterprise not primarily as a political project, but as a new version of economic rationality and the representation of the shrewd ability of capitalism to extort money from people. It can be argued that society is in a crisis with weakened ethical awareness, and many particular perceptions of corporate social responsibility have taken the place of the need for a universal morality (Rendtorff 2009a). The various programs for ethics and value-driven management for cosmopolitan business ethics in companies therefore simply express a desperate search for ethics at a time when common values no longer exist. In postmodernity, ethics is no longer a matter of duty, but cynical selfishness has taken the place of the common good.

The vision of the good corporate citizen, according to this view, does not work at all to pursue a moral imperative, but ethics has become part of capitalism's cunning efforts to legitimize itself. The politicization of the various values-driven management programs is nothing more than an attempt to promote the ideology of a particular group instead of thinking of a universal moral norm for all people. This local ethic of promoting one's own special interests secures economic power while giving the false impression of serving common ethical ideals.

This creates a dangerous illusion that the company has a "moral soul" and that it is possible to combine economics, ethics and politics in the notion of the politically correct company (Rendtorff 2009a). The problem with politicization is a tendency to turn market values into moral values. The argument is that it is not at all the task of the company, but only the legislator to define the ethical values of society, through the universal moral content of the law. And it is an illusion to think that the company can give human life the highest value.

This critical attitude emphasizes the difficulty of realizing good and ethical corporate governance with focus on social and environmental performance without making corporate ethics an instrument for smart business consultants. We face a discourse of being good rather than a reality of virtue, and this can be detected by using the critical instruments of discourse analysis (Chouliaraki and Fairclough 1999). It is difficult to avoid the critique of value-driven leadership and business ethics as a pure ideology. If ethics is to function as the integrative force in the company's activities, which also helps to create a productive interaction with the outside world, it must be based on genuine democratic dialogue with all the company's stakeholders (employees, consumers, suppliers, grassroots organizations, the local community, etc.). It is important to discuss the limits of values and ethical leadership in management in order to ensure authenticity of the ethics and value-implementation of business organizations.

Values in a political enterprise of good corporate citizenship in the perspective of cosmopolitan business ethics express a new form of management discourse that goes beyond a purely hierarchical decision-making model, based on the absolute sovereignty of the leader and top management. Here, social responsibility and ethics are integrated in the values of the firm. Political communication about values must create meaning and coherence in the political message, whereby it can also improve the organization's legitimacy in society. Ethics in the political corporation in cosmopolitan business ethics must not only be a cosmetic cover up, but a genuine and integral part of the company's business strategy. This is a condition for companies to achieve real societal acceptance and thus economic sustainability in the long term.

Applying the notion of republican democracy to designate corporate citizenship means that the social political order is conceived as democratic insofar as all participate in decisions and republican insofar as all contributes to the common good or the general interest, the "res publica" of society. Placing corporate responsibility in this order means that the company or institution or organization has rights and duties in relation to society and that it has a political, legal and economic responsibility to promote stability. and the social and political unity of society.

19.7 Conclusion

Thus, the notion of corporate citizenship is the most fundamental notion to define corporate responsibility as a "moral and political" institutional person who participates in a responsible manner in the democratic state in cosmopolitan community (Rendtorff 2009a, 2011b, 2017a, b, c, d, 2019a, b, c, d). This can be seen as an indication of the limits of the markets in business and corporations.

In principle, the notion of corporate citizenship is presupposed in the concept of CSR (corporate social responsibility) and other concepts concerning the social commitment of the business firm, for example corporate governance, corporate social responsiveness, corporate social performance, stakeholder management (management by stakeholders) etc. (Matten and Crane 2005, p. 167; Buhmann and Rendtorff 2005).

From an institutional perspective, the notion of corporate citizenship is conceived as the company's acceptance of its obligations as a member of society. This implies that companies also have moral obligations and can be seen as collective agents with collective ethical responsibility (Jeurissen 2004, p. 95). Thus, corporate citizenship is the presupposition of CSR at the same time that it is more fundamental, because it designates a global concept of responsibility which does not only include legal and economic, but more important also environmental, ethical and even global and cosmological awareness of the role and impact of the corporation on society (Rendtorff 2008, 2009a, 2017a, b, c, d, 2019a, b, c, d).

References

Axelrod, R. 1984. *The evolution of cooperation*. New York: Basic Books.
Birch, D., and G. Littlewood. 2004. Corporate citizenship. Some perspectives from Australian CEOs. *Journal of Corporate Citizenship* 13: 18–23.
Buchanan, J. 1990. The domain of constitutional economics. *Constitutional Political Economy* 1: 1–18.
Buhmann, K., and J.D. Rendtorff, eds. 2005. *Virksomheders ledelse og sociale ansvar. Perspektiver på Corporate Social Responsibility og Corporate Governance*. Copenhagen: Jurist og Økonomforbundets forlag.
Carroll, A.B. 1999. Corporate social responsibility. Evolution of a definitional context. *Business and Society Review* 38 (3): 268–296.
Chouliaraki, L., and N. Fairclough. 1999. *Discourse in late modernity – Rethinking political discourse analysis*. Edinburgh: Edinburgh University Press.
Crane, A., and D. Matten. 2004. *Business ethics. A European perspective*. Oxford: Oxford University Press.
Drucker, P. 1946. *The concept of the corporation*. New York: John Day and the Mentor executive Library.
Freeman, R.E., J.S. Harrison, A.C. Wicks, B.L. Parmar, and S. de Colle. 2010. *Stakeholder theory, the state of the art*. Cambridge: Cambridge University Press.
Govier, T. 1997. *Social trust and human communities*. Montreal: McGill Queens University Press.
Habermas. 1992. *Faktizität und Geltung, Beiträge zur Diskurstheorie des Rechts und des demokratischen Rechtsstaats*. Frankfurt a. M: Suhrkamp.
Jeurissen, R. 2004. Institutional conditions of corporate citizenship. *Journal of Business Ethic* 53: 87–96.
Katz, J.P., D.L. Swanson, and L.K. Nelson. 2001. Culture-based expectations of corporate citizenship. A proposal framework and comparison of four cultures. *The International Journal of Organizational Analysis* 9 (2): 149–171.
Logsdon, J.M., and D.J. Wood. 2003. Business citizenship: From domestic to global level of analysis. *Business Ethics Quarterly* 12 (2): 155–187.
———. 2005. Global business citizenship and voluntary codes of ethical conduct. *Journal of Business Ethics* 59: 55–67.
Matten, D., and A. Crane. 2005. Note: Corporate citizenship: Toward an extended theoretical conceptualization. *Academy of Management Review* 30 (1): 166–179.
Matten, D., A. Crane, and W. Chapple. 2003. Behind the mask: Revealing the true face of corporate citizenship. *Journal of Business Ethics* 45: 109–120.
Mattsson, J., and J.D. Rendtorff. 2006. E-marketing ethics: A theory of value priorities. *International Journal of Internet Marketing and Advertising* 3 (1): 35–47.
Mirvis, P., and B. Googins. 2006. Stages of corporate citizenship. *California Management Review* 48 (2): 104–112.
Moon, J., A. Crane, and D. Matten. 2005. Can corporations be citizens? Corporate citizenship as a metaphor for business participation in society. *Business Ethics Quarterly* 15 (3): 429–453.
Morgan, G. 1997. *Images of organization*. London: Sage Publications.
Nelson, R.H. 2001. *Economics as religion: From Samuelson to Chicago and beyond*. Pennsylvania: Pennsylvania State University Press.
Pedersen, J.S., and J.D. Rendtorff. 2004. Value-based management in local public organizations: A Danish experience. *Cross Cultural Management* 11 (2): 71–94.
Post, J.E. 2002. Global corporate citizenship: Principles to live and work by. *Business Ethics Quarterly* 12 (2): 143–153. https://doi.org/10.2307/3857808.
Rawls, J. 1971. *A theory of justice*. Cambridge, MA: Harvard University Press.

Rendtorff, J.D. 2006. Corporate social responsibility, sustainability and stakeholder management. In *Business ethics and corporate social responsibility. International conference papers*, ed. N. Duro and K. Krkac. Zagreb: Zagreb School of Economics and Management.

———. 2007. *Virksomhedsetik. En grundbog i organisation og ansvar*. Frederiksberg: Samfundslitteratur.

———. 2008. Organizational change and values-driven management: A perspective from institutional theory. In *The anatomy of change: A neo-institutionalist perspective*, ed. S. Scheuer and J.D. Scheuer, 57–79. Copenhagen: Copenhagen Business School Press.

———. 2009a. *Responsibility, ethics and legitimacy of corporations*. Copenhagen: Copenhagen Business School Press.

———. 2009b. Business, society and the common good: The contribution of Paul Ricoeur. In *Business, globalization and the common good*, ed. H.C. Bettignies and F. Lépineux, 345–369. Oxford: Peter Lang.

———. 2009c. Basic ethical principles applied to service industries. *Service Industries Journal* 29 (1): 9–19.

———., ed. 2010a. *Power and principle in the market place: On ethics and economics*. London: Ashgate.

———. 2010b. Philosophy of management: Concepts of management from the perspectives of systems theory, phenomenological hermeneutics, corporate religion and existentialism. In *Elements of a philosophy of management and organization*, Studies in economic ethics and philosophy, ed. I.P. Koslowski, 19–47. Heidelberg: Springer.

———. 2011a. Institutionalization of corporate ethics and social responsibility programs in firms. In *Corporate social and human rights responsibilities: Global, legal and management perspectives*, ed. K. Buhmann, L. Roseberry, and M. Morsing, 244–266. London: Palgrave Macmillan.

———. 2011b. Corporate Citizenship as organizational integrity. In *Corporate citizenship and new governance: The political role of corporations*, Ethical economy. Studies in economic ethics, ed. I. Pies and P. Koslowski, 59–91. Dordrecht, Heidelberg, London, New York: Springer.

———. 2012. Business ethics. In *Encyclopedia of applied ethics*, ed. R. Chadwick. San Diego: Academic Press. (2 udg., Bind 1, s. 365–372).

———. 2013a. Basic concepts of philosophy of management and corporations. In *Handbook of the philosophical foundations of business ethics*, ed. C. Luetge, 1361–1386. Dordrecht, Heidelberg, New York, London: Springer.

———. 2013b. Philosophical theories of management and corporations. In *Handbook of the philosophical foundations of business ethics*, ed. C. Luetge, 1409–1432. Dordrecht, Heidelberg, New York, London: Springer.

———. 2013c. Recent debates in philosophy of management. In *Handbook of the philosophical foundations of business ethics*, ed. C. Luetge, 1433–1457. Dordrecht, Heidelberg, New York, London: Springer.

———. 2013d. The history of the philosophy of management and corporations. In *Handbook of the philosophical foundations of business ethics*, ed. C. Luetge, 1387–1408. Dordrecht, Heidelberg, New York, London: Springer.

———. 2014a. *French philosophy and social theory: A perspective for ethics and philosophy of management*, Ethical economy, no. 49. Dordrecht: Springer.

———. 2014b. Risk management, banality of evil and moral blindness in organizations and corporations. In *Business ethics and risk management*, Ethical economy, no. 43, ed. C. Luetge and J. Jauernig, 45–71. Dordrecht: Springer.

———. 2015a. Case studies, ethics, philosophy and liberal learning for the management profession. *Journal of Management Education* 39 (1): 36–55.

———. 2015b. The need for a theoretical reexamination of sustainability in economics and business. In *Sustainable markets for sustainable business: A global perspective for business and financial markets*, Finance, governance and sustainability: Challenges to theory and practice, G. Aras (red.), 41–58. Farnham: Gower Publishing.

———. 2016. Review of Le tournant de la théorie critique, Collection Solidarité et société, Éditions Desclée de Brouwer, Paris, 2015. *Journal of Classical Sociology* 16 (3): 305–309. https://doi.org/10.1177/1468795X16646468.

———. 2017a. *Cosmopolitan business ethics: Towards a global ethos of management*, Finance, governance and sustainability: Challenges to theory and practice series. London: Routledge.

———. 2017b. Creating shared value as institutionalization of ethical responsibilities of the business corporation as a good corporate citizen in society. In *Creating shared value: Concepts, experience, criticism*, Ethical economy no. 52, ed. J. Wieland, 119–139. Cham: Springer.

———. 2017c. Perspectives on philosophy of management and business ethics: Including a special section on business and human rights, Ethical economy, no. 51. Cham: Springer.

———. 2017d. The Danish model of corporate citizenship: The novo group. In *Progressive business models: Creating sustainable and pro-social Enterprise*, Palgrave studies in sustainable business in association with future earth, ed. E. O'Higgins and L. Zsolnai, 221–240. London and New York: Palgrave Macmillan. https://doi.org/10.1007/978-3-319-58804-9_10.

———. 2019a. Sustainable development goals and progressive business models for economic transformation. *Local Economy* 34 (6): 510–524. https://doi.org/10.1177/0269094219882270.

———. 2019b. The concept of business legitimacy: Corporate social responsibility, corporate citizenship, corporate governance as essential elements of ethical business legitimacy. In *Responsibility and governance: The twin pillars of sustainability*, Approaches to global sustainability, markets, and governance, ed. D. Crowther, S. Seifi, and T. Wond, 45–60. Cham: Springer.

———. 2019c. The honest businessperson: Cosmopolitan theory and cultural praxis (the example of Denmark and Scandinavia). In *The honorable merchant – Between modesty and risk-taking: Intercultural and literary aspects*, Ethical economy no. 56, ed. C. Lütge and C. Strosetzki, 41–53. Cham: Springer.

———. 2019d. *Philosophy of management and sustainability: Rethinking business ethics and social responsibility in sustainable development*. Bingley: Emerald Group Publishing.

———. 2020a. The concept of business legitimacy: Learnings from Suchman. In *Handbook of business legitimacy. Responsibility, ethics and society*, ed. J.D. Rendtorff. Cham: Springer.

———. 2020b. Capitalism, religion, business legitimacy, and the ethical economy. In *Handbook of business legitimacy. Responsibility, ethics and society*, ed. J.D. Rendtorff. Cham: Springer.

———. 2020c. Philosophical theory of business legitimacy: The political corporation. In *Handbook of business legitimacy. Responsibility, ethics and society*, ed. J.D. Rendtorff. Cham: Springer.

———. 2020d. Principles of business ethics and business legitimacy. In *Handbook of business legitimacy. Responsibility, ethics and society*, ed. J.D. Rendtorff. Cham: Springer.

———. 2020e. Sustainability, basic ethical principles, and innovation. In *Handbook of business legitimacy. Responsibility, ethics and society*, ed. J.D. Rendtorff. Cham: Springer.

Rendtorff, J.D., and J. Mattsson. 2012. Ethics in the bank internet encounter: an explorative study. *Journal of Information, Communication and Ethics in Society* 10 (1): 36–51.

Ricoeur, P. 1992. *One-self as another*. Chicago: University of Chicago Press.

Scherer, A.G., and G. Palazzo. 2007. Towards a political conception of corporate responsibility: Business and society from a Habermasian perspective. *Academy of Management Review* 32 (4): 1096–1120.

———, eds. 2008. *Handbook of research on global corporate citizenship*. Sheltenham: Edward Elgar.

Thompson, G.F. 2005. Global corporate citizenship: What does it mean? *Competition and Change* 9 (2): 131–152.

Ulrich, P. 1998. *Integrative Wirtschaftsethik. Grundlagen einer lebensdienlichen Ökonomie* (2 Auflage). Stuttgart, Wien: Haupt, 2. Auflage.

———. 2008. *Integrative economic ethics*. Cambridge: Cambridge University Press.

Waddock, S. 2005. Corporate citizens: Stepping into the breach of society's broken contracts. *Journal of Corporate Citizenship* 19: 87–118.

Weber, M. 1987. *The Protestant ethics and the spirit of capitalism*, Introduction by A Giddens, Unwin Paperbacks. London. Translated by Talcott Parsons from: M Weber: *Die Protestantische Ethik und der Geist des Kapitalismus* (1904–1905).

Zadek, S. 2001. *The civil corporation. The new economy of corporate citizenship*. London: Earthscan.

Jacob Dahl Rendtorff born 1965, professor at Roskilde University working on philosophy of management and responsibility, ethics and legitimacy of corporations since 1999, which was also the title of his dr. Scient. Adm. Habilitation thesis from 2010. President of European Business Ethics Network (EBEN) since 2021.

Chapter 20
Climate Problems: Market and Ethics

Kirsten Halsnæs and Niels Kærgård

Abstract The climate crisis is the major global problem of our time. As markets like those for energy have had a crucial role in the development of this problem, their management is a crucial precondition for its resolution. However, this is far from simple in light of classic market failures in respect of, for example, externalities and public goods. This is not a matter of short-term effects but of longer-term impacts lasting decades and centuries. This raises ethical issues about relations between the generations, and thus long-term sustainability. As a global problem, the climate crisis also requires international burden-sharing. Finally, the uncertainties involved are huge, especially in assessing the various tipping points. The role of economics and ethics in handling these problems is the topic of this chapter.

Keywords Climate change · Sustainability · Uncertainty · Economic instruments

20.1 The Scope and Nature of the Problems

The earth's climate is determined by many factors, but the anthropogenic influence on it is a now well-established fact based on scientific evidence (IPCC 2021). Due to inertia in the climate system, climate change will continue over centuries, even if we were able to reduce greenhouse gas emissions (GHG) rapidly and significantly. Climate policy is accordingly a different challenge compared with previous environmental problems.

K. Halsnæs (✉)
Department of Technology, Management and Economics, Technical University of Denmark, Lyngby, Denmark
e-mail: khal@dtu.dk

N. Kærgård
Department of Food and Resource Economics, University of Copenhagen, Frederiksberg C, Denmark
e-mail: nik@ifro.ku.dk

© The Author(s), under exclusive license to Springer Nature Switzerland AG 2023
N. Kærgård (ed.), *Market, Ethics and Religion*, Ethical Economy 62, https://doi.org/10.1007/978-3-031-08462-1_20

The environmental problems we have worked with in the past have largely been local problems with a short- to medium-term horizon. They include, for example, polluted rivers having serious impacts on the ecosystem, smog in big cities threatening the health of the latter's inhabitants, pesticides in groundwater, overfishing of fish stocks and the overuse of arable land and animal populations. Furthermore, specific technological solutions have often been available. In the case of climate problems, however, we are confronted with what is a global common good characterized by large uncertainties, a very long-term horizon and no obvious cleaning technologies. Addressing climate change and keeping the global increase in temperature to well below 2 °C or only 1.5 °C, − targets set out by the United Nations Framework Convention on Climate Change as part of the Paris agreement of 2015 − would require large-scale transformations of economies and societies all around the world. Such large-scale changes over very long-term horizons place sustainable development at the top of the climate-change policy agenda, a point that was also strongly emphasized in the Paris agreement. In addition to the strong links between climate policies and sustainable development emphasized in that agreement, the UN 2030 Agenda for Sustainable Development underlines the importance of capturing synergies with climate change, including the Sustainable Development Goals (SDG) in several areas. Closely linked with climate actions, these include SDG 1 (end poverty), SDG 2 (zero hunger), SDG 6 (clean water and sanitation) and SDG 8 (decent work and economic growth).

Locally the 'old' problems can be extremely serious, with high mortality rates in local populations, and they can imply the threat of more or less total species extinctions. However, the effect will typically be easier to observe and control compared to global climate-change impacts because local environmental impacts often occur within a short-term horizon and can be controlled with already available technologies. The water in the port of Copenhagen suffered heavily from pollution a few decades ago, but it is now possible to swim in its clean water and to catch fresh fish in its harbour. Many aquatic environments and cities that had become heavily polluted are now healthy again. Of course, there are also local problems that have irreversible effects, such as species extinctions.

Another key challenge in relation to climate change is that we are facing several different types of uncertainty related to atmospheric processes, ecosystems, society and human response capacities. Many uncertainties for which it is impossible to calculate probabilities and mean values for their outcomes.

Response strategies also face challenges due to inertia in the physical climate system. Even if we stopped emitting greenhouse gases (GHG) entirely as of today, it would take centuries for the climate system to stabilize. There is a very long time-lag from emission reduction policies being implemented and climate change being mitigated: for example, it takes a century for CO_2 concentrations in the atmosphere to break down. This really makes climate change an intragenerational challenge: the opportunities available to future generations strongly depend on what we are doing today.

Thus, the impact of the climate threat is already emerging, and it will continue for generations depending on the GHG emission reductions that are achieved today and in the future. This, for example, implies that very small changes are to be expected in how climate change is rolled out in a time horizon of decades. From the longer-term perspective, it is, of course, very important that large efforts to reduce GHG emissions are implemented very soon.

The climate crisis is different from other crises, but we should remember that there have been global crises before. For example, the prospect of nuclear war constituted a major threat to previous generations. The timeframe of actions and the consequences were very short. A nuclear war could start in minutes, and it actually came close to doing so a couple of times (in 1962 with the Cuba crisis and in 1982 when Russia made an erroneous observation of something that might look like an attack). This could make the planet uninhabitable in a matter of days. On the other hand, the risk could also be limited more or less immediately if there was a will to do so: a direct 'hot line' telephone connection between the Russian and American leaders or a disarmament agreement could minimize the risk.

The long time-lag in respect of the climate crisis is potentially creating a conflict between the generations. The older generations will not be hit as hard by damage to the climate as future generations. Implementing very large GHG emission reductions today, making far-reaching reductions in order to meet low temperature-stabilization goals like those set out in the Paris agreement, will require the present generations to adopt altruistic preferences to care for the future as well as protect global common goods as the climate. Such care for the future is necessary for dealing with present and future climate problems.

20.2 Mainstream Economics and Climate Problems

As discussed by Peder Andersen in Chap. 2 of this book, climate problems are a typical example of well-known types of market failure involving externalities and public goods. In a market economy without green taxes, society pays all the climate costs of increased CO_2 emissions, while for those who emit CO_2 and other greenhouse gases the costs are zero: this applies to all sources of emissions, such as fossil fuel-based energy supplies, wood-burning stoves, petrol-driven cars, ruminant livestock, industrial activity and aviation.

One well-known economic instrument in this regard is to impose a green tax on GHG emission sources as a solution, a tax which corresponds to the social costs of emissions. In the climate case, however, there are a number of problems with this proposed solution due to the long-term character of the problem and the free-rider incentives that underline the control of such a public good.

A general tax could be efficient in bringing down emissions if it were implemented globally at a uniform rate on all sources of GHG emissions, and if there were no other market failures. Marginal emission reduction costs would then be minimized, and the tax would also impose flexibility in terms of allowing emitters to emit GHGs provided they either reduce emissions or pay the tax. However, it is not very likely that such an ideal tax would be implemented in this efficient way.

The market external effects are not the only climate change-related problem for the market economy. Climate effects are also what economists call a public good, that is, a good from which, once it has been provided, everyone benefits equally and cannot be excluded (cf. Chap. 2). An improved climate will benefit Africans and Chinese, as well as Europeans and Americans. Admittedly they will not get the same benefits from it, but the benefit does not depend on how much they pay to improve the climate, but on whether you live in a lowland area with the risk of flooding, in a dry area with the danger of drought or in a suitably temperate area. The climate is global, but the effects depend on local conditions, and this imposes equity issues related to who is emitting GHGs and who is vulnerable to climate change.

Thus there is a free-rider problem: even a pioneer in climate policy is affected by the same climate as a neighbouring country that has not implemented any improvements to the climate. This calls for international collaboration, which is also the basic principle behind the UN Framework Convention on Climate Change (or UNFCCC), and issues of compensation for loss and damage and equity in the distribution of the costs and benefits of climate actions have therefore played a large role in its implementation. In this context, a uniform GHG emissions tax could be a globally cost-effective way to allocate emissions reductions, though complementary policies would be needed to address the issues of equity and fairness, as well as of vital development objectives in low-income countries. Furthermore, it should be recognized that a global GHG emissions tax is only a theoretical solution: at present there is no global governance system that could implement and administer such a tax in practice.

Binding tradable emissions permits have also been proposed as an instrument for promoting cost-effective GHG emissions reductions. However, as their effect is similar to a general tax under perfect market conditions, they will suffer the same governance limitations as a tax. The conflict of interests between countries and the free-rider problem can be and have been analysed theoretically in a game-theory framework using concepts like the cooperative and Nash equilibria, as noted in the introduction to this book.

20.3 Ethical Issues: The Future and Sustainability

Climate problems are already appearing today in the form of hazards like coastal flooding, heat waves, forest fires, droughts, cyclones and melting glaciers, impacts that are expected to increase in intensity and frequency over time. As already noted, this means that there is potentially an obvious generational problem here. Those in the current older generation face climate hazards, but much more serious impacts will affect their children and especially grandchildren.

This raises the issue of how we can value effects which will happen far into the future. The traditional economic approach to this sort of issue is to discount future effects: the further in the future they are, the fewer are the effects in terms of present values. There are good arguments for this. If the ordinary consumer has to choose between receiving an amount of something now or, for example, 10 years ahead, he or she will prefer to receive it now. If indifferent between the two situations, the consumer should have a larger amount in 10 years than today. Conversely with costs, the consumer would rather pay in 10 years' time than today. Therefore, we add interest rates to amounts that are to be paid in the future. Interest is a payment for waiting. This is possible on the basis that production will increase if we are willing to wait for it. For example, if I scrape for roots and catch fish with my hands, I will not achieve very much, but if I first spend time making a fishing rod and a spade, the benefit will be much greater. If I do research first, instead of continuing with the current technology, I will have a larger production in the long run. It pays to wait, that is, to be prepared to take time and a 'detour' with the production of the final product.

This is a consistent traditional theory, but it does mean that gains far into the future will be heavily discounted, and there are also equity issues involved in the resources and opportunities we leave for future generations. Reduced climate change 100 years from now will not count for much if we then discount it at a higher rate. The discounting of future costs and benefits can in extreme cases mean that calculating the total net benefit for all future generations can be greatest if we use all the earth's resources for the next 50 years and then neglect what comes afterwards.

But obviously this is not an ethically acceptable calculation, as it neglects the interests of future generations. This has become a major point in the definition of sustainable development, as stated by the UN Commission on our Common Future back in 1987 (WCED 1987, i.e. the Brundtland Report). This stated that the needs of the present generation should not compromise the ability of future generations to meet their own needs. Leaving the intra-generational aspects of climate change to be solved by actors in markets, even if uniform GHG emissions taxes were introduced by politicians, does not necessarily address the equity issue between the generations.

Historically, the sustainability debate has largely been driven by a growing recognition that markets cannot in themselves be expected to take into account the longer-term need to preserve social, natural and environmental values. In economics, the sustainability criterion has been defined as meaning that future generations' opportunities must be at least as great as those of current generations (Arrow et al. 2004).

Research on sustainable development is typically rooted in society's productive base, which, according to Arrow et al. (ibid.), consists of man-made capital (machinery, production equipment and other investments), natural capital (ecological systems, fossil fuels, minerals, etc.), human capital (education, health and culture) and institutions (legal systems and legislation, markets, information systems such as the internet, various public authorities, personal networks, etc.).

In practice, it is extremely difficult to 'measure' society's productive base, which would mean that an estimate would have to be made of the future return of consumption opportunities, the qualities of nature and human capital. A number of leading economists such as Arrow et al. (2004) proposes to avoid these measurement problems in connection with the concept of sustainability. They propose to do so by focusing less on how large the productive base of society is at different times than on how different forms of economic policy and regulation will affect the development direction of a society in relation to the principles of sustainable development. An example of economic regulation that can be expected to influence sustainable development is taxes on pollution, for example, CO_2 taxes on energy consumption, which, through price increases, can reduce consumption and thus lower impact on the climate. However, CO_2 taxes are only part of the picture of how a range of instruments and policy reforms can help to direct economic development in a more sustainable direction.

One of the earliest contributions to the debate on long-term development and sustainability was the book *Limits to Growth* by Meadows et al. (1972). Based on calculations using a computer model of long-term change, the book concluded that, if current economic growth continued at its present rate, the earth would reach some absolute growth limits within the next 100 years. *Limits to growth* became the subject of a very wide-ranging debate immediately after its release. Thus it was criticized by leading economists such as Robert M. Solow, William D. Nordhaus, Allen Kneese and Ronald Riker, who questioned the statistical basis of the model's assumptions that certain variables such as population, man-made capital and pollution would grow exponentially, while other variables such as technological development, pollution control and access to resources were assumed to be constant or to grow only very modestly. Another criticized premise in the book's calculations related to the potential for substituting different forms of capital for one another, such as natural capital and man-made capital (see, e.g., Nordhaus 1973).

Since then, a large number of economic debates have emphasized that there are many different factors and 'forms of capital' that are crucial for future consumption opportunities and thus for sustainable development. The discussion took as its starting point a study of whether there were any absolute limits to the utilization of non-renewable resources such as fossil fuels. An important contribution was made here by Hartwich (1977), who concluded that future consumption derived from non-renewable resources could be kept constant over time if their exploitation was constantly followed by an investment in other forms of capital offering the same return. In this way, non-renewable resources could be replaced by consumption options that would be available based on other resources. Hartwick's model thus pointed to the possibilities of substitution between different forms of capital, but assumed that there are no unique values in certain forms of capital that cannot be replaced directly by other means of consumption. Again, specific natural values are a good example.

In continuation of Hartwick's work on substitution between different forms of capital and sustainable development, various principles have been invoked as criteria for sustainable development. *Strong* sustainability means that all forms of capital must be preserved in their own right, and that criteria and limits must be formulated for the consumption of these forms. *Weak* sustainability means that all forms of capital are seen as identical, that they can substitute for each other, and that they must be able to contribute overall to given consumption options over time. A key issue is whether natural capital can be substituted by man-made capital, not what happens with natural capital seen in isolation.

One of the best known proponents of strong sustainability is Herman Daly, who, in his 1990 article, proposed three criteria for the exploitation of resources:

renewable resources must not be exploited more rapidly than the resource's ability to maintain itself at constant size (e.g. in the case of the utilization of wood, enough new trees must be planted to ensure the forest is kept in being), non-renewable resources must be replaced by corresponding investments in substitutes, and pollution must be limited so that nature's capacity to absorb it was not exceeded (Daly 1990). It should be noted here that Daly does not insist that there should be no impact on natural resources at all, but he suggests a number of limits to this impact.

Inspired by the strong concept of sustainability, a number of ecologists have worked to develop a measure of how much leeway individual consumers and countries should have in their material consumption and the derived impact on ecological systems. 'Permitted' limits influencing ecological systems are intended to be defined specifically in accordance with a number of defined natural limits for what the individual systems are expected to be able to withstand while at the same time keeping each individual area intact. A similar way of thinking is found in the notion of the 'ecological footprint', which makes calculations of how much land area different countries' environmental impacts occupy today, compared to what would be the sustainable limits for consumption.

As can be seen from the above, there have been a number of controversies between economists and ecologists regarding the criteria for sustainable development. The crux of the controversy has been summarized by Arrow et al. (2004) in a joint article with leading economists and ecologists. Ecologists have focused on the fact that current consumption in the richer countries is too high in relation to sustainable development criteria, while economists have focused more on whether the economy can deliver consumption permanently at the same level as today. Arrow et al. conclude that the optimal level of consumption over time, the level that can contribute to long-term sustainable development, cannot be determined, but that it is possible to assess whether the current level of consumption in a number of areas is in conflict with a number of criteria for sustainable development. Here they propose to concentrate on examining how consumption is affected by a number of factors that are considered to be particularly important for sustainability. These factors include the size of the discount rate – an important component in the assessment of current versus future consumption – and market prices versus the social price of the commodity for consumer goods, as well as natural resources. Discount rates that are too high and market prices that are too low to take the environmental impacts into account will lead to excessive consumption that is not in line with sustainable development.

20.4 Sustainable Development and Principles of Equity

In addition to the goal of unchanged consumption opportunities for future generations, a number of economists have also emphasized that sustainable development must also address the goals of equity and opportunities across current generations, that is, between population groups and between countries. Some of the most important recent contributions in this area have been made by A. Sen (1999) and P. Dasgupta (1993). Writing on welfare and poverty, Dasgupta concludes that it is wrong to focus on consumption rather than on the freedom of all individuals to meet the needs of each one. This freedom, he continues, requires that individuals have access to a range of resources, such as income, education, health systems, water, food, energy and political rights. The recommendation that follows from this is that studies of sustainable development must consider the resources that individuals have access to in both the short and long terms.

In relation to the debates over weak and strong sustainable development, the approach proposed by Sen and Dasgupta implies that it is not enough to measure 'genuine savings' as a concept for the entire economy, as suggested by Arrow et al. (2004). Instead, it is necessary to look at the possibilities and freedom of all individuals and also to have a kind of 'absolute' measure of individual possibilities as a starting point for assessing whether such a direction of development is sustainable.

The equality-oriented angle in research on sustainability should in principle lead to regulatory recommendations that include not only the environmental costs mentioned above, discounting that takes into account long-term trends and access to natural resources, but also a number of recommendations for equity regulations that ensure access to basic human needs and political rights for all individuals. These elements in the sustainability discussion have been particularly important in connection with international cooperation on the environment and development. This is the case for climate change, where a 'broad' development-oriented concept of sustainability has played an important role. An example of this is Agenda 21, which was adopted at the Rio Summit in 1992 and the follow-up resolutions at the UN Summit on Environment and Development in Johannesburg in 2002, and which also works as an umbrella for the UNFCCC.

20.5 Ethical Issues: The Past and Its Legacy

Where sustainability is about the future, there are also ethical issues about the legacy of the past. In their development, developed countries have used fossil fuels and other natural resources, and they have cultivated the landscape in ways that have reduced biodiversity. They have also emitted GHGs without restraint. Moreover, their populations have become rich partly because of the use of these resources. It can be debated whether it is fair to make global agreements with restrictions that prevent the peoples of Asia and Africa from accessing the sorts of lives wealthy countries' populations have been enjoying for decades. It can be argued that imposing constraints on GHG emissions reductions needs fair and proper compensation.

It is obvious that there are certain issues regarding ethical distribution that need to be taken into account. But it is also obvious that the world's climate cannot be managed if the poorer countries gradually – that is, as they can afford it – adapt the ways of life that the populations of the richer countries have and have had for decades.

Thus developments in the field of food have seen a transition from plant-based foods to light meat, such as pigs, poultry and fish, and further to meat from ruminants, like beef. Large populations in Asia in particular are currently increasing this development in their own countries at the implied risk of increasing emissions of GHGs per meal.

Although climate problems can only be solved if all countries impose restrictions on themselves, there is clearly a legacy that places special obligations on the richer countries. They are the ones that still emit the most, as they have done for a long time.

20.6 Uncertainties and Tipping Points

In addition to the general sense of uncertainty, the climate crisis is also characterized by a number of crucial tipping points. These are the points at which specific systems imposed by climate change at a given level of exposure begin to act as a factor destabilizing the climate: for example, if the tundra melts and methane accrued over very long time horizons is released, climate change will be amplified. It is far from sure that any such development will be a smooth linear process. There are a number of such tipping points, such as rainforests drying out and the ice at the poles melting.

There are many uncertainties related to tipping points, and it is therefore rational to look at climate problems also from an 'insurance point of view'. It may well be that irreparable damage does not occur with a temperature rise of more than 2 °C, but we cannot be sure, and once irreparable damage begins to show, it is already too late to stop it. This is entirely parallel to a number of other situations in which one uses a precautionary principle. Even if you smoke, there is a good chance that you can live until you are 90. But you quit because there is a significant risk of contracting lung cancer or COPD, and if you wait until you actually get cancer or COPD, it is already too late to do anything about it. There may be pesticides used in agriculture the effect of which is not fully known, but which are banned because there may be a so far undocumented harmful effect. Similarly, you take out fire insurance and health insurance because when there is a fire or your health fails, the costs are extremely high, while the insurance need not cost very much.

Similar climate problems can be coped with in a more manageable way if they are handled cost-effectively, taking all options into consideration, and winning global-wide participation as early as possible. When we do not quite know where the different tipping points are, it is rational to exploit the precautionary principle. It is far better to be too careful than to be too optimistic when it comes to problems of great uncertainty involving possibly irreversible damage.

20.7 Conclusion

The climate problem is perhaps the biggest problem of our generation. It is a problem with many aspects, one that can only be assessed through collaboration between many disciplines. The relationship between the market and ethics in this area is also very complicated.

Free unregulated markets and traditional investment calculations that discount the future costs and benefits do not contribute to solving these problems. But market failures such as those involving public goods and externalities have long been an established part of mainstream economic theory. These are problems that economic theory knows how to deal with: the societal costs and benefits must be felt and made visible in private financial accounts by means of green taxes and public support.

The problem is that climate problems are made difficult because they include very long-term and very uncertain effects. The global scale of climate-change impacts and the present and future locations of past and future sources of GHG emissions implies that there is no close link between those who pay for solutions and those who receive the benefits in terms of reduced climate-change impacts. This implies that joint global policy efforts are needed, with equity issues playing a key role in implementing climate actions, including both adaptation and mitigation. The key ethical problem is to distribute fairly the burdens between the rich and the strong people on the one hand and the poor and weak on the other.

Future generations are a very weak group in relation to the current batch of rulers, whether the latter are democratically elected or authoritarian. The time horizon for markets, elected politicians and other decision-makers makes it difficult to address the 50–100-year time horizons that are relevant in connection with climate policy. Very long-term ethical and political choices are needed to take into account the interests of both presently vulnerable geographical areas and future generations. There is no doubt that today's rich generations have a great ethical obligation to take greater responsibility for climate change.

Where economic theory can only provide limited aid in making overall ethical and political choices, it can provide great help in clarifying concepts and proposing effective instruments. Precise definitions of sustainability are an example where a conceptual analysis can clarify the debate about the responsibility towards future generations and prevent 'sustainability' from becoming an almost meaningless plus word.

Once it has been decided how large a reduction in GHG emissions is needed, economics can make effective instruments available in the form of theories of taxes and tradable quotas, instruments that on many occasions have proved far more effective than moral admonitions. Resolving climate problems needs more concrete restrictions and incentives than simply appealing to people's good will. Economic instruments such as taxes and tradable quotas have often proved effective in controlling market mechanisms jointly with the use of other policy instruments. What the market and economic theory cannot do is choose climate policy goals, but they can provide a toolbox of instruments with which the chosen goals can be realized.

References

Arrow, Kenneth, Partha Dasgupta, Lawrence Goulder, Gretchen Daily, Paul Ehrlich, Geoffrey Heal, Simon Levin, Karl-Göran Mäler, Stephen Schneider, David Starret, and Brian Walker. 2004. Are we consuming too much? *Journal of Economic Perspectives* 18 (3): 147–172.
Daly, Herman E. 1990. Toward some operational principles of sustainable development. *Ecological Economics* 2: 1–6.
Dasgupta, Partha. 1993. *An inquiry into well-being and destitution*. New York: Oxford University Press.
Hartwich, John. 1977. Intergenerational equity and the investing of rents from exhaustible resources. *American Economic Review* 67 (5): 972–974.
IPCC. 2021. Summary for policymakers. In *Climate change 2021: The physical science basis*. Contribution of Working Group I to the sixth assessment report of the Intergovernmental Panel on Climate Change [Masson Delmotte, V., P. Zhai, A. Pirani, S.L. Connors, C. Péan, S. Berger, N. Caud, Y. Chen, L. Goldfarb, M.I. Gomis, M. Huang, K. Leitzell, E. Lonnoy, J.B.R. Matthews, T.K. Maycock, T. Waterfield, O. Yelekçi, R. Yu, and B. Zhou]. Cambridge: Cambridge University Press.
Meadows, Donella H., Jorgen Randers, and Dennis L. Meadows. 1972. *The limits to growth*. New Haven: Yale University Press.
Nordhaus, William D. 1973. World dynamics: Measurement without data. *Economic Journal* 83: 1156–1183.
Sen, Amartya. 1999. *Development as freedom*. Oxford: Oxford University Press.
WCED. 1987. *World Commission on Environment and Development. 1987. Our common future*. Geneva, 190pp. https://idl-bnc-idrc.dspacedirect.org/bitstream/handle/10625/8942/WCED_79365.pdf?sequence=1&isAllowed=.

Kirsten Halsnæs born 1956, professor of climate change and economics at Technical University of Denmark. Member of the Danish Ethical Council of Denmark 2013–2019 and author of a number of rapports for United Nations Panel of Climate, IPCC.

Niels Kærgård born 1942, since 1993 professor of agricultural economics and policy at University of Copenhagen. First chairman of the Danish Board of Economic Advisors 1995–2001. In the board of University of Copenhagen 2008–2013, vice-president of The Danish Academy of Science and Letters 2008–2013.

Index

A
Aage, H., 11, 57, 59, 66, 67
Afe, A.E., 8
Ahlin, L., 172
Alesina, R., 79
Aliber, R.Z., 58
Allen, J.L. Jr., 181, 182
Ambrose, 246
Andersen, E.A., 45, 47
Andersen, F.V., 142
Andersen, J.G., 172
Andersen, L.S., 142
Andersen, P., 11, 45, 49, 287
Andersen, P.B., 173, 178
Andersen, S., 12, 105, 145, 151
Anderson, G.A., 88
Aquinas, Thomas, 182, 183, 186, 271, 272
Archard, D., 212
Arendt, Hannah, 167–169, 268
Arildsen, S., 132
Aristotle, 246, 248, 271
Armstrong, Frank, 227
Arrow, K., 6, 66, 289, 291, 292
Arrow, K.J., 4, 212
Arrupe, Pedro, 190
Atkinson, A.B., 60
Attwood, F., 225
Augustin, 167
Augustine, 246, 248
Axelrod, R., 268

B
Ball, R., 75
Barnosky, A.D., 160

Bartolome de las Casas, 183
Basil the Great, 182
Bauer, C., 243
Beauchamp, 217
Beauchap, T.L., 217
Becker, G.S., 24, 51, 63, 272, 273
Beinin, J., 200
Bell, S., 223
Belser, P., 225, 230, 231
Bénabou, R., 8, 36
Benestad, J.B., 186
Benjamin, W., 85
Berg, M., 80
Bergh, T., 147
Bernard of Clairvaux, 246
Bernstein, E., 224, 229, 233
Bertina, L., 189
Besley, T., 35, 56–59, 64
Birch, D., 274
Birch, L.V., 7
Birck, L.V., 140
Bismarck, 187
Bjørnskov, C., 74, 81
Blanchflower, D., 80
Blanchflower, D.G., 73, 78
Blazier, J., 215
Boltanski, L., 86
Bomholt, J., 143, 262
Booth, P., 192
Borre, O., 172
Böss, Michael, 169
Bowles, S., 64
Boycko, M., 57
Brown, W., 233
Brundtland, 6, 289

Bruni, L., 35
Bruno, C.R., 88
Bryson, B., 35
Bucer, Martin, 243
Buchanan, Alan, 276
Buchanan, J.M., 46
Buhmann, K., 280
Burke, Tarana, 234

C

Calvin, 271
Capiteyn, Peter, 243
Caporale, G.M., 75
Carroll, A.B., 268
Castells, M., 233
Chadwick, Edwin, 35
Chapple, W., 267
Charles, R., 182, 183, 190
Charles V, 242
Chernova, K., 75
Chiapello, E., 86
Childress, 217
Chouliaraki, L., 279
Christensen, T., 238, 239
Christiansen, J., 143
Chrysostom, John, 246
Cicero, 246
Clark, A.E., 72–75, 78, 79
Claude Saint Simon, 271
Clement of Alexandria, 182
Clemmensen, V., 243, 245
Coase, R., 4, 51
Colding, J., 8
Common, M., 48
Comte, 198
Connell, R., 223, 225, 229, 232
Connell, R.W., 225
Corner, R., 44
Cox, B., 58
Cox, H., 85
Crane, A., 267, 275, 276, 280
Crone, P., 205
Crosthwaite, A., 184, 185

D

Dahl, A., 226
Dahlerup, T., 240
Daily, G., 6, 66, 289, 291, 292
Daly, H.E., 290, 291
D'Ambrosia, C., 79
Danailova-Trainor, G., 225, 230, 231

Dasgupta, P., 6, 66, 289, 291, 292
Davidsen, T., 142
Davie, G., 172
Davis, E., 200
de Mandeville, Bernard, 4
de Moor, R., 177
Descartes, R., 162
Deutschmann, C., 85, 95
Di Nicola, A., 231
Di Tella, R., 75, 79
Diener, E., 80
Dominko, M., 76
Dorr, D., 189
Dreher, A., 81
Dreier, F., 262
Drucker, P., 267
Dübeck, I., 174
Dubner, S.J., 61
Durkheim, E., 64, 65
Dyer, R., 221
Dyson, B., 126

E

Easterlin, R.A., 73, 75, 76
Eck, Johann, 239
Ehrlich, P., 6, 66, 289, 291, 292
Eichenberger, R., 8
Ekelund, R.B., 35
Elster, J., 35
Engels, F., 60, 61, 63, 135
Engelstoft, P., 132
Enuma Elish, 90
Espersen, P., 174
Eubank, N., 88

F

Faden, R.R., 217
Fairclough, N., 279
Faisal, 202
Fama, E., 58
Felton, A., 79
Fenger, O., 3
Ferguson, N., 87
Fernández-Armesto, F., 57
Ferrer-i-Carbonell, A., 75
Ffrench-Davis, R., 57
Fink, Hans, 146
Fischer, J.A.V., 81
Flèche, S., 78
Fleischmann, C., 85
Folke, C., 8

Index

Forshaw, J., 58
Francis of Assisi, 182
Franciscus, P.P., 57
Frank, R.H., 59
Fredell, M., 185, 189
Frederik II, 240
Frederiksen, N.C., 141, 142
Freeman, R.E., 276
Frey, B.S., 8, 71
Frey, F., 36
Friedman, M., 95, 272, 273
Friis, Johan, 245
Frijters, P., 72–74
Frisch, R., 147
Frydman, R., 58

G
Gabriel, K., 251
Gaihede, G.B., 232
Garbarino, E., 8
Gehring, K., 81
Georgellis, Y., 75
Gibbons, R., 46
Gide, A., 65
Gide, C., 64, 65
Gilovich, T., 59
Gilson, Étienne, 193
Glebe-Møller, J., 248
Gneezy, U., 8
Goethe, 96
Gogarten, F., 166
Goldberg, M.D., 58
Goldfarb, R.S., 59
Goodchild, P., 12, 56, 118, 119, 127, 129
Googins, B., 267
Gorz, A., 116, 117, 119–122
Gossen, H.H., 23
Goulder, L., 6, 66, 289, 291, 292
Govier, T., 267
Graeber, D., 117
Graham, C., 72, 79
Gran, P., 203
Gratian, 246
Graves, R., 223
Gregory the Great, 182
Grønbech, V., 161
Gropper, Johannes, 243
Grosbøll, Thorkild, 174
Grundtvig, N.F.S., 132, 167, 263
Gundelach, P., 178
Gunnarson, Birger, 240

H
Habermas, Jürgen, 268, 275
Haenni, P., 207
Hahn, F.H., 4
Haisken-De-New, J.P., 74
Halman, L., 177
Halsnæs, K., 14
Hammurabi, 57
Hanisch, T.J., 147
Hanley, N., 66
Hardin, G., 6, 30, 43, 49
Harkin, M., 222
Hartwich, J., 290
Hassan al-Banna, 200
Hauge, S., 132
Hausman, D.M., 212, 214
Hayek, F., 4, 149
Hayek, F.V., 120
Headey, B., 74, 75
Heal, G., 6, 66, 289, 291, 292
Hébert, R.F., 35
Hegel, 86
Heiberg, Johan Ludvig, 132
Heiberg, Johanne Luise, 132, 136
Heidegger, Martin, 167
Heiene, G., 182
Hemmingsen, N., 240, 245–248
Hervada, J., 186
Higgs, P., 58
Hirdman, A., 221
Hitler, 161
Hobbes, T., 2, 4
Hochschild, A., 228, 229
Høffding, Harald, 142
Hoffmeyer, E., 56
Holm, B.K., 7
Homans, G.C., 63
Honeyball, Mary, 232
Hörisch, J., 85
Hornsby-Smith, M.P., 184
Hørup, Viggo, 140
Humphrey, Caroline, 117

I
Inoue-Murayama, M., 78
Irudayam, Sheeba Jem, 181

J
Jackson, A., 126
Jacobsen, L., 244
Jaime Diez Medrano, 252

Jansen, C.R., 3
Janssens, R., 215
Jegen, R., 8
Jensen, J., 169
Jensen, J.V., 165
Jensen, O., 13, 145, 154, 164
Jensen, S., 81
Jerome, 246
Jeurissen, R., 280
John Paul, 190, 259
John Paul II, 184, 185, 187, 189, 190, 192–194, 259
John Paul III, 183
John Paul VI, 184, 189, 191, 193
John Paul XXIII, 184, 185, 188, 189, 194

K
Kahl, S., 252, 262
Kant, I., 95, 119, 216, 218, 219
Kantian, 212, 215, 217, 218, 274, 275
Kærgård, N., 7, 12, 14, 131, 140, 142, 146, 147, 153, 263
Katrine, K., 221
Katz, J.P., 277
Keen, S., 125
Kesebir, S., 80
Keynes, J.M., 94, 96, 271, 272
Keynesian, 272
Kielos, K., 222, 233
Kierkegaard, S., 117, 118, 129, 132, 167
Kindleberger, C.P., 58
King Christian III, 240, 242–245, 247
King, J.E., 78
Kjærgaard, T., 164
Klein, M., 255
Kneese, Allen, 290
Knight, Frank, 273
Knight, Richard, 272
Knudsen, W.S., 65, 66
Koch, Ph., 110
Kok, J.G.E., 142
Konow, J., 60
Koopmans, R., 204–206
Korobov, V., 57
Kováts, E., 233
Kraaykamp, G., 81
Krekel, C., 72
Kuran, T., 202–206
Kurschat, A., 251

L
Lacetera, N., 8
Lactantius, 246
Lang, Mads, 241
Lange, O., 20
Lassalle, 139
Lausten, M.S., 14, 240, 242, 245, 248
Lavigne, J.-C., 189
Layard, R., 59, 72
Lazear, E.P., 24
Lee, D., 65
Leibold, S., 251
Lein, B.N., 132
Lembke, U., 234
Leontief, W., 59
Levin, S., 6, 66, 289, 291, 292
Levitt, S.D., 61
Lewis, B., 201
Lia, B., 200
Lindbeck, A., 59, 64, 65
Lindberg, C., 257
Linderberg, Fernando, 142, 143
Lindhardt, P.G., 132
Lindsnaes, B., 45
Littlewood, G., 274
Logsdon, J.M., 274, 277, 278
Løgstrup, K.E., 3, 13, 112, 145–155
Lüchau, P., 13, 173, 175, 176, 178
Luckmann, T., 85
Lund, M., 66
Lundager Jensen, H.J., 161
Luther, M., 103–112, 145–147, 149, 162, 237–248, 253, 255–258, 262–264, 271
Lutheran, 110–112, 237, 252, 253, 263–265
Lutheranism, 110

M
Ma, Y., 48
Macchabaeus, Johannes, 242
MacCulloch, R., 75, 79
MacIntyre, A., 118, 146
Macis, M., 8
Maddison, D., 48
Madsen, E.M., 248
Mäler, K.-G., 6, 66, 289, 291, 292
Mallat, C., 201
Malthus, 135
Malthusian, 135
Manow, P., 252

Mao, 161
Marcal, K., 222
Marianne Aagaard Skovmand, 222
Marshall, A., 32, 33, 37
Martensen, H.L., 131–143, 146, 149
Marx, K., 56, 60, 61, 63, 64, 67, 92, 135, 138, 198
Marxian, 154
Marxism, 190
Marxist, 135, 192, 201, 202
Massaro, T., 183, 184, 189, 191
Matsuzawa, T., 78
Matten, D., 267, 275, 276, 280
Mattsson, J., 269
Mauss, M., 107
McCloskey, D., 96
McGilvray, J., 48
McPherson, M.S., 212, 214
Meadows, Dennis L., 290
Meadows, D.H., 290
Melanchthon, Ph., 242, 243, 246, 247
Milgrom, P., 63
Mill, J.S., 32
Mirvis, P., 267
Møller, B., 45
Møller, M., 60, 62
Monrad, D.G., 131–133, 136–141, 143, 146
Moon, J., 275
Morgan, G., 275
Morgenstern, O., 5, 46
Mortensen, K.M., 167
Moss, L.S., 4
Muffels, R., 75
Muhammad Baqer al-Sadr, 201
Mühleisen, W., 223, 226
Musculus, Andreas, 244
Mustafa al-Sibai, 201
Mykle, A., 63

N
Napoleon, 203
Nash, John F., 5, 6, 9, 46, 288
Nasser, 202
Nayyar, D., 57
Nelson, L.K., 277
Nelson, R., 85
Nelson, R.H., 268, 270–273
Newby, H., 65
Newton, I., 58
Nguyen, V.T., 187
Nielsen, E.-B., 13
Nielsen, Frederik, 142

Nielsen, N.C., 60, 62
Nikolova, M., 72
Nobel, A., 61
Nordhaus, W.D., 290
Nørgaard, F., 132
Novak, M., 86, 96, 192
Nyholm, A., 132

O
Oberholzer-Gee, F., 8
Ocampo, J.A., 57
Occam, 33
Oishi, S., 80
Oksanen, S., 226
Okun, A., 31
Olsen, E., 151
Olsen, F., 234
Ostrom, E., 8, 30, 50
Oswald, A., 80
Oswald, A.J., 73, 78

P
Pahuus, A.M., 167
Palazzo, G., 267, 276, 277
Palladius, Peder, 242–244
Pareto, V., 24, 27–29
Parish, H.R., 183
Parson, Talcott, 201
Pasternak, Boris, 59
Paul, A., 85
Peach, L., 223
Pedersen, J.S., 269
Pedersen, P.J., 12, 77, 81
Pérez-Álvarez, E., 129
Perman, R., 48
Petersen, H., 14, 233
Petersen, J.H., 7, 14, 145, 147, 151, 152, 257, 258, 262, 263
Petersen, L.H., 147, 151
Petræus, 142
Petty, W., 62
Pian, C., 183
Pickett, K., 72
Piketty, T., 60, 233
Pimm, S.L., 160
Pius XI, 184, 185, 187
Plato, 168, 246, 271
Plesner, S., 58
Ploug, C., 142
Ploug, T., 14
Plutarch, 246

Pöim, M., 233
Pol Pot, 161
Polanía-Reyes, S., 64
Ponting, C., 66
Pontrjagin, L.S., 59
Ponzo, M., 75
Pope Benedict, 190, 191
Pope Benedict XIV, 183
Pope Benedict XVI, 181, 184, 185, 187–192, 194
Pope Francis, 184, 185, 190–193
Pope Leo X, 183
Pope Leo XIII, 184–186
Poppen, P.J., 59
Posner, Richard, 272, 273
Post, J.E., 278
Powdthavee, N., 76
Prasad, Monica, 224
Puel, H., 189

R
Raewyn, 229
Rahbek, J., 136
Randers, Jorgen, 290
Rasmussen, Louise, 132
Rawls, J., 60, 111, 112, 149, 268, 276
Regan, D.T., 59
Rendtorff, J.D., 14, 268–270, 274–280
Rerup, L., 141
Reuter, H.-R., 251
Ricoeur, P., 275
Ridley, M., 93
Rifkin, J., 95
Riis, O., 178
Riker, Ronald, 290
Roberts, J., 63
Rodinson, Maxime, 201
Rørdam, H.F., 241, 245
Rosa, H., 160
Rözer, J., 81
Rubin, J., 204
Rubin, M., 141, 142
Rustichini, A., 8

S
Salvatore, A., 201
Samuelson, P.A., 2, 5, 43, 65, 272
Sandel, M., 36, 116
Sandel, M.J., 56–59, 61, 64, 66
Sandler, T., 44
Sandmo, A., 26, 28

Sayyed Qutb, 201
Schanz, H.-J., 167
Scharling, W., 141
Scheible, H., 243
Scheider, S., 66
Scherer, A.G., 267, 276, 277
Schindler, David, 192
Schluchter, W., 198, 199
Schmidt, T.D., 77
Schneider, S., 6, 289, 291, 292
Schneider, S.M., 81
Schnellenbach, J., 81
Schuck, M., 183
Schürff, Hieronymus, 242
Schwarzer, A., 231
Scoppa, V., 75
Scorsese, Martin, 227
Sedlacek, T., 12, 87, 88, 95
Sen, A., 60, 212, 215, 216, 219, 292
Senik-Leygonie, C., 78
Shakespeare, 61
Shetty, P., 214
Shields, M.A., 73, 74
Shiller, R., 58
Shogren, J.F., 66
Sidgwick, 35
Silecchia, L.A., 190
Simmel, 65
Simonsen, David, 141
Singer, P., 212
Skidelski, Edward, 96
Skidelski, R., 96
Skidelsky, 96
Skovgaard-Petersen, J., 13, 200, 204
Sløk, J., 155
Slonim, R., 8
Smith, A., 4, 23, 26–29, 37, 57, 86, 94, 95, 116–118, 125, 134, 135, 138, 139, 146, 215, 222
Socrates, 168
Sofokles, 61
Solow, R.M., 212, 290
Sombart, W., 86, 139
Spiegel, S., 57
Stalin, 161
Starrett, D., 6, 66, 289, 291, 292
Steincke, K.K., 143
Stern, N., 62, 63, 66
Stevenson, B., 75, 76, 78
Stewart, J., 132
Stigler, George, 273
Stiglitz, J.E., 57
Stiglitz-Sen-Fitoussi, 72

Strohm, T., 238, 239, 255
Stutzer, A., 71
Sugden, R., 35
Svarer, M., 63
Svenstrup, T., 132
Swanson, D.L., 277
Swedberg, W., 227

T
Tanner, K., 118
Tausen, Hans, 245
Tawney, R., 34
Taylor, F.M., 20
Thaler, Richard, 150
Thatcher, Margaret, 9
Thompson, G.F., 275
Thorkildsen, D., 264
Tillich, P., 95
Timms, O., 214
Tirole, J., 8, 36
Titmuss, R., 8
Titmuss, R.M., 212
Tomasi, S.M., 194
Tönnies, 65
Tripp, C., 203, 204, 206
Troeltsch, E., 103–105, 110
Tsitsianis, N., 75

U
Ulitskaja, L., 226
Ulrich, P., 275, 276

V
van Keesbergen, K., 252
van Kooten Niekerk, Kees, 146
Varian, H.R., 42
Vatican II, 184, 185, 188, 190
Veenhoven, R., 80
Verbic, M., 76
Verme, P., 80
von Hagen, J., 61
von Hayek, F.A., 60

von Mises, L., 4, 87
von Neumann, J., 5, 46
von Trier, Lars, 227, 228
Vormordsen, Frands, 241

W
Waddock, S., 267
Wagner, F., 85
Walker, B., 6, 66, 289, 291, 292
Walras, L., 22
Wang, C., 8
Warming, J., 49
Weber, M., 34, 65, 86, 103, 139, 198–199, 201, 204, 205, 207, 274
Weberian, 205
Weberianism, 201, 207
Webers, M., 270
Weiss, A.S., 78
Weitzman, M.L., 9, 48, 62, 66
Welker, M., 61
Werner, R.A., 124
Westergaard, Harald, 142
White, B., 66
Widmann, P., 152
Wilkinson, R., 72
Willis, J., 87
Woeff, A.A., 142
Wolf, J., 145, 154
Wolfers, J., 75, 76, 78
Wood, D.J., 274, 277, 278
Wooden, M., 75
Woods, T.E. Jr., 193
Wray, L.R., 126

Y
Yezer, A.M., 59
Yin, Y.P., 75

Z
Zadek, S., 277
Zetterberg, H., 262
Zia ul-Haqq, 202